Social Work: A companion to learning

Social Work: A companion to learning

Edited by
Mark Lymbery
and
Karen Postle

Los Angeles | London | New Delhi
Singapore | Washington DC

£25.99   656646
7.DAY

First published 2007. Reprinted 2013

SAGE Publications Ltd
1 Oliver's Yard
55 City Road
London EC1Y 1SP

SAGE Publications Inc.
2455 Teller Road
Thousand Oaks, California 91320

SAGE Publications India Pvt Ltd
B 1/I 1 Mohan Cooperative Industrial Area
Mathura Road, Post Bag 7
New Delhi 110 044

SAGE Publications Asia-Pacific Pte Ltd
3 Church Street
#10-04 Samsung Hub
Singapore 049483

British Library Cataloguing in Publication data

A catalogue record for this book is available from the British Library

ISBN 978-1-4129-2001-8
ISBN 978-1-4129-2002-5 (pbk)

Library of Congress Control Number: 2006931846

Typeset by C&M Digitals (P) Ltd., Chennai, India
Printed in Great Britain by the MPG Books Group
Printed on paper from sustainable resources

MIX
Paper from
responsible sources
FSC
www.fsc.org
FSC® C018575

This book is dedicated to the social work students, past and present, who have informed our thinking and taught us more than they probably realise.

Contents

List of illustrations

Boxes

Figures

Tables

Notes on contributors

Advocacy in Action: Some of us use services, some of us resist, others have been denied or are invisible. We are from diverse backgrounds and work across the boundaries to promote social justice and welfare. We challenge existing services to accommodate and respect us and have been involved in social work education for sixteen years. You can telephone us on 0115 947 408 or 07715 099 278.

Paul Bywaters is Emeritus Professor of Social Work at Coventry University and Honorary Professor at the University of Warwick. He co-founded the Social Work and Health Inequalities Network and is the author (with Eileen McLeod) of *Social Work, Health and Equality* (2000) and (with Gayle Letherby) of *Extending Social Research* (2007).

Tina Eadie is a qualified social worker with considerable practice and management experience. She was a lecturer in social work at the University of Nottingham and is currently a senior lecturer in community and criminal justice at De Montfort University. She has researched and published on social work education, social work in the voluntary sector and professional issues.

Jan Fook is Professor in Social Work Studies at the University of Southampton. Some of her books include: *Radical Casework* (1993), *Professional Expertise: Practice, Theory and Education for Working in Uncertainty* (2000) with Martin Ryan and Linette Hawkins and *Social Work: Critical Theory and Practice* (2002).

Martin Gill is a freelance independent practice teacher who also works as a practice teaching mentor for the University of East Anglia, a distance-learning tutor in community and criminal justice for De Montfort University and a lecturer in social work at City College Norwich. He has also presented workshops for prospective candidates for the Post Qualifying Award in Social Work.

Helen Gorman is a consultant in educational development at the University of Central England, Birmingham and tutor for the Centre for Labour Market Studies, University of Leicester. A qualified social worker, she has taught and published on social work including, with Karen Postle, *Transforming Community Care: A Distorted Vision?* (2003).

John Harris is a Professor in the School of Health and Social Studies at the University of Warwick. He worked as a social worker, training officer and district manager before moving into higher education. His main teaching and research interests are in the fields of management, citizenship and community care. His publications include *The Social Work Business* (2003).

Vicky Harris is Director of the Practice Teaching Programme at the University of East Anglia and responsible for practice learning opportunities on the social work programmes. She has published in the areas of youth offending (juvenile sex offenders) and women's health.

Kaeren Harrison is currently in the social work department of Southampton Solent University. Her main research interests are in the sociology of the family, friendship and personal and social relationships. She has recently contributed to and edited (with Graham Allan, Jean Duncombe and Dennis Marsden) *The State of Affairs: Explorations in Infidelity and Commitment* (2004).

Nigel Horner is Head of Division of Social Work, Human Services and Counselling at Nottingham Trent University, with a background in residential child care, community work and social services staff development. He has researched and published widely in the areas of social work practice and education.

Richard Hugman is Professor of Social Work at the University of New South Wales, having worked at the University of Lancaster until 1995. His publications span mental health, community welfare and social work for older people, as well as the professionalisation of social work and professional ethics. Currently Richard is Asia-Pacific representative to the IFSW permanent committee on ethics.

Beth Humphries is a researcher and writer in social work-related topics. She has worked as a social worker in Northern Ireland, Scotland and England and has taught in a number of universities in the UK. She is currently preparing a textbook on research and social justice and a jointly authored book on social work and asylum seekers, with Debra Hayes

Robert Johns is Head of Social Work at the University of East London. He teaches social work law and leads the qualifying Masters programme run jointly with the Tavistock and Portman NHS Trust. A registered social worker, his practice includes ten years as a children's guardian. He is the author of *Using the Law in Social Work* (2005).

Bill Jordan is Professor of Social Policy at Plymouth and Huddersfield Universities, and Reader in Social Policy, London Metropolitan University. He has held visiting chairs in Germany, the Netherlands, Denmark, Slovakia, Hungary and Australia. He has written over twenty books on social policy, social work, social and political theory and political economy including, most recently, *Social Policy for the Twentieth Century: New Perspectives, Big Issues*, (2006). He was a front-line social worker and has been an activist in social movements for twenty years.

Juliet Koprowska is a senior lecturer in social work at the University of York. She has published in the areas of social work education and the mental health service experiences of adult survivors of childhood sexual abuse. She is author of *Communication and Interpersonal Skills for Social Work* (2005).

Mark Lymbery is Associate Professor of Social Work at the University of Nottingham. He is a registered social worker and has published in the areas of community care, social work education and interprofessional working. He is the author of *Social Work with Older People* (2005).

Jonathan Parker is Professor of Social Work at Bournemouth University. He is a qualified social worker and specialised in mental health and dementia care. He is co-editor of the highly successful *Transforming Social Work Practice* series and has published widely in social work education, practice learning, dementia and palliative care.

Malcolm Payne is Director, Psycho-social and Spiritual Care, St Christopher's Hospice, London and Honorary Professor, Kingston University, St George's Medical School. His books include *What is Professional Social Work?* (2006), *Modern Social Work Theory* (2005) and *Teamwork in Multiprofessional Care* (2000). He has recently published research on adult protection, welfare rights and day care in palliative care.

Jeremy Peach teaches public service management at Nottingham Trent University to social work and human service students in addition to managers and professionals from health and social services. Previously he worked in local government specialising in leadership practices and individual and group development. He is a member of the Chartered Institute of Personnel and Development.

Karen Postle lectures on the social work programmes at the University of East Anglia. A registered social worker, she works voluntarily as a neighbour mediator. Karen has researched and published in the areas of community care and social work education and practice including, with Helen Gorman, *Transforming Community Care: A Distorted Vision?* (2003).

Jackie Rafferty is a principal research fellow in the School of Social Sciences at the University of Southampton, Director of the Centre for Human Service Technology and Director of the Higher Education Academy Subject Centre for Social Policy and Social Work (SWAP). She has researched and published extensively on the use of information and communication technologies in social work education and practice.

Gillian Ruch is a lecturer and Programme Director of the MSc in Social Work at the University of Southampton. She has researched and written about the personal and professional welfare of practitioners, interprofessional working and therapeutic work with children.

Shaping Our Lives is an independent, national user-controlled organisation with a strong track record of undertaking user-controlled and emancipatory research and development work as well as working to improve the support service users receive and to increase their say and involvement in their lives at local and national levels. We include and work across a wide range of service user groups and place an emphasis on working in an inclusive and accessible way, to support as wide involvement as possible. See http://www.shaping-ourlives.org.uk.

Steven M. Shardlow is Professor of Social Work at the University of Salford and Director of the Institute for Health and Social Care Research. Additionally, he is Professor II (Social Work), at Bodø University College, Norway. He has published widely in the fields of evidence-based policy and practice, professional ethics, comparative practice and social work education and practice, including fourteen books.

Jan Steyaert is Professor of Social Infrastructure and Technology at the Fontys University of Professional Education in Eindhoven (The Netherlands) and a research fellow at the University of Bath. His research interests are technology and quality of life, information management in social services and active citizenship. He can be reached through Jan@steyaert.org and his publications are available through http://www.steyaert.org/Jan.

Vicky White is an Associate Professor in the School of Health and Social Studies at the University of Warwick. She is involved in qualifying and post-qualifying provision at the university and elsewhere. She has researched and published in the areas of management developments, women's perspectives on statutory social work and feminist social work. She is the author of *The State of Feminist Social Work* (2006).

Colin Whittington is an independent consultant (http://www.colinwhittington.com) working with national organisations – such as SCIE, the DH and CAIPE – local agencies, and individual managers and professionals. He is a registered social worker and an experienced researcher, manager and teacher. He has published widely on inter-agency and interprofessional issues, which he researched for his doctorate, and they feature regularly in his consultancy.

Acknowledgements

We would like to thank the members of Advocacy in Action and Shaping Our Lives whose presentations at the 2003 JSWEC Conference in Warwick inspired us to see the need for this book. Along with the service users with whom we worked when in practice, they were a constant reminder of what social work education should be about. Zoë Elliott-Fawcett and Anna Luker at Sage have been continually helpful, supportive and encouraging throughout the book's production and we are grateful to them for this. Our thanks also go to Tina Eadie and Tony Postle for their patience and support throughout this endeavour.

Part One

Introduction

The purpose of this part of the book is to:

- introduce the book as a whole;
- identify its various themes;
- clarify the intended readership of the book;
- introduce various educational features of the text.

1 Social work in challenging times

Mark Lymbery and Karen Postle

Social work in Britain

The future of social work in the context of British society is hard to predict. Social workers will need to accept, and adjust to, periods of intense change in the organisation and management of their work. Practitioners must therefore retain clarity about their role and contribution to welfare services and be prepared to argue for the continuing relevance of their role within environments which they may find harsh and unforgiving. The fundamental changes that have been set in train for social work education confirm the fact that social workers must simultaneously operate in ways that deliver a good quality of service, while also being prepared to amend their practice in accordance with frequent adjustments to their organisational locations.

Although this appears a daunting task, this book argues that it is achievable. However, we are not underestimating the task's intensity, scale or complexity: rather, we suggest that in order to accomplish it practitioners need to identify and adhere to key tenets of social work that have been neglected in recent years. In this way, we can start to transform social work practice and its education. The starting point lies in recognising the breadth of the social work task, well captured in the International Federation of Social Workers' (IFSW) definition of social work, which suggests that it should not be limited to the narrow discharge of statutory functions that has characterised its recent history in the UK:

> The social work profession promotes social change, problem solving in human relationships and the empowerment and liberation of people to enhance well-being. Utilising theories of human behaviour and social systems, social work intervenes at the points where people interact with their environments. Principles of human rights and social justice are fundamental to social work.
>
> (IFSW/IASSW 2000)

This definition conceptualises the social work role in a broader way than is usual in much practice in the UK: the notion that social work is concerned with 'empowerment and liberation to enhance well-being' is not one which accords with the reality of much practice, certainly as regards statutory agencies. However, much social work in developing countries does clearly fall within this general category. Indeed, if we consider the origins of social work within the UK and the United States of America, it is possible to discern such an orientation, particularly in the work of the Settlement Movement (Payne, 2005a). However, one of the things that distinguishes the development of social work in the UK from practice elsewhere in the world is the distance that social work has travelled from its origins (see Chapter 9; implicitly, this thought also underpins the other chapters in Part II).

What we can conclude, therefore, is that the nature and scope of social work practice – as well as its structural location – must be regarded as capable of being changed. The way in which social work has developed in the UK is not a given and does not represent the final stage of its development. The book therefore seeks to enable both students and practitioners to reflect on the circumstances of their work and to consider possible alternatives to the way in which it is organised. While we define these as 'challenging times' for social work, we emphatically do not believe that they render good quality practice an impossibility. What the book does seek to achieve, however, is the challenging aim of both enabling students and practitioners to function effectively in current practice contexts, while also providing them with the awareness of critical perspectives that can equip them with a vision of alternative ways of organising, coordinating and carrying out their work. It is certain that the structure of social work will remain untouched unless students, practitioners, managers and academics are able to articulate a reasoned case for substantive change to occur.

The educational and professional framework

In terms of current contexts for practice, there have been many changes to the shape of both qualifying and post-qualifying education for social work. At the qualifying level, significant changes were implemented in the UK from 2003, following years of discussion and negotiation. All social workers are now educated to the level of at least a bachelor's degree with honours, and all social work courses follow a curriculum combining the Department of Health (DH) Requirements (DH, 2002a), the Quality Assurance Agency's Subject Benchmark Statement for Social Work (QAA, 2000) and the National Occupational Standards for Social Workers (TOPSS, 2002). These documents have combined to create a 'prescribed curriculum' for social work. Most of the new graduates from these revised courses entered the world of social work in 2006.

In 2005, the General Social Care Council (GSCC) published a revised framework for post-qualifying education in social work (GSCC, 2005a), building on changes already incorporated in the revised qualifying programmes. Also in 2005, social work was established as a registered occupation with a protected title. This was after many years of campaigning by social work's professional body (the British Association of Social Workers); social workers are now required to register with the GSCC. This has two particular consequences:

1. There is now independent scrutiny of the standards of practice and behaviour of practitioners on the register with the possible outcomes that practitioners can be removed or suspended from the register (see Community Care, 2006a).
2. Because employers are no longer the sole arbiters of what counts as acceptable practice, it is possible that what they require of practitioners may be subjected to more scrutiny than before.

Taken together, the requirement that social workers must possess an honours degree in order to enter the profession, the strong encouragement to undertake post-qualification education and training (never previously a characteristic of the occupation) and protection of title all appeared to point towards a positive future for the development of social work in the British context. They are all characteristics of more established professions (Macdonald, 1995), pointing towards an improved status for the occupation of social work.

However, at the same time that these major changes to the professional structure of social work have taken place, the occupation has had to operate in the context of numerous initiatives that have served to constrain the scope of its activities and to fetter the discretion of its practitioners. For example, the promulgation of managerialist thought (Harris, 1998; see also Chapter 22) represents a major challenge for practitioners. At the same time, the emphasis on interprofessional education and partnership working (see Chapters 8, 14 and 20) presents another fundamental test to the way in which social workers operate. In addition, the reconfiguration of child care services that has occurred from April 2006, when combined with an ongoing consideration of the social work role in adult services, will affect the organisational locations within which social workers operate. In some parts of the UK, considerable thought has already been given to clarifying the future social work role (Scottish Executive, 2006). However, the powerful presence of performance measurement in social work (as in most public sector organisations) has also had a major impact upon social work practice and has – arguably, at least – distorted the priorities that govern social services organisations (de Bruin, 2002; see also Chapter 17).

There is an obvious risk that a reductive reading of the *Requirements for Social Work Training* (DH, 2002a) could lead practitioners and educators to ignore the more emancipatory potential of social work. Indeed, the very notion of a prescribed curriculum for social work presupposes that some elements will be included and others excluded. As constructed, this curriculum appears to favour a narrow interpretation of social work roles and functions and downplays the breadth of knowledge and understandings that should characterise the most effective practice. It is particularly worrying that little attention appears to have been given to the impact of poverty and inequality on the lives of people needing social workers' support and to establishing a clear commitment to a positive value base for social work. As a result, this book contains material at its start that addresses these concerns (see Chapters 2 and 3). It is our view that a more positive future for social work can only be secured by the re-establishment of a broader, more critical conception of its possibilities. We also believe that this has the potential to provide a more positive outcome for those people who use social services, an essential outcome if the commitment to service user involvement is to move beyond mere lip-service.

About the book

Considering this, this book operates on two levels. Written primarily but not exclusively for the British reader, it engages with the key elements comprising the prescribed curriculum for social work training in England – comparable to similar documents applicable in other British countries – providing a critical overview of what is required of social workers in their practice (see Chapters 10–16 in Part Three). However, it moves beyond this to provide an analysis of the political and social contexts within which social work practice takes place, as well as engaging with ongoing themes and debates (see Chapters 2–9 in Part Two). Thus, the book will enable students and practitioners of social work to understand not only how to practise social work effectively but also how to locate this practice within its broader societal context.

The book adopts a critical and questioning approach to its subject matter. It accepts that much of the development of social work in the UK can be contested and points out some of the difficulties that attend its current practice. It can therefore provide a particularly useful resource for students in the later stages of their undergraduate social work training and for postgraduate qualifying students. It is also intended for use by post-qualifying students, in that it addresses issues that are of particular interest to practitioners as part of their professional development (see Chapters 17–23 in Part Four). Similarly, practice teachers will find that the book helps them connect the worlds of theory and practice, while social work lecturers should find elements in the book that can stimulate their teaching and thinking about social work.

A number of educational features have been incorporated into the text. Each chapter contains an introductory section, highlighting the key themes to be addressed. This is balanced by a summary of learning points at the end of each chapter, immediately before suggestions for further reading in a 'Taking it Further' section. Another feature of the book is the deployment of questions that encourage the reader to reflect on her/his understanding of the text, relating it to personal or professional experience or both. These inserts, requiring a process of reflection on the part of the reader, are introduced thus:

 To what extent does the depiction of social work in this introductory chapter connect to your personal or professional experience?

Students on qualifying courses can use these to help make connections between practice and theory, which can be of value both in relation to the academic – in relation to essays and classroom discussions – and practice elements of the curriculum. Post-qualification, practitioners will find that the text has continued meaning for their experiences within social services agencies and will be of relevance in the world of post-qualifying education and training. Several chapters also include case studies that enable the reader to understand the complexities of the subject matter through the medium of concrete examples.

The book is organised in five parts beginning with this introductory chapter, establishing the broad scope of the book, placing subsequent chapters in the context of the reform of social work and its education in the UK. The second part is entitled 'Contexts', and contains chapters that examine the perspectives through which social work education can best be understood. The third part is entitled 'Requirements and Processes', and focuses on those elements that should characterise all social work courses, building on concepts identified in the first part and taking account of the 'prescribed curriculum' for social work training (DH, 2002a). The fourth part is called 'Thriving in Practice', and concentrates on what social workers need to sustain productive and fulfilling careers, hence shifting the focus from the qualifying to the post-qualifying levels of education and training. The fifth part contains a chapter summarising learning from the book overall. Each chapter can be read in isolation from the others; however, there are close and direct links between chapters within different parts of the book.

In accordance with the requirement that service users should be considered as central to the delivery of social work education (DH, 2002a) and, by extension, to the whole of social work, two chapters – 6 and 20 – have been commissioned from service user organisations, reflecting a commitment that the experiences and knowledge of such groups of people should be integral to the development of social work. This is also a reflection of the commitment to inclusion and participation that underpins the production of the book as a whole.

There are numerous references to internet sources throughout the text. While all of these references were correct when the book was written, it is possible that websites have subsequently been renamed or discontinued. In such circumstances, we encourage readers to use a reputable search engine to locate the various documents to which reference was made. Any changes to website addresses will be amended in future reprints of this book.

Part Two

Contexts

This part of the book discusses some of the contexts that provide the background of social work practice. These chapters introduce key concepts that underpin the discussion of several subsequent chapters and focus on the following themes:

- the political, societal and economic context for practice;
- values;
- uncertainty;
- the use of 'self';
- the engagement of services users;
- research mindedness;
- interprofessional working;
- social work in an international context.

A number of the chapters introduce themes that are further explored later in the book. For example, while Chapter 4 introduces the theme of values, the conflicts that may exist between different sets of values are explored in Chapter 23. Similarly, while Chapter 8 introduces the theme of interprofessional education, Chapter 14 explores issues of partnership and interprofessional working in more detail. Chapter 6 introduces the place of service users in the provision of social work education, a theme that is considered further in Chapter 20, which also examines more generally issues of partnership working with service users, hence picking up themes also discussed in Chapters 8 and 14. Given the nature of social work and its education, Chapter 6 provides a lens through which all the chapters in subsequent parts of the book should be viewed. In general terms, chapters in this part tend to focus on more abstract ideas than the chapters in Part Three and most of the chapters in Part Four.

2 The political, societal and economic context of practice

Bill Jordan

This chapter will:

- aim to clarify the external forces at work on the lives of both practitioners and service users, shaping their interactions;
- argue that these forces are largely invisible and taken-for-granted cultural processes, which come to determine the ways that practitioners and service users think about their encounters;
- explain how these forces become internalised as common sense, unquestioned and influential notions of relationships, needs, responsibilities and powers.

Introduction

The external forces shaping the interactions between practitioners and service users are all the more influential because they are usually unquestioned; our organisations and cultures 'do our thinking for us' (Douglas, 1987). This is because of a continuous transformation of our society which began in the late 1970s and which the Third Way governments of Tony Blair have reinforced. Our political leaders have picked up themes in economic and social relations (such as property ownership, security and choice) and developed these into a network of mutually confirming ideas and symbols. These in turn help us make sense of anonymous processes of change, such as deindustrialisation, flexible work and globalisation. The prescribed curriculum for social work education mainly reproduces an uncritical version of these concepts and linkages; it takes an effort to step out of the framework of institutionalised categories and programmes.

My starting point is the idea of a 'context' for practice. The word 'context' is usually taken to mean background or setting, which is not the main focus of the picture. I shall challenge this interpretation, both by arguing that the political, social and economic forces surrounding social work have shaped practice, and that context itself (the now largely ignored *collective* elements in exchanges between practitioners and service users) is an essential element in successful and ethical practice.

The main thrust of change in organisation, management and training for the profession has been towards delivering services to individuals, assessing individual needs, addressing individual behaviour problems and deploying evidence of effectiveness in these aspects (Macdonald and Sheldon, 1998; Sheldon and Macdonald, 2000). This has served to define practice in ways which insulate it from local and national politics and from other policy initiatives for the economy, community and citizenship. It has also separated it off from such obviously related areas as social inclusion, urban regeneration and the integration of refugees. It can be understood in an overall context of the 'modernisation' of public services (DH, 1998) and, hence, is not as marked in the voluntary sector (Jordan with Jordan, 2000).

The ultimate rationale for the transformation that informed this agenda is the improvement of human well-being – the same as that driving social work itself. The collapse of collectivisation, first in the UK in the 1970s and then in the Soviet Bloc in 1989, was taken as decisive evidence that the most reliable basis for improving well-being was individual choice, whether in markets for consumption goods or in quasi-markets for such 'public' goods as health care, education and social care. Behind this, in turn, lay social relations based on private property (share ownership and pension rights, and also housing assets) and a political programme for expanding 'personal prosperity' (Blair, 2005). It was therefore logical that personal social services, like the whole public sector, should be reformed in line with these requirements, to give service users more choice between suppliers in a 'mixed economy' of provision and to groom deviants and idlers for participation as competent, self-responsible citizens in an expanding market.

However, there are already signs that this formula is becoming less convincing, and the new evidence has direct relevance for social work. First, systematic international data shows that although self-assessed well-being continues to grow in line with national income per head in countries (such as China and India) where industrialisation and urbanisation are taking off, it has failed to do so in affluent societies (Kahneman et al., 1999; Frey and Stutzer, 2002). Where per-capita gross domestic product (GDP) is $15,000 or more, at current prices, subjective well-being remains stalled as income rises (Layard, 2003); it responds more directly to factors such as family relationships, community involvement and religious faith than to earnings and consumption (Argyle, 1999; Myers, 1999). All this is highly significant for practice and points away from individual preference as a criterion for satisfying the needs central to well-being.

The government has come to recognise this in several ways, none of which yet directly impact on the organisation of personal social services or the curriculum for professional training. For example, the Home Office (2005) has researched and promoted the building of 'social capital' – the norms underlying everyday transactions between members of groups, neighbourhoods and organisations. It has also pioneered initiatives on 'community cohesion' (Blunkett, 2004) in the aftermath of intercommunal violence in northern English towns and on civil renewal, to counter political apathy and non-participation in civic affairs (Blunkett, 2003). The third Blair administration consolidated these in the office of the Deputy Prime Minister along with the Social Exclusion Unit and New Deal for Communities, under a minister (Ruth Kelly) with cabinet rank.

Finally, alarm about 'yob culture' and 'anti-social behaviour', which played such a large part in the General Election of May 2005, and informed the Queen's speech a fortnight later, is symptomatic of the same set of concerns. The idea of 'respect' as a basis for a better civic culture has been captured in programmes for tougher enforcement in criminal justice and for stricter school discipline. Again, although there is a faint recognition of cultural and collective elements in these issues, the measures to address them are chiefly individualised and entrusted to agencies with responsibility for social control. Local authority social services are sidelined, at least from the new elements in these initiatives.

In this chapter I argue that social work will remain in a 'ghetto' of service delivery, defined along narrow criteria and isolated from important developments in public policy, unless these assumptions and categories can be challenged. Service users will be disadvantaged unless the profession can make new links with an agenda that recontextualises the services we provide and show connections between issues – poverty, exclusion, resistance, 'stalled well-being' – which are kept separate by current orthodoxies.

   How do you respond to what you have read here?

Individualism, choice and self-responsibility

The New Labour government has made explicit a change taking place in the UK from 1979 onwards. There was a shift from public services as the appropriate arena for interactions between interdependent citizens (Dean, 2004: Chapter 1), to a new contractual relationship between the state and individual citizens. The fundamental assumptions behind this are that citizens have a duty to 'take up the opportunity to be independent if able to do so' and must 'seek training or work where able to do so', while the government should 'make work pay' and regulate so that 'private pensions and insurance products are secure', with the welfare services reserved for those whose 'savings are inadequate' or who are 'unable to work' (DSS, 1998: 80). I shall now show how this came about.

The 'new contract' gives clear indications of the economic basis for the cultural transformation, and this in turn gave rise to the new system of governance. Margaret Thatcher's Conservative administrations aimed to break the power of trade unions, social movements and local authorities – the collective interests sustaining the welfare state. They had also opened up the UK economy to global market forces, making firms compete with foreign companies and driving down employment and wages in traditional sectors. The goal was to force citizens into being more reliant on their own skills, adaptability and private resources and, hence, on markets and property holdings.

These trends were reinforced by greater geographical mobility, as those joining the property-owning mainstream moved away from less-favoured urban districts into suburbs, leaving concentrations of deprivation in inner cities and on bleak housing estates. Ethnic minority populations were especially vulnerable to the polarisation of life chances this created; an upwardly mobile black and Asian middle class joined the mainstream, while their former neighbours remained among the poorer residents of disadvantaged areas.

The underlying assumptions behind the transformation were derived from a long tradition of British thought about the nature of economic and social order and the basis for good government. This implied that citizens should be set free from the constraints of collective systems and encouraged to pursue their own interests; institutions and organisations would arise spontaneously from these, for the long-term benefit of all (Jordan, 2004: Chapters 1–3).

By this logic, people who looked to the state for support were – in the very act of doing so – demonstrating their lack of the necessary competences to be full members of a society built on individual choices. They required re-education, therapy, training or punishment to turn them into adequate citizens. Only those who proved incapable should be given long-term assistance. Conversely, public services should reinforce the market order of independence and choice. In education, health and social care, opportunities to select specific facilities and suppliers should be given to service users, and the private sector should supply the model of efficiency to which state services aspired. This was the rationale for the reforms of the public sector, including the personal social services, in the late 1980s and early 1990s.

Social policy theorists have pointed out that the full implications of the individualist agenda – property, markets, mobility and choice – were not turned into a coherent system for governance until they were harnessed by the Third Way regimes of Bill Clinton and Tony Blair (Cruikshank, 1994; Rose, 1996). These made explicit the idea that individual citizens were responsible for governing themselves, improving themselves and meeting their own needs (Foucault, 1988). Their programmes for 'activating' claimants of social assistance or for fostering independence among service users deployed professionals' skills to nurture self-esteem, adaptability and the desire to realise potential, within a logic of self-responsibility that was more radical than Reagan's or Thatcher's (Rogers, 2004).

None of this could have carried conviction as a political programme without the cultural shift towards individualism among the mainstream electorate. With decline in collective mobilisations, citizens' attention had shifted to 'identity politics' – the expression of diversity, difference and aspirations for personal self-fulfilment. It is one of the ironies of recent history that much of the vocabulary of Third Way politics is borrowed from counselling, or even social work.

The positive part of Third Way programmes has been a much stronger commitment to including disadvantaged citizens in the mainstream – a dimension which the neo-liberal regimes of the previous era neglected. But this thrust to inclusion is structured by the logic of individual and family self-responsibility – skills training, flexible employment and mutual reliance. While tax credits give more generous support to those willing and able to take the low-paid work available, access to savings, pension rights and home ownership is beyond the reach of many. The contradictions of the programme began to emerge in New Labour's second term.

These include the persistence of inequality (*Guardian*, 2005a) and low rates of social mobility (*Guardian*, 2005b). The personal social services have been implicated in the failures of Third Way programmes to improve the lot of those remaining outside the mainstream. Because resources have flowed to new initiatives associated with the inclusion of relatively able, more active, fitter citizens, social workers have been involved in rationing those in greatest need and tackling the deviance of those most resentful of being left in society's margins. I shall move to show how contradictions and failures in Third Way approaches have led to rethinking priorities and launching fresh initiatives.

 What examples of the issues discussed here can you identify?

Community, morality and 'respect'

The paradox of New Labour's programme has been that, although committed to a mainstream order of choice, it has always been simultaneously concerned to 'remoralise' society, through many interventions. This side of its policies has been demonstrated by its emphases on 'responsibility' and 'community', in each term of office. The specifics have changed frequently, in response to a series of emerging issues.

New Labour's determination to be seen to be tackling law and order, drugs and alcohol, truancy, homelessness and family breakdown stem from its researches before the 1997 election, when focus groups revealed the Conservatives' vulnerability on these matters. To reconcile its stances in relation to social control with proclaimed values, the government's initiatives pursued a spirit of 'tough love' (Jordan with Jordan, 2000; Jordan, 2001), combining community development and regeneration in deprived districts with enforcement measures against deviant behaviour. However, despite detailed attention given to these programmes, new problem phenomena and new buzz words have continued to proliferate.

The Blair administration cannot be accused of having been negligent of the communal dimension of these districts' problems, even if it has adopted a socially conservative version of the goals it pursued. Influenced by Putnam's (2000, 2002) ideas on 'social capital', it tried to strengthen networks and associations, as well as families. The difficulty was that, even where it had success in building local 'bonding' capital, it has found it far more difficult to make 'bridging' links with the mainstream (Leonard, 2004). This was most clearly revealed in violent riots in Bradford, Oldham and Burnley in the summer of 2001, when white and Asian groups from rival deprived neighbourhoods clashed over mutual resentments. The 'community cohesion' initiatives which followed the reports on these events (Home Office, 2002; Blunkett, 2004) indicated that the government was keen to build bridges between members of such rival communities but unclear about how to bridge between them and the mainstream.

The central difficulty for all these initiatives is that the norms and practices they seek to instil – reciprocity, cooperation, honesty and responsibility – are assumed to arise spontaneously in mainstream society, through everyday interactions in employment, civil society and family life. They are taken to be by-products of self-interested choices in markets and other institutions of liberal democracy; hence only deprived communities need these special interventions. In fact, the dominant culture of individualism produces many of the behaviours defined as especially problematic. Binge drinking, drug abuse, yobbishness and lack of respect are far more widespread than the policies presuppose; they are not confined to poor districts. They go with the cult of the individual, as do obesity, promiscuity and political apathy.

Each new wave of policies under New Labour has tried to back positive initiatives with cracking down on targeted problem behaviour – 'zero tolerance', anti-social behaviour orders, curfews and parenting classes. Tough measures against individuals (or even whole groups, such as teenagers in 'hoodies') do not create a culture of civic engagement between citizens. The new emphasis on 'respect' adds nothing, unless it convinces those who feel alienated that their membership and contribution are valued, within a coherent view of how common interests are fulfilled. Policies to shame and stigmatise, such as making offenders on community service wear distinctive uniforms, have the opposite effect (Bunting, 2005).

The planned reforms of services for children and young people put these, with education, as part of the overall goal to ensure that all reach their full potential (DfES, 2004). But education itself is now recognised as a sphere where competition for advantage, rather than cohesion, is the dominant theme. Research suggests that the most successful state schools are colonised by more resourceful middle-class families, and children from poor districts are least mobile, hence losing out under regimes for 'choice' (Sutton Trust, 2005). Similarly, schools in many cities are even more segregated on ethnic lines than are residential districts (Phillips, 2005).

In other words, the professional training of social workers cannot afford to treat the dimensions of individual choice and community cohesion as parallel desirable objectives. Social work education must engage with the contradictions between individual autonomy and communal solidarity. In the process of development to adulthood, children and young people draw on cultural resources from their neighbourhoods and societies, but this dialogue between identity and belonging is complex and problematic.

 Think about communities you know. Does what is said here ring true for them? What, if any, social work practice is happening within communities rather than with individuals?

Well-being and social services

An important recent development in the social sciences, significantly for social work practice, is that the concept of 'well-being' is under fresh scrutiny. In the post-war welfare state era, it was taken to lie in full membership of society, with rights to protection against risks associated with a capitalist economy. This protection consisted partly in belonging to a trade union or civic association and partly in claims on fellow citizens though social insurance and public services.

When collectivism seemed to fail in the mid-1970s, and Margaret Thatcher's programme won majority support in 1979, well-being was redefined to consist in the steady increase in personal prosperity, hence the widening of command over private resources. Expressions like 'consumer sovereignty' and 'consumer empowerment' demonstrated the political dimensions of the new policies, which spilled over into the public sector and linked choice to well-being. New Labour has endorsed these connections.

Research by psychologists now casts doubt on the reliability of long-standing association between economic growth and increased well-being. If people are asked to assess overall satisfaction with their lives, they produce rather robust assessments, which can be compared over time and between countries (Kahneman, 1999). While rich individuals in all societies report themselves as happier than poor ones, the data for the past thirty or forty years show that citizens of affluent societies are not making gains in subjective well-being corresponding with gains in increased incomes per head (Kahneman et al., 1999; Frey and Stutzer, 2002: 9–12; Layard, 2003).

These findings confirm what has been suspected for many years – that the pursuit of further material affluence in rich societies puts people on a 'hedonic treadmill' in which they become victims of their own rivalrous desires to own and consume more than others and, hence, of stress and overwork (Bunting, 2004). Many writers have concluded that a competitive market environment, threatening everyone with insecurity and demanding more and more effort to 'get ahead' causes unhappiness (Lane, 2000; Pusey, 2003). The obverse is that individual self-realisation does not equate to happiness unless it also leads to better relationships with others. The same set of researchers showed that the main determinants of subjective well-being are close relationships (Myers, 1999) and wider community membership (Argyle, 1999). In the UK, there is disturbing evidence of declines in both dimensions among certain sections of the population. For example, rates of dissatisfaction with their partners by first-married people aged thirty in 2001 were almost ten times higher than those recorded among the same age group at the start of the previous decade, with similar large rises among cohabiting and second-married couples (Ferri and Smith, 2003). Psychosocial disorders among children and young people have risen continually since the 1950s (Rutter and Smith, 1995). Men in Social Class V, almost half of whom were members of trade unions in the post-war period, are now less than half as likely to be members; indeed, a larger proportion of them have been arrested than belong to these or other organisations (Bynner and Parsons, 2003).

One important question which research has not addressed is how these findings relate to the emergence of the 'service economy' in affluent societies. Whereas industry, especially manufacturing, was the largest source of employment in the immediate post-war period, particularly in the UK and Germany, most of these jobs have now gone to the East Asian countries, leaving services as the employers of around 70 per cent of the workforces in affluent countries. The comparative success of the US and UK economies, in terms of employment growth, is said to be in the creation of new service jobs, especially in the private sector (Iversen and Wren, 1998). This trend in the labour market, visible since the mid-1960s, has been further reinforced by New Labour's policies.

This shift has been achieved by drawing more women into the labour market, thus providing the 'flexibility' that was missing in old industrial structures. Women are also often the main consumers of the new services, which employ mainly women. The Yellow Pages record a growth of over 500 per cent in aromatherapists and cosmetic surgeons between 1992 and 2002 (BBC Radio 4, 2004). On New Labour's assumptions, the greater use of private services for personal self-realisation should express exactly the kind of freedom, choice and self-development that enhances well-being.

Why it has not done so should be a question of urgent and intense concern for social workers. On the face of it, the quest for self-improvement through individual projects of awareness (counselling, therapy, experiential learning) sounds like the adoption of our professional philosophy on a societal scale. I would argue that it misses an essential part of social work's contribution, the cultural and collective context of wider relationships.

This same element is missing from the service-delivery, evidence-based and managerialist style of public services. In focusing on efficiency, targeting and outcomes for individuals, it has neglected the contextual features of services, which give experiences meaning and integrate them into the membership of communities and into citizenship itself. In my conclusions I shall consider how individual freedom and choice might be offset by a more contextual approach to the personal social services.

Conclusions

New Labour is conscious of the issues raised in the previous section. The launch of Layard's (2005) book on the topic is also coordinated with a policy initiative on mental health; Layard himself addressed a seminar of the Downing Street strategy unit on 'Mental Health: Britain's Biggest Social Problem?' (Brindle, 2005).

At present, all that is happening is that 'well-being' has entered the long list of buzzwords which pepper government documents, along with 'participation'. For example, the Department of Health Green Paper (2005) on social care is entitled *Independence, Well-being and Choice*. Not only is there no attempt to analyse the relationship between these notions; there is no clarification of what well-being might mean, or of how it has come to be a contested concept.

Both curriculum design and the cultural environment of public services obscure the tensions between individual choice and community cohesion. The *Requirements for Social Work Training* (DH, 2002a) simply lists tasks, risks and skills in relation to 'individuals, families, carers, groups and communities', without acknowledging any such issues. I have argued that the collective context requires attention in its own right.

Professionals cannot simply blame the government, businesses or mainstream culture for public services' shortcomings. For instance, the scandalous quality of school dinners was exposed by a celebrity chef, Jamie Oliver (Channel 4 TV, 2005), not by teachers, education officials or catering workers. Furthermore, Oliver demonstrated that, with energy and charisma, it was possible to change the whole context and culture of the school kitchen and canteen. Professionals have colluded in a system rationalising the malnourishment of children as 'choice'. There is a similar scandal waiting to break in geriatric wards and care homes, with the added dimension of withdrawing all nourishment from selected patients, deemed no longer viable.

Oliver did not just denounce the lack of nutritional value of 'turkey twizzlers'. He involved a whole class (eventually a whole school) in picking, preparing, cooking and eating healthy food. Thus, he provided a coherent education and social experience, in which they all shared. Whereas the idea of individual choice counts sharing as a cost, not a benefit, Oliver showed it was a necessary feature of creating a meaningful context for healthy eating.

Fortunately, there are successful models to follow, both in the voluntary and community sector, and in public policy initiatives – but practice must embrace something far broader than 'service delivery'. For example, one of the strongest forces driving the local authorities in Oldham, Burnley, Halifax, Slade Green and Stoke to re-engage with local communities has been the rise of the British National Party (BNP). It is as part of a political process that people have again been consulted and involved in improving the quality of their lives (Muir, 2005). Support for the BNP consequently fell sharply. Since our welfare state was founded on the attempt to win citizens' loyalties for democratic politics, and against totalitarianism, this revives post-war tradition.

Social work cannot wait for the political culture and landscape to change to its advantage; it must also be proactive in making opportunities. This requires alliances with other human-service professionals, and between agencies and sectors, to identify contexts for potential development. At a theoretical level, social work academics can also collaborate with other social scientists in re-examining the nature of services, and their particular contribution to well-being (Jordan, 2005). And practitioners can re-examine the basis of their daily work, in relationships and cultures of warmth and acceptance.

Key learning points

1. The 'choice agenda' in public services is in conflict with the 'community cohesion' agenda.
2. Individualism and independence in social care are not easily reconciled with the well-being of service users.
3. The collective context of practice deserves attention in its own right.
4. Relationships are the most important component of well-being, and social work should focus on these.

Taking it further

Readers who want to know more about this will find the following helpful:

Davies, L. and Leonard, P. (eds) (2004) *Social Work in a Corporate Era: Practices of Power and Resistance*, Aldershot: Ashgate.

Jordan, B. with Jordan C. (2000) *Social Work and the Third Way: Tough Love as Social Policy*, London: Sage.

Layard, R. (2005) *Happiness: Lessons from a New Science*, London: Allen Lane.

3 The place of values in social work education

Richard Hugman

This chapter will:

- address the place of values within social work and its education;
- argue that social work is a necessarily value-laden activity and that practice cannot be understood unless the values underpinning it are fully recognised;
- suggest that practitioners must engage in a continued process of critical thinking and the development of 'moral fluency' to give practical expression to these values.

Introduction

Social work is a value-laden activity. Its central concern with 'social change, problem solving in human relationships and the empowerment and liberation of people to enhance well-being' (IFSW/IASSW, 2000) means that, at its core, social work focuses on aspects of life that embody people's hopes and fears, their dreams and struggles. The structures of a society and institutions within it, such as the family, are things about which people hold very clear and strong views concerning what is right and wrong. The goals people have for their lives and the choices they make in action also express values. Thus, values are an integral part of every element of social work, whether at the micro, the meso or the macro level, in direct or indirect practice and in every imaginable setting.

For this reason, it is essential that social work education should explicitly recognise and respond to values in practice. This chapter explores the place of values in social work, particularly the way in which effective practice is grounded in a clearly articulated set of values, and considers how values can be addressed in professional education.

Which values?

As Koehn (1994) has argued, all professions can be understood as the pursuit of particular sets of values. The values to which Koehn refers are very broad. For example: the values of medicine, nursing and the allied health professions are those of health; the values of the legal profession and the courts are those of justice. Of course, none of these professional areas has a monopoly on the core value set associated with them. Neither is any core set of values exclusionary of others. For example, social workers in some settings may share health as a value with colleagues from other professions, just as they will also identify justice as an important value (especially if seen as *social* justice).

In this sense, values, considered broadly, can be seen as goals or objectives of a profession. They represent what the profession regards as important and, therefore, what it should be seeking to achieve overall. Embedded in the IFSW/IASSW (2000) definition of social work are four values that define social work globally: social change, (social) well-being, human rights and social justice. Let us look at each of these in turn.

Social change

In framing social change as a goal or objective of social work, an implicit assertion is made that the causes of problems in everyday life and a lack of well-being arise from social relationships and the structural arrangements of society. Indeed, from its beginnings, social work has had achievement of social change as a value, in the sense of it being a primary objective. Early pioneers, such as Hill, Addams and Richmond, all emphasised that social change was both desirable and possible to ensure the development of a good society (Fook, 2002). Addams, particularly, saw social work as a profession necessary for achieving a fair and democratic society (Addams, [1907] 2002). These early writers disagreed among themselves on the focus of change. The continuing debates within social work have concerned whether change should be pursued at the micro, meso or macro level, and the resulting difference in the type of methods which are seen as appropriate.

In the past two decades, especially in Western countries, this value has increasingly been challenged by shifts in political and economic ideology. The rise of neo-liberalism, emphasising individual responsibility for all aspects of life, has seen an attack on the value of social change. Along with the wider human services and social welfare field of which it is a part, social work has been required increasingly by governments to show it can provide services as commodities for consumption, and the focus on social change has been recast as illegitimate within this context (Hugman, 1998). Thus the value of social change has to be seen as highly contested, both from within the profession (in terms of focus and methods) and in the wider society (in terms of ideological legitimacy).

 Do you think social work has a role in bringing about social change?

Social well-being

The objective of social change is not held for its own sake. It is inherently bound up with achieving social well-being. It could be seen that another primary goal of social work is to address social need. Doyal and Gough (1991) define human need in terms of those things that people require in order to be able to live within their society. Fundamental to this are health and autonomy. Health (including physical and psychological safety) is a basic need, because without this it is much more difficult to achieve other things, such as happiness, good relationships and success. Similarly, unless people also have a sufficient degree of autonomy in thought and action, the achievement of these other more specific life goals will be much harder.

In practice, social work addresses needs that tend to be defined more specifically. In many cases social workers respond to needs for 'independence', 'care', 'protection', 'improved family relationships', 'avoidance of self-destructive behaviours' and so on. However, all of these can be seen as specific forms of the broader values of health and autonomy. As with social change, some of the debates within social work and about social work in the wider society concern the way in which the value of social well-being is understood and expressed. It is in the operationalisation of this value that the present neo-liberal political and economic climate attempts to limit the capacity of professions, including social work, to make choices about practice goals (Hugman, 1998). In as much as well-being is seen as the responsibility of each person for her- or himself, it follows that decisions about someone's needs and how to achieve them should also rest with the individual. Where people pay directly for services, professionals have a strong role in setting goals and agendas directly with service users. However, where the state provides services for citizens, contracts, service specifications and other managerial devices may serve to provide accountability, but at the same time they set practice agendas and remove the definition of professional goals from professions.

Human rights

For Ife (2001), the value of human rights is the core of social work. A rights perspective begins from the moral claim that to deny human rights is to deny people their humanity. He points to five elements in the idea of human rights as it shapes social work values (pp. 10–11):

- Rights concern the basic requirement for a good human life.
- Rights are universal or are universally applied to specific social groups (such as 'all people who are disadvantaged by a specific problem').
- There is widespread consensus on the legitimacy of a right.
- A right can be achieved for all those to whom it legitimately applies.
- A right is not in conflict with other rights.

For Ife, human rights can be seen in three 'generations' (in other words, stages of thought): civil and political rights; economic, social and cultural rights; and community and national rights. Social work, he argues, is affected by all of these.

What human rights issues can you identify in your area of practice?

The value of human rights in social work can be seen, for example, in the practice objective of 'empowerment' (Burke and Dalrymple, 2002). This is founded on the principle that everyone has the right to make decisions about their own lives to the greatest extent of their capabilities. The value of human rights points to the responsibility that social workers have to ensure the rights of service users are identified and promoted. Difficulties may be encountered in relation to Ife's fifth element, because the reconciliation of conflicting rights places great demands on social workers to grasp the nature of rights and the ways in which they connect. Hence, to achieve empowerment in situations where different service users' interests are (at least potentially) in conflict, it may be necessary for each to receive assistance from separate social workers.

Social justice

As Banks (2006) demonstrates, the value of social justice is widely held in social work. Many national codes of ethics make strong statements about the pursuit of social justice as a primary objective for social work. This may take the form of asserting a duty for social workers to oppose inequality, oppression and exclusion. However, what this means often differs, as justice refers to many ideas that are not the same and can even conflict with each other. Examples include the notions of equality of rights and of desert as a basis for the allocation of scarce resources (including the use of a social worker's time). Clearly, social workers' actions will be very different if working from an understanding that social justice is based on human rights compared to one where it might be based on views about desert.

One form of attention to social justice apparently shared globally by social workers is opposition to racial and ethnic discrimination and oppression. As a value position, anti-racism begins from the premise that all human beings have equal moral value. Thus, beliefs or actions that confront or undermine this value should be opposed. Racism, like other forms of oppression such as sexism, ageism, homophobia and disablism, is pernicious because it takes a fact about a person (such as skin colour) and turns this into a moral category, which is then used to deny the humanity of that person in some way. Moreover, the use of such categories is then applied to whole groups of people in a way that denies the individuality of each, their identity, values and beliefs. The injustice of racism lies in this denial of humanity in others and in the way such a value leads to oppression. Anti-racism does not ignore differences existing between cultures, or between groups within cultures. Rather, it asserts that to take such differences as the basis of moral distinctions which are then used to oppress and exclude people is an injustice.

Multiple values

The four values indicated in the IFSW/IASSW (2000) definition of social work are derived from two particular traditions of ethics (Banks, 2006). The first is usually associated with the work of Kant, who postulated that each human being is of absolute moral worth solely on the grounds of being human and so should always been treated as an end in her- or himself, never as a means to an end. The idea of human rights is primarily based on this position. The other tradition is that of consequentialism, usually associated with utilitarianism (as in J. S. Mill's work), in which an act or idea is evaluated according to its outcome and on a balance of the consequences for the majority of people who are affected. The idea of social justice is primarily based on this position.

Resolution of these debates is often found in a pragmatic response bringing together the principles that derive from these positions, simply placing them alongside each other. The work of dealing with conflicts between them is then left to the interpretation of principles in practice situations (see Chapter 23). However, this is not an arbitrary process; Banks (2006: 34) calls it a 'common morality' perspective, arguing that in everyday life most people use 'considered judgements' that build up coherent positions through experience. Indeed, sometimes values may conflict, and each of us finds ways of reconciling our values so that we maintain a plausible sense of integrity (we return to this below).

Understanding diversity in values

Each individual social worker brings a unique set of personal values to the professional role. At the same time, each service user will hold another unique set of personal values. So to what extent is it possible to speak of a shared set of values defining social work? Beyond that, given the cultural differences involved, to what extent is it even thinkable that there could be a global set of values that could be said to be held across the 84 countries in which formal professional social work exists (defined by membership of the IFSW)?

One answer to this question has been to assert that values are always particular to the position of individuals and groups within a given society or culture. This position is known as 'relativism' because it argues that values are always *relative* to social or cultural contexts. For example, in contemporary Western societies, many people regard individual autonomy as extremely important. This is reflected in ideas about choices people might make about their lives, such as their careers or their close personal relationships. In contrast, in many Eastern and indigenous societies, the value of group membership (such as family or clan) may be regarded as much more important than individual autonomy. This can be seen in situations where life choices are viewed as the responsibility of significant others rather than of an individual, seen for example in the influence parents and other family members might have on the choice of a career or a spouse.

An example of value relativism in professional practice is the different meaning cultures might give to the notion of 'confidentiality'. While the individualism of Western culture affords it high value, as an expression of privacy for the individual and control over life choices that follow from managing who knows what about oneself, in some other cultures the idea of 'confidentiality' challenges the importance of social relationships such as family. Carrese and Rhodes (1995) provide an example of this in the context of health care for Native Americans, where it is expected that poor prognoses are shared with senior family members who then decide what the person with the illness should be told. This directly contradicts notions of the centrality of the individual that are at the core of the principle of 'confidentiality' found in professional codes of ethics (Banks, 2006).

Against this position, however, questions may be asked about the extent to which human beings differ from each other at a fundamental level. This position is known as 'universalism', because it argues that there are foundational values that are *universal* across all social and cultural contexts. For example, as noted above, the idea of 'human rights', central to the Universal Declaration of Human Rights (UN, 1948), applies to all people, irrespective of their origins or location. These rights include the right to life, the right to education, the right to freedom from slavery, the right to protection in law, the right to freedom of conscience and religious belief, and the right to freedom of movement. Where people cannot enjoy these rights, the universal position argues, it is not simply a matter of cultural difference but of the denial of values inherent in being human. For Doyal and Gough (1991), these rights link to common human needs; for Ife (2001), the assertion of rights is the only way to achieve those things that are needed.

An example of a universal approach to values is provided by Browne (1995) in her discussion of nursing practice. As a white Canadian working in an Inuit community, Browne observed how the meaning of 'respect' between the professional and service users was communicated in the same practical way that it would be in a Western social context, even though in conversation the idea might appear to be different. Allowing service users modesty in clinical examinations, discussing with them what was significant for them in terms of 'confidentiality', and so on, were all part of the cross-cultural practice she describes.

To complicate matters further, it can also be argued that both relative and universal claims have some merit. Cultural differences do impact upon the values that people hold and act on, while at the same time there are some values that appear to be important for all people. A resolution to this dichotomy can be found in the idea of 'ethical pluralism' (Kekes, 1993). In summary, this approach distinguishes between *primary* and *secondary* values. The former are those that can be understood as the values that are foundational to a moral framework, expressing broadly common human goals. They might include, for example, valuing the importance of children being able to grow up healthy or being able to enjoy the capacity to love and be loved. Secondary values, in contrast, are those that operationalise the primary values, expressed, for example, in having appropriate family structures or a particular health and social welfare system. These are attachments to particular cultural manifestations of ways to achieve primary values. So, it must be emphasised that 'ethical pluralism' is not simply relativism in disguise. It rejects the claims of both relativism and universalism in their pure forms.

Ethical pluralism as explained by Kekes (1993) also recognises that values are not neat and tidy. Rather, it accepts that the values we hold may at times be *incompatible* or even *incommensurable*. Incompatible values are those that are contradictory. That is, although we may hold such values, we cannot express one without denying another. Examples that Kekes gives include 'freedom and equality, solitude and public spiritedness, good judgement and passionate involvement' (1993: 54). Incommensurable values are those that cannot even be compared, an example of which is the choice between duty and well-being

(Kekes, 1993: 56). It is not that we cannot choose (otherwise we could not act) but that all such choices remain subject to debate and are thus impermanent. I expect that many readers will have had the experience of struggling within themselves between two strongly held values which cannot be compared but which make competing demands on life choices. This is the nature of a genuine 'ethical dilemma'.

 Can you think of an example of this from your work? How did you resolve it?

This complexity is especially important for social work because the profession focuses on the individual and the social context, responding to both and to the connections between them. Both primary and secondary values form part of the field of practice understood like this. Social workers must be prepared to work not only with their own incompatible and incommensurable values, but also with those of service users and where there are differences between individuals and their communities. This calls for a combination of practical wisdom and skill that has been called 'being morally active' or 'having moral fluency' (summarised in Hugman, 2005: 163–4). A vital element in developing such capacities is the way in which values are addressed in professional education, so we now turn to this question.

Values in social work education: frameworks

Because values are such a central facet of social work, it could be expected that they would form a similarly important component of social work education. To consider how this is achieved, we will look briefly at the guidance from two countries, the UK and Australia, before proceeding to look at the educational issues arising from explicit recognition of values in social work practice.

In the UK, several bodies exert influence on social work education. First, the Quality Assurance Agency for Higher Education (QAA) in its benchmark statement for social work (QAA, 2000), Section 2.4, under the heading of 'Defining Principles' begins 'Social work is a moral activity [...]' and proceeds to specify respect for persons, honouring cultural diversity and combating discrimination and social exclusion as examples. In Section 3.1.1, it itemises 'values and ethics', noting three broad themes: the nature and history of social work values; specific values (related to concepts of rights and responsibilities and of justice); and philosophical and conceptual material to enable the student to develop a capacity to think about values. However, the document also itemises other value-laden standards. These include, for example, reference to the implications of cultural diversity, anti-discriminatory practice and the connections between policy, law and professionalism. For the QAA, quite clearly, values are not only a core dimension of social work but also can be specified distinctly.

Similarly, the Training Organisation for the Personal Social Services (TOPSS) UK Partnership (2002) document specifying the national occupational standards for social work makes its assumptions about values quite explicit. The opening section repeatedly makes statements such as, 'social workers must be open and honest', 'social workers must respect confidentiality' and 'social workers must challenge injustice' (TOPSS, 2002: 2–3). These ideas are summarised in Sub-section 6, 'Values', where empowerment of service users is added to notions of respect, honesty, confidentiality and challenging injustice (TOPSS's 2002: 4). In the following sections, which detail in considerable minutiae the standards of every type of practice, values and ethics are placed at the centre of the explanatory models. This part of the document is the GSCC, 'Codes of Practice'. As the GSCC is now the statutory registering body for social workers in England (there are other councils for the other constituent parts of the UK), the terms of these codes should be known and understood by all graduates.

Ironically, the DH (2002a) *Requirements for Social Work Training*, which is the UK government policy statement on social work education, makes only one very brief mention of values and ethics, in the appendices, where it summarises the headings from the QAA and TOPSS UK documents. Other components of social work education are provided in explicit terms (such as the number of hours of assessed practice, the teaching of law and so on). Thus it would seem that for the UK, although values in social work have been specified, the formal policy statement has assumed but not addressed them.

In contrast to the UK, the framework for social work education in Australia is established by the Australian Association of Social Workers (AASW, 2000). Although in most other respects this document is like the DH (2002a) statement of requirements, it is more like the QAA (2000) and TOPSS (2002) papers because it specifies qualifying degree programmes must include '[m]aterial on the recognition and thinking through of ethical issues' (AASW, 2000: 8). It further states that social workers should be able to 'think critically within a framework of commitment to ethical practice', stating that: 'particular attention [should be] paid to dimensions of power and disadvantage, and the influence of class, gender, age, intellectual and physical disability, heterosexism, race and ethnicity [and there] must be a focus on empowering and non-oppressive practice' (AASW, 2000: 8). So, like the QAA and TOPSS, the AASW commits social work to a definite values framework, consistent with the IFSW/IASSW understanding of social work (see above) and the international framework for professional ethics established by the IFSW and IASWW (2004). In this sense, we can say that there is wide agreement about the core values of social work and their place in social work education. These values are very specific.

Values in social work education: practice

 If you are a manager, lecturer or a practice teacher, how might you help beginning practitioners to become 'morally active' or 'morally fluent'?

Being 'morally active' or 'morally fluent' was seen earlier in this chapter as the purpose of values education. (Issues introduced here are pursued further in Chapter 23.)

There is a problem arising from the way the educational documents that have been reviewed here specify a very distinct set of values. This problem concerns the implication that values education should therefore be didactic. That is, if social work values can be specified in this way, is the educational issue therefore one of ensuring that 'correct' values are learned? To answer this affirmatively suggests that values can be learned like this. It also denies the validity of other values that any individual beginning social work might quite reasonably hold and generally fails to deal with the complexities of reasonably competing values.

In contrast, I argue that values education in social work has to accomplish a very difficult task: it needs both to address the values that form the basis of social work (globally) and to allow for difference, incompatibility and incommensurability. So it is insufficient, although necessary, to present the list of core values as something to be learned as a set of facts, no matter how wide the agreement throughout the profession that the list is definitive. Learning what is widely regarded as the core values of the profession can only be a starting point for values education.

Beyond this, the professional social worker must be able to think through values as they are encountered in practice and theory, to weigh them, to grasp the incompatibilities and incommensurabilities and to learn to work with these as a reality. One very common way of structuring learning of this kind is through the use of case discussions or vignettes of 'ethical dilemmas'. These can be structured in order to avoid the possibility of there being just one 'correct' answer and, instead, to require students to engage in a reasoned way with value differences and value incompatibilities. Even in doing this, we should consider how students are to be equipped to engage in a reasoned discussion about values.

The approach proposed by Plath et al. (1999) is to provide students with learning in 'critical thinking'. This approach combines the use of case studies or vignettes with clearly articulated learning about social work theories and values. Plath and her colleagues tried two different ways of doing this. The first they call 'immersion', in which the theories and values are embedded in the case study material and students are assisted to learn inductively by teasing them out. The other they call 'infusion', in which theories and values are taught separately and then students address case study material using these as tools. Plath et al. conclude that the second approach, that of 'infusion', is more effective as a learning strategy. The point of this is that students learn to identify values in all aspects of social work and the capacity to engage critically with their own and others' value positions. The underlying ethos is that there are clear strongly shared primary values underpinning social work, while there is considerable diversity at the secondary level; at both levels, however, there will be many times when values are in conflict, even those held by an individual.

Being clear about values

As we have seen, it is possible for individual social workers, and for the profession as a whole, to hold values which may at times be in conflict or which may even be impossible to compare. However, at the same time, the profession globally has reached a strong degree of consensus that certain values are more congruent with the technical objectives of practice. In other words, it is not possible to separate values from technique or, to put it differently, to detach ends and means. We began with the observation that social work is value laden. To conclude, we should add that it is values (ends) that give meaning to the techniques of practice (means) and not the other way around. Unless social workers are equipped to grasp the values dimension of theory and practice, then they will be poorly prepared for the complexities of their role. For this reason, values education (introduction to critical thinking about values) as opposed to values instruction (didactic learning of given values) is an essential part of professional training. Only when social workers can engage as members of a professional community in the constant process of dialogue about values can we be said to be clear about the values of the profession.

Key learning points

1. Social work globally embodies four value dimensions, which are the moral goals of the profession: social change, social well-being, human rights and social justice.
2. Within every society and for each person there are usually multiple and competing values, some of which are primary and some secondary. Thinking about professional values and ethics must take account of this complexity.
3. Guideline curriculum documents provide very clear support for values education in social work, emphasising specific core values.
4. The task of social work education is not only to teach beginning practitioners about the core values of the profession but also to prepare them to engage in the moral debates surrounding social work.

Taking it further

Readers who want to know more about this will find the following helpful:
Banks, S. (2006) *Ethics and Values in Social Work* (3rd edn), Basingstoke: Palgrave.
Hugman, R. (2005) *New Approaches in Ethics for the Caring Professions*, Basingstoke: Palgrave.
Ife, J. (2001) *Human Rights and Social Work*, Cambridge: Cambridge University Press.

Uncertainty
The defining characteristic of social work?

4

Jan Fook

This chapter examines:

- how uncertainty affects our practice, and what it means for
  - how we construct social work professionalism
  - frame our practices and theories
  - educate future social workers.
- whether uncertainty is a useful concept for framing our contemporary understanding of social work.

Introduction

- Is it possible to be effective social workers when much of the context we work in is uncertain?
- Can you think of instances when you were sure of what needed to be done, only to find that you were not able to control the situation?
- Have there been times when the information which you needed to make a clear decision about action was ambiguous?

I argue that although the idea of uncertainty pervades thinking about our social and global contexts, it may not be a sufficient framework for defining the social work profession's contemporary mission. There may also be more certain and definable characteristics of social work, which, although taking account of uncertainty, nonetheless remain relatively constant in guiding how we approach practice.

I begin by reviewing the idea of uncertainty, first as conceptualised by social theorists and then as discussed by professionals. I then look at what these conceptions mean for our understanding of professionalism, professional knowledge and practice. Last, I outline some specific directions the social work profession needs to take in order to remake itself for current times.

Uncertainty

Thinking about uncertainty is aptly captured by Beck's (1992) description of contemporary times as 'reflexive modernity', which involves:

- a breakdown of predictable life stages, social rituals and norms because of uncertain social conditions;
- increased access to information, both through educational opportunities and technological advances;
- resulting shifts in social boundaries and categories and increased opportunity to remake them;
- emphasis on the importance of individual identity-making and life choices;
- contexts becoming more important;
- the breaking of traditional boundaries, people deriving their sense of community from a wide range of networks;
- different sources of power, less hierarchical and more mixed.

However, in this climate of greater choice and fluidity, there is also increased risk in charting a life course through uncertain conditions. Social institutions themselves cannot monitor and control these risks in personal lives, so there is a greater need for individuals to find their own sources of meaning and solidarity. Overall, the construction of the self within these fluid social contexts becomes the crucial task of living. Thus the self is a reflexive project (Giddens, 1991) in which 'critical reflection and incoming information are constantly used by people to constitute and (re)negotiate their identities' (Ferguson, 2001: 45). In reflexive modernity, this task of living, to create a meaningful sense of self in relation to changing social conditions, is what is uncertain.

Turner and Rojek (2001) add another dimension, 'vulnerability', to the idea of uncertainty: the vulnerability of our embodiment. Yet vulnerability also has positive aspects: it 'suggests an openness to the world and our capacity to respond to that openness in ways that are creative and transformative' (Turner and Rojek, 2001: xi). Furthermore, they argue that frailty implied in vulnerability is central to humanity, having the capacity to unite human beings. Uncertainty in this sense is borne out of our own physical vulnerability, carrying both positive and negative opportunities.

In broad terms, uncertainty experienced by individuals involves the interplay between breakdowns in taken-for-granted social institutions and people's need to make a meaningful sense of themselves in charting a successful life course in this context. This situation holds both positive and negative potential: positive in that opportunities may exist for creating new alliances and options and reaffirming universal bonds between people; negative in that increased competitiveness and fear of risk may lead to greater self-protection, narrowness, rigidity and social intolerance.

Uncertainty and implications for professional knowledge

There are specific implications of such uncertainty for the role of knowledge in society. Beck (1992) further theorises that within a 'risk society', *risk*, but also the *perception of risk*, becomes important. This perception fundamentally depends on external knowledge. Therefore, the nature of knowledge, its fallibility and control over its production become increasingly important in managing perception of risk. This has specific implications for professionals and their knowledge base, particularly for the expert knowledge base upon which professionals are presumed to practise.

Expert (scientific-technical) knowledge is coming under mounting public criticism, questioning its alleged value neutrality and, thus, emphasising the role of different political interests in determining knowledge, its interpretation and use. Pellizoni (2003: 328) terms this as 'radical uncertainty', characterised by problems whose very premises are indeterminate, in which knowledge may be interpreted in fundamentally different ways and about which there may not even be consensus on what is relevant. In this realm, 'facts and values overlap' (Pellizoni, 2003: 328).

How might some of this uncertainty play out in the daily dynamics of professional practice? 'Radical uncertainty' may provide a useful framework for understanding much indeterminacy that social workers experience. Banks (2001: 17–21) suggests that, for social workers, uncertainty may arise when 'technical rational' and 'moral' realms become confused – essentially technical-rational decisions gain moral overtones, and morality itself may become defined solely in terms of outcomes. This latter point refers to cases where the 'right' action may be determined by whether the 'right' outcome was achieved (only knowable in hindsight). To exemplify, she cites cases where a child protection worker may be deemed to have made the wrong decision (in not removing a child from parental care) only after the child is murdered. If the child appears to be subsequently unharmed, the decision is deemed right.

Charles (2001) notes uncertainties in the medical profession, which is primarily uncertainty regarding limitations of knowledge experienced by medical students. This is experienced as a gap between what is known and what is needed to be known. What makes it more uncertain is the uncertainty of whether the gap results from personal inadequacy or from an inherent problem with the nature of medical knowledge (Charles, 2001: 64). Other types of uncertainties include those regarding: treatment outcomes and patient responses (Light, 1979); patient preferences for participation in decision-making (Charles et al., 1998); and patients' understanding of treatment benefits and risks (Charles, 2001: 64). Further uncertainties exist due to the clinician's subjectivity (emotions, intuition, biases of social and personal background) and the fallibility of test technology (White and Stancombe, 2003: 16).

To summarise: uncertainty exhibits itself in several key ways. Broadly, there is uncertainty for individuals in both surviving and succeeding in life – this is the project of making selves and life courses when social structures are changing and no longer provide sufficient guidance. In this context arise particular uncertainties for professionals in trying to minimise risk and the perception of risk in situations and individuals' lives within uncertain environments. Professional knowledge is uncertain in several ways:

- There may be inadequacy in addressing new and changing situations.
- Outcomes may be unpredictable since contexts (and factors involved in those contexts) change.
- Meaning is indeterminate – since there may be multiple differing interpretations which may change according to context.
- Meaning systems may become confused so that moral and technical realms overlap.

Clearly, uncertainty of outcome is one of the major uncertainties facing professionals. Not only is it unclear which specific professional actions may lead to which specific outcomes (all other conditions remaining static), but having certain preconceived outcomes in mind may actually work against successful professional practice (Fook et al., 2000: 134). Yet despite a wealth of research indicating the *certainty* of uncertainty, some practitioners still assume that uncertainty is something to be eliminated or controlled (Gibbs, 2002: 154–8).

Given clear acknowledgement of uncertainty in professional practice, how do we understand this persistent need for certainty? Perhaps professional status is somewhat dependent on management of risk or, at least, the perception of it – the conundrum for professionals is whether (and how) their knowledge can be made and applied in ways that effectively reduce these uncertainties, despite the fact that they are integral to current human and social experience. We might say that *the paradox of professional practice is the certainty of uncertainty, and the corresponding need to provide certainty within uncertainty*.

Recognising this sort of dilemma points to key ways to develop our characterisation of professionalism:

1   We need a better understanding of how we work and develop knowledge in relation to specific contexts, as opposed to how we develop more abstract and generalised knowledge. I term this *contextuality*.
2   As a result, we need to reconceptualise the nature of learning as contextual.
3   We need to develop openness and tolerance for difference in the light of vulnerability – this is not only a challenge but also a necessity.
4   We need to frame uncertainty and lack of control as positive opportunities.

New professionalism and the nature of professional knowledge and expertise

'New professionalism' (Leicht and Fennell, 2001) is a way of reconceptualising professionalism to incorporate some of these issues and challenges. It is presented as an alternative to 'old professionalism', in which it was assumed that professionals, as experts, could master the requisite knowledge in imposing order and reducing uncertainty (Gallagher, 2005). By contrast, 'new professionals' recognise there must also be openness to scrutiny. The 'new professionalism' therefore 'blends control through expertise with an openness to inspection and evaluation by peers and the public at large' (Leicht and Fennell, 2001: 14). We see calls for increased accountability in current trends in the UK towards service users (GSCC,

2002a) and inclusion of their perspective in research, service design and delivery. This may entail recognition that scientific knowledge 'becomes more and more necessary but less sufficient' (Beck, 1992: 156), so that professionals must consider new ways of creating, using and reviewing knowledge. This has led to calls for a more reflective approach to practice (Sullivan, 1995: Chapter 6) valuing the role of intuition and the ability to develop expertise directly from experience itself (Gallagher, 2005).

The idea of working with uncertainty provides a useful conceptual framework to underpin our understanding of the expertise of the 'new professionalism'. How do professionals make certainty out of uncertainty, that is, act with relative confidence and commitment in situations where knowledge, outcomes and conditions are indeterminate?

Studies of social workers' actual practice indicate that they work in a large range of settings requiring diverse and multiple skills and knowledge. These situations often involve an array of competing interests, so it is not always clear who the client is, and workers' practice may be in part determined by context (Fook et al., 2000: 111). These complexities lead to the need to develop the following features of expertise (summarised from Fook, 2004a: 35–8):

- contextuality;
- knowledge and theory creation (transferability);
- processuality;
- critical reflexivity;
- a transcendant vision.

Contextuality refers to the ability to work in and with the whole context and in relation to it. This involves appreciation of how specific contexts may influence actions and interpretations of players in it, but it also involves ability to work with the whole context, rather than focusing solely on individual players (Fook et al., 2000; Fook, 2002).

Transferability involves the ability to create knowledge/theory relevant to context and the ability to take learning from one situation and make it relevant to a new situation. In this sense, it differs from generalising knowledge across situations. The former's focus is on using prior knowledge to illuminate new meanings, whereas the latter's focus is more on imposing meaning from other contexts.

Critical reflexivity (Fook et al., 2000: 189–92) and an ability to critically reflect is important in this theory-creation process. It involves not noly creating theory directly from practice by exposing the assumptions embedded therein but also an ability to locate oneself and one's own influence in the situation, particularly in relation to existing power arrangements. I will clarify what I mean by critical reflection later by elaborating on a particular approach to critical reflection which I consider crucial to the 'new' social work profession.

It is vital in social work to retain a value position, and there are increasing calls to maintain the integrity of professional work by doing this (Sullivan, 1995). 'New' professional expertise must therefore include ability to maintain a higher order of values, termed a 'grounded yet transcendent vision' (Fook et al., 2000: 196). This involves the ability not only to respond to daily conflicts in particular situations but also to continue to work, at another level, in terms of broader goals (what might be termed a 'calling' (Gustafson, 1982)). This broader vision gives meaning and allows a sense of continuity despite uncertainty.

In summary, the expertise of the new professional requires not only a contextual ability to make and remake appropriate knowledge but also an ability to ground this knowledge in specific contexts and yet to transcend those contexts through maintaining broader values. Professionals use values to provide continuity and certainty and as a guide for remaking contextual knowledge and practice.

Social work theory, practice and education in uncertainty

Social workers must be prepared not only to make and remake (through regular scrutiny) their knowledge in ways which are relevant in changing contexts but also to share some congruency with higher order values which may transcend specific workplace contexts. In many ways, this imperative differs little from how many of us may have understood the social work profession's ideals: as being contextual, accountable and value based. Where new demands enter, however, is in understanding and valuing knowledge and approaches to knowledge-making. Whereas former approaches to professionalism were based on more static, rational and hierarchical approaches to knowledge, new professionalism demands new understandings of knowledge-making. Whilst social work's ideals may remain similar, the ways these are enacted, learnt and developed may change radically.

We can understand these better if we focus on the implications of new ways of understanding professional knowledge and its use. For instance, practising from a principle of contextuality may mean that although social justice is valued, the social worker may need to recognise that this may be interpreted and enacted in many different ways and from many different perspectives, according to context and in relation to different players in that context. Given unpredictability of outcomes, the new social worker will need to recognise that what are assumed to be social justice practices may not necessarily result in social justice outcomes in all contexts, or for all players in all contexts. Effective practice based on social justice principles therefore needs to involve a spirit of openness and flexibility, a co-creation of meaning and actions in a particular context. This may mean that not all players agree on what practices or outcomes are appropriate, and, therefore, meanings of social justice must be reinterpreted and reformed during the process. Empathic and listening abilities, communication, cooperative skills, creative abilities and flexibility are vital to this process. This approach points to different forms of accountability which are partially created through processes of dialogue. Values in this sense, whilst having abstract meaning, must also be understood as being co-created in context.

Pause here to think about:

- What are some examples of similar broad values you hold?
- How do you enact these values?
- How can you be sure that the way you enact these values is interpreted and experienced by others as you intend?

More specifically, this means that much has been made of the current importance of reflective approaches in developing new professionalism. Reflective practice (as used in the professions) is attributed to the work of Argyris and Schön (1976) and later to Schön (1983). Although there is considerable confusion about what this actually means in practice (Fook et al., in press), it is possible to delineate a clear model for use by practising social work professionals. I therefore focus attention on critical reflection, as both an approach and a practical process highly compatible with my approach to critical social work (Fook, 2002). I will now briefly elaborate on what this involves, both in theory and in practice.

Critical reflection

Critical reflection is a specific form of reflective practice. Reflective practice involves a process of exposing assumptions which are embedded in the way practice is actually enacted (Argyris and Schön, 1976). In the process of exposing these assumptions, practitioners also engage in unearthing the thinking (or theory) implicit in what they do. The process therefore also functions as a process of articulating and developing practice theory, directly from the practice experience itself. Third, the process acts as a form of evaluation of practice, in that, when implicit theory is exposed, it also becomes available for scrutiny. This in turn presents opportunity for practice to be changed and improved based on this scrutiny. The degree to which the process changes and improves fundamental practices will necessarily vary depending on the fundamentality of the implicit theory exposed and changed.

The process of reflective practice becomes *critical* when it is able to expose a deep level of assumptions which function to preserve dominant power structures or relations (Brookfield, 1995). Many types of assumptions may do this, of course, and they do not necessarily appear to be explicitly about power. For instance, apparently straightforward assumptions about types of knowledge used in professional practice may hide assumptions about which (and whose) knowledge is legitimate and, therefore, also disguise assumptions about who is powerful. Connections between knowledge and power, as developed in notions of discourse, are relevant in understanding how critical reflection can work.

The process of critical reflection can be transformative (that is, it can allow for a reworking of fundamental thinking and power structures and relations) by:

- exposing implicit thinking that unwittingly supports dominant power structures/relations;
- allowing scrutiny of this thinking;
- allowing a remaking of this thinking to support remaking practice in relation to structures and relations in more empowering ways.

I have discussed the details of this process elsewhere (Fook, 2004b; Fook, 2004c), but there are many different ways to critically reflect. The method I use is an example of only one of these. This process is conducted in small groups, in which participants deconstruct 'critical incidents', using questions based on ideas of reflective practice, reflexivity, discourse and deconstructive analysis, and critical theory.

Some research I conducted with participants in these groups indicated that professionals can use critical reflection to remake themselves as potentially powerful, able to exercise agency in influencing situations (Fook and Askeland, 2006). This involves revaluing themselves by recognising many different types of power, and more inclusive conceptions of professionalism. They also remake their choices, moving usually from framing choices in 'forced choice' terms to creating multiple choices, and sometimes moving from a more fatalistic frame (framing practice situations as 'dilemmas') to a more empowered frame (seeing sticking points as potential 'opportunities'). Reframing understandings of practice provides more opportunities for the development of new practices. In this process, participants also experience 'liberation' or empowerment, as if freed from ways of constructing situations that restrict options and ways of doing and being.

These are characteristics vital to the practice of new, and critical, social work. Not only is critical reflection based on new approaches to the creation of professional knowledge, it also appears to foster some of the very values which we have for so long regarded as integral to the social work endeavour and which are now being recognised as crucial in times of uncertainty. In some senses, what remains constant with critical reflection is fundamental social work values but what becomes flexible is the process of creating practice knowledge about these and the types of practice knowledge created.

Critical reflection, contextuality and social work education

Clearly our notions of learning, what is involved and how it best happens need to be reworked to some extent with such an approach.

Learning, from this point of view, may be conceptualised in terms of meaning. This is similar to transformative learning, developed by Mezirow (1994), which is 'the social process of construing and appropriating a new or revised interpretation of the meaning of one's experience as a guide to action' (Mezirow, 1994: 222–3). Following the idea of reflexive modernity, everyone makes meaning of their experience in their own contexts (personal, social, cultural, material). Learning is therefore holistic, involving a range of features, including emotions, activities, social expectations and hidden impulses, and 'is thus an integrated experience and involves the ability to integrate experience' (Fook, 2001: 21).

In this approach, the culture and context of learning become much more integral to aspects of the learning process. How people learn from and in context is important. However, what is of equal importance, and perhaps easier to modify, is how the context of learning and the culture of learning that develops in that context also influence learning. Learning in this sense involves a much broader set of activities than what takes place in a classroom or even in a university and what takes place in direct interactions between students and teachers. How a context and culture of learning is co-created, between sets of players and institutions, becomes vitally important. Of course, the more hidden ways in which cultures develop and are maintained, and the implicit values which are condoned, are especially significant. The processes of teaching and learning, what is communicated about social work in the ways we relate with each other, and the implicit values these support, are a necessary focus in this approach. The ability to critically reflect on how learning contexts and cultures are co-created (often unintentionally) is vital.

Such an approach to learning also places shared responsibility on all who are part of the learning context to co-create a vision of social work through processes and contexts which are congruent with this. There may be less emphasis on specific and set curriculum content and more on learning the processes of learning from experience; accordingly, there may be less emphasis on the location of learning and more emphasis on facilitating learning in a variety of contexts. Established ways of teaching and learning need to be scrutinised for their capacity to foster ability to learn from practice experience, to formulate contextual knowledge, to be open to differences and to reaffirm the broader values and mission of the social work profession.

Possibilities of critical reflection in current contexts?

Given the uncertainty of the current social and global environment, critical reflection is an absolutely vital skill. Nevertheless, it may be difficult for professionals to be reflective when many national and organisational contexts work against reflective cultures. For instance, it might be argued that current trends in the UK are towards more standardised forms of practice that restrict professional discretion and creativity (Parton, 2004). For example, the framework for the assessment of children in need and their families (DH, 2000a) provides necessary guidelines for assessment. Yet there is also a danger that such frameworks may serve primarily as checklists, limiting the ability to recognise less predictable factors. The hidden message is that workers simply need to perform an assessment along preconceived lines, rather than be open to a range of less determinable factors which may also have a bearing on the situation. The end point is emphasised, rather than the process of how relevant information is obtained and interpreted. In some senses, it may feel as if workers are not rewarded for their own thinking but more for arriving at right outcomes.

Yet this climate does not work counter to critically reflective stances per se. Workers still need to engage with service users to conduct assessments in ways that allow them to elicit a complexity of information and the possibility of different viewpoints. They also must make decisions about interpreting information. These remain aspects of practice requiring critical reflective abilities and a degree of predetermined rigour. From this point of view, it may be argued that critical reflective abilities may allow better outcomes. Being critically reflective is not necessarily mutually exclusive with producing set outcomes: this depends at least partly on what the outcomes are and how they are framed and understood. Research indicates that there is much room for professional discretion, even when it is assumed that policies are clear and perhaps rigid (Baldwin, 2000).

Conclusion

How well does the concept of uncertainty work as a framework for social work in contemporary times? Uncertainty is most clearly an integral part of the contexts of social work practice, providing a key way of formulating our understanding of the profession, especially in terms of the ways in which professional knowledge is created and used. However, there are also some clear and ongoing values, approaches and skills relevant in current contexts. In fact, I have argued that some key guiding principles become more certain. Our foregoing discussion has thrown some aspects into sharp relief according to their relative certainty or uncertainty. For instance, if we recognise knowledge and practice situations are uncertain, there is one certainty that follows: knowledge and practice must be flexible. Also, uncertain and changing situations do not undermine the relevance of more abstractly conceived values. These still provide necessary guidance in diverse situations; they remain a constant, but what may change are their specific expressions as they are co-created in different contexts.

It is possible, and necessary, to frame social work as a profession whose fundamental values are certain, but which uses flexible processes to co-create meaningful expressions of these in various contexts. In this sense, I would conclude that rather than *uncertainty* being the defining characteristic of social work, *contextuality*, or *the ability to respond meaningfully in relation to different and changing contexts*, is a more useful and relevant framework for understanding its contemporary mission.

Key learning points

1. Uncertainty is an important, but not the only, defining characteristic of social work.
2. For individuals, uncertainty is inherent in charting a life course and a meaningful sense of self within changing social structures and conditions.
3. A particular challenge for professionalism and professional knowledge is how to minimise uncertainty (risk) when contexts are uncertain.
4. A 'new' professionalism needs to include the ability to critically reflect upon practice experience in order to create knowledge responsive to context.
5. Professional education needs to be based on an approach that supports the idea of learning in context.
6. Professional social work needs to be contextual, not only grounding itself in context but also transcending uncertainty through maintaining higher order values.

Taking it further

Readers who want to know more about this will find the following helpful:
Fook, J. (2000) 'Deconstructing and Reconstructing Professional Expertise', in Fawcett, B., Featherstone, B., Fook, J. and Rossiter, A. (eds) *Practice and Research in Social Work*, London and New York: Routledge, pp. 104–19.
Fook, J. (2002) *Social Work: Critical Theory and Practice*, London: Sage, Chapter 11.

Social work and the use of self
5 *On becoming and being a social worker*

Kaeren Harrison and Gillian Ruch

This chapter will:

- introduce the notion of the social worker's use of 'self';
- counter reductionist ways of working which imply that the quality of social work relationships are irrelevant to efficient practice;
- argue that the impact of the 'self' on others is critical for contemporary social work;
- advance ideas of how social workers can develop and sustain use of self.

Introduction

A first-year student who had missed several lectures and who had failed to turn up for an appointment with her personal tutor struggled to see why this was of concern to staff. In an e-mail response to her tutor's letter asking after her general well-being and reminding her about the importance of attendance, she stated 'I do not feel that missing a tutorial is in any way related to how I behave professionally at work.'

This vignette succinctly illustrates the focus of this chapter: the complex and challenging nature of the social work practitioner identity. On starting a social work qualifying programme, few students fully understand what being a professional social worker means or fully appreciate the standards and expectations involved in a professional social work course. From the outset, students are required to understand that standards around conduct and behaviour in classroom and placement learning environments are identical. The principles of professionalism apply in the two settings, and students need to be aware that they are accountable for their actions in both. What the student above seems to be overlooking is the importance of demonstrating congruence between what someone says, what they feel and what they do. The suggestion here – for this student, anyway – is that there is a clear distinction between 'being' and 'doing'. It is almost as if the person they are in an academic setting is not the same person they are in a practice setting, and somehow or other they are in training to qualify as someone other than themselves. The problem is, of course, that there is a much closer 'fit' between the personal self and the professional self than students recognise and that 'locating and exploring the gap between the students' private self and their (imagined) professional persona' (Clapton, 2001: 157) is a critical task facing social work educators.

The challenge for educators is to enable students to assimilate essential and useful professional strategies without suffocating their personal 'selves'. This challenge is heightened by a trend since the late 1980s that places less importance on the 'self' in social work practice and education. This stance appears to be reinforced by negligible references to the 'self' in the National Occupational Standards informing the degree assessment procedures. Paradoxically, we argue, the changing nature of the social work student population, with a larger number of younger students and students with minimal previous social work experience, strengthens the case for placing greater attention on developing self-awareness and an appropriate professional identity. The risk of a 'self-less' approach is that social work students and qualified practitioners resort to 'doing' social work as opposed to 'being' social workers. In the current climate, there is more pressure than ever to evidence what social workers 'do', a trend manifested in endeavours to 'professionalise' social work – registration, codes of conduct, etc. – with little engagement with the complex nature of professionalism, professional identity and the professional self. In this chapter we seek to counter the prevailing and, we think, unhelpful and inappropriate 'self-less' understandings of professional identity (Ruch, 2004). We suggest that 'self-centred' understandings of professional identity, rather than being perceived derogatively as might conventionally be the case, are appropriate and necessary for effective and ethical practice. To explore these issues further, the chapter is structured around three fundamental questions which you could consider now:

- What do we mean by the 'self'?
- Why is the 'self' important in social work?
- How can 'self-centred' practice be maintained, and what gets in the way?

What do we mean by 'the self'?

Considerable thought has been given to the nature of the self and the significance of nature versus nurture as primary influences on the developing sense of self (Colton et al., 2001). Like all potentially polarised debates, the most helpful outcome is one that acknowledges the importance for the construction of the self of both nature and nurture and the inextricably interconnected relationship between them. In social work, writers have engaged with the concept of the 'self' in various ways but with a common acknowledgement that polarised understandings are unhelpful and that the 'self' is more than simply a rational being (Ash, 1992; Howe, 1998). By focusing on two particularly important aspects of the self in social work, the cognitive and affective aspects of the self and personal and professional identities, we seek to reduce the risk of polarised responses to such debates and to enhance the possibility of social workers developing as integrated, holistically informed, reflective practitioners.

Thinking and feeling

Two central aspects of human behaviour are the capacity to think – intellectual or cognitive development – and the capacity to feel – emotional or affective development. The danger underpinning any polarised ideas, such as the nature–nurture debate, or thinking and feeling, is that one of the identities is forced to adopt an inferior position to the other. All too often in relation to the thinking–feeling binary, 'head' activities of thinking are valued more highly than 'heart' activities of feeling. A duality of superior and inferior 'ways of being' is constructed, privileging rational, cognitive behaviours over emotional, affective behaviours. Phrases like 'I think therefore I am' and 'mind over matter' illustrate this. Healthy and holistic understandings of the 'self' require individuals to integrate their affective and cognitive capabilities.

Wilfred Bion's (1962) work as a psychoanalyst with individuals and groups helpfully tackles dualistic ideas associated with the thinking-feeling binary. For Bion, feelings and thoughts are inextricably interrelated. He coined the phrase 'containment', which refers to an individual's unbearable feelings being contained – 'thought about' – by another person in such a way that they can be returned to the individual in a more manageable form. Bion suggested that in the process of being contained, feelings are translated into thoughts. By being contained emotionally, individuals can bear to face their feelings and, over time, develop thinking structures that enable them to internalise the containment process. Containing relationships facilitate integrated emotional and cognitive development.

Inevitably, in placement settings, students will encounter issues that trouble them personally, perhaps because they evoke memories of upsetting things which have happened in their own lives or because they are topics that challenge their existing 'common sense' understandings and beliefs. If they can learn how to deal with these issues in a safe 'containing' environment, this will help them become better practitioners. As Lister (2000) has pointed out, on social work programmes, the exploration of personal experiences, values and political beliefs is fundamental to social work training and involves students in questioning their histories, relationships and identities: 'For many students, this is the first time they have been afforded the opportunity for such exploration and this has a profound effect on their sense of self' (Lister, 2000: 166). 'Containing' educational experiences allow students to explore potentially threatening personal and professional issues in safe contexts and help them to critically analyse their previous experiences in the light of newly acquired learning.

Similarly, 'containing' work settings enable practitioners not simply to survive but to thrive in practice. The associations between practitioners not being able to cope with the demands of the job, not least its emotional impact, and levels of stress, long-term sickness and burnout are well documented (Charles and Butler, 2004). The recruitment and retention difficulties facing the profession link to these realities. 'Containing' contexts create opportunities for practitioners to make more informed and, by implication, potentially more effective interventions, which in turn generate job satisfaction and professional well-being.

Personal and professional selves

The vignette of the student in the introduction to this chapter illustrates how it is possible to develop an understanding of professional identity divorced from the person behind the professional façade. Separation of personal and professional identities generates another binary relationship evident in comments such as 'in my professional opinion'. Remarks such as these imply that the professional viewpoint being expressed is in no way related to the personal views held. Understandings of the 'self' and enhanced self-awareness help to challenge these dualisms and to encourage practitioners to recognise when, how and why practice encounters resonate with personal experiences and trigger unexpected responses. Ash (1995: 25) presents a clear argument for the inseparable nature of the personal and professional, thinking and feeling aspects of the self: 'It is both wasteful and perilous to ignore feelings and life experiences in the belief there is some unsulliable "professional" mode of being.' She goes on to challenge practitioners 'to know thyself' as 'there is more of oneself in every interaction than meets the eye' (Ash, 1995: 26). Given the social work curriculum, it is almost inevitable that some of the subject matter will resonate, on occasions in disturbing ways, with students. By introducing students in their qualifying programmes to holistic models of the self, a firm foundation is laid for their continuing professional development.

Why is the 'self' important in social work?

The place of 'self' in social work practice is a dynamic one (Howe, 1998). In the decades between 1930 and 1960, social work was rooted in psychodynamic case-work traditions that recognised the place of relationships and 'self' in professional interventions. The 1960s onwards saw the ascendancy of behaviourism and radical social work that placed a greater importance on rational behaviours and collective responses than on the professional relationship. In recent decades, managerialist perspectives have dominated social work practice and the relationship and the 'self' in social work practice has been pushed to the margins. Encouragingly, there is evidence of renewed interest in relationship-based practice (Sudbery, 2002; Trevithick, 2003). Howe (1998) emphasises the important contribution of recent work undertaken within developmental psychology to the shifts in thinking about the complexity of the self and its social nature. This contemporary thinking highlights how understandings of human behaviour cannot be simplified and rendered one-dimensional or divorced from an individual's social context.

The resurgent interest in the professional relationship can be partly understood as a response to the expansion of economically driven and managerially dominated practice contexts. Such contexts foster a reductionist perception of individuals (service users and practitioners) as rational consumers or commissioners of services, perspectives irreconcilable with the renewed recognition of the complexity of human behaviour and its social and relational foundations (Howe, 1998). For practitioners to practise ethically and effectively, a model of practice is required which is coherent and congruent with professional realities. The model we propose that meets these requirements is one built on relationship-based and reflective practice.

Relationship-based practice

In essence, relationship-based practice involves:

- recognising the complexity of human behaviour and relationships, i.e. people are not rational beings;
- considering human behaviours and the professional relationship as an integral component of any professional intervention (Ruch, 2005).

This perspective suggests that social work encounters cannot be a-relational or relationship-less, but they can pay more or less attention to the relationship. From this relationship-based perspective, practitioners need to acknowledge that social work is complex, unpredictable and full of uncertainty and that engaging effectively with disadvantaged and distressed individuals and families requires the establishment of meaningful professional relationships. It is not possible to simply complete the necessary paperwork and retreat, although some might argue this is the required approach as engaging in the relationship simply disrupts the 'care management' process. Relationship-based practice is demanding and requires practitioners to develop creative professional strategies that do not restrict their professional responses to procedurally informed and narrowly conceived understandings of evidence-based practice. It requires engagement with the whole self – the personally professional self and the professionally personal self. To achieve such responses and to sustain relationship-based approaches, practitioners need to develop as reflective practitioners.

Reflective practice

Reflective practice is an increasingly familiar term in social work but not always well understood. The literature refers to various different types of reflective practice (Ruch, 2000). Reflective practice requires practitioners to recognise each encounter as unique and informed by an inclusive range of knowledges embracing not only 'hard' knowledges such as orthodox theory and research evidence but also 'soft' knowledges associated with practice wisdom, personal experience and intuition. An important distinction between different types of reflective practice relates to the extent to which practitioners can move beyond forms of reflective practice that simply ask 'What did I do and how?' to the more complex question 'Why did I do that and why did that happen?' By engaging with knowledges derived from professional training and personal experience, practitioners can begin to answer the 'why' questions and model professional responses that are informed by their holistic 'professional self' and are specific, dynamic and responsive to the unpredictable and complex nature of human behaviour.

An encouraging aspect of the degree assessment processes is the expectation that students undertake reflective analyses of their practice. This expectation, along with the requirement for students to compile a portfolio with reflective dimensions incorporated into it, provides an important foundation on which reflective and relationship-based practice can be built. However, as outlined above, neither the curriculum content encapsulated in the benchmark statement (QAA, 2000), or the National Occupational Standards (TOPSS, 2002), refer directly or indirectly to the role, place and significance of self. All the more reason, perhaps, for social work education to reclaim the 'art of being' from the competence-driven 'science of doing', and to promote the use of self in social work education and practice.

In social work training, there is broad agreement on educational models that stress the importance and value of learning from experience, since these are congruent with the aims and objectives of social work practice (Yelloly and Henkel, 1995). Indeed, learning theories suggest that previous knowledge is the foundation on which students build new understandings and, as such, it is good practice to encourage individuals to identify their own stories and to work from this starting point (Cree and Davidson, 2000). Alongside pedagogic approaches relevant to qualifying practitioners, it is equally important that systems exist to enable qualified practitioners to sustain their self-centred practices. The challenge lies in enabling students and practitioners to integrate *personal* knowledge and experience with *professional* knowledge and experience and to recognise the individual and organisational conditions that can promote or impede this professional developmental process.

In thinking about challenges to sustaining integrated and informed professional identities and reflective and relational practices, it is possible to identify two sources of potential opposition: first, internal obstacles associated with individual responses to being invited to develop enhanced levels of self-awareness with the concomitant self-exposure and vulnerability that they imply; and second, external obstacles associated with the absence of reflective spaces and places that encourage practitioners to stop, reflect and think. The following section explores both internal and external obstacles to reflecting and relating and outlines ways that opportunities for promoting and sustaining 'self-centred' practice can be found in educational and practice settings.

Internal obstacles and opportunities

An integral and unavoidable dimension of developing and maintaining a 'self-centred' reflective professional identity is the willingness to be open to self-examination. By definition, this involves becoming vulnerable and dependent on others in order to grow in self-awareness. These are exposing positions to adopt and challenging tasks to engage in. Perhaps one of the hardest realities to accept is that the task is never fully accomplished. Underpinned by relationship-based and reflective practice, self-awareness and professional development are ongoing processes. This realisation, while initially daunting, is also the reason why becoming a social worker has the potential to be so professionally and personally fulfilling.

The challenges of developing internal strategies to develop and sustain a 'self-centred' professional identity are exacerbated by two features of contemporary social work training and practice. First, within social work education, the creation of an undergraduate degree in social work has opened up opportunities for widening participation. Experience of social work or social care is not an entry requirement, and minimum age at qualification is no longer relevant: successful applicants can be accepted if they are eighteen before the course starts. Consequently, many students – especially the younger adult learners – arrive on qualifying programmes soon after leaving secondary education with little in the way of relevant work experience or appreciation of the standards and expectations of a professional social work course. While their peers on other non-vocational degrees are enjoying the experience of 'being a student', social work undergraduates have to quickly adapt to 'being a professional'. With younger cohorts of qualifying practitioners, it is vital that the essential ingredients of 'self-centred' professional development are established in the early stages of their training and that on qualification practitioners are encouraged to continue developing their professional identity. Early emphasis on the 'use of self' on qualifying training programmes should set a precedent for all subsequent academic and practice-related learning and enable internal barriers to such personally-rooted pedagogic approaches to be tackled as soon as possible.

At the other end of the professional development continuum are those qualified practitioners who have found ways of coping with the demands of practice in essentially 'self-less' ways, ways that minimise the attention paid to the contribution of the 'self' to professional practice. This group can be divided further into two subgroups: first, well-established qualified practitioners whose initial training and early professional development 25 years ago may have embraced more 'self-centred' approaches to practice, but who, with the attrition of supervision to what is now often merely a case management exercise, have become entrenched in a bureau-professional role with little attention to the professional self. Second, the more recently qualified practitioners whose experience of training and practice has provided little incentive to develop a more reflective and 'self-centred' stance and who, in a similar way to the first subgroup, operate from a position of bureaucratically-driven practice. For both subgroups, continuing their professional development by embarking on post-qualifying social work courses can be sobering.

In some ways, it is understandable that focusing on the importance of self can be seen by others as (quite literally) self-indulgent and irrelevant. For one thing, it is time-consuming. Given the pressures in social work education and practice, there is an argument that qualifying and qualified practitioners should be prioritising 'learning and doing' and not 'thinking and feeling'. For many qualifying and qualified practitioners alike, reflective spaces where they can explore the affective impact of their work are all too rare, and the temptation to resort to 'doing' social work is strong. The combination of the negligible reflective opportunities and the emotionally demanding nature of practice make it unsurprising that practitioners resort to bureau-professional responses that emphasise procedures and paperwork and minimise the amount of interpersonal contact. When reflective opportunities do arise, they are an unfamiliar professional resource and can be unnerving. Practitioners can exhibit resistant and reluctant behaviours that prevent them from being able to realise the potential of reflective forums.

In order to overcome these obstacles to holistic and self-centred professional development and to feel more confident about engaging in 'self-centred' practice, practitioners need to develop internalised professional identities on which they can draw when work challenges them. By this we mean an internal working model enabling practitioners to draw on all the diverse sources of knowledge that inform their professional decision-making and actions. Such a model has two central characteristics. First, it emphasises that who and what we are, together with our life experiences, is likely to impact on how we practise as social workers. Second, that learning to share relevant personal information is part of developing good practice and becoming a competent, reflective practitioner (Furness and Gilligan, 2004). From the outset of their social work education, practitioners need to learn about their purposeful use of themselves and to develop their self-awareness (see Chapter 19 for an explanation of this process). Adult learners on a social work course should be expected to participate in experiential exercises that reveal something about themselves in a safe environment. Sometimes concerns are expressed that exercises in which students have to disclose information about themselves might be 'risky' and 'exposing'. These concerns may be raised despite such exercises being handled carefully, with clear provisos that students disclose as much or as little as they choose. Such concerns are understandable but questionable, as social workers very often expect (and require) service users to disclose personal details about themselves to others. The principle being adopted is that sharing information about the self with peers (students or colleagues) is a way of allowing further exploration and analysis and establishes a precedent about how professional identities are developed. Indeed, to facilitate discussion (and to model good practice), it can sometimes be useful for tutors and supervisors/managers to engage in the process too. After all, tutors/supervisors/managers who are reflective about their own selves and their own practice, and who can model the process of reflection, are also people who can facilitate the transfer of learning.

This philosophy can be replicated in a variety of forums across education and practice contexts. Examples include:

- case studies requiring scrutiny of personal values and political beliefs;
- required reading that addresses the perspective of service users and carers;
- keeping a reflective diary of thoughts and feelings;
- process recording and regular analyses of critical or significant incidents.

These are all constructive strategies for promoting the use of self as an analytical tool. Overcoming internal obstacles to professional development and enabling practitioners to create an internal structure that assists them in engaging with complex practice issues should not be done in isolation. Research (Ruch, 2004) has highlighted how vital it is that practitioners have internal and external support systems that are complementary and that jointly facilitate a practitioner's reflective capabilities.

There is a dilemma here, however. In order to develop an internal reflective space, practitioners need formal support forums that promote the development of a reflective professional stance. To take advantage of formal reflective spaces, however, practitioners need to have begun to develop their own individual reflective understanding. This dilemma highlights the importance of both sources of professional support being encouraged to coexist. They are complementary and compatible and the existence of one type of reflective space does not diminish the importance of the other. What might these external reflective spaces look like?

External obstacles and opportunities

As acknowledged elsewhere in this volume (see Chapters 2, 17 and 21), the current climate in which social work is practised is hostile to thoughtful practice and prioritises throughput and outcomes rather than process and effectiveness. To counter these circumstances, practitioners need well-developed and well-resourced formal support systems receiving solid organisational backing. It is the noticeable absence of such systems in many social work settings that creates one of the most serious obstacles to the development and maintenance of sound reflective and relational practices. It takes a self-aware, resilient and determined practitioner to challenge prevailing expectations and to demand better support.

Addressing the antagonistic and 'self-less' aspects of contemporary social work requires formal sources of professional support that complement the individual strategies practitioners can put in place to sustain their professional development and 'self-centred' practice. Historically, supervision fulfilled this role. An unfortunate, but perhaps unsurprising corollary of the shift towards increasingly bureaucratic and managerial(ist) practice contexts has been the reconfiguration of social work supervision. In its original format, the model of supervision found in social work settings was based on a tripartite structure that addressed the management, educational and support needs of the practitioner. Over the past two decades this model has been pared down with the sole objective of the supervisory process often becoming case management (see Chapters 21 and 22).

In the late 1990s and early 2000s, a heightened awareness from various stakeholders of the complexities of social work practice and the shortfalls in case management supervision have prompted new responses to meet the professional support needs of practitioners. Whilst not yet comprehensively available for all practitioners, these emerging supportive systems represent an important re-recognition of the demanding nature of social work practice and the implications of such practice on the 'professional self'. Examples of creative initiatives include:

- consultation forums for individuals or teams provided by external consultants who are free from case or line management responsibilities;
- two-tier supervision structures within teams, enabling line managers to address case management issues and senior practitioners to encompass the broader developmental needs of practitioners and cases under discussion;
- co-working systems, encouraging practitioners to engage in conversations about their differing perspectives on practice issues and which, by implication, promote more informed and potentially more effective interventions;
- peer supervision, a practice comparable with co-working, but one which, by formalising and structuring commonly occurring informal conversations about a case, recognises the significance of what can often be an undervalued professional support mechanism;
- group supervision or case discussion – similar to peer supervision, but involving teams or groups of practitioners engaged in similar work having opportunities to explore in depth and collectively case-related concerns;
- professional development seminars, forums supporting practitioners in developing their competence in evidence-informed practice.

The common characteristics of these forums are that they create reflective spaces in which practitioners can be encouraged to take time to reflect and think. Reflective spaces are crucial if the prevailing 'doing' culture in social work practice is to be effectively challenged. In such places and spaces, the emotional dimensions of the work and its impact on the personal and professional identities of practitioners can be addressed. It is essential that such spaces receive organisational attention and backing. The importance of these diverse reflective forums is threefold:

1. They ensure practitioners can sustain an integrated personally professional and professionally personal identity that maximises the use of self as an effective resource in chronically under-resourced professional contexts.
2. A direct repercussion of the above point is that practitioners with integrated and attended-to professional identities are less likely to experience overwhelming stress, ill health or burnout – professional risks all too common in contemporary practice.
3. With reflective opportunities available there is greater scope for practitioners to develop more thoughtful and potentially ethical and effective responses. Such responses are capable of embracing the uncertainties, complexities and challenges inherent in the lives of service users with whom they are engaged.

Conclusion

In this chapter, we have sought to demonstrate how the professional self and relationship-based and reflective practice can be promoted and sustained. If practitioners do not pay attention to these aspects of professional development and practice, we believe they will fail to realise their professional potential and, consequently, will reduce the likelihood of giving effective responses to service users. To show why the use of 'self' is important in social work, and to promote a more 'self-centred' understanding of what it means to have a 'professional identity', we have explored obstacles to the emergence of holistic practitioners and have described the formal and informal conditions that help sustain this integrated professional identity. We believe that it is imperative that social work practitioners, educators and students take the necessary risks in the process of continuing professional development to ensure that a sound transition is made from simply having a professional identity to being and sustaining a professional self.

Key learning points

1. The relationship between the personal self and professional self is important and unavoidable.
2. Critically reflective learners are required to be open-minded and self-aware.
3. Qualifying and qualified practitioners should be encouraged, through formal and informal support mechanisms, to develop 'self-centred' understandings of professional identity.
4. Who you are, how you feel and what you do shape professional development.
5. Reflective and relationship-based practice are integral to effective and ethical social work.

Taking it further

Readers who want to know more about this will find the following helpful:

Cooper, A. and Lousada, J. (2005) *Borderline Welfare: Feeling and Fear of Feeling in Modern Welfare*, London: Karnac.

Gould, N. and Baldwin M. (eds) (2004) *Social Work, Critical Reflection and the Learning Organization*, Aldershot: Ashgate.

Schön, D. (1987) *Educating the Reflective Practitioner: Toward a New Design for Teaching and Learning in the Professions*, San Francisco, CA: Jossey-Bass.

Journal of Social Work Practice http://www.tandf.co.uk/journals/titles/02650533.asp.

6 Why bother?
The truth about service user involvement

Advocacy in Action

This chapter will:

- explore the various reasons why the involvement of service users and carers in social work education is a positive development;
- argue that it will only be successful if undertaken from a position of mutual respect, allowing individuals to benefit from being involved in the educational experience;
- discuss the possible reasons for diminishing service users' involvement;
- counter these by emphasising the developmental opportunities that have been experienced by group members.

Introduction

This chapter focuses on the requirement, specified by the DH (2002a), that service users should be actively involved in the provision of social work education in England. We argue that service user involvement is not solely a response to guidance from above – far from it! The voices of people fighting for justice have long insisted on a hearing on their own terms. Government legislation was preceded by, and is partially the outcome of, grass-roots energy, passion, commitment and innovation.

However, the establishment has responded predictably through the tactics of incorporation. 'Participation' is the seductive invitation to join in, but who sets the values and agendas, and who draws up the guest list? If we join in, will the experience of participation have relevance to our lives, or will inclusion just leave everyone frustrated? For some, experiences of top-down participation activities have resulted in cynicism and the urge to avoid partnership at all costs. How, then, can service users be involved to make partnership a cornerstone of professional learning?

While the involvement of service users within professional learning undoubtedly brings improvement, there is still considerable resistance to equitable partnerships and the power shifts they require. There are many reasons that have been advanced for not involving service users more fully within social work learning. The purpose of this chapter is to tackle some of those apparently well-intentioned but ever so dangerous excuses for not involving people. We challenge them through the sharing of our personal experiences (a process that reflects the way in which we teach). The next section outlines some of the personal histories that we bring to teaching; the following section applies these to the excuses we have encountered.

 Think about your own work experience; what would promote or block the involvement of service users?

What involvement means for me

Leigh

I joined Advocacy in Action in 2000 when they said they'd pay me for speaking to the students. To be honest, the money was the only reason I joined at the time: it was an easier option than begging it. I was on heroin and crack and needed every penny I could get. The group knew where the money was going, but no one ever judged me for it. They just accepted me for who I was. That meant a lot to me. I made friends who weren't addicts and I talked about my life in group settings that weren't about therapy or behaviour modification. Over time, the talking and the teaching and the friendship became more important to me than the money. I enjoyed the impact that my story had on students. I felt I was helping them to be better supporters to other vulnerable people. I was able to build on my 'people skills' and my teaching abilities. I found I built myself up at the same time. The experience has contributed to my present situation, now illegal drug-free for four years and living in my own home after twenty years on the streets. Lots of students mention my input as memorable and important when they evaluate the teaching. Knowing I have helped them makes me feel worthwhile.

Jonathan (with Julie)

I have been teaching students for fifteen years. Some students like me; some are frightened. I always know which students feel uncomfortable when I go and sit next to them. I stare at them hard and stick out my tongue. I like going to different universities. I like meeting people. I sit with Julie and talk about my life. I shout all the names of the people who hit me in hospital. I shout them out loud: I tell them to 'get lost'. When I first came to the university, I needed lots of help to join in. Over time I have become more independent and confident in my own abilities. I now use the toilet by myself and I can sit still in a group without interrupting everyone. I like being part of things. I like watching the students. I am a very good judge of human nature. I love having a practical joke. It is impossible to ignore me!

Stuart

I was sleeping rough when I first started teaching in 2004. I let my partner do all the talking; I never said a word. The first time he spoke to students, I held up the pictures about his life. I learned to use the photocopier and the laminator. I helped make all the teaching materials. I learned to operate the console and took responsibility for the video slots. I worked out the overhead projector and learned when the acetates were needed and which ones to use. The group told me they couldn't manage without me. I felt proud for the first time in my life. When I got my confidence up I started speaking to students in small group work. I helped them do the work. My stammer got less and less, even though it was always there. I felt good about my work with students. I felt good about my skills. I felt good in myself.

Christine (with Julie)

I have been teaching students for sixteen years. I don't use many words. But I nod and smile a lot. I use gestures and touch. I can tell people what I am good at. I tell people what my brother did to me. I show photographs about my job at Scope. Julie asks me questions and I answer or nod. I always smile. I tell Jonathan 'lay off!' when he's annoying the students. I like to help people. I hand out marker pens and picture cards. I don't like it when I get left out because I'm quiet. I'm sad if I don't get a chance to join in and help others. Sometimes all students want to do is hold my hand and help me. People don't always make the opportunity for me to give my strengths and assistance.

Brian

When I was sleeping on the streets I didn't have a social worker. I hated 'em ever since they let me down when I got put in a care home and abused by staff. No one ever helped me in my life what was supposed to help me. Only my partner Stuart helped me and I helped him. It was Stuart what got me off all the drugs when he locked me in his flat. That was before we got chucked out for not paying the bills. When I met Advocacy in Action they said, 'Why don't you come and join the group?' Then I got asked to go to Birmingham with Julie and Kevin. So me and Stuart said 'yes'. We was both very nervous but I stood up and told my story to the students and they was all very proud of me. I was that scared my hand was shaking, but I said to myself, 'Brian! This is your chance – you got to tell 'em about what it's like on the streets'. I was proud of myself to tell you the truth. Then I wrote my story out proper with help from Julie and I did a drawing for the first time in my life and now I got my own book and overheads and display cards. In my story I said all the things I never told anyone before. It felt like letting the poison out and it felt better for me to tell my story after all these years. The students said I did brilliant. What being a trainer means to me is that now I got my life back. I've got a book and people want to buy it from me. I'm making a video about my life. I speak at conferences and teach students. I don't feel depressed all the time like I used to. I got a flat and I won the right not to be evicted. I even got a diary because I've got a life to look forward to. Being involved has made me powerful in my life.

Jeeja

I came from Calcutta to work with Advocacy in Action via the British Council. I wanted to help Indian disabled people to set up a group and become trainers. I learned a lot of teaching skills in Nottingham. I enjoyed working with students at the universities. It amused me when they spoke to me like a child because I was physically disabled. As a woman with a masters degree in social work from Delhi University I found that very amusing and amazing. At one place, a lecturer said to me, 'Have they brought you out for the day?' She should have known better!

Julie

I have worked at universities in England and abroad for sixteen years. As a carer and person with incapacity, I am pleased with all the skills and capacities I have built up. Without a single qualification in health or social work, I think I now have expert knowledge and have contributed much to student learning.

Haji and Gultan

As asylum seekers, we have had very little chance so far to contribute to our new land or repay the huge assistance given us since we fled from Turkey. We were both professionals in our own country but even so, felt frightened when Advocacy in Action suggested we should talk to students. What had we got to offer them? Working at Nottingham University for two years has been great. We told about the cruel oppression of Kurdish people. We shared our experiences in a strange new country. We challenged the bad opinions held about migrants.

Trevor

I was very angry at the way the police treated gypsies on our site. They beat up all the men in front of the women and children. I told the students, 'if I had a shotgun I would have let it off there and then when the police upset the dear little children'. The students was nervous of me – I could see they was – but you got to live in the real world not the classroom!

Loveleen

As an Asian disabled woman, living independently in my own bungalow, I like the chance to come to the university. I enjoy being paid for what I do. It's important for me to be paid. I get on with some people better than others. Sometimes I get challenged which is difficult. But I have learned about myself. I like all the friendship and support.

Andrea

I want to join in. I require personal transport and an assistant. It is quite difficult for me to talk about some issues if the assistant is there – because though I am supposed to be in charge, I live in fear of my carers. Sometimes I feel I had more freedom in the hostel before I went into the independent living. I have lots to tell students. Sometimes they feel uncomfortable. They want to think that community care is working when I know it isn't working well for me. I'm not being negative. They just need to hear the truth.

Kevin

It took me a long time to do what I want. I spent a long time from the 1960s to the 1980s institutionalised and unrecognised. People didn't know what I was capable of. I was a founder member of Advocacy in Action and one of the first teachers in the group. I remember it was nerve-racking the first few times I spoke to large audiences. I'm so good at it now, I forget it wasn't always this easy. But speaking out gave me the chance to say everything I had inside me and got me recognition for it. I started to see myself in a different way. I saw I could prove people wrong. I saw myself as a person to be listened to. Then I found out I could draw and paint. My pictures about Balderton Hospital became famous. Drawing the pictures and telling the story healed my suffering and made me feel better, happier, stronger, proud. That's how people became interested in me. And I was a brilliant presenter on my life because it belonged to me and no one else. And the story has helped students become better social workers. When I was made Visiting Lecturer at the University of Nottingham, that felt very important to me. It was brilliant to know I'd got the skills and knowledge and was a recognised expert.

- How does reading the stories enhance your understanding of power and powerlessness and help you make links between your own and service users' experiences?
- What do the stories tell you about the potential of service users as problem-solvers and partners?

The experience of our involvement in social work learning is hugely positive for everyone concerned: students, presenters *and* academics. Student and professional feedback and reflective evaluation testify that the messages hit home and stay there, informing and influencing practice over the ensuing years. This provokes a serious challenge to all the reasons for not involving service users and citizen stakeholders in social work education.

Why bother with involvement?

The definition of 'bother' is 'to give trouble to oneself and others' – so why bother? We take the trouble to get involved because in the long term it is worse for everyone if we don't. Our experience of the quality of services provided is essential if professionals want to get things right. Where served well, we are quick to praise. We are also magnanimous and forgiving of human error. So let us test out, in the light of our personal narratives, all the reasons for not making use of our valuable experience.

We don't want to exploit you

This suggests that benefits are one-sided, the partnerships manipulative, and contain an element of professional control. Yet, for many of us, involvement has enabled a reclaiming of control and an accumulation of benefits. Leigh, now a settled householder, is making huge choices around her lifestyle. Since the early days, her confidence and self-worth have increased dramatically. Stuart has learned all sorts of skills and appreciates that his disabilities need hold him back no longer. Julie knows more about teaching and good social work practice than she could ever have learned on a formal degree course. Everyone gets paid, although some choose not to make personal use of reimbursement. Christine, Haji and Gultan and Jonathan have all had the opportunity to 'give', which is a powerful thing to do if customarily on the receiving end of help. Kevin has forged out a career and a name in service user history. Involvement has given him a lectureship, television appearances, power, a lifestyle hitherto only dreamed of. Exploitation? We absolutely disagree! We have made the partnership work well for us and are reaping its benefits.

Your involvement is tokenistic

In its broad sense, this excuse reduces all partnerships to trivial and marginal concessions, to be got out of the way of the 'real' work in hand. But it also singles out those people judged 'less able' to get involved. Our experience demonstrates that when academic partners commit to the incorporation of community partners within allegiances built on trust, mutual respect and dignified resourcing, then involvement not only *becomes* the 'real work' but makes *all* work more productive and highly satisfying. Where tokenism is used to devalue the involvement of people of 'difference', this becomes downright oppressive. We have always worked on the margins and sought out the least well heard and well served. It is important that our teaching group reflects this. But the presence of Jonathan, Christine and Stuart has caused sufficient unease to prompt occasional accusations of tokenism.

In the months that Stuart sat wordless in the group, we had no indication of how involved he felt. All we knew was that he turned up for everything. Once we found his technical competence, we built on it. Stuart had place and purpose in the group without need of spoken word. Jonathan will never give a presentation without Julie's help. But he still plays a vital part in the group. An astute judge of human nature, Jonathan enables us to assess the quality of student engagement with him. Christine embodies the right to witness and be witnessed. Intellectually different, she has wisdom, sensitivity and compassion and offers colleagues and students patient, kind support with the world's best smile.

Understanding has many layers. Where abstract ideas and concepts may fly over people's heads, human feelings are shared, empathised and cared for. Involvement may be on many levels, not just the visible spoken interactions. Inclusion is a universal entitlement. We have never met anyone anywhere who was not capable of joining in. To hoist involvement on the spear of 'tokenism', however, indicates a calculated decision on the part of detractors *not* to join in. It shows the lack of value afforded to difference and flaunts an unwillingness to enter humbly and respectfully into the diverse worlds of others.

Hearing your experience feels so voyeuristic

A furtive consumption of the 'service user peep show' by passive spectators on a titillating and transient guilt trip? We beg to differ! Invariably where presenters expose intimate personal stories, listeners feel uncomfortable and worried. Issues of confidentiality and protection arise and are discussed. It is important to confirm that storytellers are aware of the impact of their stories and of the consequences of disclosing them. And it is as natural to feel moved and upset by the appalling things that human beings have done to one another in the name of care as it is to be inspired by the resilience, strength and spirit that survived it all.

Brian hopes that disclosing his history of childhood abuse and his present status as a gay learning-disabled recovering addict will help people learn how to treat one another better, protect the most vulnerable in society and force professionals to confront the terrible betrayals and neglect that kept him on the streets. Christine also insists on disclosing what happened in her own home – when an over-protective mother locked her indoors, where the real danger lay. That she tells her story without words makes it even more powerful. Kevin talks of the strength that comes with the telling of the story and of the challenges it throws out to the 'experts'.

Without a doubt, these tales are painful to tell and painful to hear. But there is mutual healing and reconciliation to be found within. Some people say we need 'professional therapists' to sort us out. That is a subtle way of blame-shifting! By attempting to confine and redefine the evidence within professional territory, it is thus the 'vulnerable storytellers' who become the problem, rather than the cruel testimonies they carry. This is a clever invalidating mechanism and an utter abnegation of the responsibility to hear the truth and to do something about it. Far from voyeuristic, we engage others in open honest interactions that demand personal and professional change, described by one student as 'face-to-face, nowhere-to-hide connection'.

Isn't it upsetting for you to keep going over the past?

It is often suggested that we should leave the past behind. But reclaiming the past and making sense of it is the platform on which we build our today and tomorrow – and it is our past that celebrates this survival. The past is important as our individual and collective history. It represents our anger, our pride and our power.

Haven't you got any happy stories?

It's not that we don't share the happier experiences within our teaching – some listeners only focus on those that upset them. Yet even within our darkest accounts, there are moments of joy, inspiration and strength. People just need to look. Stuart and Brian, Haji and Gultan, Kevin and Christine particularly embody hope and optimism. But Andrea feels, 'some social workers always want clients to be happy – perhaps it helps them feel they're doing a good job!' Loveleen hates being told 'cheer up, it's not that bad', when sometimes it *is* that bad! Is sadness allowed – or does 'happy and content' equal 'grateful and compliant'? We don't want social workers to try and make us happy. We want social justice, social welfare and good life opportunities. And we reserve the right to be fed up when we want to be!

You have such negative perceptions of professionals!

Occasionally, someone will get angry and accuse us of 'bashing the workers'! We've been told we undermine the good work of professional services. The underlying gripe seems to be, 'After all we've done for you!' In reality, we commit ourselves to help people improve. We would not have spent so long in social work education if we were in it for retribution. Presenters rarely speak badly of workers – they just tell the truth. Where listeners reject the validity of our stories, it may herald for them the beginning of that struggle where they must confront their own personal values. It is remarkable that many storytellers are extremely forgiving of the suffering endured. They have great generosity, mercy and tolerance. However, for certain individuals, like Andrea and Trevor, the pain is too raw to do more than share it. And as with the rage of all denied human rights over time, theirs must be accommodated and respected. The skilled facilitators within our group enable this to happen safely and lead reflective discussions afterwards.

It is good when we can support learners to work through these dilemmas and to find ways forward together. We deny the accusation that we are negative: in the main, service users are positive and supportive. But professionals need to learn *why* others mistrust them. Avoiding involvement because people *may* be negative only allows workers to build up unrealistic views of themselves and the value of their work to others.

You are over-emotional and under-intellectual

Personal feelings are important to us. We like everyone to share their feelings as they learn with us. Social workers are not often encouraged to do that, although they expect other people to do so. A student said her previous 'intellectual' social work training had led to detachment and disconnection of her own experience and with those of clients. She now felt herself rattling the chains that prevented her from opening up. Some people in our group *can* be quite intellectual; others have different intelligence. We make no distinction between intellectual people and people labelled 'slow'. The most important qualification for us is greatness of heart. We are proud to be feeling human beings. We want to trust that our feelings will be respected. We want to be sure our workers connect to their own hearts and to ours. Our aim, in fact, is to help put the heart back into social work.

We use services ourselves – we KNOW how you feel

Do you? The number of people like us who make it onto social work degree courses is small, and the future looks less rosy as social work becomes more procedure driven and less about human experience and justice. We know the practitioners who identify with us, survivors of oppression themselves. But in general, although student life is hard, we challenge anyone who claims to 'know' what it feels like to sleep on the streets or to return to a restrictive bullying group home. Avoiding involvement on the pretext of 'knowing how service users feel' fools no-one.

You speak for yourselves – but do you represent other service users?

We get this excuse all the time. It manifests as, 'our clients are different – you can't speak for them', or 'you're just pushing your own agenda, you're not bothered about anyone else!' We argue that the experience of exclusion feels similar to the refugee, the homeless citizen, the Traveller, the carer and the learning-disabled person. As a group we transcend the boundaries that separate us and we support one another. Although each of us can only tell our personal story, we make links with the experience of others and join with them to ask for justice. Kevin relates Jonathan's shared experience of Balderton Hospital. He recalls those whose stories died with them and brings everyone into the problem and its solution. Julie and Leigh share the experience of domestic violence with Christine. They draw on what Jeeja has taught them about Asian women and link in with Kevin's experiences as a battered husband and Brian's insight of violence within gay relationships. Loveleen talks of mental health in the Asian community and Julie compares it with her Irish experience. When we advocate for better services, we demand consideration of diversity, to accommodate faith, race and culture, sexual-preference and lifestyle choice, age, disability, gender and life circumstance. Until everyone gets a fair share, we will perservere. If 'unrepresentative involvement' excuses professionals from hearing our stories, they run the risk of hearing nothing at all.

What professional credibility does your teaching have?

As we set up to challenge the credibility of professional control, it is amusing that we are now asked for our professional credentials. Although we *do* have *some*, the credibility of the learning we facilitate is through the expertise of our own personal experience. It has far more impact than second-hand delivery by an eminent practitioner or received wisdom from some academic book – like this one! While learners can debate or challenge theory on an abstract level, it is impossible to avoid the challenges that Leigh's or Andrea's stories throw out or to refrain from thinking about their implications in terms of professional practice. Our concern, if any, is that service user involvement becomes too professional and loses its uniqueness and its integrity.

What training or qualifications equip you to do this?

Our experience suggests that it is usually the academics and other providers who need training when it comes to partnership, not service users (see Chapter 20)! Involvement *does* require support. We have helped individuals and groups worldwide who wished to share their experience to help others learn. Kevin expresses his joy at supporting others – there can be surely no better role model. Jeeja took her learning back to set up a national network of disability action groups, educating Indian professionals and society through theatre and teaching. People require presentation skills, assessment techniques, an equalities input and the confidence to speak of their own experience, promoting other's learning from it. We already have the potential. There are excellent user-led organisations to lead design and delivery of this support, but, as usual, the lucrative industry, building up around our involvement, is one where the control and the rewards remain with others. Demanding user 'training and qualifications' as a prerequisite for involvement is simply a way of controlling it and ensuring that no real challenge will result.

It isn't a proper part of the course

This suggests service user input is benevolently tolerated as an amusing sideline or a break from serious study. It marginalises the importance of what we do. There is a responsibility on the part of academic colleagues to challenge this. There is an urgent need for academic staff training and support around involving service users in their teaching programmes. Student feedback to our teaching suggests that not only is the service user input valued, it can be *the* most important component. Demeaning user-led teaching as marginal or second-rate is an excuse that says much about the values, abilities and understanding of its detractors.

Your condition worries us

This is the defence that implies 'What if it all gets out of hand and you damage yourself or one of us or harm our reputation?' Superficial words of concern mask both fear of difference and the discrimination it promotes. What is really meant is, 'You are not suitable to be working with us!' Often, nothing is actually said: there is an attitude, a glance, a tone of voice. Jeeja has experienced this quite blatantly on a number of occasions, Jonathan also. For those of us used to living in our own skins, our personal conditions are not the problem, it is other people's response to them.

Teaching is demanding: can you keep up with our documents and meetings?

These suggest that we're not really up to involvement and that it will only mean more work for other people. In reality, service user educators are among the most committed and hard-working groups around and contribute a great deal for very little reward. We may require things to be done differently to accommodate our requirements, but this is an entitlement not a concession. Kevin and Brian's insistence on taped documents has been met with an implicit grumble: 'Service User Value? Nuisance Value!'

We're not able to change our way of working

All this really means is *you* are not willing to try! Our experience of working with forward-thinking universities is that change brings innovation. We have developed new assessment frameworks and teaching methods that empower previously marginalised students. We know we may make mistakes, but we are always willing to *try* things differently. There is much learning in this approach.

Won't paid work affect your benefits? Paying people like you is irresponsible

The first is a legitimate concern. However, it should not be used to excuse the non-payment for valuable work done nor to avoid involvement on the grounds of compromising people's financial arrangements. Service user teachers are quite capable of declaring earnings without supervision and are also skilled at creative problem-solving in respect of earnings versus entitlements. Discussions around payment-in-kind may also be judged appropriate within the teaching partnership. Concerns, on the other hand, about the 'irresponsibility' of paying 'using' addicts or street drinkers, for example, suggest that people aren't doing 'real work' or earning 'real pay'. Would 'conventional' educators be withheld payment until they could guarantee its 'responsible' disposal?

But in the short term, compromises on payment must be agreed by the people working together, respecting one another's personal and professional situations. We have systems of volunteer expenses and staggered wages that keep paid involvement 'legal'. We can and do use our payments collectively. Nevertheless, we must never underestimate the huge importance of even humble sums of money earned through work. Loveleen, Christine and Leigh all appreciate their small cash payments, and the uses they put them to are no-one else's business once the job is done.

We can't really afford your involvement

Advocacy in Action are valuable people. We charge a professional rate for services provided and give excellent value for money. But, like many groups, we are open to negotiation. We are confident of what we're worth and we choose whether to work for less or no cost sometimes – that's our decision. We respect genuine concern about not exploiting our good nature and we understand that some budgets are finite. So we generally tell partners the financial worth of our involvement and ask them to look at what they can afford. We have never refused genuine partnership because of limited resources, but we challenge those who begrudge each precious penny wasted on involvement to tot up the long-term losses that non-involvement accrues, and we ask, 'Can you afford *not* to get involved?'

 How does reading this make you feel about the reasons you came into social work? Reflect on this in the light of what you understand the social work role to be.

Conclusion

In our considered opinion, there *are* no valid reasons for non-involvement. As experts on ourselves and wise judges of our experiences of service provision, we are essential partners in the education of those who would serve us. We need to challenge both the professional detractors and those disillusioned or disempowered amongst our own ranks. We hope we've convinced you to bother about involvement if you're not already doing it. And yes – everyone needs to bother. Partnership won't happen overnight. We all have to work at it. To the query, 'Is it honestly worth the effort?', we would wholeheartedly reply, 'Immeasurably so'.

What do you think?

Key learning points

1. True partnership with service users will improve the quality of education of social workers.
2. With support, any person can contribute to the process of learning.
3. The diversity of a teaching group will enhance the learning of students.
4. Social work is as much about the 'heart' as it is about the 'head'.
5. There are many obstacles that can be put in the way of meaningful partnership.
6. With time, effort and goodwill these can all be overcome.

Taking it further

Readers who want to know more about this will find the following helpful:
'Themed Issue: Service Users and Carers in Social Work Education' (2006) *Social Work Education*, 25 (4).

7 Research mindedness

Beth Humphries

This chapter will:

- engage with the idea that social workers need to be 'research minded';
- explore the relationship between social work and research, emphasising the contested place of 'knowledge' and 'evidence' within social work practice;
- discuss how greater service user involvement in research processes changes not only what is researched but also how research is undertaken.

Introduction

- Why do you need to use research in your work?
- How can it make a difference to what you do?

Social workers and other welfare and health professionals have increasingly been urged to develop a research mindedness, to inform themselves and be alert to research findings and to apply these to their practice. The term has also been interpreted to refer to the need to develop research skills in order to evaluate their work, to collect statistics and generally to be aware of the significance of understanding the impact made by their efforts as professional workers (see Fuller and Petch, 1995), although this latter meaning is not extensively promoted in official social care literature (e.g. Walter et al., 2004). The government has insisted on these developments in various ways, notably through the QAA statement about expectations of standards of degrees in social work (QAA, 2000), within National

Occupational Standards, the requirements for the degree in social work and in post-qualifying training. Also significant here was the establishment of the Social Care Institute for Excellence (SCIE), whose remit is to promote 'useful and relevant knowledge' (Walter et al., 2004: Preface) and to gather and publicise knowledge about how to make social care services better. Along with this, a plethora of government-supported organisations has been established, dedicated to promoting research mindedness, and the Economic and Social Research Council (ESRC) has brought together a number of universities around the UK Network for Evidence-Based Policy and Practice. This chapter addresses some of the issues raised by the notion of 'research mindedness' that students and practitioners will need to consider if they are to approach this aspect of practice in a critical and analytic way.

Models of research mindedness

SCIE's *Knowledge Review*, 'Improving the Use of Research in Social Care Practice' (Walter et al., 2004) reports on the uses made of research in social care and recommends how the effectiveness of this process can be improved. The report identified three models that embody different ways of thinking about and developing the use of research in social care (mainly in social services departments). According to the report, there was little by way of promoting research within the independent sector, and the role of service users or their representative organisations was very marginal. The models are

- the research-based practitioner model, where it is the role and responsibility of the individual practitioner to keep up to date with research and to apply it to practice;
- the embedded research model, where research use is achieved by embedding research in the systems and processes of social care, such as standards, policies, procedures and tools. Responsibility for this lies with policy-makers and service-delivery managers;
- the organisational excellence model, where the key to successful research use rests with social care delivery organisations. Research use is supported by developing an organisational culture that is research minded.

The authors outline a number of possibilities and limitations of each of these models, ultimately rejecting them all in favour of what they name a 'whole systems approach' to research use (Walker et al., 2004: Chapter 4). They say that 'a systems approach assumes that initiatives to improve the use of research are more likely to be successful if they complement one another and if together, they address the whole care system' (Walker et al., 2004: 44).

The framework of three models is helpful in examining how 'research mindedness' is variously interpreted within organisations, and it emerged in the report that the 'research-based practitioner' and 'organisational excellence' models are much less in evidence than the embedded research model. In other words, research findings are interpreted and incorporated at policy and managerial level and, indeed, may be invisible to practitioners, whose role is to carry out instructions about practice, and where there are low levels of practice autonomy. Adoption of resulting policies may be reinforced by, for example, performance measurement, inspection and appraisal regimes. This finding is not surprising given the extent of managerial control evident in other aspects of practice.

However, the linear process of implementation of research findings initially envisaged by the report's authors was not matched by practice. In an example given of a study bringing together two multi-stakeholder groups whose remit was to gather relevant information to formulate policies to improve services for the over-fifties, they noted:

1. Certain forms of knowledge became accepted currency, primarily knowledge based on professional and personal experience rather than research knowledge.
2. Existing relevant research was never accessed by the groups and on occasions research findings presented at meetings were devalued.
3. Research was re-presented and 'transformed' through individuals' experiences or agendas.
4. Research use was haphazard and depended on organisational features and on changing agendas, roles and power relations.

This suggests complex factors are at play in all negotiations about social reality including competing views of 'legitimate knowledge', different agendas, roles and power relations and the reinterpretation, negotiation and renegotiation that inevitably takes place. In other words, the implementation of policy can never be the result of 'pure' research, but many factors are at play in the process. These need to be appreciated by producers and users of research.

 Which of the four models best describes how research is used where you work?

Whose knowledge?

There are many kinds of knowledge and in our society some are regarded as more acceptable than others. The knowledge produced by some researchers, for example, is regarded as more legitimate than that of other researchers and of lay people, because it is based on scientific principles and systematic and rigorous methods. However, it has long been acknowledged that different kinds of knowledge are produced by people according to their location in structures of class, gender and ethnicity. Certain powerful views of knowledge (largely male, white and Western) have come to be seen as the most rational and scientific, along with the devaluing of knowledge born out of women's experiences and those of colonised peoples. This, it is argued, has led to the ascendancy of a scientific rational-technical model of research resulting in inappropriate methods and distorted policy initiatives that have contributed to the subordination of these marginalised groups and which have not been in their interests. Feminists and others have argued that what people know through the experience of their daily lives must be brought centre stage and valued as a contribution in informing research and policy (Beresford and Evans, 1999; Humphries, 2004).

The SCIE Review offered clarification about the nature of knowledge, aiming to 'forge a "constructive consensus" on what counts as social care knowledge' (Popay and Roen, 2003: 7), categorising knowledge as,

- organisational knowledge;
- practitioner knowledge;
- user knowledge;
- research knowledge;
- policy community knowledge.
    (Popay and Roen, 2003: 22)

The authors say their categorisation does not privilege one type of knowledge above another, declaring that it 'sends a powerful message that all are of potential value' (Popay and Roen, 2003: 24). But because this list is produced in a vacuum, there is no acknowledgement of structures of power in that 'knowledge' produced by research is negotiated through the various interests of policy-makers, managers, practitioners and users, and that these interests have more or less influence on research outcomes. Research-based knowledge is 'transformed' as a result of reframing and reinterpretation linked to a range of agendas, roles and power relations. Indeed, research findings can be *ignored* if they do not support dominant agendas (see Humphries, 2004). In the hierarchy of knowledge, certain perspectives are clearly privileged. It is important for social workers not to be naïve about the politics of social research that affects their practice.

 Think of a piece of research you have read. Whose interests did it reflect?

Not only are power relations ignored but the model of research assumed by the SCIE review is also the one most favoured by the government, based on behavioural social work and the empirical practice movement, of which Webb has written a powerful critique (Webb, 2001). All the examples Popay and Roen rate highly in their section measuring quality (2003: Appendix 5) are experimental or quasi-experimental studies or surveys. The appropriateness of such approaches for *social* research has long been challenged as incapable of taking account of the context in which people live their lives and the meanings they attribute to events and actions. The implication for the knowledge produced by these methods is that they take no account of the subjective knowledge of research subjects and position the researcher as arbiter and interpreter of legitimate knowledge.

What sort of research mindedness?

The discussion so far has been concerned with the politics of research mindedness, raising questions about the knowledge produced by research. This in turn demands an examination of what we mean by 'research'. Hammersley (2003) claims a distinction between 'basic' and 'applied' research, the former concerned to pursue truth and to contribute to the accumulation of a body of knowledge about a topic, the latter concerned with an immediate commitment to practical improvement in the world. Hammersley also insists that research must be 'distinguished sharply from other activities' (2003: 33) including professional activities such as education or social work.

Hammersley's binary division between basic and applied research is a useful one in an analysis of the 'evidence-based practice' movement – highly influential in social work – since, clearly, managerial and government priorities are focused on urgent answers to practical problems, and the dominant model of evidence-based practice fits that agenda very well. Evidence-based practice has 'making decisions' as its priority, and the emphasis is on the very practical goal of discovering 'what works' (see Butler and Pugh, 2004). The ascendancy of the applied model is linked to its immediate relevance for policy-makers, and the favoured method of intervention is cognitive-behavioural change in individuals.

A limitation of Hammersley's concept is that it implies that basic research in its search after truth is somehow divorced from political interests and is (at least potentially) 'pure' in the sense of being uninfluenced by other concerns. The insistence on such objectivism ignores decades of debate about the problems with claims of research to be, or at least to aim to be, 'value free', neutral and impartial (Humphries, 2003). It posits 'emancipatory' and other 'politically influenced' approaches to research as an abandonment of the obligations of the researcher to 'preserve some autonomy from the state and other powerful social interests, thereby destroying the conditions in which research can flourish' (Hammersley, 1995: vii). However, as I have argued elsewhere (Humphries, 2004), there is no conflict in a researcher's being committed to an opposition to injustice and a concern to alleviate and even prevent suffering. It is when research attaches itself to *factions* (whether right or wrong) and not to these *values* that 'taking sides' becomes a problem. Moreover, the separation of 'basic' from 'applied' research leads to a narrow focus on 'what works' to the exclusion of explanations of why the issue became a problem in the first place or of the meaning of behaviour to groups and individuals. One may justify a concern in social care for lessons about application of research, but such research is not value free, and the values underpinning it should be declared. Further, such research is 'best practice' when it is set in a context that takes account of inequality and injustice. An understanding of these debates will help practitioners to question 'one size fits all' models of research and to insist on considering a wider range of approaches that will involve service users and will seek to include the social factors that impact on people's lives.

 How can people using services benefit from research?

Whose interests are served by research mindedness?

The above discussion touches on a central dilemma of contemporary research in social work, its relationship to social policy and policy makers. To what extent are researchers, including social work researchers, enslaved to the demands of their paymasters? This is not a new dilemma, but its examination has gained greater significance in the light of the knowledge economy and the urgency of a push towards evidence-based practice. Here I am concerned with the tensions among stakeholders who may have competing objectives and, particularly, with the expectations of those commissioning and using research in making and implementing policy. As I have argued, much current research is funded with the requirement that it is useful for informing practice, which translates into studies attempting to measure the impact of interventions regardless of their relationship to the wider social context. It is not interested in the inequalities and injustices that have contributed to particular social problems, but only in what is effective in changing the resulting problematic individual behaviour. This pattern exists not only in social work, but also in probation, education and health, where 'lifestyle' and personal responsibility are prioritised. In this sense, many studies are context-specific, examining the impact of interventions in very narrow settings and attempting to generalise these to other environments. What policy-makers require here are simple, straightforward answers, specific conclusions (preferably those they themselves have already reached) and concrete recommendations for practice. This leads to a research mindedness that reduces complexity, that risks significant distortion and that is so influenced by the interests of politicians that it betrays the uncertainty and the contingency that is inherent in all constructions of knowledge (see also Chapter 4).

The problem goes beyond policy-makers' insistence on definitive answers because if the answers are inconvenient or contradictory of policy makers' preferences, they can be ignored and discarded. In the field of asylum for example, government policy and legislation have ignored the evidence (enshrined in the Children Act 1989) that children need the stability and consistency of family life, by enacting (amongst other damaging legislation) Section 8 of the 2004 Asylum and Immigration (Treatment of Claimants, etc.) Act. This withdraws benefits from failed asylum seekers and provides for their children to be taken into care if destitution results. In other words, families are deliberately plunged into poverty to force them to leave the country, and children are likely to suffer most as a result. The Children Act was explicitly designed to prevent children being taken into public care for reasons of poverty and destitution. The research evidence is ignored in the 2004 legislation. The ideological and populist goal of needing to be seen to be tough on asylum leads to the setting aside of any available research (Humphries, 2004) and to the serious consequence of damage to children's lives and futures.

The point made here is that research mindedness may not result in the free choice for individual researchers or practitioners of what is to be studied, or even how the research problem is to be constructed. The expected outcome may have to be geared to the information needs of managers rather than the practice or political interests of the researcher. Indeed, there will be times when the pressure is towards directions which are unpalatable to the researcher or the practitioner but over which they have limited control.

Research mindedness requires a commitment – even a passion – on the part of researchers, which may lead them towards thinking that is beyond common sense and conventional knowledge and towards exploring a range of perspectives on social issues about which they care deeply. Or they may want to inquire into intellectual problems which will not necessarily have an immediate application to practice. They will have to face the reality that their interests will not always coincide with the interests of policy makers. They will confront the choice of being true to their commitment and risk losing their credibility and support for their current and future research, or of succumbing to a different and alien view of research and losing their integrity as researchers. Likewise, practitioners may find themselves in conflict with their managers.

This is a stark view of a reality that is managed differently by different researchers and practitioners. Some are relatively successful in pursuing their personal commitments whilst somehow satisfying their political masters. One high profile person like this in the UK is Hilary Graham who has brilliantly managed the tension over many years (e.g. Graham, 2000). Other researchers deny the dilemma by separating the technical aspects of research from its uses in social policy. However, as I have commented elsewhere, 'research that attempts solely to measure the impact of interventions regardless of their relationship to the social context, is not value free. Rather it has taken the side of whatever values have inspired the interventions it uncritically evaluates' (Humphries, 2004: 114).

All research is political, and those with a mind to study social problems will need to confront the questions of who their political ruler will be, and of the cost of giving them what they demand.

Which user perspectives and what involvement?

 How can people who use services be involved in research?

I turn now to some questions about the aims of research to achieve user involvement and to 'bring to voice' marginalised voices that have been silenced through relations of power in society (see also Chapters 6 and 20). It is a universal aim of social work to enhance possibilities for 'empowerment', an aim that is shared by government at all levels. In policy terms, this is expressed in the ideal of 'participation', where professionals are expected – indeed required – to involve service users and carers in planning and delivering services and in making a central contribution to research. A new paradigm of research has been developed under the rubric of 'participatory research' (see de Koning and Martin, 1996; Beresford and Evans, 1999), appropriated by government. Few people would argue with or oppose the notions of 'empowerment' and 'participation', and Chapters 6 and 20 in this book are devoted to the implications of service user involvement. I confine myself to asking a number of questions about participation as it is expressed in the research process.

First, consider the notion of 'bringing to voice'. Inspired by critical and feminist perspectives, this is intended to capture the idea of researchers in fields such as education, community work and social and health work from their position of relative power, facilitating and making spaces for poor, old, disabled, young or ill women and men to speak out about their oppression in ways that will be heard and heeded by those in power.

Empowerment comes through the act of speaking and through recognition that their knowledge is legitimate and valid. Any research that is conducted is designed in their interests and for purposes they define. The researcher and the service users or carers act cooperatively together.

A problem with this perspective is that empowerment is treated in a depoliticised and generalised way. It is 'defined in the broadest possible humanist terms, and becomes a "capacity to act effectively" in a way that fails to challenge any identifiable social or political position, institution or group' (Ellesworth, 1989: 307). As a result, everyone can agree that it is a 'good thing'. At this level, participation in research – with its language of 'sharing', 'giving', 'redistributing' – is regarded as unproblematic. However, as I have been arguing here, research in social work and other areas of social policy is not free of context or political considerations. In the current climate, most funded or approved research is hedged around with conditions related to targets, budgets, resources – those considerations that are of vital concern to managers, all of which may be antagonistic to service users' interests. Moreover, the New Labour government has favoured social research almost exclusively based on a model that sees knowledge in terms of producing evidence of what works in controlling and changing the behaviour of people defined as 'social problems'. The dominance of this powerful agenda leaves little space for other voices.

This leads to the question of *whose* voices are to be heard? It is unlikely to be those of people who are most profoundly affected by social policy initiatives. Further, in inviting participation of service users and carers, researchers may feel that involvement of those who are least likely to be awkward is the most expedient route. Researchers too are interested actors and have their own priorities and prejudices. The question needs to be asked, 'What diversity do we silence to gain an easy intimacy with participants?' In this case, 'participation' becomes a patronising tokenism. It cannot be assumed that the aims of researchers and users will coincide. Indeed, a genuine engagement of service users can be conflictual, angry, frightening and antagonistic – a space of instability through which struggle and change can take place, which can be time-consuming and exhausting, but which is central to progressive practice. Moreover, any discussion of participation in research needs to come to grips with issues of trust, risk and the operation of desire around identity and power, in which both service users and researchers are implicated – that is, division amongst service users and between them and the researchers. Dynamics of subordination operate within this context as they do in wider society and need to be taken into account in any efforts towards empowerment through participation. Few publications about research tackle these aspects of participation.

A particular dilemma for critical and feminist researchers in involving service users in research is that the 'voice' that speaks may not, in the researcher's view, be an oppositional one. Not all women or gay people or disabled people, for example, will believe that they are oppressed and will recognise the 'truth' of their exploitation, as understood by researchers. They may not perceive their situation in the same way or construct similar social situations as problems. Indeed, the voices heard may be racist, homophobic and sexist. Is there a legitimate place for their views in the designing and implementing of research? The thorny question of whether all views of users and carers should be regarded as being on equal terms, requires to be confronted in any research project that aims to be participatory. In the rush to obey the injunction to 'involve users and carers', what values and measures of acceptability may be sacrificed?

A related problem is that some voices may *choose* to be silent as a result of cultural and social practices of power. There is evidence that the voices of marginalised groups are often silent by choice, from a reluctance to act as educator to dominant groups by sharing their experiences of pain and humiliation (e.g. Williamson, 2000). They may also have made a judgement that the environment is not a safe one in which to speak. The silence about these dilemmas in research reports could be related to researchers' definitions of 'empowerment' and 'participation' that exclude possibilities for struggle and for challenging political positions and social institutions. What diversity do we exclude, then, in the name of liberatory practice? It might be argued that one role of the critical researcher is to help bring to light issues of power and oppression as they emerge in the stories, histories, experiences and accounts of participants. This assumes of course that researchers are free from their own learned homophobia, disablism and racism. Even where this is the case, all our voices are partial, multiple and contradictory. Our experiences of oppression do not necessarily make us immune from acting in oppressive ways. We are all self-interested, and often our survival leads us to speak in partial narratives that exclude others. Such voices may be legitimate and valid, but they should not be without response, without challenge. As Ellesworth (1989: 305) points out, oppositional voices are both partial and partisan and must be made problematic because they hold implications for other social groups and their struggles.

There are no glib answers to these dilemmas. A research mindedness that seeks to be participatory needs to embrace these complexities. This will lead to an uncertain and unstable research environment, but one within which change can take place, within a framework of principles of social justice. All our opinions and perspectives can be measured against these principles rather than some being regarded as more valid than others because of who speaks or all being absorbed into the lowest common denominator without challenge or response. One of the fundamental negotiations that should take place in agreeing a participatory model concerns the values and the political ends that will inform any research study. Such a way forward offers profound challenge in a political climate where a very different view of research mindedness holds sway.

Finally, there is a desperate need for the establishment of alternative research communities to support individual researchers and practitioners. A number of establishment-approved organisations have grown up, financed and encouraged by government departments demanding quick answers to their version of social problems. If practitioners are to resist the research implications of this, they require the backing and authentication of like-minded colleagues. It is time to show that they can be an oppositional force.

Conclusion

In this chapter I have raised questions about 'research mindedness' in relation to the meaning of research, research knowledge, research approaches, political influences and user participation. I have been concerned to emphasise that dominant and political interests shape the development of the social sciences and that their 'autonomy' is always problematic. Many questions remain and are the stuff of struggle on the ground, and my intention has been to disrupt the taken-for-granted nature of some of the discussions around them. In drawing attention to what might otherwise remain invisible, I hope to alert researchers and practitioners to the contested nature of the concepts and practices they use in their work.

On the larger canvas, a research mindedness that points to the possibility of analysing agency and structure as intertwined and mutually implicating one another goes beyond the objectivism/subjectivism debates about social reality. A focus on the interplay between meaning and structure requires research tools that are not imported from the natural sciences but that are grounded in a critical social science. Fostering a critical practice developed from the issues raised here will contribute towards research decisions about the scope and context of a study, legitimate knowledge and appropriate methods and participation and will alert practitioners to the political nature of all research.

Ultimately, research mindedness is not about discovering a single 'truth' about an aspect of practice, since truths are constructed through powerful discourses. It is concerned to nurture an appreciation of many possible truths and to ask questions such as, 'In whose interests are needs being named in this way?', 'What other truths are suppressed in the process?', 'How do these constructions measure against values of democracy, justice and equality?'

All this is not to advocate that social work ignores the contemporary political economy with its emphasis on value for money and targeting. Social work is part of and, indeed, is shaped by that reality. It is also, and always has been, concerned about social casualties and social justice. Research mindedness should have this goal at its core, and its quest should be to nurture critical intellectual and political skills to make it central to ways of thinking about evidence-based practice.

Key learning points

- Acknowledge different kinds of knowledge, and hold knowledge produced by the subjects of research as legitimate and valid.
- Seek to understand and use models of research that are appropriate to accessing this knowledge.
- Locate social problems in their wider social context rather than pursuing narrow behaviourist ends.
- Be committed to a view of democracy, social justice and equality to guide research practice, rather than commiting to privileged or powerful voices.
- Make space for the voices of oppressed groups, and enter into dialogue with them, but be prepared to question both one's own and others' understandings.
- Seek out a research community that will share and attempt to implement similar principles.

Taking it further

Readers who want to know more about this will find the following helpful:

Fawcett, B., Featherstone, B., Fook, J. and Rossiter, A. (eds) (2000) *Research Practice in Social Work*, London: Routledge.

Lovelock, R., Lyons, K. and Powell, J. (eds) (2004) *Reflecting on Social Work: Discipline and Profession*, Aldershot: Ashgate.

Popay, J. and Roen, K. (2003) *Types and Quality of Knowledge in Social Care, SCIE Knowledge Review 3*, Bristol: Policy Press.

Research Mindedness for Social Work and Social Care, SWAP website: http://www.resmind.swap.ac.uk.

8 The rise and rise of interprofessional education?

Colin Whittington

This chapter will:

- define interprofessional education and trace some important steps in its progress;
- give the appearance at first that interprofessional education has progressed along a linear path, while later contesting the impression;
- question the idea of the rapid rise of interprofessional education;
- challenge assumptions of an ever-upward trajectory, suggesting that trajectory is dependent on many factors and is hard to predict.

Introduction

Interest in interprofessionalism in care services is reaching new, higher levels while interprofessional education continues its relatively recent progress from the margins towards the mainstream. Long-term champions of interprofessionalism greet the trend with a justifiable mix of satisfaction and caution. At the same time, some newer observers may be tempted to think of the present state as a point in a rapid, perhaps linear and ever-upward trajectory, a vision that also requires caution. Exploring these aspects in the development of interprofessional education will indicate its complexity and help in appreciating more fully what has been achieved so far.

Definition and discourses

The chapter is concerned with interprofessional education in the UK (and describes policies mainly in England), but the enterprise has also been recognised internationally for many years (Barr et al., 2005). Interprofessional education may be referred to in different forums as 'multiprofessional' or 'multidisciplinary' education rather than 'interprofessional', sometimes with unspoken differences of meaning. Despite differences, the terms have a common objective, namely, 'learning for collaborative practice' (Whittington, 2003a). This expression helps in looking more broadly at interprofessional education by removing the exclusive focus on profession or discipline so that two other major aspects of collaboration, the inter-agency aspect and the service user and carer dimensions, may enter the field of view. The idea also lowers the barrier that 'inter*professional*' can erect between occupations, a barrier that tends to marginalise people without recognised professional training despite contributions to care services.

This wider, collaborative perspective is useful in connecting to the related idea of 'partnership'. The lexicon of partnership and collaboration embraces two subsets of terms. The first subset relates to *organisations* and includes terms such as 'inter-agency', 'multi-agency' and 'inter-organisational'. The second subset is concerned with *professions or disciplines* and consists of terms already introduced, including 'interprofessional'.

These two subsets are more than analytical categories; they represent two parallel discourses. The organisational, or rather *inter-organisational discourse*, speaks particularly of inter-agency partnership, multi-agency working, organisational and service integration and 'whole systems'. Inter-organisational discourse tends to link explicitly to national social legislation and service policy. Research and development within the discourse reflect these preoccupations, being oriented towards solving problems of management, governance, common systems and service user outcomes. The discourse inclines towards 'training' more than 'education' and speaks of workforce development, 'toolkits' and occupational standards.

By contrast, the *interprofessional discourse* is expressed in terms of practice and education between professions and among multidisciplinary teams, especially in health care. Research is predominantly in health or health and social care and is both national and international. The discourse tends to speak of education, learning and assessment, addressing learner attitudes, skills and identity, professional culture and contexts of professional learning at pre-registration and post-registration levels.

They are parallel discourses, but their boundaries are not sealed. Nevertheless, the discourses are represented in broadly different social networks. This separation presents a particular challenge to social workers whose work is strongly defined by their organisational base and inter-agency network, but whose effectiveness depends upon managing interprofessional relationships as well. Social workers have to bridge the two discourses themselves, although there are models that help to make the connections (Whittington, 2003b). The present chapter implicitly reinforces the separation, yet the interprofessional discourse is significant and expanding and demands study in its own right. The first requirement is a definition of interprofessional education: 'Occasions when two or more professions learn with, from and about each other to improve collaboration and the quality of care' (Barr et al., 2005: xvii).

The essence of interprofessional education in this definition concerns interactive learning between different professions. This view distinguishes interprofessional education from 'uni-professional' learning, in which there is little or no direct contact with other professions, and 'multiprofessional' learning involving learning alongside other professions but without designed interaction. Learning for interprofessional practice can occur in all three types (Whittington and Bell, 2001) although interactive learning is increasingly the method of choice. One further point on terminology: 'interprofessionalism' is used to mean the state of working and learning with other professionals and the schools of thought and movements that support that state.

 Which 'discourse', interprofessional or inter-organisational, most closely reflects your own learning and practice experience, and what learning opportunities would assist you in integrating the two in your practice?

Social policy and interprofessional education in social work

Two concepts already mentioned, 'collaboration' and 'partnership', have become wide-spread in public policy and key drivers in the development of interprofessional education (Whittington, 2003c). Partnership is especially associated with New Labour policies which, from 1997, gave the idea a key place in the 'modernisation' of public services. By then, however, the concept was hardly new. Service cooperation formed a part of much social legislation under the preceding Conservative governments in the 1990s and was central to their NHS and Community Care Act 1990.

Even then, the importance of 'close liaison between social workers and colleagues in related services' was scarcely novel, dating at least to 1959 (Younghusband, 1959: paragraph 125). The following decades saw numerous Acts and public reports advocating collaboration along with publications theorising collaborative practice and the case for underpinning learning (Whittington, 1983; Loxley, 1997).

The evidence that collaboration has long been advocated leaves two compelling arguments unaltered: first, that Conservative community care policies in the 1990s stimulated unprecedented levels of attention to joint working; and, second, that New Labour's far-reaching emphasis on partnership had even greater impact. Each government had its own contrasting agenda, but they shared a motive to maximise service value while containing costs and loss of effectiveness caused by dysfunctional professional, organisational and service boundaries (Whittington, 2003c). Until partnership and collaboration were perceived as servants to this cause, they remained secondary policy ideas to parties in power and gave little leverage to champions of interprofessional education.

By the late 1990s, the numbers of interprofessional education champions in education and practice had grown, but still they needed patience. While New Labour policies on public sector modernisation burgeoned and partnership ran through most of them, the focus was primarily strategic and framed by the inter-organisational discourse described earlier (Whittington, 1999: Appendix 1).

This focus was strongly represented in the wide-ranging White Paper *Modernising Social Services* (DH, 1998). The White Paper confirmed the promise of grants and flexible financial rules on joint working, joint national service frameworks and a statutory duty of partnership between the National Health Service (NHS) and local authorities. Two new organisations were announced, the long-awaited General Social Care Council (GSCC) in England (with similar councils in other UK countries) and the Training Organisation for Personal Social Services (TOPSS) – later encompassed in Skills for Care and Development. Among their many functions, these new organisations would have a role in supporting partnership.

The White Paper's injunctions to joint working implicated all services but gave particular attention to the social services' relationships with the NHS. The 'Berlin Wall' that was said to divide them had to come down to create a system of integrated care and a better service to users (DH, 1998: paragraph 6.5). In a direct response, TOPSS England commissioned a strategy on partnership to supplement the first national social care training strategy (Whittington, 1999).

The NHS Plan brought modest encouragement to IPE with proposals for joint training 'in communication skills' as part of a new core curriculum for NHS staff (DH, 2000b: paragraph 9.18). Subsequent consultation on NHS workforce development supported multi-disciplinary approaches and cross-boundary teamwork (DH, 2000c).

In social care, a further step came with *A Quality Strategy for Social Care,* which predicted the growth of joint working and the need for effective local partnerships (DH, 2000d). Supplementary reports recommended the extension of social work training to three years to strengthen specific areas, including learning for joint working. Concurrently, modernisation of teaching in higher education led to a subject centre in social policy and social work (SWAP) whose role includes promotion of interprofessional education in cooperation with others.

In 2001, the DH established groups to lead work on the reform of social work education in England and the introduction of a three-year degree. There was no group for interprofessional learning, but the DH commissioned research to inform development (Whittington, 2003a). The DH also announced pilot development of the New Generation multiprofessional common learning programmes.

When the *Requirements for Social Work Training* appeared, they comprised the 'prescribed curriculum for the social work degree' and drew together academic benchmarks from the QAA and National Occupational Standards (DH, 2002a). The requirements specify learning and assessment on 'partnership working and information sharing across professional disciplines and agencies' (DH 2002a: 4). The QAA benchmarks expect student knowledge and skills in collaboration and in partnership and understanding of service-providing networks. The National Occupational Standards give standards for multidisciplinary and multi-organisational work and cite the GSCC code, which requires work in partnership with colleagues from other agencies (GSCC, 2002a).

Concurrently, changes were in progress that would transform the organisation of care services. New partnership requirements, changing service vision for particular groups and new flexibilities in the use of budgets saw a continued differentiation of the conventional social services department model into adult and community services, joint trusts for learning disability and mental health and care trusts combining primary and community care. The failures in the care of Victoria Climbié led to the Children Act in 2004 and a major programme of change, including children's trusts and a new statutory duty on inter-agency cooperation (DfES, 2004).

In social work education, attention turned to post-qualifying learning and a new framework in England to take effect in 2007 (GSCC, 2005a). The framework includes an unprecedentedly strong and explicit commitment to interprofessional education, promoting a combination of joint learning with other professions and the study of the knowledge and skills of interprofessional and inter-agency practice.

The foregoing account confirms the rise of interprofessional education but shows it to have been slow. If the rise is to be sustained, the momentum must be maintained. In education and training domains, there are a number of drivers:

- the injunctions of regulators and course requirements;
- the experience gained since the 1990s of pioneer joint training programmes and later from New Generation pilots and other projects;
- the promotion of interprofessional learning by individual and collective champions, organisations such as the Centre for the Advancement of Interprofessional Education (CAIPE) and government-supported initiatives (Creating an Interprofessional Workforce (CIPW) 2005);
- specification of common core skills for the workforce in particular services (DfES, 2005);
- national and international cooperative initiatives (Health Sciences and Practice, 2005).

Yet the momentum these sources provide seems secondary to more fundamental driving forces that are underwritten in government rhetoric and policy and include:

- demands upon managers and professionals to innovate and cooperate as necessitated by the combined effects of:
  - recurrent change in services and organisation led by government,
  - the dynamics of a mixed economy of care,
  - and new political and participatory relationships;
- 'whole-system' theories of management and governance in which system members are required actively to facilitate cooperation;
- a history of enquiries that blame failures of collaboration for the death or harm of service users or other members of the public;
- the prioritisation of consumer choice and responsiveness to service users, who demand that services cooperate effectively;
- a mix of assumption and evidence that partnership and collaboration can deliver solutions in more effective and efficient services and that education can make an important contribution.

Regarding this last position, if the rise of interprofessional education is to be sustained and extended, stronger evidence of effectiveness is needed. One group of researchers has sought to review that evidence. The next section will consider their findings.

 Do you observe rising or falling levels of attention to interprofessional education, currently, and what factors account for what you see?

A systematic review of research on interprofessional education

The first systematic review of studies of interprofessional education was published in 2005 by Hugh Barr and colleagues in the Joint Evaluation Team (JET) (Barr et al., 2005). The review asked: 'What types of interprofessional education under what circumstances result in what types of outcome?' (Barr et al., 2005: 42). The team confines the review to interprofessional education in two service domains, defining interprofessional education as: 'Members (or students) of two or more professions associated with health or social care, engaged in learning with, from and about each other' (Barr et al., 2005: 43).

Extensive electronic searches and analysis of research quality produced a sample of 107 qualifying papers in which interprofessional education had been evaluated (Barr et al., 2005: 46). Papers covered a thirty-year period and most had been undertaken in the USA (54 per cent) and UK (33 per cent). The majority reported interprofessional education that extended over more than seven days of interprofessional contact, usually spread over several months. Few initiatives led in themselves to a qualification, and only ten linked directly to pre-registration or similar awards (Barr et al., 2005: 49). One fifth took place at pre-qualifying level while most occurred after qualifying. Most initiatives involved nurses (89 per cent) and doctors (88 per cent). Social workers were involved in 36 per cent (Barr et al., 2005: 51). The majority of studies focused on, or included, the learners' perspective of interprofessional education and a quarter included a 'patient/client' perspective (Barr et al., 2005: 55).

A typology is described of six levels of outcome reported in the studies. These levels covered learners' reactions to the experience, modification of attitudes to other groups, acquisition of collaborative competence, behavioural change, changes in organisational practice and benefits to service users. Most studies reported outcomes at more than one level. Quality of outcome was assessed by the team as positive, neutral, negative or mixed. There was a clear predominance of positive outcomes in all six categories.

At the heart of the review are efforts to 'evaluate evidence regarding the effectiveness of interprofessional education' (Barr et al., 2005: xv). If effectiveness is defined as reports of positive outcome, then the review gives encouraging evidence of effectiveness. However, the research team are generally cautious in the findings they report. They observe that the studies, which were predominantly experimental or quasi-experimental (66 per cent), assist more in answering 'what?' questions than questions about 'how?' and 'why?' (Barr et al., 2005: 54).

This conclusion is put to good effect by the reviewers who develop a range of descriptive (or 'what') classifications and typologies of interprofessional education from their data. Yet limitations in the review studies restrict the team in answering particular 'what?' questions too, including the research question seeking the relationship of types of interprofessional education and types of outcome (Barr et al., 2005: 42). The report says that a key element of interprofessional education, namely interactive learning, 'can achieve' improvement in 'collaborative practice and the quality of services' but that 'data are incomplete, and numbers too small, to show which interactive learning methods are more or less effective' (Barr et al., 2005: 140).

Similar caution is expressed in the finding of 'some evidence' that interprofessional education 'creates positive interaction' and 'encourages collaboration between professions', and also 'improves client care' (Barr et al., 2005: 139). The caution is needed because the reviewers found problems of methodology or interpretation in a number of studies reporting these kinds of outcome (Barr et al., 2005: 78–9).

Barr and colleagues explore interprofessional education more comprehensively than can be shown here. Confining attention to the evidence of effectiveness of interprofessional education, it is notable that, within the terms of the reviewed studies themselves, positive outcomes were the predominant result. Nevertheless, the reviewers remain cautious, concluding that 'nothing … leads us to expect a dramatic break through in establishing the evidence base for interprofessional education' (Barr et al., 2005: 141).

There is little in the reviewers' findings to suggest that interprofessional education has risen on an evidence-based platform. The position strengthens the case for seeing the rise as being driven primarily by policy and politics and, it follows, as vulnerable to their changing priorities.

Factors in the progress of interprofessional education: empirical evidence and theory

This section takes up two aspects of the idea of 'rise and rise'. The section notes, first, the earlier observation that the rise has not been rapid and, second, argues that it has not been nearly as linear as the description earlier of progression from social policy to social work education might suggest. The discussion seeks to account for aspects of a more typically slow and erratic progress as follows:

- by describing empirical evidence of the wide and complex agenda that the development of interprofessional education entails;
- by theorising on the significance of the professional 'knowledge base' as a source of underlying tensions for interprofessionalism.

A study of interprofessional education in social work

In 2002, with courses for the new social work degree soon to start, the DH commissioned a study of learning for collaborative practice, to inform development of the degree. This subject had not been systematically researched in UK social work programmes for a decade (Whittington and Bell, 2001). The new study took as its population the providers of Diploma in Social Work (DipSW) programmes who represented a rich but untapped and directly transferable source (Whittington, 2003d).

All DipSW programmes in England were contacted to identify work in progress and to learn of experience gained. Survey questionnaires were returned by 39 programmes (a 50 per cent response rate) representing all main categories of provider, route and type of programme and all regions. Follow-up interviews were held with nine programmes.

The study was primarily qualitative and exploratory, using mainly open-ended questions to learn: *what factors, respectively, assisted and hindered the development of opportunities for learning to practice collaboratively with other professions and agencies?*

All respondents recounted both factors that helped and hindered. The factors related to provision or deficits on five broad dimensions:

1. *Resources:* the availability of resources such as placements, teachers' skills and development time, and the budgets to support them.
2. *Organisational and professional cultures and environments:* the nature of structures, cultures, attitudes and relationships affecting collaboration within and between educational institutions, agencies and professions.
3. *Regulatory and assessment expectations:* the degree to which expectations of learning for collaborative practice are clear in regulations and assessment requirements.
4. *Knowledge base:* the availability and accessibility of models and concepts of collaborative practice and of methodologies for how it may be taught, learned and assessed.
5. *Conceptions of professional and interprofessional identity:* social work identities that training seeks to develop, and how to facilitate their formation and manage the tensions between them.

 Which factors above have had the greatest effect in assisting or hindering your interprofessional education and are there others that you would identify?

The experiences and practices reported were grouped into pointers to assist courses in action planning for the social work degree. They are adapted from the original in Box 8.1 below (Whittington, 2003d: 11–12).

Box 8.1   Twelve pointers to action in developing interprofessional education.

1. Clarify models of collaboration and of professional and interprofessional identity.
2. Foster commitment to, and expertise in, interprofessional education among course staff.
3. Develop practice teacher commitment to interprofessional education and support creativity in accessing relevant practice learning opportunities.
4. Make interprofessional education a core criterion of course design.

(Continued)

(Continued)

5. Build the local resource base for teaching and learning methods and content in interprofessional education.
6. Seek practice learning opportunities and links across a range of agencies.
7. Strive for clarity of roles, language, criteria, standards and evidence in practice assessment.
8. Invest in partnerships with local agencies and professionals.
9   Work for collaborative university structures and climate.
10. Seek dedicated resources for development.
11. Apply the requirements, standards and codes of the professions involved and build on the leverage they give for developing interprofessional education.
12. Provide and seek leadership that cultivates and models collaboration.

The guidance in Box 8.1, based on the experience of half the social work programmes in England, indicates the range and complexity of the interprofessional education agenda. It is hardly surprising that the path to interprofessional education has been neither rapid nor, in the experience of respondents, straightforward, although many nevertheless reported interprofessional education initiatives (Whittington, 2003a: 45–60).

Professional and interprofessional projects

The idea of profession is highly contested both among sociologists and occupations. Nevertheless, most of the occupations involved in interprofessional education tend to think of themselves as professions and have been implicated in the institutional strategy of job control called 'professionalisation', or the 'professional project' (Macdonald, 1995). The strategy includes, centrally, two elements: first, claims to esoteric knowledge and expertise, that is, the 'knowledge base'; and, second, efforts to convert these claims into the relative autonomy, income security and the other rewards associated with professional status such as recognition, valued identity and, in care professions, rights and influence in pursuing goals of human service.

The strategy has important organisational and political dimensions, but the discussion here concentrates on the knowledge base, to cast light on the idea of the 'interprofessional project' and to illuminate some of the underlying structural tensions. Plainly, occupations pursue professionalisation with varying success and differ in the models of profession pursued. Furthermore, the outcomes are increasingly conditioned for all care professions by organisational employment, management control and governance systems that recognise the right of service users to participate. Nevertheless, ideas of profession and aspects of professionalisation are found across sectors such as health, social care, education and criminal justice. This scenario is an alert to the intensely occupation-specific and potentially competitive environment within which a cooperative enterprise, the 'interprofessional project', is pursued.

The goals of the interprofessional project are, for most of its adherents, different in order from the professional project. The purpose is not to replace professional identity or to gain recognition of some new hybrid practitioner, multi-skilled across professional domains, although this idea has been aired. The aim is, rather, to construct and lodge within each participating profession a revised discourse and identity embracing interprofessionalism.

Macdonald (1995) argues that the origins of a profession rest in the identification of an area of abstract knowledge which those who possess it can isolate from social knowledge generally and to which they can establish a special claim. Claim to an esoteric knowledge base is a necessary, although not a sufficient, condition of professionalisation. The base comprises not only theories but also associated skills and techniques which are typically accompanied by ethical codes that guide their use. The success of some occupations, such as medicine and the law, in establishing knowledge claims and accompanying social power, contrasts with the mixed fortunes and lower status of occupations such as teaching, social work and nursing, whose knowledge is viewed as practically based, closer to everyday social knowledge and more subject to routinisation by the employing organisation.

There are increasing calls for the development of a base of theory and evidence that will inform interprofessional practice (Barr et al., 2005: 143; Whittington, 2003d). The objective creates a paradox. The pursuit of an esoteric professional knowledge base is a procedure of *exclusion* that separates occupations. The interprofessional project seeks a knowledge base that *unifies* aspects of professional education and practice and underpins a unifying ideology that bridges participants' professional separateness. This is by no means to say that the two states, professional and interprofessional expertise, cannot exist simultaneously; manifestly, that is achieved, but there is a tension to be managed.

In addition, theories and an evidence base come with their own, far from neutral, baggage. The knowledge culture of medicine and, more broadly, of health, is based primarily in scientific positivism. Research and evidence in social work and some other professions are more eclectic and include a significant strand of qualitative, interpretive theory and method. Positivist and interpretive paradigms embody different and potentially conflicting assumptions about how people and the social world are to be understood and the respective roles of professional and service user in constructing and acting on that understanding. These conflicting assumptions underlie aspects of the familiar debate between 'medical' and 'social' models of illness, disability and care. The research and evidence base of interprofessional education and practice thus become arenas for working out the tensions between different paradigms espoused by the professions involved and imported from the 'parent' professional culture.

The knowledge base and dominant paradigms of a profession are allied to a third dimension: the profession's value priorities. This association is particularly noticeable in social work where competent practice has long been portrayed as reliant on explicit values to bind the knowledge and skills that practitioners require (O'Hagan, 1996). Professions do not own their values yet they do sometimes claim a special relationship as 'early adopters' of particular values. Social work and social care have taken this stance in promoting equal opportunities, anti-discrimination and diversity and have sought to lead in building values of involvement of service users and carers into professional method (Higham, 2005). These values and the ethical codes they generate are likely to be reflected in priorities for the interprofessional knowledge base and methods. The result is potential conflict with professions who give a lower priority to 'equalities' or who take a more hierarchical view of the relationship with service users.

Plainly, the pursuit of the interprofessional project introduces tensions. A valued professional identity has to shift to accommodate new dimensions. Working cooperatively modifies autonomous decision-making and flattens familiar professional hierarchies. Taken-for-granted knowledge, values and established paradigms are exposed to alternatives.

Conclusion

Interprofessionalism is, in the deceptively simple phrase, working together. It is also the intersection of multiple systems of policy, occupations, education and practice. Discussion of aspects of these systems and their history has endeavoured to show the limitations of the idea that the rise of interprofessional education has been rapid or linear, or is reliably ever upward.

In particular, the idea of a linear rise of interprofessional education must give way to one that recognises the inherent *complexity* of the systems, concepts, intentions and interactions that bear upon the interprofessional project (Cooper et al., 2004). Complexity theory is not the new panacea, however, and needs debate. In the meantime, the factors strewn in the path of the interprofessional project can seem like insurmountable obstacles. Yet evidence of interprofessional cooperation in practice and education continues to grow, driven by the sets of forces described in the policy discussion earlier and encouraged by evidence of gains for service users and professionals (Whittington, 2003b: 31; Barr et al., 2005). Like the professional project, the interprofessional project does not have a secured end point and must be continually renewed. There are actions that participating professionals can take, individually and collectively, to help in sustaining the process; key points are suggested below.

The final point in the list concerns professional values that are congruent with interprofessionalism. Relevant social work values include respect for persons and commitment to reflect critically on power structures, including professional institutions, in pursuit of emancipatory goals. Values also include professional accountability, partnership and service user-centredness. These values combine to modify the traditional model of the independent, elite professional and to promote the actively collaborating, interprofessional professional. They also direct attention to what should be the primary purpose of the interprofessional project: a quality service for users and carers.

Key points in sustaining the interprofessional project

1. realistically appraise the challenges posed by interprofessionalism;
2. strengthen and diversify the research and theory base;
3. share knowledge and learning from successes as well as problems;
4. publicise the gains for service users, professionals and other stakeholders;
5. cooperate to support colleagues engaged in professional and interprofessional change;
6. sustain professional motivation by playing to professional values that are congruent with interprofessionalism.

Taking it further

Readers who want to know more about this will find the following helpful:

Colyer, H., Helme, M. and Jones, I. (eds) (2005) *The Theory–Practice Relationship in Interprofessional Education*, retrieved on 4 December 2005 at http://www.health.heacademy.ac.uk/publications/occasionalpaper/occ7.pd.

Leathard, A. (ed.) (2003) *Interprofessional Collaboration*, Hove: Brunner–Routledge.

Weinstein, J., Whittington, C. and Leiba, T. (eds) (2003) *Collaboration in Social Work Practice*, London: Jessica Kingsley.

9 Social work in an international context

Steven M. Shardlow

> **This chapter will:**
>
> - address social work in its international context, noting how, in the United Kingdom, only certain elements of the social work role (IFSW/IASSW, 2000) are accorded value and status;
> - consider the more emancipatory and liberatory potential of social work common within many societies across the world;
> - identify several social problems that can only be resolved through collective international action;
> - suggest that an understanding of the development of social work in the UK can be enhanced through an understanding of its growth elsewhere.

Introduction

In the UK, the construction of social work is often grounded upon the idea of an *individual* social worker engaged with an *individual* person or *individual* family, albeit frequently working interprofessionally. Social work is, then, a local, culture-bound activity (Lorenz, 1994: 45), specific to time and place (Lyons, 1999: 2). The focus of the service user, carer and social worker are likely to be highly particular, localised and to centre upon the immediate locality of residence or a community sharing ethnicity, sexual orientation or another unifying aspect of individual biography. For practitioners, localised practice has many advantages, particularly acquiring knowledge of local context and resources. Yet, localised practice carries the danger of myopic practice, where custom and local policy define the bounds of both competence and presumed excellence. For true excellence in practice, something all service users should aspire to receive, practitioners need a broader vision, a questioning about how social work is practised in other countries, a questioning about lessons to be learned from elsewhere and directly applied to a given local area. This is one major reason, among many reasons, to take careful account of international social work. This chapter explores the nature of international social work not from vicarious interest but from genuine desire to create a better and more informed practice in our localities.

Towards an international definition of social work

Social work is a differently constructed activity across the world. This can be seen by comparing illustrative statements about social work. The Indiana School of Social Work produced a 'fridge magnet' that gave seventy-five reasons for when you might need a social worker (see Figure 9.1).

You'll Need a Social Worker...

When you come into the world too soon • When you hate the new baby • When you get into fights at school • When you are left home alone • When you get poor grades • When you miss your big brother • When you don't want mommy and daddy to divorce • When you can't find anyone to play with • When you don't think your teacher likes you • When you are bullied • When you don't like how the neighbor touches you • When you don't make the team • When your best friend moves away • When you always fight with your siblings • When your friends pressure you to get high • When you can't adjust to the move • When you can't talk to your parents • When you want to quit school • When your friends don't like you anymore • When you didn't want this baby • When you feel like running away • When your friend swallows an overdose • When you are the only one that thinks you're fat • When you wonder if you are drinking too much • When you can't find someone who speaks your language • When you can't stick to a budget • When you can't forget the assault • When you can't decide on a career • When your family pressures you to marry • When your boss is hitting on you • When you want to adopt • When you can't find good day care • When you think you are neglecting your kids • When you are hated because of who you are • When you lose your baby • When your community has gang problems • When your kids want to live with your ex • When your kids won't listen • When your partner is unfaithful • When you want to meet your birthparent • When your disabled child needs friends • When your mother won't speak to you • When you just can't face moving again • When you want to be a foster parent • When your city officials don't respond • When your best friend has panic attacks • When you find drugs in your son's room • When your brother won't help care for dad • When your job is eliminated • When your mother-in-law wants to move in • When your neighborhood needs a community center • When you find there is no joy in your life • When your car accident destroys your career • When you sponsor a refugee family • When your legislature passes a bad law • When your partner has a mid life crisis • When you are stressed by menopause • When your spouse wants a divorce • When your mom gets Alzheimer's • When you are caring for parents and children • When you want to change careers • When you lose your home in a fire • When you are angry all the time • When your nest really empties • When your partner insists you retire • When you can't afford respite care • When you can't find a job and you're sixty • When your kids demand you move in with them • When your daughter suddenly dies • When you are scared about living alone • When you can't drive any more • When your children ignore your medical decisions • When your retirement check won't pay the bills • When you learn you have a terminal illness • When you need a nursing home •

Life's Challenges: Social Workers Are There For You!
Indiana University School of Social Work
© 2001 Darlene Lynch and Robert Vernon, All Rights Reserved

Figure 9.1   Indiana University School of Social Work fridge magnet.

How do you relate this to what you know of social work? What do you know about how social work happens elsewhere in the world?

Irrespective of content, the very idea of a 'fridge magnet' suggests commercialism, combined with locating social work in such a familiar setting, the 'kitchen'. Some of these points of crisis in *individuals'* lives may surprise the reader as reasons to request social work help, and some are doubtless recognisable and familiar. This construction of social work contrasts with a conception from Africa. For example, Rampal (2000) identifies the impact of HIV/AIDS on society as loss in the prime of life, poverty and dependence, drop in productivity and greater demands on public services, suggesting a key role for social workers:

> Social and community workers are particularly well positioned to serve as co-ordinator, and network people and resources and to render assistance at different stages of the illness.
>
> An important element in the social worker's networking system is the traditional healer. Traditional healers are local medicine men and women who utilize basic traditional medicines and spiritual principles in effecting cures. *Sangomas* and *Inyangas* fall into this group. Health care systems which include traditional healers are likely to be effective ...
>
> (Rampal, 2000: 39)

Here, social work is a community resource drawing upon traditional structures to mobilise action for HIV AIDS sufferers and their families. Contrasting strongly with the highly individualised US approach, this view from Africa is collective and grounded in social-development models. Nor are these the only constructions of social work: in a Dutch context, van der Laan suggests that social work in the Netherlands is developing an increasingly strong economic focus whereby its primary purpose is to assist people back into the workforce (van der Laan, 2000).

Recognising these differences around the world in the way that social work is constructed, IFSW jointly adopted a definition of social work with IASSW[1] (IFSW/ IASSW, 2000: see Chapter 1 for the full definition).

The heart of this globally applicable statement concerns professional values; it may be at that level of abstraction that social work can be seen as a global and united profession despite the different constructions of practice.

 Look at the IFSW definition of social work at http://www.ifsw.org/en/ p38000208.html; how well does it fit with what you know as social work?

The scope of international social work

Can we confidently assert that *international* social work can be differentiated from other forms of social work? Midgley (2001) suggests three distinct areas delineating the scope of international social work. First, as specialist social work conducted by international agencies (for example, International Red Cross, UNICEF, Oxfam). Their work includes providing immediate assistance following disasters, development programmes to relieve problems such as water shortage and ensuring food security and assisting with the impact and management of HIV/AIDS. Because these agencies are international, the nature of the work they undertake constructs a non-nationally grounded social work. Second, contacts and exchanges that take place between social workers from different countries are, by their very nature, international social work. Such contacts have a long tradition, with the first international social work organisations developing in the 1920s. A range of international organisations, notably IFSW and IASSW, work to facilitate knowledge transfer at a global level, develop global policy statements, encourage discussion and debate between social workers from different nations and, most importantly, seek to influence international and national governmental and non-governmental organisations. Third, social workers need to acquire global awareness to enable them to 'transcend their concern for the local and the particular' (Midgley, 2001: 25) due to the impact of globalisation. This is well illustrated in the economic sphere where, as a consequence of globalisation, jobs are exported from Western companies with high labour costs to developing countries with much lower wage costs. Social workers in countries that lose jobs may face having to deal with an increasing number of social problems deriving from unemployment. Similarly, social workers in developing countries may have to deal with problems about the workers' health, due to exploitative working conditions, or problems deriving from family stresses arising from adults who care for others often being employed for long hours. Helping strategies in both contexts can only be developed by fully understanding the cause of these problems.

Specific international issues?

 Can you think of ways in which global problems are social work issues?

We need to consider whether there are problems or issues particular and unique to international social work. For some problems, where the issues are all a consequence of globalisation, although they are manifest within one nation state, their cause or resolution does not rest fully within that nation state's jurisdiction.

Global abuse of children

The availability of pornography involving children on the internet highlights an issue. Paedophiles have used the internet with increasing sophistication to access images of child pornography, while availability of cheap international airfares has led to the extensive development of sex tourism involving the sexual exploitation of children. Social workers, the probation service and police authorities may have responsibility for catching and supervising paedophiles, but the victims are often children living in a different country to where the internet-based crime is committed or to where the paedophile lives. The control and regulation of the internet and the need to protect children abused in this manner are international issues.

Global exploitation through enslavement of adults

The development of 'human trafficking', a form of slavery, has emerged as a major problem due to the growth of mafia-type crime organisations, particularly in eastern and central Europe, and the ease of travel from parts of the world where many are desperate to escape poverty. These organisations frequently promise people work but, on arrival in western Europe force them into domestic service or prostitution. People may be intimidated and controlled by being forced to take drugs or to make enormous loan payments, ensuring they can never become 'free'. They become chattels to be used and may be 'sold' to other individuals or organisations (Roberts, 2006). In response to this and similar forms of organised crime, the UK government introduced SOCA (Serious and Organised Crime Agency) in April 2006.

The movement of peoples

We live in an age where many people are displaced through famine, civil strife, fear of detention and torture, natural disaster and war. There are many migrants, refugees and asylum-seekers – terms often confused and misused.

Migrants

The United Nations (UN) defines a migrant worker as a 'person who is to be engaged, is engaged or has been engaged in a remunerated activity in a State of which he or she is not a national' (UN Convention on the Rights of Migrants, 2003): the term does not refer to those who are displaced or forced to leave their home. Hence, migrants make, albeit constrained, choices.

Refugees

A refugee has protected status according to international convention (in particular the Geneva Convention 1951 and subsequent protocols) and is defined as someone who, 'owing to a well-founded fear of being persecuted for reasons of race, religion, nationality, membership of a particular social group, or political opinion, is outside the country of his nationality, and is unable to or, owing to such fear, is unwilling to avail himself of the protection of that country' (Article 1, the 1951 Convention Relating to the Status of Refugees).

Asylum-seekers

According to the Immigration and Asylum Act 1999 (IAA) § 94 (1), people are defined as asylum-seekers if:

1. they are at least eighteen years old;
2. they are in the UK;
3. they have registered a claim for asylum at a place designated by the Secretary of State;
4. the claim has been recorded by the Secretary of State; and
5. their claim has not been determined, i.e. when the appeal to the Adjudicator has been disposed of (IAA §. 94 (3)).
    Note: If an asylum seeker has a dependant as part of their household, they continue to be defined as an asylum seeker even if they don't come within the above definition (IAA §.94 [3A]).

Practitioners need to be aware of these differences and to act accordingly when working with migrants, refugees and asylum-seekers. (For some practice implications of working with asylum-seekers, see Chapter 7.) There is growing evidence of a social construction both unifying and demonising all three groups by the term 'bogus'; similarly, assumptions that migrants have choice should not stand uncontested. Service users and carers who have come, in whatever circumstances, to the UK bring a distinct cultural heritage and are likely to need services reflecting their heritage, including interpretation.

The international movement of peoples also affects professionals: registered social workers may come to the UK as long- or short-term migrants. Community Care has detailed an increase in the number of qualified social workers from overseas (excluding other European Union (EU) countries) working in England, as measured by numbers of GSSC letters of verification issued: 1,175 in 2001–2 compared with 1,390 in 2002 (an 18 per cent increase). If historic trends continue, approximately one third of these will be social workers from Australia and New Zealand (Community Care, 5 February 2004). This is a much smaller proportion than in the nursing profession, where approximately one third of all new registrations are from overseas. The same article reports the South African Minister of Social Development as criticising the UK for recruiting South African social workers and nurses when there are shortages there. Certainly, international recruitment agencies operate through internet sites specialising in overseas recruitment from such countries, raising profound ethical questions about international relationships.

Natural and human disasters

There are a large number of natural disasters (such as earthquakes, hurricanes and floods), and human disasters (particularly terrorist incidents). When disasters are large and cannot be contained within the nation state, then relief, either cash or labour, will be donated from around the world. In the immediate aftermath of disaster, initial needs are primarily practical, providing medical care, locating all survivors and re-establishing disrupted major services (water, food and shelter) – much of which requires technical knowledge and equipment. Depending upon the nature of the disaster, there is a variable but crucial period when emergency help must be provided to maximise survival rates. Social workers are then centrally involved in the processes of counselling relatives and survivors, attempting to locate relatives and to reunite them with survivors (post-disaster disruption may result in movement of large numbers of people). Large-scale disaster, the purview of international social work, requires that these tasks are well coordinated, problematic when teams are likely to speak different languages and have incompatible equipment.

These are four truly international issues as the causes, impacts and possible solutions are too diverse in a global sense for any national government to deal with adequately.

Professional boundaries

Differing terms are used for 'social worker' in various countries such as *Der Sozialarbeiter* (Germany), or *l'assistant sociale* (France). The fact that the words 'social worker' find equivalence in other countries should not be taken to imply that conceptualisations of social work, job descriptions or the professional boundaries with other social professions are the same as in the UK. For example, in Russia the term 'social worker' is often, although not exclusively, applied to the person who provides services such as cooking and cleaning for people living in their own homes – elsewhere termed a 'home carer' or domiciliary support. In some countries (e.g. Finland), the social worker may deal more with direct provision of income support than happens in the UK, where this is the responsibility of a separate central government department whose staff do not term themselves 'social workers'.

Differences between the boundaries of social work and other professional groups in various European countries are particularly evident when considering the professional group known as social pedagogues (termed *Der Sozialepedagogue* in Germany and *L'éducateurs spécialisé* in France), found in a group of European countries, especially in the northern and central regions. According to Hämäläinen (2003: 69), 'social pedagogy is based on the belief that you can decisively influence social circumstances through education'. This profession originated, in the nineteenth century, by providing holistic *social* (not academic/classroom) education to children – often those living in institutional care. This has been extended to include work in the community. Whereas in Anglo-Saxon contexts, the term 'pedagogy' has a laboured, heavy and slightly negative connotation, the concept of *l'éducation* in French is a broad concept including children's emotional, intellectual and social development. The conceptual underpinning of social pedagogy relies upon providing assistance to, essentially, natural processes of maturation and development and on helping people achieve their full potential. This contrasts with the central tenets of social work, which are the problem-focused, grounded responsive management of social or individual problems.

Social work as an export – towards theoretical unity?

Recent years have seen a thriving international trade in social work. For example, following the collapse of communism in the Soviet Union and eastern Europe, as these countries establish capitalist economic systems, democratic governments and civil societies, they have developed forms of social work that draw upon Western models. These models have been exported through EU-funded programmes such as TEMPUS (see, for example, a learning exercise called 'Gulliver's Travels' (Doel and Shardlow, 2006)). These exports may or may not be desirable but, as a strongly culturally grounded profession, transposition of methods and practices from one country to another may not be the most helpful way to develop social work in other parts of the world. For example, successful social work in South Africa can only be developed in harmony with a sense of the collective – the notion of *Umbutu*, a term lacking exact translation, whose approximate meaning is 'I am because we are' – differs considerably from social work's development in individualised consumerist societies. In the UK, we may be most concerned about the export of social work but should be equally concerned about importing culturally inappropriate models of practice. In the 1950s, the UK received a substantial Carnegie-funded programme to establish a form of 'casework as social work' (Hartshorn, 1982). This form of social work was highly influential and not overthrown until the radical social work movement ushered in the development of a distinctly UK-constructed social work practice and a very substantial UK-based literature.

We should not presume that either Western models of social work or indigenous welfare practices are inherently superior and therefore preferable: social work remains a culture-bound activity. There is no single Western model, Western societies are pluralist and care must be exercised not to assume that a single dominant Western model of social work practice exists. Yet Western knowledge is often privileged (Midgley, 1981). It is most desirable that there is a mutuality of influence flowing easily, in both directions, across national and cultural boundaries. One of the best known examples of such transcultural influence in social work is that of family group conferences; these derive from Maori decision-making practices in Aotearoa (New Zealand) and have had demonstrable impact in the USA (see, for example, Kemp et al., 2000) and UK (see, for example, Lupton and Nixon, 1999). Less well known, but considerably significant, is the development of an approach to the provision of services for unemployed female workers in a neighbourhood of Beijing based upon the integration of indigenous practice and professional knowledge (Yuen-Tsang and Sung, 2002). Here, a team of practitioners and educators conducted a research-based project leading to the establishment of a women's cooperative and the construction of a communally based support network. Yet despite such professional interactions, no single global theory of social work is likely to emerge, as Payne suggests: 'any act of social work, any organisation of any agency, or any welfare system represent a mixture of elements … in a different recipe reflecting social expectations and cultures' (Payne, 2005b: 15).

He draws upon diverse cultural traditions of social work from India, China and Africa to introduce a range of alternative theoretical practices to those produced in the West. Different approaches to professional development should be celebrated; we should be careful about yearning for uniform social work practice, except perhaps in one respect. Not all cultural practices are equally to be valued. For example, the genital mutilation of young girls can have no moral justification, yet it is culturally sanctioned in certain parts of the world. Social work theory should not condone such practices on the grounds of cultural relativism. Social work can, whatever form it takes, be consistent with internationally ratified conventions on human rights – particularly the UN Universal Declaration of Human Rights (1948). Such declarations and charters provide a benchmark for good professional practice wherever social work is found (Freeden, 1990) and provide a means for social work to challenge morally unacceptable practices.

Researching and building knowledge about international social work

Numerous publications describe social work in different countries; some take a world perspective (see, for example, Tan and Envall, 2000; Tan and Dodds, 2002; Tan, 2004); others take a regional view (see, for example, regarding Europe, Adams et al., 2000 and 2001). Many accounts provide a description of social work in one country juxtaposed with a similar account from one or more other countries. The premise that underlies such juxtaposition is that through comparison, however informal, lessons can be learned about the constituents of good practice and, therefore, the quality of practice can be improved in our own country. Importantly, these juxtapositions should challenge our views about the very nature of professional ethics, practice modalities and conceptualisation of social work. In that sense, international social work is radicalised social work as it is inherently reflexive.

Various approaches have been used to sharpen the value of such juxtapositions, restricting the juxtaposition to a particular aspect or theme of professional practice (for example, social work with a particular service user group) in each country. Another approach is to develop a framework for comparison that helps to structure understanding. Two prominent approaches can be characterised as the 'ideal-type model' and the 'profiling model'.

The 'ideal-type model' is strongly associated with the work of Esping-Andersen (1990 and 1996), providing a framework to compare welfare regimes of which social work forms part. Critics of Esping-Andersen's work have drawn attention to the model's ability to accommodate a wide range of types of welfare regime. Abrahamson (1992) has developed a slightly more expansive categorisation, which is firmly grounded on the work of Esping-Andersen (see Box 9.1 below).

Box 9.1   An 'ideal-type model' of welfare regimes based upon Abrahamson's model.

Ideal type of welfare regime	Characteristics
Corporatist	*Developed welfare provision* Provision through the labour market or churches; those outside the reaches of the labour market may experience relatively low levels of provision Examples: France, Germany
Latin model	*Limited public provision of welfare* Major providers of social care: families, the churches and charitable foundations Examples: Spain, Portugal, Ireland

(Continued)

Residual	*Principled ideology that the state should not be the primary provider of welfare*
	Where possible the state should retreat from the provision of welfare, often adopting a commissioning or quality-monitoring role; provision by families
	Examples: UK, USA
Social democratic	*Universal provision of welfare to all citizens*
	The state is the key provider, little provision may be available by the not-for-profit or private sectors
	Examples: Denmark, Finland, Norway, Sweden

Within any welfare regime, the form of social work is likely to be constructed in line with the dominant welfare ethos. Using this 'ideal-type model', it is possible to compare examples of welfare regimes to the extent that they conform to particular idealtypes. The real difficulty with the 'ideal-type model' is that no one country will possess all the characteristics of a particular ideal type and may possess characteristics of several.

The profiling model is a different approach to developing a taxonomy for types of welfare regime, drawing upon Kahn and Kamerman's (1976) study of eight countries' social services (Canada, France, Israel, Poland, Yugoslavia, the USA, the UK, West Germany). This study has methodological currency and draws not on conceptualised 'ideal types' for comparison but on a series of dimensions along which countries can be compared to provide a profile of any given country. These dimensions were developed by reviewing the areas of maximum variance between regimes and then formalising these into distinct dimensions. Three key dimensions were, for example:

1. the degree of independence of welfare organisations (may be free-standing or integrated with health services);
2. the form of services (may be integrated and generalist or discrete and specialist – as when there are separate structures for the provision of children and families services from those which are provided for older people);
3. the responsibility for service (may be for the commissioning, the provision or both).

Using a 'model' based on these and other similar dimensions a profile can be constructed of any welfare regime which can then be compared with any other. Profiles can be modified and adjusted according to the dimensions selected. A profile of social services developed using Kahn and Kamerman's approach would emphasise organisational aspects of social work.

If structured comparison of social work generates helpful knowledge, it is important to be aware of the nature and extent of knowledge so derived. Regrettably, not very much work has been undertaken in this field. First, much of the work that has been completed concerns broad policy and organisational themes rather than a detailed study of professional social work practice. Second, a substantial volume of published work in English about international social work practice is based upon the accounts of observational visits to other countries. Hence, these accounts are, by definition, produced by outsiders. In an exercise to map the extent of comparative studies that collected new data about social work in two or more European countries in the twenty years prior to 2000, Shardlow and Wallis (2003) found only fourteen such studies, although this was an underestimate due to the method used to identify published materials (including only those recorded in electronic databases). This number will have grown since the mapping exercise; however, the low number of studies emphasises how little detailed knowledge we have in this field other than through purely descriptive accounts of social work.

This account may leave the reader somewhat deflated because of the lack of an extensive body of rigorous methodologically sound comparative studies of international social work practice. There are, nonetheless, some exemplary studies: see Box 9.2.

Box 9.2   Example of comparative study of social work practice: protecting children.

In a European study of child protection (Belgium – the Flemish and Francophone communities – France, Germany, Italy, the Netherlands, the UK – England and Scotland), Hetherington et al. (1997) used a creative methodology based around a series of seminars in each country (consisting of social workers who were citizens of and practising in that particular country) to consider a case example, constructed in order to be free of 'specific national organisational landmarks' (1997: 45). Participants were asked to comment upon how they would have responded to a similar situation had it arisen in their own country. A second seminar was held for the same social workers, who were given the responses of social workers in the other countries (as derived from the first seminar) to comment on. This process revealed a rich texture of similarity and difference across the countries. As might be expected, the study revealed considerable differences in legal requirements and administrative systems but also fundamental differences concerning interpretation of the individual's rights and the role of the state and the family, apparently grounded in historical and cultural traditions, which greatly affect social work practice.

Conclusion

Elements of international aspects of social work affect all social work practitioners, however localised they may believe their practice is. Hence, understanding something of the nature of international social work is not a luxury – something that can be avoided. It should be a requirement for all practitioners. Nor is international social work something restricted to those who have international contacts or who travel overseas as part of their practice – that is a relatively small aspect of international social work. A chapter such as this can only provide an overview of certain aspects of international social work: the next step is to read some of the accounts of how social work *is* different in other countries and to consider how social work *might* be improved in this country.

Key learning points

1. The international dimensions of social work are integral to localised practice.
2. Excellence in social work requires an understanding of lessons to be learned from practice in other countries. comparison generates new knowledge and new ideas.
3. There are particular types of international social work issues.
4. Relatively little international empirical research has been undertaken about social work.
5. Social work may be unified at the global level through a shared sense of professional values; nevertheless, it remains differently constructed in different countries.
6. There is a need for global action to deal with some of the problems that social work has to address on the local level.

Taking it further

Readers who want to know more about this will find the following helpful:
Adams, A., Erath, P. and Shardlow, S.M. (eds) (2001) *Key Themes in European Social Work: Theory, Practice Perspectives*, Lyme Regis: Russell House.
Healy, L.M. (2001) *International Social Work*, Oxford: Oxford University Press.
Lorenz, W. (1994) *Social Work in a Changing Europe*, London: Routledge.
Lorenz, W. (2006) *Perspectives on European Social Work*, Opladen: Barbara Budrich.
Lyons, K. (1999) *International Social Work: Themes and Perspectives*, Aldershot: Ashgate.
European Journal of Social Work http://www.tandf.co.uk/journals/titles/13691457.asp.
International Social Work http://www.sagepub.co.uk/journalsProdDesc.nav?prodId=Journal200781.

Note

1 The definition, adopted by the IFSW General Meeting in Montreal, Canada, July 2000, is also available in Danish, Finnish, German, French, Norwegian, Portuguese, Spanish and Swedish. A commentary on this definition includes discussion of 'values', 'theory' and 'practice'.

Part Three

Requirements and processes

This part of the book focuses on the requirements that have been created for qualifying-level social work education in England and on the educational processes that will enable these requirements to be delivered. The chapters focus on the following themes:

- social work law;
- the social work process of assessment, planning, intervention and review;
- communication skills;
- understanding the life course;
- partnership working;
- practice learning;
- social work and information technology.

Taken together, the chapters in Parts One and Two provide an introduction to the elements that comprise qualifying-level education and training in social work. Given the nature of social work and its education, Chapter 6 provides a lens through which all the chapters in this part of the book should be viewed. It is clear from the book overall that we consider that the engagement of service users should run through all aspects of the curriculum.

10 Social work law

Robert Johns

This chapter will:

- contribute to your understanding of the legislative basis of social work;
- engage with the range of legal issues practitioners encounter;
- help you to gain sufficient understanding of legal issues to ensure safe practice within an increasingly complex and challenging legal framework.

Introduction

At an international social work conference, following a presentation on teaching social work law in the UK, a Canadian social work educator approached the presenters and confessed, 'We don't teach law on our social work courses', but then added, 'although perhaps we should'.

In the UK there is little debate about whether the law should be taught on social work courses: it is obligatory. In designing the parameters for the new degree in social work in England, the DH (2002a) stipulated that law was to be a compulsory subject, alongside human growth and development, assessment, communication skills and partnership working (DH, 2002a: 3–4). However, whereas each of these other categories is amplified in the requirements, law is not: the requirement is simply baldly stated as 'law'.

Each of the other countries that constitute the UK has also stipulated that law must be included in the social work curriculum (Care Council for Wales, 2004, Northern Ireland Social Care Council, 2003, Scottish Executive, 2003). Reference to legal rules and skills is also made in subject benchmarks and National Occupational Standards (QAA, 2000; TOPSS, 2002). The formulation of the requirements of the new degree suggests that, whereas there is a degree of latitude with subjects such as assessment or communication skills, there is something definitive and absolute about the law that needs to be conveyed to social workers.

Yet this is far from being the case. The remark from the Canadian colleague underlines the lack of international agreement about the role of law in social work, and, indeed, a recent comprehensive survey of all recent research into social work law teaching conducted for the Social Care Institute for Excellence (Braye et al., 2005) revealed a paucity of social work law literature in some countries.

This chapter begins by explaining how law came to be central in social work and social work education in Britain, offering a brief overview of developments that help to explain its current pre-eminence. The discussion then focuses on contemporary approaches to and issues concerning teaching the subject on professional qualifying courses in the UK, drawing on research that examines how the subject is taught and assessed. The chapter then concludes by setting out a number of reasons as to why intending practitioners should be enthusiastic about learning about the law.

The law and social work in Britain

Social work history attests to the lack of any kind of social work law in the nineteenth century, since there was no legislation that created 'social work' as such (Clarke, 1993; Midwinter, 1994). The origins of social work organisations lie in voluntarism, meaning not that social workers were volunteers (although nearly all of them were), but that social work organisations were non-statutory voluntary agencies, not created by 'the law', who chose to operate in certain areas of social need and secured financial support by direct appeals to the public for charity. Many of the nineteenth-century and early twentieth-century pioneers in social work were motivated by strong religious principles (Bowpitt, 1998).

The lack of statutory regulation meant that voluntary organisations could be selective in the kind of work that they did, often being highly innovative and creative, but the result was piecemeal and patchy in terms of organisation of services. For service users, the consequences could be dire, since the quality of care received, being unregulated, was unpredictable, and occasionally practices took place that today would be unthinkable: for example, the practice of arranging the emigration of children who were cared for by charities (Bean and Melville, 1989).

At this time, the law allowed limited intervention in family life and therefore no real remit for social workers to protect the vulnerable from harm. As a consequence, children, for example, sometimes suffered extreme abuse (Hendrick, 1997). Attention drawn to abuse by social workers and others eventually resulted in legislation that regulated family life at least to some extent, allowing the courts to declare some parents to be 'unfit' to care for their children (Children Act 1908, Children and Young Persons Act 1933).

The creation of the welfare state in the period 1945–8 heralded the move away from a social work service offered primarily through voluntary organisations to one which was provided principally through the state, namely, in Britain, local authorities. The creation of children's departments in every local authority in 1948 was a significant milestone, and social workers employed in these departments built up expertise in this particular area of social work (Parker, 1990).

At the same time, social workers began to gain a foothold in areas where hitherto the law had simply been oppressive. For example, the much-reviled legislation that compelled anyone who was destitute to plead their case before a Board of Guardians and seek admission to a workhouse was repealed by the National Assistance Act 1948, which created a role for social workers working in local authority welfare departments, laying on them a responsibility to make provision for vulnerable adults. Social workers were made responsible for dealing with the detention of people under the Mental Health Act 1959, and this promoted a greater emphasis on voluntary treatment and community care.

Up until the 1970s, social workers, including those employed in statutory agencies, worked in specialist fields. The landmark Local Authority Social Services Act 1970 introduced generic social services departments, one port of call for help, and with it – perhaps unintentionally – came generic social workers. It was clearly going to be difficult for generic social workers to have an in-depth knowledge of the law as it related to all of their work, and deficiencies soon became apparent. Complaints began to emerge that social workers did not know enough about the law as it affected their work with families, and this lack of legal knowledge was regarded as one of the principal casualties of the dilutions of specialisms (Parker, 1980).

A series of high-profile child abuse cases, beginning with that of Maria Colwell in 1974, directed media attention to the acclaimed deficiencies in social work practice, often connected to poor inter-agency cooperation but also linked to knowledge gaps (Parton, 1985). Concern, specifically about the lack of legal knowledge in the field of child protection, came to the fore in the 1980s with the publication of the Beckford Report (1985), quickly followed by the Carlile Report (1987). These inquiries into the deaths of young children subject to court orders revealed ignorance about the requirements of orders and the powers social workers held but failed to exercise, with fatal consequences. This dramatically confirmed anxieties already highlighted concerning practitioners' inability to understand the legal component of their cases and their confusion between their own agencies' procedures, resource limitations and exact statutory requirements (Grace and Wilkinson, 1978).

Likewise, there was concern about the lack of availability of suitably trained and knowledgeable social workers in the field of mental health, specifically those (mental welfare officers) empowered to arrange compulsory admissions under mental health legislation. This had serious consequences for service users in terms of the protection of civil liberties and for the public in terms of assumed lack of protection and possible danger and led to the move to recreate a mental health specialism in the guise of 'Approved Social Workers' who were required to undertake specific legal tests as a prerequisite of being approved by their local authorities (section 114 Mental Health Act 1983; Central Council for Education and Training in Social Work (CCETSW) 2000).

Social work law teaching in the dock

Naturally, this identified lack of legal knowledge in social workers was connected to the quality of social work education more generally, which stood accused of failing to accord sufficient attention to law. Questions were asked about the extent to which qualifying courses in social work taught their students about the legal basis of practice. How much law was taught, what aspects of law were taught, and how good was the teaching and learning? How could a situation arise where student social workers did not understand what powers local authorities had, or were unaware of legal ways in which children could be protected from harm?

These and other deficiencies were highlighted in a composite law report prepared by Ball and colleagues (1988), which represented a turning point in the development of social work law teaching. For while the Beckford Report asserted the centrality of law in social work practice, *The Law Report* argued for its prominence in social work education, not in the sense of supplanting social work theory or values, but in reaffirming the reality that the majority of UK social workers were engaged in practice in statutory agencies. Thus, intending practitioners needed to be clear about what the law said, and they needed to be assessed appropriately on their legal knowledge and skills. Subsequently, clear guidance was provided on this (Ball et al., 1995; CCETSW, 1995).

In response to criticisms levelled at social work educators, significant changes were made to the curriculum in many higher education institutions with the intention of moving law, if not centre stage, at least out from the wings. As a consequence, discernible improvements have now been noted in the quality of law teaching in many social work courses, although many questions remain as to exactly what should be taught, how it should be taught, who should teach it and how it is to be assessed. It is these questions which will now be addressed.

What is social work law?

 Think about where you are working now, or your last placement:

- What legislation governed the way you worked?
- What other legislation was relevant for the people with whom you worked?

What should be taught in a social work law course? Given that the commissioning and regulatory bodies in the UK have determined that 'law' should be taught, it may come as something of a surprise that none has stipulated exactly what this means. There is no national curriculum, simply a mandate in each of the constituent countries of the UK. This being the case, decisions about the construction of the curriculum in social work qualifying courses are effectively devolved to the programme providers themselves. The literature suggests that there is a significant debate about its precise boundaries, partly reflecting an underlying question concerning the whole purpose of teaching social work law. This fundamental question is crystallised in the 'Pericles and the Plumber' debate initiated by Twining (1967) concerning the purpose of legal education for law students.

In essence, this debate revolved around whether law taught to law degree students should be jurisprudential – that is, concerned with the philosophy and principles – or whether the focus should be on what the law says and how it should be applied. In social work terms, the philosophical 'Pericles' approach might translate into learning and teaching about how the law generally promotes principles of justice, equity and anti-oppressive practice, whereas the 'plumber' approach might test students on the content of the Children Acts of 1989 and 2004, requiring students to apply current statute law to real or fictitious case studies. So, in essence, should law teaching reflect the bigger picture, or should it concentrate on how it applies to individual service users? Posed in this way, the question clearly presupposes that social work law is either one or the other. However, the consensus appears to be that social work law needs to be both.

In a key text that explores the relationship between social work and the law, Cull and Roche (2001) underline the importance of the broader context, suggesting that social workers do not study the law for its own sake but do emphatically need to understand the legal context in which they operate as professionals and its impact on service users' everyday lives. This point is echoed in the heartfelt cry, 'I want to be a social worker not a lawyer!' (Johns, 2005).

 List the reasons why you think you need to know about the law as a social worker.

Yet social workers do need to know what the law actually says about what they can and cannot do and most certainly do need to understand how specific laws can help or hinder the empowerment of service users. For example, how can social workers truly understand oppression unless they have some awareness of the kinds of inquisition facing claimants for income support or jobseekers' allowances? How can social workers understand homelessness without a nodding acquaintance with housing legislation? How can social workers address domestic violence without knowledge of processes for seeking protection through the courts? This point was emphasised in service users' comments to the SCIE researchers who conducted a comprehensive overview of social work law teaching in 2004–5. Service users believed that social workers should have accurate knowledge of the law as it affects their work and users' lives and should be able to integrate their knowledge so as to be able 'to respond to the complexity of people's lived experience, because "families don't fall into boxes"' (Braye et al., 2005: xiii). Hence, social work law teaching should be directed to this goal.

Adopting this approach, social work law becomes more than the sum of all social services legislation, that is, more than just the laws that set the parameters of social work practice in local authorities. The law's attempts to address discrimination issues (especially the Disability Discrimination Acts 1995 and 2005 and the Race Relations (Amendment) Act 2000) illustrate the relationship between the legislative, executive and the judiciary, underlining that the law can be both empowering and disempowering in service users' everyday lives. Analysis of this aspect of legislation exposes a vital weakness: the law is only really effective in individual cases where discrimination can be proven to have taken place. At the same time, general duties are imposed on the executive (public bodies) to take active steps to promote what social workers would call anti-discriminatory or anti-oppressive practice. The potential for making a difference is certainly there.

Furthermore, examination of the operation of the legal system and of the implementation of the Human Rights Act 1998, which adopted the European Convention on Human Rights as a benchmark for legal decisions, shows how legal provision may facilitate (or impede) good practice. Perhaps a couple of examples will help demonstrate this.

1. In a landmark case in 1999 (*Z. and others* v. *the United Kingdom* Application No. 29392/95, often referred to as the 'Bedfordshire case'), the European Court established that children do have rights of redress where local authorities patently fail to protect them by ignoring persistent complaints of abuse. This potentially empowers children but may also lead to local authorities being over-cautious in their child protection practice, too anxious to intervene for fear of being sued for not taking appropriate action.

2. In 2004, the European Court clarified issues of capacity and consent in relation to people with learning disabilities and mental health problems (*H. L.* v. the *United Kingdom* Application no. 45508/99, often referred to as the 'Bournewood case'). This may have halted the potential abuse of people who were unable to give fully informed consent to decisions, but may also result in an increase in the use of compulsory powers in order to safeguard the professional from accusations of abusing that lack of capacity to consent. The balance may thus have shifted from an implicit assumption that professionals will generally act in people's best interests to a position where they have to demonstrate explicitly that they are doing so. Consequently, there may be an increase in the use of formal legal authority to clarify or 'prove' this.

Therefore, intending social work practitioners must understand the legal parameters within which they work, the limits of their powers and the expectations and responsibilities of their role. This will promote their confidence and ability to work in both statutory and voluntary agencies. Furthermore, social work students in all agencies need to be able to articulate the rights that citizens have in their relationship with the state, mediated through public bodies. In order to achieve this, students might need to know something of the historical development of law and, especially in the UK context, be aware of the role of common law. In addition, the consensus amongst social work programmes surveyed for SCIE (Braye et al., 2005: 74) is that law is interpreted to mean:

- an overview of the legal system, usually including court structures, human rights principles and conventions;
- anti-discrimination laws;
- local authority duties generally;
- service provision for older people and people with disabilities;
- mental health legislation and principles concerning detention and treatment;
- support for families, together with the law promoting services for children in need including permanency planning for children who cannot be cared for by their own families;
- means of resolving conflicts within families;
- child protection;
- court work;
- youth justice.

How do social work students learn about the law?

 If you are a lecturer or a practice teacher reading this chapter, consider:

- How is law currently taught?
- Are there any things which could be done differently to enhance students' learning?

If social work students are to become both academically able to analyse the contexts in which they work and skilled technicians competent in the application of law, the question then arises as to how that aim should be attained. Preston-Shoot (2000) contends that social work students should become confident, credible, critical and creative – confident enough to challenge decisions and interpretations, credible in presenting or defending themselves, critical in the sense of being able to analyse and assess and therefore navigate through the complexities of the law, and creative in responding to practice dilemmas and conflicting demands. This would appear to argue for high order academic skills, empathy for service users' experiences, sensitive interpretation of anti-oppressive practice principles together with demonstrable competence in interpreting the law and applying it in real life.

Can this be achieved solely by having a discrete, specialist course in social work law or is a diffuse approach appropriate where the law is part of a number of different modules? There is a lack of empirical evidence to demonstrate conclusively that one approach is better than the other, but again the question presupposes a choice of two, whereas there is much to be said for both having a specialist module and for integrating the law into all aspects of the curriculum, including the practice learning curriculum (Ward and Hogg, 1993). Dickens (2004) suggests that the four principles underlying social work education, derived from research analysis of child care law teaching, should be:

1. acknowledgement of the wider context;
2. specific discrete teaching of law complemented by teaching in other areas;
3. clear linkages between law and practice;
4. demonstration of knowledge and skills in practice.

This indicates that social work students need to learn about the law not just by studying current legal rules and provisions, but also by engaging in analyses of policy and reflecting on ethics and key social work principles. Above all, they ought to learn through practice about the law as it operates on a day-to-day basis and be able to assess its impact on service users.

This being the case, there will need to be a number of people involved in the student learning process. Students should not really expect to learn all they need to know about the law through one module or one book. Efforts will clearly need to be made to ensure that the centrality of law in contemporary UK social work practice is recognised in the other modules the students undertake and that there is specific provision for demonstrating learning about the law in the student's assessed practice.

Not only are a number of people involved in facilitating student learning, but evidence also suggests that programme providers deploy a variety of methods in promoting learning. These range from use of case law and case studies to hearing service users' accounts, problem-based learning, video, project work, individual research exercises, observation, role play and simulation exercises, computer-assisted learning and distance learning (Braye et al., 2005: 26–7). Traditional lectures and seminars are still a popular means of teaching, but there does appear to be a trend to move towards enquiry-based learning (Braye et al., 2003) paralleled by a growing interest in the potential opportunities afforded by e-learning (Oliver and Huxley, 1988; Johns, 2003; see also Chapter 16).

How is learning about social work law assessed?

If you are a lecturer or practice assessor reading this chapter, consider:

- How is law currently assessed?
- Could anything be done differently to ensure students can apply their learning to practice situations?

Use of case studies for assessment is popular. Generally, these consist of fictional true-to-life scenarios about which students have to answer questions, either as a piece of coursework or under time limited constraints. Such an approach enables students to demonstrate an integrated and flexible approach to implementation of the law. Preston-Shoot et al. (1998) suggest that the use of case studies enables students to develop and demonstrate responsiveness and flexibility to situations that they are likely to encounter in real life.

The comprehensive review of social work law teaching (Braye et al., 2005) uncovered a multiplicity of assessment methods, including:

- oral tests;
- portfolios comprising project work, case summaries and reports;
- library research tasks;
- peer assessment of seminar presentations;
- multiple-choice questions;
- assessed debates;
- reflective logs;
- reports on the legal implications of specific cases;
- self-assessment.

One particularly innovative idea came from Blyth and colleagues (1995), who proposed that students should write a guidance or briefing note for service users on a specific legal point.

The message overall from research is that students enjoy a variety of assessment methods, especially those that do not overlap with what is taught elsewhere in their programmes, and that learning is particularly effective when students understand the connections with real-life practice. In this respect, assessment of legal knowledge and associated empowerment of service users ought to feature in the practice curriculum and in the assessment of practice learning, despite the lack of confidence some practice teachers and assessors have expressed in their ability to assess law competence (Preston-Shoot et al., 1997).

Conclusion

This chapter set out to offer a flavour of social work law teaching in the UK. Underpinning all of it has been the assumption that in the UK it is an absolute necessity for social workers to know and apply the law in their everyday social work practice, and evidence has been put forward to show how this need is being met by social work educators. While it may be obvious why social workers employed in the public sector need to know their legal duties and responsibilities, the incorporation of the broader context implies that law is a prerequisite for all social workers who are serious about their commitment to social justice. Knowledge of the law is essential in order to be able to promote the empowerment of service users, for it is clear that social work law is wider than just the content of statutes, and a radar scan of the curriculum deployed in qualifying social work programmes suggests that concerted efforts are being made to imbue a sense of confidence in social workers both in implementing the law and in challenging it.

It seems appropriate to conclude by summarising a number of key reasons why social work students ought to be enthusiastic about learning about the law and should most certainly adopt a very positive approach to it. Undoubtedly the operation of the law really matters in service users' lives, and this in itself offers sufficient rationale for its central place in the social work education curriculum in the UK. Law is rightly and justifiably a cornerstone in the new qualifying degrees in social work.

Key learning points

1. Wherever they practise, social workers must be certain about the legal basis for their practice and sufficiently confident about legal processes for them to know what they can and cannot do.
2. Social workers must be able to promote empowerment by acting as advocates when service users need to navigate their way through legal and administrative systems.
3. Social workers need to understand their accountability to service users, their employers and the courts. This includes supporting service users in having their voice heard and responding appropriately, including when service users make complaints.
4. Defensiveness, overcautious practice and resistance to people exercising their rights are all signs of workers who are not confident about their own knowledge and skills.
5. Social workers must open up their own practice to scrutiny and be able to give a clear account of themselves when their decisions are challenged.

6. Social work law is an interesting and vibrant topic of study in its own right. It should be taught constructively and imaginatively, using a variety of learning and teaching approaches to both capture students' imagination and to influence their everyday social work practice.

Taking it further

Readers who want to know more about this will find the following helpful:

Braye, S., Preston-Shoot, M., Cull, L.-A., Johns, R. and Roche, J. (2005) *Teaching, Learning and Assessment of Law in Social Work Education*, London: Social Care Institute for Excellence.

Cull, L.-A. and Roche, J. (eds) (2001) *The Law and Social Work*, Basingstoke: Palgrave.

Johns, R. (2005) *Using the Law in Social Work*, Exeter: Learning Matters.

The process of social work
Assessment, planning, intervention and review

11

Jonathan Parker

This chapter will:

- introduce a systematic approach to practice;
- provide a critical understanding;
- review assessment, planning, intervention, review and evaluation;
- promote a holistic art/science integration for social work.

Introduction

The importance of high quality education for social workers is high on the UK agenda, as indicated by the development of degree level first qualification and the revision of the post-qualifying education framework (Burgess, 2004; GSCC, 2005a). Social workers, from students to qualified professionals, display their anxieties by asking and reframing the questions, 'How do you do it?' or 'What is it that you do?' Understandable questions, maybe, but ones which suggest that there is a right way to do or practise social work and, as a consequence, a wrong way. Whilst this may fit with some more restrictive pronouncements concerning evidence-based practice or with those who believe social work is defined by its legislative or bureaucratic purpose alone, social workers practise in ever-changing situations and varied fields, and it is not possible to provide a discrete definition of social work nor to prescribe a set of correct processes and procedures to follow. This does not mean there are not better ways of working that rely on a continuously developing evidence base and acknowledge change and context. A process for social work practice that is not prescriptive about methods used or field of practice may form a useful framework for such an evidence base whilst deriving in part from requirements for practice from legislation, guidance and policy.

Questions concerning what social workers do have much to do with how we conceptualise social work itself. It may be that social workers in a UK local authority hospital team for older people will 'do' certain things because of their legislative base and procedural conventions. This does not, however, provide a universal understanding of what social workers do, nor does it define social work itself. Neither does, of course, the development of a behavioural programme with a young mother and her children, although both examples may be described as social work. So, if social work cannot be defined in terms of what social workers do, can it be understood in other more concrete ways? Since April 2005, in England, the title 'social worker' has become protected under the Care Standards Act 2000, section 63. This means that social work can only be practised by those who are registered. However, legal recognition and protection does not provide a clear understanding of social work. It is not possible to rigidly define what social workers do, but it is possible to delineate some of the processes that frame their actions. In this chapter, we will explore a four-stage process model, concerning assessment, planning, intervention and review and evaluation which provides a framework to describe social work practice in varied and multiple settings. The term 'process' may, at first, suggest a linear model which is constraining by its movement through set stages to reach a desired end goal. In social work, this does not adequately delineate practice as we have already suggested, and the model proposed is entered and re-entered at varying stages throughout the social work relationship that encompasses it (see Figures 11.1 and 11.2).

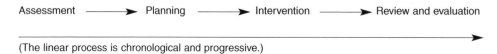

(The linear process is chronological and progressive.)

Figure 11.1   A linear approach to the social work process.

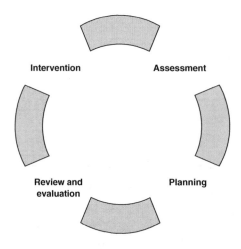

(The process may repeat or be entered and re-entered
at various points within the cycle.)

Figure 11.2   A cyclical approach to the social work process.

Tensions between methods that locate problems with individuals and their actions and communitarian models, based on social justice, that understand that problems of living result from structural and political factors permeate debates about social work. For instance, political ideologies tend towards individual, problem-focused concepts as seen in self-help and individual responsibility promoted by the New Right whilst New Labour has promoted technical bureaucratic performance and target-based approaches to social issues. Whilst simplistic to associate social work process with left- and right-wing ideologies, both concepts have influenced social work thinking about and responses to individual and social problems and continue to do so.

Changes to social work education in the UK have done much to respond to the need to enhance its quality and to standardise it. However, such changes are never neutral and are also politically motivated, as shown by the then Minister for Health's statement when introducing the English degree: 'Social work is a very *practical* job. It is about protecting people and changing their lives, not about being able to give a fluent and theoretical explanation of why they got into difficulties in the first place' (Smith, 2002, italics in original).

We might dispute the rather naïve implication that it is not important to have knowledge and an ability to theorise and test resulting hypotheses if social workers are to produce successful outcomes. Indeed, Parker and Bradley (2003: ix) conceptualise social work education as 'knowledge ... that develops by your active involvement in using it rather than being given a set of instructions and understanding developed by others'. However, the minister's statement located social work education within a particular context emanating from the crucible of New Right attacks on welfare and social work and New Labour's promotion of 'best value' and the modernising agenda. Social work is promoted as a means of helping individuals take their place in society and protecting the vulnerable. This agenda might be criticised, as it was by earlier radical social work theorists arguing that social work acts as a buffer to defend the status quo and prevent radical social and political solutions. Smith's statement is somewhat at odds with the more holistic sentiments of the IASSW/IFSW definition of social work, which clearly balances individual problem-solving with the need to confront issues of social justice, although notions of social justice in the UK relate largely to the Social Exclusion agenda than espousing a liberationist perspective (IFSW/IASSW, 2000; see Chapter 1).

 How do you conceptualise social work and what place do you believe theory has within effective practice?

The process model can be used across the range of contemporary roles carved out for social work, not only to 'fix' what might have gone wrong (Howe, 1987; Davies, 1994) but also to promote change; it is flexible. Social work is both an art and a science in which practitioners draw on knowledge(s) and evidence in reflexive and creative ways, applying ethical approaches to make a difference in the lives of vulnerable or marginalised people. The DH

(2002a) requirements for social work education identify the importance of social work processes and specifically include learning about assessment, planning, intervention and review. This process allows the social worker to practise systematically, creating a pathway to connect the individual and society.

Theorising in social work practice and process

Thompson (2005) argues that 'systematic practice' provides one way of militating against charges, justified or otherwise, of vagueness and drift. Systematic practice involves clarity about the objectives of the work and the methods to be employed. It must be remembered in this desire to systematise practice that social work is not and can never be an exact science; as Thompson (2005: 65) puts it, 'systematic practice is not to turn social workers into robots who slavishly follow a rigid sequence of stages'. Equally so, a more scientific and technical approach to practice must not be dismissed. It is easy to do nothing, hiding behind the false belief that because social work deals with complex and dynamic human problems, nothing can be predicted, managed or theorised in a way that makes a difference based on best evidence available at the time. This is increasingly important in the changing world of practice in which social work is in a state of flux, moving from local authority social services departments to a mix of private, voluntary and integrated services within health, education, housing and justice services. In order for social work to survive, it needs a process that helps to delineate its practice whilst recognising its context.

Munro (1998) is optimistic concerning the possibilities of developing an integrated practice in which experiential wisdom is intertwined with a logical and 'scientific' approach. Views are divided and epistemological debates rage, but an integrated approach seeks to transcend that debate, making it more human, acknowledging complexity, diversity and striving for rigour. Social work depends on a skilful use of learned knowledge and its application with wisdom. What makes it come alive and defines it is its association with values and ethics. The social work process as described is ethically neutral: it can be applied to control, regulate and manipulate in ways that deny the agency of those involved or subjugate cultures and communities. It can also be used to explore and develop with people alternative ways of being, developing and challenging. The social worker's role within this is defined by his or her ethical beliefs and directives: professional, organisational and personal. In seeking to eradicate oppression and discrimination, working collaboratively with people will permeate each stage of the process.

Tensions are no more clearly exposed than in debates about theories and models with sharply polarised views from the extreme non-directive, person-centred approaches to the more active, but nonetheless collaborative and negotiated models – such as task-centred, cognitive behavioural work and 'expert' psychodynamic approaches and 'atheoretical' rigidly bureaucratic and procedural models. A common way in which social workers and students deal with the complex array of theories identified is to employ a personalised amalgam of parts of models which seem to work, described as eclecticism (see Payne, 2005b). This may seem to represent a mature and evidence-based approach but is, unfortunately, often an excuse for either the uncritical application of partially known or misunderstood models or laziness in searching the knowledge to underpin models or to develop practice. On the other hand, eclecticism can represent a powerful evidence-based and research-minded approach which uses the practitioner's knowledge and practice wisdom. An understanding of social work practice can be systematically explored by reflection on experiences and the constant testing, challenging and reinterpretation of assumptions in practice. Conscious reflection on practice as a process in which one constantly strives for improvement is an important tool in developing the practitioner's evidence base, which may draw on a range of perspectives. This form of eclecticism is ripe for research and fits with the social work process model which can accommodate tacit as well as explicit and rigorously researched theory bases.

 Do you think social work is more of an art than a science or vice versa? What impact might your thoughts have on your practice?

Assessment, planning, intervention, review and evaluation: a model for practice

Central to all aspects of social work is *assessment*, whether this is child protection, mental health, care management or any other area of practice. There is, however, no clear theoretical articulation of assessment and often a technical-bureaucratic understanding of assessment as a task to be completed or key role to be performed. Assessment in social work is much more than this and can be conceptualised, within an art/science integration, as relational, involving joining and journeying through a situation, discussing together ways to make a difference.

Assessment frameworks to follow are increasingly prescribed in social work practice. For instance, in work with children and families, the assessment framework (DH, 2000a) has introduced core areas to explore the ecological environment in which children, and their families, live. These include an examination of health and development, capacity to parent and environmental factors. The framework is fluid enough to take individual circumstances into account and requires social workers to deploy their skills and artistry in working with people, identifying issues and delineating core information. The framework itself is built on a theoretical perspective that understands children as subsystems of family systems which interact with wider suprasystems, the environment (Bronfenbrenner, 1979). It is also policy-driven, highlighting the importance of inter-agency sharing of information and cooperation in working, while emphasising the principles of person-centred, strengths-based practice. This has been continued in the strategy to develop a Common Assessment Framework for Children and Young People as part of the Every Child Matters initiative. The ideological driver here concerns assessment across agencies and professions as an aid to prevention and early identification of problems or concerns.

There are a wide range of tools that are useful in the process of moving from the general to the particular, including genograms, or family trees, across and between generations, ecomaps, in which people locate the panoply of relationships important to them and the strengths and stresses associated with them. It may be useful to chart an individual's, family's or group's history and interactions with their living system or social world using a 'life-road map' or a 'flow diagram' of key events (see Parker and Bradley, 2003). It is also possible, using a variation of the ecomap, a culturagram, to explore the impact of culture and belief systems with people. What is important, however, is to recognise the power imbalances in the assessment process, to acknowledge these and to work collaboratively and openly.

There are core characteristics of any assessment model. Accepting a number of variations on a theme, these include:

- preparation, planning and engagement;
- data collection and creating a problem profile;
- preliminary analysis of data;
- testing the data, deep analysis;
- use of data, creating an action plan.

(Parker and Bradley, 2003)

If such a general theory base concerning assessment were to be developed, it would necessarily include a consideration of power relations. Assessment is a powerful method of collecting personal and sensitive information which can potentially be used at a range of levels, some of which follow:

- to 'assist' individuals, families or groups to identify issues for change;
- to identify and label 'problematic' individuals, families or groups to change, control, regulate or punish;
- to identify partial issues central to one participant only;
- to assess 'need' as defined by social work agencies, legislation and policies and to neglect or marginalise other interpretations.

Social workers in England are required to work to a code of practice that delineates key guiding precepts (GSCC, 2002a). These militate against the excesses of punitive, over-regulatory approaches to assessment, but each social worker operates at the tense interface between marginalised individuals or groups and pervading social structures and *mores* and needs to reflect continually on these tensions.

Smale and Tuson (1993) use a helpful understanding of assessment types as *questioning* in which social workers are seen as 'experts', a *procedural* approach which is formulaic and uncritical, and the preferred *exchange* model where people using social work services are seen as 'experts by experience', able to identify needs and negotiate strategies to account for them. In this reciprocal exchange of information, power imbalances are redressed, and it is this model social workers should seek to develop rather than using an eclectic mix of the three which may simply dilute the value of exchanges that see the service user as 'expert'. While social workers necessarily employ procedures, they can still use an exchange model in their work. Indeed, the spirit underlying many procedures demands that social workers advance collaborative exchanges that put users centre stage (see Chapter 6)!

Assisting people to identify issues for change allows social workers to plan with them how they might recognise it and determine what they need to achieve it. Planning, of course, begins to some extent before assessment but needs to involve those people most affected by the process and to draw on identified issues, needs and goals. Planning in social work is akin to creating a route map to get from one place to another; it 'presents a detailed picture of a situation, those involved and what action might be taken, and by whom these actions might be taken in order to meet assessed or identified needs' (Parker and Bradley, 2003: 64).

However, the route is not always linear and there may be a number of detours on the way. Changes in plans make assessment a continuous process that develops throughout the social work relationship.

In ethical approaches to social work, people using services are centrally involved and able to direct the planning process as far as this is practicable. Where they are not able to direct the process, they should be informed at all stages about what is being planned and why. There are a number of factors that need to be taken into account when working collaboratively to plan social work. In particular, it is fundamental to be realistic, to set feasible and achievable goals and to detail any risks associated with the plan. An example of this can be found in the DH guidance on care planning within the single assessment framework in adult care (DH, 2002b).

A useful mnemonic acronym has been developed that encapsulates the core elements required in successful planning, **SMART**:

Specific and clear roles, tasks, aims and goals;
Measurable outcomes;
Achievable targets and goals that those involved can reasonably expect to reach;
Realistic and relevant outcomes that address the central issues affecting those involved;
Time-based, that is, they have a time limit that is clear, agreed and not too far in the future (see, for instance, DfES, n.d.).

The following case example concerns an independent programme plan with Marissa, a woman of twenty-five who has a learning disability.

Case study

Marissa was living with her parents and taking a course in independent living at her local college. She was described as having moderate learning difficulties, and both she and her family had been supported by the community learning disability team for a number of years. Her aim was to have a flat of her own, and the social worker had begun an assessment with her to identify her needs, resources and goals. It was important for Shaistah, Marissa's social worker, to use a range of techniques – drawing, telling stories and general discussion – to identify and

(Continued)

(Continued)

check that she understood what Marissa was saying and to continue to frame her understanding in a clear, feasible, realistic and measurable way that involved Marissa at all stages. Setting a realistic timescale to achieve her goal of having her own flat was central to Marissa's motivation to continue, but it also allayed some of the anxieties expressed by her parents that it would not happen immediately and without planning. The plan developed between Shaistah and Marissa included her family and the college and agreed tasks and roles for those involved in the process. This helped all concerned to measure and identify what had been achieved.

Intervention follows from and is bound together with assessment and planning and relates to the methods and models to be used to achieve changes or outcomes that have been identified and agreed. There are many different forms of interventive method (Payne, 2005b). These include individual models such as psychodynamic, cognitive-behavioural, crisis intervention and task-centred models; social approaches based on systems thinking, social psychology and social and community development; and socio-political frameworks including critical theories, feminist theories, anti-discriminatory and anti-oppressive practice.

Interventive approaches can be analysed and classified in various ways as coming from identifiable philosophical and political perspectives (Howe, 1987), and it is important that practitioners take a critical and analytic approach examining why they are using a particular model and the impact this may have on those with whom they are working. The analytic framework proposed by Payne (2005b: 12), while acknowledging that no theory can be defined by one category alone, is helpful in delineating the theoretical orientation and philosophical position of theories:

- reflexive-therapeutic;
- socialist-collectivist;
- individualist-reformist.

The central importance of this analysis lies in the purposes of social work as intra-psychic help, individualised help or social change. In practice, all aspects interweave with one another as the individual constructs and is constructed by the social world, but such heuristic devices are important to our conceptualisation of social work.

Each social worker's views and perspectives will be important to the approach adopted; this will be partly derived from beliefs, experiences and developing practice wisdom, but will also be influenced by the agency's perspective and purpose and legislative base. Task-centred work is common in many fields of social work practice, because it is systematic and participatory, moving through assessment and exploration, planning and reaching an agreement on goals and tasks, completing tasks and reviewing and evaluating achievements. Task-centred practice fits the social work process model well, although other models of intervention also progress through these elements. While the following example concerns a man with depression, the model is equally transferable to other settings.

Case study

Kwame worked as a teacher in a local secondary school. He had been off work for six months because of depression and had been referred to the integrated mental health team for support. Following a successful cognitive-behavioural programme which reduced his negative thinking, his social worker, Ebenezer, identified, in discussion with Kwame, a number of concerns that he wanted to address. These related to aspects of his life that were important to him, especially re-establishing links to his cultural roots.

Ebenezer explored what he meant by links with his cultural roots and, using a 'funnel-like' approach to his assessment, developed a list of issues that Kwame was able to rank in order of priority. Kwame recognised that he was someone who, in his own words, 'liked to run before walking' and agreed that Ebenezer should ensure his targets and goals were feasible and realistic. Kwame identified meeting and forming links with a local Ghanaian group would assist him in re-establishing his cultural heritage. The task-centred model allowed Kwame and Ebenezer to negotiate the steps and tasks required to achieve this goal and how to measure when these had been successfully completed. Important in undertaking this work was the emphasis on collaboration and participation in which Kwame himself chose and agreed the importance of the work to be done.

There are many cogent reasons to review and evaluate your work, some of which are personal, professional, organisational or statutory. These can be analysed further (see Table 11.1 for a non-exhaustive list).

Table 11.1   Matrix of some key drivers for review and evaluation of practice.

	Personal	Professional	Organisational	Statutory
Personal	To develop and grow as an individual	To develop practice wisdom	To meet appraisal objectives	To meet statutory obligations to assess and provide services as a social worker
Professional	To develop research mindedness	To develop and promote best practice within the profession	To meet agency targets and goals	To meet statutory responsibilities of the profession

(Continued)

Table 11.1   (Continued)

	Personal	Professional	Organisational	Statutory
Organisational	To develop practitioners conscious of the need for evaluation	To develop an evaluation focused and skilled workforce	To demonstrate success in key purposes and roles	To meet statutory responsibilities of organisation
Statutory	To encourage personal skills development and competence	To ensure professionals are competent, up to date and actively involved in the development of the profession	To regulate the workforce and demonstrate that the public are well served	To promote evidence-based social policies

The terms 'review' and 'evaluation' warrant some explanation. Social work is reviewed throughout the process of working together with others. It is not something that simply occurs at the conclusion of a piece of work, although it has its place here as well. Each session or task is open to review; that is, what has happened and where the work is going can be summarised, shared and reflected upon to ensure that the assessment is capturing the needs of those involved, that the plans are relevant and feasible and that the methods to achieve goals are agreeable to all parties. At the end of a piece of work as a whole, it is important to go through this process again.

There are forms of statutory and procedural review that sit alongside the process of review. Reviews in child care, adult services and mental health, for example, are set in terms of timing, regularity, contacts to be made and people to be invited to contribute. Whilst this form of review is prescribed, it is consistent with reviewing work throughout the process of the social work relationship. The two can operate in concert.

Evaluation relates to a more evidence-based approach to developing research-mindedness and critically analysing practice with a view to improving it and outcomes for those receiving social work services. It is difficult to determine how research is used within social work practice but important to promote its value in ensuring there is an adequate and relevant evidence base for practitioners to use and develop to improve practice. Evaluation may be undertaken across the team or organisation in part to meet externally imposed targets or performance indicators. This may be resisted by some social workers on the grounds that it restricts and constrains practice to fulfilling political or ideological wants rather than responding to individual or community need. The debate will continue, but it is important to remember that evaluation of performance is central to contemporary social work and important in attracting funding. It is perhaps at the micro level, that of the practitioner, that evaluation is most appreciated by individuals, as this can be seen to relate to improvements in practitioner performance, providing the best possible service and improving as a social worker. It is less common to find practitioners actively involved in evaluation of their own practice in a systematic way, however, and most 'evaluation' remains at the tacit level of reflection rather than the rigorous analysis of practice that can derive from reflection or practitioner based research. Whilst there are many approaches to inquiry in social work of which practitioners may avail themselves (see Alston and Bowles, 2003), the skills involved in identifying issues, examining their meanings, forming hypotheses about why things happen in the ways they do and testing these in practice are all important to rigorous evaluation.

 Do you think of systematic practice as linear or non-linear? What are your reasons and how might this impact on your practice?

Conclusion

Core elements within the social work process concern: assessment of the situation, the needs and capacity for resolution; the planning necessary to achieve goals or to meet needs; the models and interventions that might be appropriate in the work; and a review and evaluation of that which has been achieved, the reasons for the outcome and how this can be generalised. While this indicates, on the surface at least, a linear process starting at one end of a line and working forward systematically to the other, social work is not like that. The model is better conceived as a circle or even a sphere in which social workers and those people with whom they work join at different points and move around those points continually oscillating backwards and forwards as situations, events and perceptions change (see Figure 11.2). A different metaphor is taken from the jigsaw. *Assessment* concerns the sorting of pieces into some beginning semblance of order before attempting to place them. *Planning* can be construed as a task-oriented piece of work akin to preparing to fit the jigsaw pieces, with *intervention* being the completion of the jigsaw. *Review and evaluation*, in this analogy, would constitute a reflection on how the jigsaw was completed and what learning could be transferred to other situations. Throughout its completion, one may return to any previous point to refocus, and this is likely to happen a number of times. social work practice, however, is not as simple as completing a jigsaw (and there are some extremely complicated jigsaws!).

Key learning points

1. The social work process is fluid and dynamic.
2. Social workers use a mix of artistry and science in their practice.
3. There are many different models and theories for social work practice.
4. Eclecticism has dangers and benefits and must be used with caution.
5. Reflective practice is central to personal and professional development.
6. Partnership and collaboration are important in working through the social work process.

Taking it further

Readers who want to know more about this will find the following helpful:

Coulshed, V. and Orme, J. (2006) *Social Work Practice: An Introduction* (4th edn), Basingstoke: Palgrave.

Parker, J. and Bradley, G. (2003) *Social Work Practice: Assessment, Planning, Intervention and Review*, Exeter: Learning Matters.

Thompson, N. (2005) *Understanding Social Work: Preparing for Practice* (2nd edn), Basingstoke: Palgrave.

12 Communication skills in social work

Juliet Koprowska

This chapter will:

- offer endorsement for the view that communication skills are essential to sound, effective social work practice;
- argue that, despite the increasingly bureaucratic nature of much social work, the individual practitioner's ability to engage with service users is vital.

Introduction

To paraphrase Jane Austen: 'It is a truth universally acknowledged that a well-educated social worker with a qualification should not be in want of communication skills.' However, concern about the communication skills of social workers has arisen in a number of quarters, hence their prominence in the agenda for social work education.

- Why are communication skills so important?
- What makes for good communication?
- What makes it hard to achieve?

These are the questions which this chapter seeks to address, with a primary focus on interpersonal communication, rather than on written or electronic means. It is based on the premise that communication and relationship are inextricably entwined.

The chapter starts by making the case that communication skills are at the heart of social work and explores the contradictions and tensions that challenge this contention. The chapter then turns to aspects of good communication and proposes that an approach-avoid axis offers a framework for evaluating communication in a wide range of social work contexts. Finally, the evidence that communication often founders is discussed alongside the need to recognise and respond to those with different communication. Although it would be helpful also to discuss how communication skills are learnt and evidenced, and there is much written about the subject, little has been established with certainty (Trevithick et al., 2004).

The heart of social work?

It is often said that communication skills lie at the heart of social work. This view is espoused in descriptions of and prescriptions for the education of social workers (Lishman, 1994; Kadushin and Kadushin, 1997; Koprowska, 2003, 2005; Richards et al., 2005; Trevithick, 2005).

It is also evident in service user literature, which consistently highlights the importance of warmth, interest, giving time, taking concerns seriously, accepting people's perspectives, providing information, and offering choices (e.g. Barnes et al., 2000; de Winter and Noom, 2003). These are the approaches most likely to create the trust and confidence in services which social workers are expected to engender (GSCC, 2002a). Furthermore, as the conception of service users as 'experts by experience' gains currency, their influence should be gaining ground, through increased involvement in social work education, service development and policy-making.

The DH (2002a) requirements for the social work degree make special mention of these skills, specifically skill in communicating with children, adults and people with different communication (referred to elsewhere as 'communicative minorities' (Koprowska, 2005: 124)). Indeed, the DH puts such a premium on communication skills that it provided short-term funding for universities to establish 'skills laboratories' for the degree. Meanwhile, the academic subject benchmark for social work devotes a section to communication skills (QAA, 2000), and since interaction with service users and colleagues is integral to social work's key roles identified in the National Occupational Standards, they could not be achieved without communication skills.

Additionally, exhortations to improve communication with service users and between professionals and agencies arise from inquiries into preventable deaths such as those of Jonathan Zito and Victoria Climbié (Ritchie, 1994; Laming, 2003; Scott et al., 2005). The inference is that sound communication is the bedrock for good practice, and for safer practice. Communicating with Victoria herself might have revealed her true circumstances; better communication between professions and across agencies' geographical and administrative boundaries might have produced better care both for her and for Christopher Clunis.

There appears, then, to be consensus that communication skills are at the heart of social work, or are perhaps the heart itself. Yet this heart is under threat and has long been so. "Reductionism, managerialism and the bureaucratisation of practice" constitute a major threat, according to Richards et al. (2005: 412). They propose that these factors, and pressure of time, turn social workers away from empathic engagement with the service user as a person, and away from the reflective process which would entail too painful a consideration of what they are failing to do. Educators are challenged to examine the ethics of teaching skills that leave students ill-equipped for the workplace. Whilst arguing that skills in communicating sensitively with service users must remain in the curriculum, since social work practice changes over time and relationship-based work may once again be in the ascendant, other skills should be taught to prepare students better for employment.

This portrait of social work is confirmed anecdotally through contact with current and former students. Most social work students train because they wish to engage with people and to enhance their lives. The learning of communication skills with individuals, families and groups is frequently described as one of the more valuable aspects of their university experience, yet many comment that on placement and in subsequent employment they are scarcely able to make use of them. They report that in the main, the 'real' work with service users is undertaken by support staff. As case workers have morphed into case managers, the need for direct work of therapeutic value is met by people arguably less well-trained to provide it. The social work process of assessment, planning, intervention and review frequently involves delegating assessment and intervention to others, retaining only planning and review – the elements depending more on cognition than on emotional engagement with service users.

It is noteworthy that the voice of employers is less clearly articulated in this debate, perhaps since social work itself forms only a small part of their remit, with social care a far larger responsibility. Additionally, employers are accountable for implementing policy, legislation and frameworks for practice, with their proliferation of deadlines, targets and performance indicators. The need to comply with these demands, which are introduced with the explicit goal of improving service delivery, may perversely result in the impoverishment of authentic communication with service users by social workers on the ground, as the pressure to complete the paperwork on time becomes imperative.

Cooper and Lousada put it like this: 'Our belief is that a complicated conjunction of forces has created a state of affairs in which a substantial retreat from engagement by people with people has come to seem both legitimate and inevitable' (2005: 27). They emphasise that it is people who provide welfare services – people who are inevitably affected by their relationships with service users. Engagement is unavoidable, and, anyway, is the essence of what service users value; the question is to what extent welfare providers and their supervisors are able to recognise its value and to foster such engagement.

McCluskey (2005), in a detailed study of interactions between professionals and service users, argues that the instinctual attachment behaviours of care-seeking and care-giving identified by Bowlby in infants and their care-givers are present also in help-seeking encounters between adults. Just as infants cease exploration when experiencing care-seeking needs for comfort, reassurance and food and only resume when these have been met, so with adults. Just as caregivers of infants instinctually try to understand and meet the infant's needs, so with adults. Distressed individuals attempting to tell their story and explore their issues will intermittently show signs of care-seeking, thus activating the instinctual care-giving system of the workers, which will only be 'switched off' by successful care-giving. Success is measured in terms of meeting the service user's care-seeking needs and the resumption of exploration. McCluskey emphasises the satisfaction and relief on both parts when these care-seeking goals have been met.

McCluskey's findings offer a compelling psychobiological insight into the dissatisfaction felt by both service users and social workers when these instinctual systems are frustrated in favour of 'getting the job done'. They have important implications for the well-being and retention of staff, as well as for service user satisfaction.

Social work practice and education are no strangers to paradoxical and conflicting demands, yet it is hard to countenance the idea that, whilst it is widely acknowledged that good communication skills are a prerequisite for sound practice and research evidence such as McCluskey's (2005) is helping to explain why, they are simultaneously becoming surplus to requirements, sometimes through the very means designed to improve them. Has social work outsourced its heart?

Moving away from the bleakness of that question, I will turn to the role of communication in human relationships at large.

The interpersonal core of communication

Communication skills are learnt in the cradle, or perhaps more often in the arms and on the laps of those who care for us. Eye contact, play, the earliest forms of turn-taking conversation and affectionate and responsive care-giving are now known to be the means by which the infant brain develops and, with it, the ability to regulate our own emotions and to recognise and regulate the emotional states of others (Schore, 2003a). We become who we are through relationship.

Neglect, abuse and trauma can alter neurological development in infants and young children and affect their ability to process information, to regulate emotional states and to relate to others. These effects are not confined to childhood. Early adversity, particularly abuse and trauma, are implicated in the aetiology of 'psychotic' experiences such as hearing voices and seeing visions (Schore, 2003a; Escher et al., 2004; Read et al., 2005), and adult experiences of abuse, for example domestic violence, combat or torture, may alter an individual's functioning and impair communicative ability. The diagnostic divisions between post-traumatic stress disorder, dissociative identity disorder and psychosis are being eroded (e.g. Kilcommons and Morrison, 2005), with the 'symptoms' reconceived as coping strategies resorted to in unbearable circumstances. Having left their neurological marks, these coping strategies persist beyond the presence of the threat, and beyond their apparent utility, affecting intra- and interpersonal communication. Individual adversity takes place in a social context which may alleviate its impacts or exacerbate them, so that the interpersonal impacts of experiences such as economic disadvantage and discrimination also need to be understood and taken into account.

Concomitantly, a growing body of evidence supports the long-held belief that therapeutic relationships can be reparative (summarised by Schore, 2003a and 2003b). The brain's plasticity, even into adulthood, means that communication itself, both in formal and personal relationships, can bring about neurological, psychological, emotional and physiological change. This sheds light on the origins of resilience, since a reliable relationship is a key factor in preventing long-term mental health problems in children who experience adversity (Rutter, 1985). In short, it is our relationships that create us, harm us and have the potential to heal us.

Other factors which are not inherently relational may nonetheless influence a person's ability to communicate, such as head injury, stroke, dementia and congenital or acquired impairments. The social consequences of serious obstacles to communication, whatever their origin, are significant. Segrin's research (cited by Hargie and Dickson, 2004) into the experiences of people with poor communication skills, showed that their contact with others, social achievement and sense of well-being were adversely affected.

It is perhaps self-evident that many people numbered amongst the users of social services will be contending with these difficulties. It therefore seems reasonable to suggest that social workers need better-than-average skills in communication. And we are, of course, not exempt from the experience of trauma, impairment or injury, nor immune to their impacts.

Good communication

 What does good communication involve?

Communication takes place in several dimensions at once. It is both verbal and non-verbal, cognitive and emotional, of the mind and of the body. Whilst it is helpful to distinguish between these dual dimensions for the purpose of thinking about them, they are inseparable. Speech is the primary means of conveying cognitive information, yet is never solely verbal; it carries emotional content in voice tone, speed, volume and pitch (paralanguage). Similarly, non-verbal behaviour conveys emotion but can also be used to underscore spoken words.

Communication is fundamentally interactive. Almost without exception, we respond to those with whom we communicate and make adjustments accordingly. Individuals demonstrate greater and lesser degrees of sensitivity (people with autistic spectrum disorders may be much less able to do this than others). Flexibility, adaptability and responsiveness appear to be key components of successful professional interactions, and social workers therefore need to take a metaperspective during encounters, so as to be able to change direction and steer communicative exchanges purposefully. This process entails awareness of our own verbal and non-verbal contributions and their impact on service users, and also awareness of our emotional responses to the content and manner of service users' communications.

Verbal behaviour (spoken, written or signed) is under a high degree of personal control. Within the limits of our vocabulary and means of expression, we can choose to say whatever we want, or to say nothing at all. Although much speech is experienced as spontaneous, verbal expression is amenable to change. Personal habits which are an impediment in social work, such as frequent interrupting or predominantly asking closed questions, can, with effort, be altered once identified.

Body language contains innate and universal elements, and learnt and culturally determined elements (and some non-verbal behaviour seems to belong to neither group with certainty). Although emotion is experienced in concert in body and brain, it is made visible through the body. The facial expression of certain emotions is universal – of sadness, happiness, anger, fear, surprise, disgust and, some say, contempt (Darwin, 1998; Ekman, 2003), though we have partial control over its display (suppressing a cry of fright, refusing to smile). Other emotional responses may be less evident in the face: there is no special 'look' that accompanies jealousy. The fact that we have less control over our physiological and emotional responses than our verbal ones means that, if we attend to them, they furnish us with knowledge unavailable through speech and cognition.

Here are three examples from my own practice:

1. Visiting a woman with long-standing depression, I always left with painfully tense shoulders. When I told her this, her extreme tenseness came to light, mine vanished, and we were able to work to reduce hers.
2. Filled with dread about visiting a woman whose involuntary admission to hospital I had arranged, I overrode my fears on the basis that I was 'too senior' to take account of them and was assaulted for the only time in my social work career.
3. Asked to observe the mother of a severely disabled child through a two-way mirror, I quickly found myself doubled up with pain. I had the thought that she was hurting from hatred and misery; as a student at the time, I felt unable to approach her and never discovered the meaning of my pain.

The approach-avoid axis

Communication runs along an 'approach-avoid' axis. (This axis is used by Simon and Agazarian (2003) for analysing verbal interaction, discussed in Koprowska (2005).)

Approach behaviours include:

- explaining working methods so that service users understand what is expected of them;
- giving information;
- asking open questions;
- answering questions where possible;
- responding empathically to emotional information;
- accepting the service user's perspective as valid (even if holding a different view);
- reflecting on one's own emotional experience as a source of information.

Avoid behaviours include:

- relying on paperwork and procedures instead of, rather than alongside, interpersonal responsiveness;
- concentrating on closed questions and cognitive information;
- chasing open questions with closed ones, thus preventing open questions from being answered (Calman et al., 2005);
- fleeing from emotional information, especially distress and anger, into cognitive and factual realms;
- defensive practice, i.e. taking action to protect yourself or the organisation rather than in the service user's interests.

Neither list is intended to be comprehensive. Approach behaviours are almost without exception more functional than avoid behaviours, since fostering interpersonal connectedness produces more comprehensive information. They are more likely to satisfy the wishes of service users and to meet the care-giving needs of the workforce, thus protecting against burnout. Conversely, they can take their emotional toll, and an appreciative and tolerant organisation is needed to sustain and retain workers over time (Meyerson, 2000).

Approach behaviours may be criticised for being time-consuming and untenable given the constraints within which social workers operate. Yet I contend, first, that inadequate communication wastes valuable time, since service users end up dissatisfied and flawed or even dangerous decisions are sometimes made; and, second, that time is psychological as well as temporal. Giving time is about the atmosphere between people, not just the number of minutes spent together. It stems from an aura of calm, not haste; from interested attention, not preoccupation with the next task; from eye contact rather than pen-pushing. These are not inherently time-consuming but entail a level of personal containment and focus which are hard to achieve when workers are stressed.

By contrast, Richards et al.'s (2005: 412) "[r]eductionism, managerialism and bureaucratic practice" depend upon avoid behaviours. Approach behaviours generate more information than is strictly required, uncover needs which cannot be met within current resources and may, on occasion, consume more time. Avoiding emotional information is easily accomplished by never asking open questions. Since closed questions elicit yes/no answers, or offer narrow alternatives, they are excellent for obtaining factual information and useless in enabling people to tell their story or to describe their feelings, thereby inhibiting the emergence of unpalatable realities.

Social work sometimes faces us with situations that induce fear for ourselves or others, and avoidance of engagement may stem from this. In an incisive analysis of the Climbié Inquiry, Ferguson (2005) argues that the workers involved with Victoria prior to her death were affected by fear of her abusers and disgust regarding her diagnosis of scabies. He suggests that their inability to manage these feelings or use them to understand the child's experience meant they distanced themselves from both her and her 'carers'.

In other instances, avoidance may be of knowledge that challenges our preferred world view, illustrated in the following case study.

Case study

Jenny is in her first placement, working with women who have been subject to domestic violence. Eager to view the women as 'more sinned against than sinning', she offers esteem-building responses and reassurance to Michelle, who repeatedly expresses concerns about her parenting ability. Only when Michelle abandons her children for a day does Jenny start to recognise that she is struggling as a parent. It emerges that Michelle and her partner's relationship was peaceable until she became pregnant, and at one level she holds the children accountable for the violence she experienced and the demise of her partnership.

Jenny has avoided information that does not fit with her preferred perception of Michelle and failed to make space for her to explore her thoughts and feelings about her children. Although her methods appear to be positive and supportive, without this exploration, it will be hard for either of them to know whether Michelle can parent her children adequately.

By way of contrast, social work can be so preoccupied with problems that, despite its value base, it falls foul of pathologising service users, their strengths and capabilities excluded from awareness in favour of maintaining a construction of them as inadequate or ill (and preserving a construction of self as competent and unimpaired), an outlook challenged by the strengths perspective (Saleebey, 2005).

 What do you know about your own approach-avoid behaviours?

Communication errors, communication needs

A great deal is to be learnt from where communication goes wrong, and communicative incompetence is rife. Stumbling over words, misinterpreting behaviour, saying things we regret, misjudging the context, being stumped by impossible questions: these are commonplace experiences, and mostly we learn to weather them and repair our mistakes (Cupach and Spitzberg, 1994). McCluskey (2005), too, observes that errors are continually made and repaired in a flow of communication. The essential difference between successful communication and that which founders is this 'cycle of rupture and repair' in which mistakes are made and quickly made good, leading to "evident relief … and … mutual delight and pleasure" (McCluskey, 2005: 190).

 Do you change your communication style to suit a service user's communication needs?

There is certainly some evidence that health and social care workers use communication ill-suited to those with whom they work, leaving service users' communicative needs unrecognised. For example, communication impairments in children and their complex links with social, emotional and intellectual development and behavioural problems appear often to be overlooked (Cross, 2004). Overestimation of comprehension stands out: in other words, adults overrate a child's understanding and may then interpret their behaviour as truculent. Whilst some children's difficulties resolve as they mature, inevitably others will join the ranks of adult service users – perhaps to be found especially amongst the minority with complex needs identified by Keene (2001) who are frequent users of multiple services. How often are their communicative needs recognised at these points in their lives?

In a study of adults, Henry and Strupp (1994) noted that therapists were often unable to adapt their style to accommodate 'difficult' clients and instead responded with hostility. Meanwhile, less articulate service users may be disadvantaged in their dealings with childcare social workers where there is over-reliance on verbal communication, since articulate clients appear more 'plausible' and 'insightful' (Holland, 2000: 161). Bradshaw (2001), researching communication in institutions between staff and service users with learning disabilities, dismayingly found that scant time was spent interacting with service users (2 per cent in her own study), that complex language was used instead of signs and signals known to be intelligible to service users, communication tended to take the form of instructions, and hearing impairments went unrecognised. Deaf people, too, report that colleagues who sign revert rapidly to talking when another hearing person is present, even where both hearers are competent signers (Young et al., 1998).

What is happening in these interactions? Certainly all these are 'avoid' behaviours par excellence. Some of these studies suggest that professionals lack training and skill in recognising that communication has gone awry, while others identify something more pernicious, where the difficulty is understood and the skills to respond are present, but the socially dominant (excluding) means of communication is used in preference by those with access to it. A further possibility suggested by McCluskey (2005) is that workers recognise their predicament, are distressed by the rupture, but lack skills in repair, creating patterns of interaction characterised by loss of vitality and satisfaction. It is noteworthy that the recognition of and response to fleeting non-verbal cues is central to the difference, an observation that lends support to Holland's (2000) concern about over-reliance on verbal communication.

Conclusion

This chapter has discussed some fundamental tensions in social work – between the primacy accorded to communication skills by all stakeholders, the perils of inadequate communication skills (for both service users and social workers) and the work demands that depend upon dispensing with these very skills. In considering the idea that communication can be charted along an approach-avoid axis, it seems that approach behaviours provide the satisfaction with services sought by service users, agencies and the GSCC alike, and the rewards of the work sought by social workers – not to mention providing the rich all-round picture on which thorough social work assessment and intervention rest. However, avoid behaviours are commonplace, for reasons encompassing personal, individual, professional and organisational factors. These include characterological preferences, individual lack of skill, the move towards managerialism in much social work practice and pressure to accomplish tasks within timescales which are poorly matched to overall workload in the context of limited resources.

So where do we go from here? Do we continue to hold a beacon for relationship-based skills, rather than just fact-finding skills? It appears to me that we must, that the conflict cannot be resolved by abandoning this ambition. But rhetoric is never enough; we need to undertake much more research into the learning of communication skills and their evaluation in practice to discover how they make a difference – to our own lives and those of service users. Then we will be able to make the argument where it counts and make an impact not just on provision but also on the recruitment and retention of sensitive and capable staff.

Key learning points

1. Communication might seem a dispensable luxury or in conflict with fact-finding to determine eligibility for a service, but failing to be emotionally responsive blocks communication, generates partial information and increases the risk of poor decision-making.
2. In interaction there are always choices about what to say and do that will serve to approach and engage the service user or to distance them.
3. The fewer communication skills the service user possesses, the greater those needed by the social worker. Communicative impairments often go unrecognised.
4. Successful communication is rewarding for service users and social workers alike. This interpersonal dimension should be acknowledged and valued.
5. More research is needed to ascertain the effectiveness of training social workers in communication skills.

Taking it further

Readers who want to know more about this will find the following helpful:

Koprowska, J. (2005) *Communication and Interpersonal Skills in Social Work*, Exeter: Learning Matters.

Thompson, N. (2003) *Communication and Language: A Handbook of Theory and Practice*, Basingstoke: Palgrave Macmillan.

Trevithick, P., Richards, S., Ruch, G. and Moss, B. with Lines, L. and Manor, O. (2004) Knowledge Review 6, *Teaching and Learning Communication Skills in Social Work Education*, London: SCIE, http://www.scie.org.uk/publications/knowledge reviews/kr06.pdf.

13 Understanding the life course

Paul Bywaters

This chapter discusses health inequalities throughout the life course and, in doing so, it:

- challenges notions of the 'life cycle', advocating instead a critical engagement with the concept of the 'life course';
- argues that this approach makes more sense of each individual's transition through life;
- indicates how understanding the 'life course' also draws attention to causes and consequences of inequalities relevant to social work practice.

Introduction: why study the life course?

A key factor behind the UK government's decision to endorse degree level social work training was the child protection inquiries that have haunted the profession since the early 1970s. Repeatedly, inquiries into these cases, from Maria Colwell to Victoria Climbié, called for improved social work training, a crucial element of which should be child development (DfES, 2005). As a result, 'human growth and development' is one of the few subjects training programmes have to teach and assess (DH, 2002a). Understanding service users' biographies and how factors in their past lives and circumstances shape their current experience and aspirations underpins assessment and intervention planning across adult, as well as children's, services. Therefore, human growth and development across the life course is a core aspect of underpinning knowledge for social work.

However, the study of human development is not just a matter of learning an established body of knowledge. Like so much 'knowledge' underpinning social work, human development involves contested ideas and values. The primary aims of this chapter are to highlight key questions for a critical study of human development and to introduce epidemiological approaches to the life course as a neglected source in the social work literature. For a comprehensive or detailed account of human development, students should look to other texts, such as Crawford and Walker (2003) or Aldgate et al. (2005).

Developing a critical understanding

This contested understanding of human development is exemplified by a number of central debates.

?

Consider your own positions on these questions before proceeding:

- To what extent are human lives determined rather than self-directed? When we talk about our life course, is it something we control, we learn, we follow or we experience?
- Are the primary influences on human development 'natural' or social, economic and environmental? How do we draw on biology, physiology, psychology or sociology to understand the life course?
- Are dominant understandings of human development in the UK Eurocentric, overemphasising the individual and assuming that particular cultural patterns are 'normal'?
- Is human life best understood as a series of commonly experienced stages or as a fluid, individual progress?
- To what extent does childhood determine adult experiences or can adults remake their lives?

From the 1960s until relatively recently, the work of Erikson (1965) was central to teaching about human development on UK social work courses. Erikson's account of eight developmental stages and associated critical tasks was welcomed partly because it suggested a move away from narrowly individual models of human development to an approach integrating social and psychological influences. It also looked beyond childhood and recognised that people continue to develop through adult life and into old age.

Despite the social dimension, the underlying idea of staged development originated from biological models of the life cycle. The study of the life cycle of butterflies or frogs, for example, is often understood as a series of discrete and dramatic changes producing clearly different forms and stages of life: egg-larva-chrysalis-butterfly, or egg-tadpole-frog. While that degree of differentiation and fixity was not suggested to apply to humans, the ideas that each successive stage of development built upon the successful management of earlier ones and of the successful completion of maturation was clearly present in Erikson's work. He suggested a fixed order to the stages, which was assumed to operate across generations, gender or culture. People were expected to have similar developmental experiences to others in their age cohort and to previous generations at the same stage of life. It was recognised that these stages were not just biologically founded but reinforced by social policies (health, education, work, pensions) and cultural institutions (births, weddings, funerals) that bind societies together.

The influence of these underlying assumptions is clearly seen in two classic texts widely circulating in social work education in the 1980s onwards: Vera Fahlberg's (1982) *Child Development* and the British Agencies for Adoption and Fostering (1986) collection of articles entitled *Working with Children*. While it was made clear that 'there is a wide range of "normality" and the detail of each child's development is special to him or her' (Cooper, 1986: 5), a core set of ideas was unmistakable.

Consider how many of these arguments, if any, you disagree with:

- Development usually takes place in a more or less orderly sequence from conception to maturity. At different ages children are said to have reached a particular stage of development and there are certain general characteristics at different ages [...] Heredity determines the limits of an individual's capacity [...] The environment will determine the extent to which each individual is able to fulfil his or her inherited potential [...] Physical development usually progresses smoothly [...] Emotional development also goes along a regular path [...] Children have certain basic physical and psychological needs and if these are not adequately met, growth and psychological development will be distorted in various ways and may never be complete [...]

(Cooper, 1986: 5–6)

- As children develop normally, they pass through a number of stages of development. At each of these stages, the child has to accomplish certain major developmental tasks.

(Fahlberg, 1982: 5)

Many of these elements continue to be reflected in major government policies for children and families such as *Every Child Matters* (DfES, 2004). The assumption that the early years are vital building blocks for education, health and social success has been reinforced in UK social policy in recent years. This approach focuses attention both on the significance of key stages and on points of transition between them, such as birth, entry to school, adolescence and transition to adulthood, becoming a parent and retiring from paid work. Social institutions and policies are said to deal with problems in 'sequencing, unjust transitions, inattention to individual development rights' (Mayer, 1988 in Priestley, 2005: 26).

However, almost every assumption outlined by Cooper and Fahlberg above has now been questioned as the concept of the life course has replaced the life cycle. Five questions to consider:

Is the idea of normal fixed stages of development and transition tenable in the face of the fluidity and diversity of contemporary experience?

As Hunt (2005) argues, stages have been abandoned in sociological discourse in favour of considering how 'stages' are socially constructed. Stages have lost their deterministic qualities providing – at best – only broad markers of experiences and expectations. For example, transitions from education to work and into parenthood take place for some before reaching 20 (Graham and Power, 2004). Care leavers – particularly – commonly find themselves out of education and having responsibility for managing a home and for parenting in their late teens. However, the *average* age for first becoming a mother is now over 29 in the UK (OECD, 2005). For teenage parents, grandparenting beckons at an age when others will first have a child. Similarly, the idea of a fixed stage of adult work followed by retirement at 60 or 65 is also evaporating as the pensions crisis takes an increasing grip on the imagination of Western societies. Some commentators ask whether social changes conflict with 'natural' human development.

Do such fundamental social and economic changes also undermine the idea that similar age cohorts will have common experiences at different points in history?

For example, widely available contraception and abortion, in-vitro fertilization (IVF) treatment, divorce and greater equality in access to paid employment have contributed substantially to changing relationships between men and women since the 1960s.

Can the idea of fixed stages be sustained in the face of growing inequalities of experience within cohorts resulting from differences in economic, environmental and social resources?

Average life expectancy for a boy born in East Dorset in 2001–3 was eleven years greater than for a boy born in Glasgow (ONS, 2005). Almost four fifths of children in Pakistani and Bangladeshi families in the UK are living in poverty compared to under one in three white children (Karlsen and Nazroo, 2000). For many in low-paid and health-damaging work, early 'retirement' is brought about through ill health, while gender disparities in old age are starkly seen in the five years greater average life expectancy women enjoy compared to men with correspondingly greater chances of living alone and in poverty (Arber et al., 2003).

 Does the idea that once a stage has been completed it cannot be revisited or altered reflect current experience?

With increasing changes in the labour market fuelled by globalisation, adults are now expected to embrace a culture of lifelong learning and career change rather than jobs for life. New patterns of divorce and remarriage mean that men commonly start new families in their fifties and sixties. Meanwhile, grandparent roles increasingly return others to intensive child-rearing. One in three grandparents care for their grandchildren for more than 21 hours per week (Prasad, 2000). Remedial operations such as hip or knee replacements, inserting heart pacemakers and simple measures, such as ensuring older people's feet and teeth are kept in good condition, can significantly help to reduce or reverse the biological effects of ageing – although not the impact of ageist expectations.

 Does the life cycle thinking imply passivity in the face of biologically and socially constructed events?

The idea of fixed and largely immutable stages, of set tasks that have to be completed, seems to deny human choice, the idea that we can control the trajectories of our lives. As we turn now to explore life course approaches, individual agency becomes a central issue.

Life course or life courses?

Life course, rather than life cycle, thinking usually emphasises the importance of individual pathways rather than normal stages and so is better able to account for diversity in human behaviour and outcomes within and across age groups and generations. The concept of the life course focuses attention on the interactions between individuals' biological make-up and the influence of social, economic and environmental factors at micro, mezzo and macro levels across their lifetimes. It also often emphasises individuals' capacity to shape their own destinies or to construct their own identities (Davey Smith, 2003; Hunt, 2005; Priestley, 2005).

For example, Wiggins et al. (2004) describe the primary 'legacy' of the life course for quality of life in old age as adequate pension provision, choice about retirement age, owner occupation, access to a car and ongoing health. Each of these elements is – in large part – a consequence of a lifetime's actions and choices, influenced by external factors, perhaps dating back to the foetal environment or even earlier. The combination of human agency and external influence is unique for each individual, so personal trajectories and transitions are arguably more significant than common patterns.

However, as Hockey and James (2003) and Priestley (2005) observe, the life course concept has many varied interpretations, with different emphases on the relative importance of individual agency, biological make-up and social structures. Three alternative sets of ideas will be discussed here. First, for some authors, the idea of stages still holds value, but life course thinking requires greater understanding of the dynamic and fluid nature of lives 'driven by individual decision making yet shaped by public institutions and policies' (Priestley, 2005: 27). Mayer (1988) argues that supposedly individual choices are influenced by shared cultural scripts underpinned by immense collective social investments. The social policy framework is shaped around and shapes key life stages and transitions – pregnancy and childbirth; pre-school, school and further and higher education; adult employment and parenthood; retirement and old age – notwithstanding the growing New Labour emphasis on choice (for example, DH, 2004).

A critique of this retention of an age and stage model of the life course emerges from experiences of groups of people who do not 'fit'. For example, Arber et al. (2003) argue that both life cycle and life course approaches have tended to see human development as gender neutral and underplaying difference. Similarly, Priestley (2000) argues that a critical examination of the lifetime experiences of disabled people makes it clear that, for many, 'normal' assumptions of the life course do not apply. From before birth, cultural expectations, biological development and the impact of social policies take many children with significant impairments or illness along different pathways or trajectories to able-bodied children. These trajectories are not just a function of disability or impairment but also of the interaction between these and other aspects of identity, such as ethnicity (Ali, 2005). An examination of the position of disabled people raises fundamental questions about assumptions built into much life cycle and life course thinking that privilege a particular construction of adult life, involving full-time employment, financial and personal independence, long-term relationships and parenting, none of which may be available to severely impaired individuals and which are also compromised for their families (Beresford et al., 1996).

The life course and postmodernity

Second, late modern or post modern writers make a more radical rejection of the stage model. For these authors (for example, Giddens (1991), Featherstone and Hepworth (1989 and 1991)), identities are chosen and negotiated, not fixed. Choice, individuation and risk are the key motifs in a world in which the individual can create a personal pathway and in which anything is possible. It is not that individuals plot their way through life stages differently but that it no longer makes sense to think in terms of stages or cohorts. Featherstone and Hepworth argue that reliance on age as a key dimension of social stratification is no longer adequate. The focus of contemporary culture on youth, lifestyles and consumerism cuts across age barriers and is reflected in populist views that we are all capable of being young now. This feeds fears of ageing and may be particularly disadvantageous to older women as looks and sexuality are emphasised in this focus on youth (Hockey and James, 2003). It is also disadvantageous to those who cannot purchase the lifestyle that they might like to choose.

The questionable assertion that the life course is not at all a function of age (and of bodily realities) also masks material realities. If contemporary life course trajectories are as much a product of individual agency as is implied, then one would expect to see increasing social mobility as individuals moved within and between social strata across their lifetimes. However research (Blanden et al., 2005) suggests that, far from becoming more fluid over the past 30 years, UK intergenerational social mobility has declined markedly. One reason is that the rapid growth of higher educational opportunities has disproportionately benefited those from better-off backgrounds with an increased relationship between family income and educational attainment continuing into the generation born in the late 1970s and early 1980s. There is evidence of causal links between increasing inequality in income and in educational attainment. While undermining the primacy of individual choice, this also suggests divergence of experience within and between age cohorts and, as such, does not necessarily imply support for an age/stage model of development.

Epidemiology and the life course

A third strand of life course theory, developed within the discipline of epidemiology (the study of health patterns within populations), has significant potential interest for social workers because of its focus on avoidable socially created inequalities. Krieger (2001: 695) defines the life course perspective within epidemiology as follows:

> how health status at any given age, for a given birth cohort, reflects not only contemporary conditions but embodiment of prior living circumstances, in utero onwards. At issue are people's developmental trajectories (both biological and social) over time, as shaped by the historical period in which they live in reference to their society's social, economic, political, technological, and ecological context.

For Davey Smith (2003: xiii) the life course approach is about relating 'socially patterned early-life exposures (like birth weight) to socially patterned health outcomes (like heart disease)'. But it is not only in early life that disadvantage and discrimination have an impact on later life chances as '[d]ifferent social trajectories across the life course [...] lead to the differential accumulation of negative exposures among those who start life in less affluent circumstances' (Davey Smith, 2003: xiii–xiv).

Epidemiological research in the UK and the USA has been instrumental in generating evidence linking 'cumulative environmental insults' to poor health and reduced life expectancy. Social conditions are literally embodied, reproduced biologically in living bodies (Krieger, 2005) and can be seen to have direct human consequences. Poor health, lives cut short or lived with unnecessary physical and mental suffering, is perhaps the sharpest marker of social disadvantage and has been insufficiently recognised as a focus of social work practice. Almost all social work service users are either already suffering from poor physical or mental health or are at risk of developing poor health because of their disadvantaged circumstances and history (McLeod and Bywaters, 2000).

While this epidemiological work focuses on *health* outcomes, the primary influences on health are the *social* factors comprising the everyday experience of most service users: poverty, poor housing and environmental conditions, poor nutrition, reduced educational opportunities, discrimination, inadequate health and social care, low and insecure income, physical and sexual violence. Thus, disentangling epidemiological evidence requires understanding the causes and consequences of *social* inequalities (Graham, 2002). This has the potential to illuminate service users' lives and to inform social work responses.

Ben-Shlomo and Kuh (2002), discussing life course influences on chronic illness, have developed a useful pair of models to explore ways in which disadvantage across a lifetime can result in poor outcomes. These models are not mutually exclusive and not only applicable to health outcomes (see Box 13.1).

Box 13.1   Conceptual life course models.

Critical period model

- *with or without later-life risk factors*
- *with later-life effect modifiers*

Accumulation of risk

- *with independent and uncorrelated insults*
- *with correlated insults*
  - *'risk clustering'*
  - *'chains of risk' with additive or trigger effects*

(Ben-Shlomo and Kuh, 2002: 287)

The *critical period model* points to circumstances occurring during a specific period in a person's life which have lasting or lifelong effects. In epidemiology, these concern effects on 'the structure or function of organs, tissues and body systems' (Ben-Shlomo and Kuh, 2002: 286) which are not substantially modified later. Ben-Shlomo and Kuh give the example of maternal exposure to thalidomide in pregnancy damaging limb development. HIV transmission from mother to child is another. Poor maternal nutrition in pregnancy or exposure to damaging levels of toxic substances including tobacco and alcohol can affect the foetus's biological development, resulting in low birth weight and other conditions with long-term consequences. Maughan and McCarthy (1997) present evidence that insecurity and instability in childhood and infancy can have long-term effects on cognitive function and psychosocial disorders in later life, although social work has – as an article of faith – believed that change and personal growth can always occur.

This simple form of the model can be developed by recognising that some effects in a critical period may only emerge as significant when there is also secondary exposure to a later risk – poor muscular development may be of negligible influence until late old age when, for example, incontinence might result. Additionally, some critical period effects may be positively modified by later-life exposures or opportunities. The protective effects of the welfare state generally are relevant here, as Davey Smith (2003) argues. Parenting a child as a teenager may have lifelong consequences for a care leaver's structural position: their education, accommodation, social relations, job opportunities and pension. However, the quality of care, support and opportunities provided during and after pregnancy may substantially modify the potential disadvantage, turning a negative experience into a positive one. The impact on quality of life in late old age of not having been able to accumulate a private pension is much less if an adequate state pension system exists. However, social work has sometimes been complicit in creating or enhancing critical-period events, for example, by requiring looked after young people, including unaccompanied refugees, to live independently at 16, often with very limited material or social resources and in hostile environments (Barn et al., 2005).

The *accumulation of risk model* focuses attention on ways in which 'factors that raise disease risk or promote good health may accumulate gradually over the life course'. Davey Smith (2003: xvi) explains this as follows:

> A woman in a low income household is more likely to be poorly nourished during pregnancy and to produce a low birth weight or premature baby. A child growing up in a low-income household is more likely to be disadvantaged in terms of diet, crowding, safe areas in which to play and opportunities for educational achievement. An adolescent from a low-income household is more likely to leave at the minimum school-leaving age, with few qualifications and to experience unemployment before entering a low-paid, insecure and hazardous occupation, with no occupational pension scheme. An adult working in this sector of the labour market is more likely to experience periods of unemployment, to raise a family in financially difficult circumstances and to retire early because their prematurely expended health can no longer cope with the physical demands of their work. A retired person who does not have an occupational pension is more likely to experience financial deprivation in the years leading up to their death.

The development of this model involves identifying how risks work together. Risk, or 'environmental insults', may be accumulated through *independently occurring factors* or may occur in 'clusters' or 'chains' of *correlated factors*. An older person may experience a fall, the loss of a spouse and changes in eligibility criteria for services within a relatively short period. These factors are independent of one another. However, their impact on the person's life would be compounded by limited material or social resources or poor health resulting from childhood or adult exposures. A child born into poverty has a raised chance of experiencing a *cluster* of disadvantages which are correlated, although not necessarily causally linked: low birth weight, not being breast-fed and having a poor diet, being exposed to passive smoking and having poor educational opportunities. *Chains of risk* occur when one factor leads to another. For example, being abused as a child may lead to being looked after, reduced social confidence, educational attainment and low self-esteem resulting in risk of damaging sexual experiences and self-harm. As Ben-Shlomo and Kuh say, such 'links are probabilistic rather than deterministic' (2002: 287). Understanding how such clusters and chains of risk operate in creating social inequalities would be valuable (Graham, 2002).

Graham and Power (2004) present a further model – also not mutually exclusive – for linking childhood circumstances with adult health. They point to two main *pathways*. These are, first, that 'socio-economic circumstances across childhood influence adult health through their effect on circumstances in adulthood' and, second, that 'children's circumstances shape the development of health and other resources in childhood, with these resources laying the foundation for socio-economic position and for health in adulthood' (Graham and Power, 2004: 11). The research which unlocks the details of these pathways will be directly relevant to social work.

Implications for social work

The concept of the life course is subject to varied interpretations reflecting conflicting strands within social work practice and theory: individualism versus social structure; relative values versus standpoint. This complexity and difference, illustrated in outline above, precludes the possibility of single and unambiguous measures of normal development. However, these competing conceptions offer a variety of ways of understanding service users' lives. They also suggest to me a number of valuable areas of development for social work.

First, the epidemiological work linking the cumulative impact of disadvantage to health and, therefore, to social inequalities suggests that social work needs to refocus attention on basic needs such as money, housing, food and education, both in childhood and adult life.

Second, social workers should reassess the importance of history-taking as part of the assessment process (see Chapter 11). Understanding the biological, personal and social contexts of an individual's life course may give valuable clues to current experiences and future plans. For example, social workers should consider the impact of transitions and experiences on older immigrants from ethnic minorities (Burholt and Wenger, 2004) or the importance of personal narratives for maintaining identity in old age (Tanner, 2001).

Third, we need to develop our understanding of the ways in which social work interventions can influence life course transitions – for good or ill. Barn et al.'s (2005) work on care leavers from ethnic minorities is a good example.

Finally, social workers need to learn more from and contribute to social scientific understandings of how people's lifetime socio-economic position is determined. This would focus not only on individual narratives but also on populations and on social epidemiology and could make a major contribution to preventive social work.

Key learning points

1. Students should adopt a critical approach to understanding human growth and development, which is a contested subject.
2. Life cycle models suggest all human beings experience a common set of life stages linked to biological age and reinforced by social and cultural factors.
3. These models have been criticised for being too rigid and deterministic, not reflecting either the diverse realities of contemporary lives or the importance of human agency.
4. There are divergent approaches to understanding human development using the concept of the life course.
5. Some authors adopt a more fluid approach to life stages than was apparent in life cycle models. Others reject 'stages' entirely in favour of a focus on individually created identities.
6. Epidemiological studies of the life course highlight the impact of social structures and cumulative disadvantage on people's life chances, providing useful models for understanding causes and consequences of social inequalities.

Taking it further

Readers who want to know more about this will find the following helpful:

Davey Smith, G. (ed.) (2003) *Health Inequalities: Life course Approaches*, Bristol: The Policy Press.

Hockey, J. and James, A. (2003) *Social Identities across the Life Course*, Basingstoke: Palgrave.

McLeod, E. and Bywaters, P. (2000) *Social Work, Health and Equality*, London: Routledge.

Priestley, M. (2005) *Disability: A Life Course Approach*, Cambridge: Polity Press.

14 Partnership working
The interdisciplinary agenda

Malcolm Payne

This chapter will:

- develop insights about interprofessional education first introduced in Chapter 8;
- recognise that more partnership working is critical in health and social care;
- explain how good partnership working is needed because people's lives are complex;
- argue that effective partnerships depend upon understanding the nature of teamwork and accepting different professional groups' valid contribution to the joint enterprise.

Introduction: policies for partnership as a response to complexity

The lives and problems of human beings are complex. Because social work sees those lives as part of wider family and social networks, it deals in even greater complexity than many professional colleagues. Consequently, to avoid being false in how it deals with people and their lives, social work needs complexity thinking (Adams et al., 2005), seeking to understand connections within and between human lives, rather than trying to simplify.

In addition to the complexity of people's lives, social work operates in complex helping systems: social work agencies and wider social provision in, for example, health care and education have developed as states took up responsibility for the welfare of their citizens. As soon as one aspect of life requires help from social agencies, this impinges on all sorts of other social care systems. A long-standing objective of policy has been to improve how these services respond to the complexity in people's lives. An example is the 2006 government White Paper on community health and social care services, where this aspiration is clearly expressed: 'We will move towards fitting services round people not people round services' (DH, 2006: 6).

This means that professionals with different backgrounds, from different intellectual disciplines and with different roles work together to provide care and support to service users and people around them. As the ramifications of a service user's needs become clear, those working together interact with a wide range of other aspects of the user's life, and this means they interact with a wide range of other services. Some will be businesses – for example, a social worker might make contact with the user's pension fund provider. Many, however, will be other social agencies. It has always been necessary for such agencies to cooperate to achieve their aims in providing services to citizens. There have always been problems in organising that cooperation. In recent years, attempts to improve cooperation have focused on the idea of partnership, covering cooperation between agencies, between workers and between workers and service users, and on multiprofessional and interdisciplinary work as a way of organising cooperation between workers from different professions or traditions of learning, research and knowledge development.

'Partnership', 'interdisciplinary' and 'agenda' are not neutral words. They all represent aspirations, an assumption 'something needs to be done' about problems in this area of work. 'Partnership' implies an aspiration towards close mutual trust and reliance (Payne, 1995). 'Interdisciplinary' implies an aspiration towards interlocking different disciplines of learning associated with particular professions, so that they work together. 'Agenda' implies a plan to achieve objectives and refers to professional, organisational and government aims to promote partnership through interdisciplinary work. In understanding aspirations and perceptions of problems in management, professional work and policy, it is useful to keep a critical eye open for the interests of the different people and groups who are raising the need for change. The interdisciplinary 'agenda' is partly a professional movement but also connects with a government policy intention as part of 'modernising' public services, and in this case particularly health and social care. Policy in favour of partnership and interdisciplinary work may reflect a wish to destabilise existing patterns of organisation and professional practice. Any change like this will have benefits but may also present problems. Also, because even policy legitimated by government authority is often created with a broad brush, the people who implement it must look carefully to establish the best way of doing so and of avoiding the problems.

Partnership

 Identify the different partnerships in your work. What contributes to their success or failure?

Partnership working in social work refers to three kinds of partnerships:

1. Between workers and clients or service users (see Chapter 20). Here, the idea of partnership implies that users are equal to the worker, trusted to take their part in planning and making progress – not just consulted, worked with according to worker or agency priorities, or seen as objects of help or pity. Partnership implies that users are the subjects, the main actors, in meeting their own needs in their own lives. Partnership with users in practice needs to be backed up by agency and service systems that consult users about the organisation of services and organise and fund agencies so that they are focused on users' needs. Otherwise, the worker is trying to practise in an environment that does not support the openness that partnership requires.
2. Between different kinds of workers. Here, partnership implies being prepared to assume responsibility for working with the service user alongside colleagues, respecting and valuing their contribution and jointly planning the work, so that it forms a seamless whole (see Chapter 8).
3. Between different kinds of agency. Here, partnership implies organising agencies so that their aims and pattern of work fits together.

Partnership working comes from a variety of professional and policy initiatives (Weinstein et al., 2003). Perhaps the most important is coordinating provision of health and social services between separate government structures. Social services provided through local government and health care provided through the NHS are separately financed and administered with separate legal mandates. Therefore, coordination of health and social care towards common objectives is hard to organise, and this structural issue may be blamed on professional divisions (Lewis, 2001; Glasby and Littlechild, 2004). One movement was achieving financial integration through joint finance and management initiatives from the 1970s onwards. At the same time, work on interdisciplinary teams in specialist health care teams led to multiprofessional working by social workers in specialist health care settings, for example, renal, paediatric and palliative care.

Teamwork also developed in primary care, with different professions working alongside general practitioners (GPs), or family doctors, providing the first level of care to patients within the NHS. GPs are independent contractors providing their services as part of small businesses to the NHS. This system promotes independence and local autonomy but makes it difficult to finance and coordinate their work in concert with other aspects of health care – this is another structural issue in health care. However, because virtually everyone in the UK is registered with and values family doctor services, their surgeries provide non-stigmatising access to a wide range of people possibly needing social work help. Including social workers within the team is occasionally achieved but is far from universal.

Partnership has also been an issue in child protection. Early inquiries into situations where public services have failed to protect children from being abused or neglected by adults found problems of communication and coordination between different services and professionals involved. Therefore, coordinating structures, such as child protection registers and area child protection committees, were established to improve partnership (Hallett, 1995). From the late 1990s, the government approach to this has been to connect local social and other services by requiring formal cooperation in various ways. Social care services for children were mainly integrated into local authorities' education departments, and a director of children's services was appointed in each area. The Children Act 2004 lays a 'duty to cooperate' on many public bodies, requires local authorities to take the lead in creating an agreed 'children and young persons plan', to establish representative 'safeguarding children' panels and to take part in establishing a common assessment framework (DfES, 2004).

Mental health and learning disabilities work have also been important sites for developing partnership working, initially in community learning disabilities teams during the 1980s and then in community mental health teams. In these fields, interdisciplinary teams involving social workers and nurses together, sometimes with clinical psychologists and psychiatrists, have been both the forerunners and the instruments of a structural combination of health and social services agencies in organisational partnerships (Onyett, 2003).

In these areas, users' participation in decision-making that affects them and, increasingly, their right to significant influence or control of decisions has had an important influence. NHS reforms aim to achieve 'more choice and a much stronger voice for patients' (DH, 2005b). Parents and young people are now often part of case conferences about child care and protection. Patients receiving health care, particularly long-term care, are supported in relationships with the health service by 'patient advice and liaison services' (PALS). Disabled people can receive funding to pay for their own carers through 'direct payments', instead of having to accept arrangements made at one remove through care managers. Many other services aim to connect services so that they focus on people's preference to be cared for in their own homes. For example, 'health and social care services are to work together to ensure that people with long-term neurological conditions are given the care and support they need to live independently in their own homes wherever possible' (DH, 2005c). These examples all raise the importance of clear decisions about how users participate in and influence partnership working.

Health and social care agencies form a connected system of organisations, where workers from different disciplines are part of a social network of interpersonal relationships. The connections between organisations may involve:

- completely separate organisations, where joint activity relies on workers' cooperation;
- shared support functions, such as information and training, bringing economies of scale and access to scarce skills;
- shared contract processes, supporting cooperation by financial incentives;
- shared working, where boundaries and strategies are aligned;
- merger, where joint working achieves greater permanence and a single identity for users and workers.

(Audit Commission, 1993; Leathard, 2003: Chapter 7; Whittington, 2003c)

Such a range of organisational strategies for cooperation means, however, that it can be hard for service users, their carers and for professionals to know how the system is set up, how it affects individuals and what they have to do to navigate the system. Crucially, organisational systems do not create cooperation, people do. This means workers need to focus equally both on interpersonal relationships in their daily work, and also on wider links between agencies, since professionals form the social network that is incorporated into agency relationships. This has often been seen as a particular responsibility of social workers, frequently acting as agents that help users and other professionals to cross boundaries within the care system. However, it is also a responsibility of other professionals, who have connections in a network relevant to their own discipline: doctors speaking to doctors and nurses to nurses about issues affecting their specialist responsibilities. Thus, all professionals may need to take responsibility for reaching out and drawing in connections within their own disciplinary network for the benefit of others in their multiprofessional team.

Interdisciplinary work

How do you define multidisciplinary/interdisciplinary work? What contributes to its success?

Improving partnership mainly focuses on improving structures. The interdisciplinary element of this is a restructuring of relationships between different professions working together. Because it is concerned with their varying disciplines, it focuses on the different knowledge, skills and values that professionals bring to their work, rather than to their professional role. It is about how their different knowledges may be used in an integrated way to respond to the complexity of people's lives and social networks.

This can helpfully be understood by seeing each professional group as operating in a shared field of knowledge and understanding. There are centres of interest and responsibility, which are the main focus of particular professions. Some of these overlap. Sometimes there are gaps between them. Competition also occurs. Interdisciplinary work tries to define whose disciplinary knowledge and understanding can most usefully take action with particular situations which a team of workers is dealing with. Then, it will usually be necessary to decide how different team members will work together to formulate a more complete response to the user's life complexities.

A common approach to interdisciplinary working focuses on flow of work into, through and out of the service. Planning this is similar to the pattern of practice in many social care and related professions. The service user and their surrounding social network has to be taken into the service; referral, intake, admission or registration systems describe this process. In interdisciplinary work the case is not allocated to just one worker, but there may be a key worker, primary worker or sub-team that accepts special responsibility for the service user. A regular team meeting manages the work, by sharing information about different responsibilities and actions and then planning what each worker will do in the next phase. As part of this, they will also plan for transfer on to the next aspect of the service, discharge or case closure. Only some of the team may be involved in a case, and a 'core and periphery' model of practice develops (Miller et al., 2001) where a small group of professionals involved in all or most cases calls occasionally on others. Sometimes, as a result, issues arise about the relationships between the core and the periphery.

The team may be called multidisciplinary, interdisciplinary, multiprofessional or interprofessional. Thinking about a 'team' as the site of interdisciplinary work implies a focus on teamwork as an idea. As with the other concepts explored here, 'team' and 'teamwork' are aspirational ideas: people often use the terms to express the hope, wish or policy that cooperation should be improved, without thinking clearly about what working together in this context implies. The next section, therefore, looks at different forms of teamwork.

Approaches to teamwork

 Think about the team in which you work; are there ways it could work together differently?

Multiprofessional teamwork has developed since the 1970s, combining perspectives on teamwork drawn from management studies and health care. Management ideas on teamwork derive from research in the 1940s, showing that interpersonal relationships and group support improved task performance. This perspective leads to a concern for group relations between members of a work group, selecting appropriate group members and helping them to work together better. Health and social care teamwork focuses on coordination in delivering services, particularly emphasising professional boundaries and barriers. Research has shown that good communication and group relations improves collaboration between workers from different professions. This may be enhanced by training them together (Miller et al., 2001: Chapter 7).

Multiprofessional practice that focuses on group relations sees the main aim of teamwork as clarity about objectives, leadership and professional role within the team. Virtually all teamwork literature (Payne, 2000a) and, especially, a large study of the NHS emphasise the importance of gaining commitment to a clear mission for a team and being clear about leadership. This does not necessarily mean having one leader but rather being clear about who takes leadership for which tasks and ensuring things happen. It particularly means taking action to ensure no debilitating conflict about leadership exists, either generally or over particular issues. Clarity about professional role means each professional having a clear conception of the content and boundaries of their professional role, so that they can enact it as they deal with their colleagues. Then if work is interdisciplinary, where roles overlap or are shared, clarity about boundaries helps to identify responsibility. There may be gaps in responsibility for aspects of the team's work; role clarity helps identify these too.

An alternative approach to multiprofessional work focuses not on group relations but on knowledge management. The knowledge-management approach focuses on the overall aims of the team and proposes each person brings to it their personal knowledge, skills and value assumptions. This personal contribution incorporates their professional background. The task of the team is to allow the personal and professional knowledges to be expressed, as a contribution to the work. The primary focus is on the service user, and interdisciplinary work establishes a shared process enabling team members to 'speak' their knowledge (Opie, 2003). The skill of leadership is allowing all these knowledges to be expressed and included in an overall plan. In turn, the plan must incorporate the separate professional objectives of the different people and their professional responsibilities. As this process takes place for successive service users, teams establish a 'community of practice' (Wenger, 1998) in which the history of the shared experience of working together creates a joint understanding of the whole field of practice.

So, in my hospice's palliative care team meetings, doctors, nurses, social workers, spiritual care workers and others make their contributions, sharing work around. Some actions are clearly a particular profession's responsibility, but joint work helps them share understanding about other people's roles. Recently, for example, I explained to a doctor how I had arranged with the local authority adult services department a protection plan for a patient whose relative was accused of ill-treating her, and he said this helped him to understand how these things were accomplished safely and confidentially, in general as well as in this particular case. Later, I rehearsed with a nurse who was part of the adult protection meeting how to conduct a home visit. She appreciated the plan but feared the relative would confront her about what she saw as an authoritarian intervention. Here, I helped both colleagues to consider the consequences for their practice of an action in which, while they had participated, I had taken a primary role. In future, these colleagues will feel more confident in understanding how an adult protection role may be incorporated into our overall palliative care responsibilities.

The advantages of the knowledge-management approach to teamwork are the focus on the service user and the emphasis on sharing and interacting, rather than on maintenance of professional positions. The disadvantage is that responsibilities and interesting work can be leached away by more powerful professions, leaving a rump of undesirable or undervalued work and a weak implementation of the potential of alternative disciplines. This is important to professions, such as social work, which are not well understood by others and whose members are often underconfident about their potential contribution. Therefore, both approaches to teamwork emphasise the importance of maintaining clarity about the role a social worker can undertake. I find that it can be helpful to rehearse possible aspects of potential social work roles before attending case discussions and general meetings. Social work teams can also usefully rehearse together the line they will take in dealing with common situations.

Doing partnership

This discussion about issues in partnership working suggests the importance of developing a number of skills in 'doing partnership'. Four partnership roles are important (Payne, 1993):

1. liaison, making and sustaining contact with other agencies and colleagues;
2. co-ordination, ensuring through liaison that organisations work together when required;
3. representation, acting on behalf of your agency or user with another agency or person;
4. presentation, promoting and demonstrating the value of role of your work and your users' needs.

It is important for workers to plan their work in all these roles in relation to the partnerships they are responsible for. Planning should consider:

• the nature, extent and intensity of relationships required – for example, frequency of regular contacts, problem-solving approaches, how conflictual and consensual relationships are;
• making first approaches, building appropriate relationships around useful topics and deciding on the time, effort and other resources to be used;
• establishing a pattern of relationships, how you will make contact – for example, through regular meetings, or by telephone on particular cases – and the extent to which contacts will intrude upon the freedom of users and agencies to decide on their own priorities or promote involvement in other agencies' objectives.

The most obvious skill involved in these activities is communication. The boundaries between organisations and disciplines are barriers to communication. Among the differences that may need to be overcome are different timescales, priorities, language and jargon.

How can we understand what social workers need to know and do in promoting partnership with other agencies?

Two areas of understanding are useful: the fields of practice that they are likely to need to know about and the kinds of things that they are likely to be asked to do. Workers need to have enough understanding of the work, organisations and personnel they are likely to deal with when they are in contact with agencies in each of these fields and expertise in the kinds of work they are likely to undertake. Drawing on Kamerman's (2002) analysis of fields of practice in social work, Table 14.1 sets out the fields of practice that social workers are likely to be part of or relate to and the focuses of action that their work might entail in each of these fields. It is often helpful for a social work team to plan who takes responsibility for connections in each field of practice, keeping up to date with changes in personnel, responsibilities and organisation of agencies in each field. Social workers who are alone as members of a multiprofessional team can also use this as a guide to selecting knowledge about local agencies and activities they should undertake. For example, work with people recovering from mental illness might focus more strongly on health, housing and poverty and on practical help and self-help systems, while work in child protection might focus more on education, housing, development and protection. Thinking in this way allows workers to set priorities for where they make their strongest efforts in liaison.

Table 14.1   Fields of practice and focuses of action.

Focuses of action ⟹	Information, advice, referral and advocacy	Therapy, counselling and rehabilitation	Development, socialisation and personal growth	Protection	Practical help and care	Promotion of self-help and mutual aid
Health and mental health						
Education						
Housing and homelessness						
Employment and unemployment						
Justice (civil and criminal)						
Income transfers, social security, poverty						

(Kamerman, 2004)

Knowledge transfer: participation and consultation

Think about your interdisciplinary work; what knowledges about other fields would help you?

One useful way of understanding interdisciplinary work from a knowledge-management viewpoint is to identify potentially useful knowledges and to think about how to transfer knowledge from one area to another. Health care practice often refers to bio-psycho-social knowledge, to which spiritual knowledge might also properly be added. For broad social care settings, crimino-legal and education knowledges may also be useful, although organisations with a health care focus might count these knowledges as 'social' or 'psychological'. Education knowledges might also be divided into pedagogical and andragogical (respectively, learning for young people and adults), since learning processes for people differs with age. Anglo-American social work frequently views practice as a problem-solving process akin to the medical model of diagnosis and cure of an illness. However, it can be very appropriate, and often less disparaging to service users, to see it as an educational process in which workers accompany users on a journey to explore new ways of understanding (see Chapter 9 for an explanation of pedagogy). Similarly, management knowledges are helpful to workers in organising work, or in helping users, for example, with financial or time management. Nursing knowledges are beneficial when helping people provide care.

Seeing all these suggests a daunting list of knowledges that social workers might potentially need to encompass. Obviously, it is impossible for one person to have the necessary expertise in all these areas; indeed, a multiprofessional team would find this hard. The way a team might respond to this is:

- *dividing* the work with someone among team members taking up responsibility according to expertise;
- participating alongside other team members to share responsibility through *working together* on a piece of work;
- acting as *consultants* to others to share specific expertise;
- specialist *liaison* with external sources of expertise.

These options emphasise different combinations of workers accepting accountability for parts of each piece of work. This draws attention to the importance of defining clearly who takes on what in shared work.

For example, the multiprofessional home care team in my hospice recently helped a patient with Parkinson's disease, unusually for them, because their patients generally suffer from cancer. However, the Parkinson's disease specialist team wanted help with pain management, where the hospice has expertise. There were also family and relationships problems between the patient and his carer, mainly arising from severe anxiety and strong feelings of loss of freedom and satisfaction in their marriage. The consultant palliative care physician sought advice from other specialists about medication usually used with Parkinson's disease patients and worked on the pharmacological interactions. The social worker spent time discussing the patient's and carer's fears and anxieties, gaining their confidence by resolving several social security problems and responding to difficulties arising because their package of community care was insufficiently flexible for them. The clinical nurse specialist (CNS) discussed the management of episodes where the patient and his main carer became very anxious, when pain increased and he went into muscle spasm, becoming frozen in one position and unable to move. Through liaison with the accident and emergency (A&E) nurses, who developed a technique for delivering medication when the spasm resulted in inability to swallow, the CNS trained the carer to use the technique at home, and this avoided the need for anxious rushes to A&E. One area of interdisciplinary debate was whether the social worker, having formed a good supportive relationship with the couple, should do this training. However, it was decided that training by the CNS would be more accepted, because her nursing expertise and her interaction with the Parkinson's and A&E nurses gave her detailed understanding of the nursing procedures involved. The consultant worked out appropriate combinations of medication which could be given in emergencies. The social worker focused on reducing the general anxiety and increasing the mutual support offered in the family. In this example, each professional reached out and drew in the information resources from their own network; their responsibilities in the case were defined by their usual professional roles. Where there was overlap between the CNS and the social worker, they worked out a clear allocation of responsibilities which complemented each other. The patient and carer were also involved in the plan to help them learn the medication techniques, and this also increased their confidence in each other's support, thus helping the social worker's more general intervention.

Conclusion

Government, the profession and individual workers aspire to achieve progress and success in the three aspects of partnership, between workers and service users, between workers and their colleagues and between agencies. However, aspiration is not achievement. Partnership working needs careful planning, good communication and a clear understanding of effective ways of sharing knowledge across organisational and disciplinary boundaries. Good agency and political support needs to complement workers' efforts to create good interdisciplinary practice. If these aspirations are not achieved, health and social care work cannot respond to the complexity in people's lives.

Key learning points

1. Partnership working is needed to respond to complexities in people's lives and in patterns of service provision.
2. Partnership between workers and service users, between different professional disciplines and different agencies need to be considered.
3. Policy and structural advantages and constraints affect how effectively cooperation can be organised.
4. Interdisciplinary work can also be promoted through teamwork.
5. Teamwork can be improved through improved group relations in the team and service network, but a recent innovation in teamwork practice involves working on better knowledge management.

Taking it further

Readers who want to know more about this will find the following helpful:

Glasby, J. and Littlechild, R. (2004) *The Health and Social Care Divide: The Experiences of Older People* (2nd edn), Bristol: Policy Press.

Leathard, A. (2003) 'Models for Interprofessional Collaboration', in A. Leathard (ed.) *Interprofessional Collaboration: From Policy to Practice in Health and Social Care*, London: Brunner Routledge.

Payne, M. (2000) *Teamwork in Multiprofessional Care*, Basingstoke: Palgrave.

15 Practice learning in context

Vicky Harris and Martin Gill

This chapter will:

- link to the requirement, since 2003, for extra emphasis on practice learning in the social work degree;
- engage with the systemic difficulties of organising and coordinating practice learning;
- provide examples of how properly organised and managed practice-learning opportunities fulfil a vital function in each practitioner's development;
- complement material in Chapters 6 and 20 regarding service users' involvement in practice learning;
- argue for the importance of the 'practice teacher's' continued role compared with the reductive notion of 'practice assessor'.

Introduction

The IFSW states that social work promotes 'social change, problem solving in human relationships and the empowerment and liberation of people to enhance well-being' (IFSW/IASSW, 2000). Although this principle underpins different forms of social work across the world (as observed in Chapter 9), its complex and stressful nature requires practitioners in every country to integrate values, knowledge and skills with day-to-day practice; however, the detail of their practice will differ widely across the world. As specified in Chapter 1, in the context of England the requirements for social work education have been centrally directed. These requirements include the necessity that all social work students should complete 200 days of assessed practice and emphasise increased involvement of service users and carers in social work courses (DH 2002a). These changes to social work education have been matched by concurrent changes in the organisation of social work itself. Separation of adult and children's services and the increased use of multidisciplinary models of service delivery combine to present practitioners and students with the challenge of maintaining a distinct professional identity. In this chapter we explore the implications of these changes for the organisation of practice learning. After placing practice learning in a historical context, we explore the scope for new models to meet current needs and consider whether the 'practice teacher's' role remains valid.

Changing practice teaching

Training and assessment of social workers in the workplace has undergone significant change since the days when placements were provided by a social work practitioner supervising a student. The criteria for becoming a student supervisor was personal interest, and having at least two years post-qualifying experience (Lindsay and Walton, 2000). The student worked alongside the supervisor, who allocated work, provided supervision sessions and wrote a report for the higher education institution recommending whether the student had passed or failed the placement. Students were seen as being the responsibility of the supervisor rather than the team, and the range of work available to them depended in part on the relationship between the supervisor and their colleagues.

Development of the GSCC (formerly the Central Council for the Education and Training of Social Workers) Practice Teaching Award in 1987 introduced formal teaching and accreditation to this function. Since then, practice teaching has been supported by a comprehensive theoretical and practice base (Lawson, 2001: 7). The supervisory role has been supplemented by a more active approach to teaching students. Pritchard (1995: 195) distinguishes between *practice teaching* and *supervision*, with each having a specific role, that of practice teaching being to help the student to learn the job, whereas the focus of supervision is helping the student to develop his or her ability to do the job better (see Chapter 21). Doel and Shardlow (2005: 5) comment on the participative nature of the practice learning experience but note that in reality little is known about what actually takes place within the supervision or practice tutorials.

The Core Competences and Values Requirements introduced in 1996 (CCETSW, 1995) reflected a drive towards an evidence-based framework of assessment that attempted to measure outcomes rather than process or curriculum. This approach was continued in 2002, when the National Occupational Standards and the GSCC Codes of Practice were introduced (TOPSS, 2002; GSCC, 2002a).

As numbers of social work courses and social work students have increased, there has been pressure to find sufficient practice placements and practice teachers. Practice teaching is an intensive process, both in relation to the time taken supervising students and in terms of intellectual and emotional challenge. When combined with the 'ordinary' demands of the everyday social work task, it seems hardly surprising that many practice teachers only supervise one, or at most two, students in their careers. A review of practice teaching in London and the south-east found that 33 per cent of new practice teachers failed to take any students after qualification, rising to 50 per cent in the second year, and almost all respondents had stopped practice teaching after six years (Lindsay and Tompsett,

1998). Lindsay and Walton (2000) found significant differences between agencies in the extent to which planning for staff development and practice teaching was integrated into agency business plans. Some agencies regarded recruitment of practice teachers as an optional extra for staff development, and the provision of placements often relied on the goodwill of singleton practice teachers. Teaching was seen by some practitioners as a route to promotion or as a step towards gaining other qualifications; some were recruited into management positions or undertook other work in addition to their normal roles, often without systematic funding (Lindsay and Tompsett, 1998; Lindsay and Walton, 2000).

 How is practice teaching currently organised where you are based? Could it be organised differently?

Specialist and 'off-site' practice teachers

The demands placed upon practitioners, and the ad hoc way in which practice teachers have been trained and deployed, has meant that the traditional model of practice teacher and learner has been difficult to sustain. Research carried out with 139 practice learning agencies in the CCETSW England region in 1999 found that specialist and semi-specialist practice teaching posts were seen as a key way of supporting practice teaching (Lindsay and Walton, 2000). The increased use of 'off-site' practice teachers has shown that a 'learning experience' need not be confined to the work setting where the practice teacher is based. The responsibility for assessing the student remains with the practice teacher, but the teaching/supervision roles are negotiated between the on-site supervisor and the practice teacher, depending on individual skills and circumstances. Often the on-site supervisor allocates work, oversees learning opportunities and, in many ways, mirrors the line manager's role. Separating 'practice teaching' and 'supervision' enables the practice teacher to focus on active teaching of theory, specific skills and anti-oppressive practice. Being at one remove from the agency, the practice teacher is also able to help the student to critically reflect on their own value base and that of the placement agency.

Groupwork

Groupwork enables students to engage jointly in the sort of 'activity-based learning' advocated by Doel and Shardlow (2005). An evaluation for the University of Wolverhampton (PLTF, 2005) found that students enjoyed the support of group supervision, and being part of a group contributed to feeling less isolated, and more empowered. The university found that this way of working enabled practice teachers within local authority training sections or student units to manage large numbers of students and promoted greater consistency in the moderation and verification of placement portfolios. The disadvantages were finding ways to manage group dynamics where students had widely differing abilities and experiences and ensuring group discussions did not replicate work already undertaken with the workplace supervisor. There was also a concern that placement supervisors did not overlook individual students' needs. Although there are benefits to group learning, such groups can inhibit learning in individuals from oppressed groups if the group were to replicate wider social patterns of oppression (Gould and Taylor, 1996: 86).

Group practice teaching sessions could be a valuable way of addressing anxiety and organisational factors arising from 'bureaucratic requirements, inadequate resources, high workloads, competing demands of users and the organisation' (Eadie and Lymbery, 2002: 516). A properly managed group experience could provide support for students in high-pressure placements, or for those who are at risk of marginalisation because of their identity. Lindsay (Lindsay, 2003), in evaluating group learning in practice placements in Northern Ireland, proposes that group learning should be regarded as complementary to, not replacing, individual supervision. By employing principles of best groupwork practice, learners benefited from the opportunity to support each other; discussion with their peers also helped them to develop a better understanding of social work practice and underpinning knowledge.

The demands of 'real' social work on placement may present students with emotional challenges that reflect their own life experiences. Dempsey et al. (2001) developed a model for pre-placement workshops which could be adapted for workplace learning. The workshops use a person-centred framework to help students reflect on their motivation for entering social work, and to develop 'openness, honesty, and genuineness in communication as opposed to a false or "professional" persona which can happen only too easily when people are thrown without warning or support into emotionally laden situations' (Dempsey et al., 2001: 636).

Similarly, the use of a problem-based learning format lends itself to a groupwork approach. The Newcastle model enables students to share and reflect on their experiences. Students use the group to 'construct their own meanings from their own personal and cultural history … the role of the teacher is to assist learners to make links between different kinds of experiences and to make connections between areas of knowledge' (Gibbons and Gray, 2002: 532).

Changing practice learning

Traditional placements based in statutory agencies sometimes mean students only engage with service users at one remove, their experience obscured by office culture and set procedures. The Practice Learning Task Force (PLTF) was set up by the DH in 2003 as part of their modernisation initiative to increase the quantity, quality and diversity of practice-learning opportunities. A diverse range of placements is likely to widen students' understanding of the 'lived experience' of the communities in which they work, as well as exposing them to cultural differences. They will gain some understanding of the disadvantage and oppression regularly experienced by service users and receive valuable feedback concerning service users' perceptions of statutory agencies.

The PLTF initiatives led to practice learning opportunities being provided in a range of community organisations, such as faith groups, residential schools and women's aid projects (Doel et al., 2004). A distinction can be made between formal 'social work' settings, focusing on empowering others through the tasks of assessment, planning and managing interventions, and 'social care' settings, which focus on practical care tasks crucial to the well-being of clients (Barron, 2004: 26).

Group care and residential settings offer students the opportunity to engage in a more intense experience, one which is closer to the lives of service users and carers, whose voice is more rarely heard. Direct involvement in personal care tasks in a social care setting enables students to develop basic social work skills and values, provided there is clarity between the placement provider, the student and the practice teacher about the assessment criteria and the specific tasks to be undertaken (Barron, 2004: 35). A consistent assessment method is needed to ensure fairness across programmes, given the 'precarious balance between creative divergence and consistent standards' that can exist in different placement settings (Doel et al., 2004: 14).

A single placement in a community setting may not meet all National Occupational Standards assessment criteria. If the available learning opportunities do not allow the student to undertake complex social work roles, such as formal risk assessments, funding and managing complex packages of care, or working in a court setting, placements can arrange for the student to spend some placement days at a different agency, where they will gain the required experience.

Bringing service users and carers in from the cold

How can people who use services be appropriately involved in assessed placements?

A paternalistic model of social work, regarding service users as passive recipients of services, is no longer valid (Levin, 2004: 14). Service users and carers provide the basis of students' learning, yet for many years their contribution has been undervalued and their potential undeveloped. Initiatives to involve service users were often limited to gathering feedback from individuals about the student who worked with them or asking them to contribute to formal teaching sessions on their experience of social care (GSCC, 2004). Service users made an important contribution to the development of the assessment criteria on which the National Occupational Standards were based (DH, 2002c). The inclusion of the requirement that service users should be involved in all aspects of social work training (DH, 2002a) represented an important milestone in social work education. Involving service users from the outset ensures that students treat service users and carers as active participants rather than as passive recipients (Levin, 2004: 8).

An evaluation carried out for the GSCC in 2004 showed that higher education institutions had made progress in developing service users' contribution to social work programmes (GSCC, 2005b). The inclusion of service users and carers in selection processes, and the requirement for formal assessment of a student's 'readiness to practice', enabled teachers, professionals, service users and carers to create a holistic assessment of a student's potential at the early stages of the course.

Developing meaningful involvement of service users requires careful planning with them which is not imposed from above (see Chapter 20). Service user involvement can be placed on a continuum from information exchange at one end to having power to control outcomes at the other. It will continue to be limited while 'exclusionary structures, institutional practices and attitudes [...] still affect the extent to which service users can influence change. It appears that power sharing can be difficult within established mainstream structures, formal consultation mechanisms and traditional ideologies' (Levin, 2004: 14). For higher-education institutions and practice learning co-ordinators, this means that service users and carers should be included in the planning, management and assessment of practice-learning opportunities. This could be achieved through finding more placements with user-led organisations or by developing structures in statutory agencies that enable service users to work directly with students, as well as contributing to the final assessment (Doel, 2005).

Clarity about the assessment process and how decisions are validated is therefore essential. Service users and carers should have access to training and other resources to enable them to make a full contribution. Arrangements to ensure that service users can access venues for meetings, and that payment issues are resolved, need to be made. A culture of inclusion should be fostered so that barriers to communication, such as the use of jargon, are recognised and addressed (Carr, 2004; Levin, 2004; GSCC, 2004; GSCC 2005b).

Practice assessing or practice teaching?

The SCIE (Kearney, 2003) suggested a four-stage model for practice learning, which tracks a social work student through a three-year undergraduate degree course. The structure of some two-year postgraduate courses would require the model to be condensed. In this model, the assessment of students in the workplace is seen as being a generic function in its own right (GSCC, 2002b). Rather than students being assessed by a GSCC-accredited practice teacher, students would be assessed at different stages by a workplace assessor who might not be a qualified social worker.

1. Students at stage 1 would shadow and observe a practice assessor, who could be a social worker or someone in a related area, including a service user in a user-based or user-led organisation, and who would contribute to the higher education institution's assessment of the student's capacity to act appropriately and safely in a practice environment prior to the start of formal practice learning (Kearney 2003: 7). A student who has prior experience of social care may not need as long a period of assessment for readiness to practice as a school leaver, who is likely to have had less relevant experience prior to entering training. In a postgraduate programme, that previous experience could be incorporated into written assignments or otherwise reflected upon by the student and used – with a range of other criteria – as valid material for 'readiness to practice'.
2. Stage 2 would be provided by 'an experienced social worker, or other social care worker' (Kearney, 2003: 7), who would have undertaken a short training programme, such as that in the 'Workbook for Assessors', provided jointly by Skills for Care and the PLTF (Beverley and

Coleman, 2005). This model allows for practice learners to be supervised by non-social work staff for a significant proportion of their 200 days of assessed practice.

3. Stage 3 is provided by an experienced social worker and practice assessor providing students with experience of legal intervention and statutory risk assessments following which a final assessment of competence is made.

4. At stage 4, an experienced social worker or practice assessor would oversee problematic placements, co-ordinate practice learning opportunities within their agency and supervise and mentor assessors at Stages 1, 2 and 3. SCIE envisage that practice assessors at stages 3 and 4 should have undertaken a 'full programme' to qualify for the role, but this may not be equivalent to the GSCC Practice Teaching Award, which incorporates anti-oppressive practice as a fundamental concept of social work (GSCC, 2002b: 20).

We would argue that this model does not acknowledge the complexity and richness of the practice teaching function which has been developed. Dominelli (2002: 15) argues that practitioners need to integrate their understanding of anti-oppressive practice intellectually, emotionally and practically. Performance, in the sense of practical skills and tasks accomplished, is only one element on which the assessment of competence is based. Social workers operate in a dynamic and uncertain world, in which the ability to undertake complex assessments of risk and need is paramount. Policies such as the *Assessment of Children in Need* (DH, 2000a) and *Fair Access to Care Services* (DH, 2002d) use an evidence-based model, but also emphasise the role of professional judgement in reaching assessment decisions (Horwath and Thurlow, 2004: 8). Decisions have to be taken in the light of multiple perspectives in an environment where uncertainty is more likely than certainty about the probable outcomes of intervention (or non-intervention). This is of particular importance when the concept of the 'internal market' means that social workers are managers of 'packages of care', negotiating with providers from the commercial and voluntary sector, as well as from other statutory agencies, and monitoring the quality of their services. In a time of scarce public resources, managers in social care departments with budgets to protect may be under pressure to opt for short-term solutions which are not in the service user's long-term interests.

Horwath and Thurlow describe legislation, procedures and empirical research as 'rational-technical' activities, whereas 'practical-moral' activities 'recognise that people do not fit neatly into boxes and [that] personal and professional values and beliefs influence judgements' (2004: 7). Students need to develop the ability to critically reflect on their work in order to reach informed, professional decisions. A 'tick-box' type assessment of their competence to undertake a specific task, or to acquire a particular skill, will not furnish practice learners with the critical analysis, complex value base or reflective acumen necessary to function as a professional social worker. Students could learn the paperwork to be completed without developing the reflective skills that provide an understanding of the principles that support their proposed intervention. These outcomes are enabled by directed teaching in the workplace, not just within higher education institutions.

We argue that the concept of reflective practice should be incorporated from the beginning of the social work course and developed through the entire practice learning experience, rather than only being addressed at the later stages of assessed practice. The need for social workers to have an awareness of ethical dilemmas and conflicts of interest, and the impact of their own values and prejudices, was recognised by CCETSW (1995) in the Core Competences for the Diploma in Social Work and has been carried forward into the National Occupational Standards (TOPSS, 2002: 56). Learning is a graduated and incremental process; theory, activity and values are integrated through reflection, enabling the learner to build on past experience (Schön, 1983; Kolb, 1984).

Ixer argues that although the concept of reflection is often mentioned in social work literature, there is no shared sense of what this involves. He suggests that students might engage in *'expedient learning'*, doing what is necessary to achieve their objective of passing the course rather than risk failure (2003: 12). He warns that a model of reflection based only on a Westernised, northern-hemisphere tradition may exclude service users whose views and experiences have not been recognised as legitimate knowledge (2003: 9). In order to facilitate a dialogue with the student, whereby student and teacher can explore values and assumptions together, practice teachers need to be confident and comfortable with their own value base so that students can understand their own positions without fear of failure (2003: 14).

By delegating the practice assessor role to non-social work colleagues at Stage 2, there is a risk that assessors will focus on processes and procedures, rather than helping students to develop their own professional identities. The absence of an explicit commitment to accredited practice *teachers* seems, on the face of it, to risk returning to a fragmented and uncoordinated model of practice learning, which fails to meet the needs of students and service users. We question whether a five-day training programme for practice assessors, particularly if the assessor is not from a social work background, would provide them with the skills to teach students the values and knowledge base that would challenge oppression and promote social change. If practical skills are taught at the expense of reflection, which we argue is an essential process for the practitioners' development of a firm social work value base, there could be serious implications for the future of social work as a profession. There is thus a continuing role for skilled and accredited practice teachers, who can enable students to identify and address the dilemmas and conflicts inherent in social work.

Conclusion

Changes in the arrangements for social work education in England and Wales resulted in increased practice days to complement the teaching curriculum provided in higher-education institutions. We have identified opportunities and challenges for work-based learning to ensure it is fit for purpose. Approaches such as those discussed here retain the concept of the practice teacher in a more complex model, which has developed from an individualistic, historically supervisory, approach. Practice teachers will therefore have an increased role to play in the management of placements, but we believe that these additional demands will be amply compensated by enhanced workplace experiences, providing a rich source of learning for students. In this context it would not only be counterproductive to return to a simplistic model of assessing students but would also be swimming against the tide of international developments in social work education.

Key learning points

1. Practice learning is an evolved concept rather than one which has been designed.
2. The primacy of 'practice' asserted in recent policy guidance ignores the multidimensional nature of the learning process.
3. Scope exists for developing more innovative and creative ways of providing practice-learning experiences.
4. Such new developments need to be fully evaluated.
5. If social work is to retain its role as a champion of oppression, the role of the practice teacher needs to be maintained and developed.

Taking it further

Readers who want to know more about this will find the following helpful:

Kearney, P. (2003) *A Framework for Supporting and Assessing Practice Learning*, SCIE position paper No.2, London: SCIE, http://www.scie.org.uk/publications/positionpapers/pp02.pdf

Journal of Practice Teaching in Health and Social Work Education http://www.whitingbirch.net/p002.shtml.

16 Social work in a digital society

Jackie Rafferty and Jan Steyaert

This chapter will:

- conceptualise social work as taking place within the 'digital society';
- explore how information and communication technology (ICT) impacts on the individual, families and communities;
- argue that technological change has irretrievably altered the nature of the social world and, hence, practitioners need to understand it.

Introduction

We live in a digital society which has significantly changed the information landscape affecting every aspect of our lives. The current wave of technological innovation is part of the context in which social work students, practitioners and service users and carers operate. Technology can improve the quality of our lives and learning and can potentially enrich social work practice, but the extent to which it does so depends on our active involvement. It will not happen without social workers moulding technology developments and uses to their own and service users' needs. However, the technology can also pose challenges and dangers.

In this chapter we outline some of the major issues when thinking about the digital society from a social work perspective. Starting from the position of individuals or households, three issues emerge:

1. the digital divide (which can sometimes be a bridge);
2. digital literacy;
3. the new information environment.

This new information environment is also part of the new meeting place between service users and social workers which necessitates changes in social work practice, as well as in social workers' skill sets. Finally we outline an extra digital skill social workers need, which we label 'innovation through resistance'.

 Think about the ways you use information and communication technologies (ICT). What are they? What issues of inequality can you identify when you think about the use of ICT?

Digital divide

To make progress in using ICT for social work and social care requires practitioners, service users and carers need to be digitally literate and to have access to the technology. In 1995, the North American magazine *Newsweek* described the average internet user as politically conservative, white, male, single, native English-speaking, living in North America and a professional, manager or student. Much has changed, mainly through the widespread availability of the internet in Western countries. Technological innovation has rarely undergone such a rapid diffusion process. Although the speed of diffusion seems to be slowing down, the community of internet users still grows.

Amidst rapid diffusion of computers and the internet, we should remember that there are huge inequalities concerning who benefits from innovations. The digital divide surfaces at a global (Finland has more internet connections than the whole of Latin America), geo-political regional (far less computer diffusion in southern Europe than in north-west Europe) and at the household level. At each level, different dynamics play and specific solutions need to be identified. In this chapter, we focus on the latter level: households.

There are no less than seven significant socio-demographic factors that indicate social exclusion. These include:

1. income;
2. educational level;
3. gender;
4. age;
5. employment status;
6. ethnicity
7. type of household (e.g. single-parent).

Access to the internet follows the same pattern: the higher the household income, or the younger its members, or the more Western its ethnicity, the more internet access it will have. The only surprise is how unsurprising it is that precisely these seven variables influence internet access. There is a strong argument that the digital divide is not digital at all, but another facet of social exclusion. As such, having access to the new media differs little from having access to health care, education or employment.

The digital divide is in permanent flux. Gender is one of the seven indicated fault lines and used to be a very strong divide. However, there has been a shift, and gender is no longer a strong indicator for access to technology. Men and women have similar levels of access to, for example, mobile phones and internet connections. While some divides narrow, others increase. Over the past five years there has been a considerable shift away from income and education level as prime factors in the digital divide towards age. While younger age groups earlier indicated high costs and opportunities elsewhere (school and work) as a significant reason not to have home internet access, older age groups cite lack of both interest and digital skills. This raises the distinction between diversity and a divide. If older people are comfortable using the old media and see no interest in acquiring access to new media, should we still define this as a digital divide or as an informed choice?

Benefiting from computers and the internet is not only based on access but also relates to usage. It is reasonably safe to state that, on average, time spent using the internet continues to increase. (However, one has to bear in mind that people's responses are notoriously unreliable when asked about how they spend their time, and time-diary surveys are complex and expensive.) Such developments go together with the shift from metered to unmetered access, from dial-up connections to broadband or cable. It also generates a debate on time displacement, whether the internet is taking time from 'television time', 'social time' or 'work time'.

Finally, to understand the balance of benefits from computers and the internet, in addition to quantity of usage, we also need to look at 'quality' of usage. It makes quite a difference to someone's quality of life whether they spend an hour online to increase their employability by e-learning new skills or to increase their social networks by catching up with old friends and 'weak ties' (Granovetter, 1983), or by playing online games, browsing pornography or chatting with unknown partners in a chat room.

Research on internet use amongst Swiss households found that its use for entertainment varied across socio-demographic groups. Less-educated people used the internet predominantly for entertainment, while more educated people used it in a more information-oriented way (Bonfadelli, 2002). This finding also related to low-income households being surprisingly well represented among broadband users as a consequence of peer-downloading music or movies.

In attempting to 'deconstruct' internet usage, the Dutch Dialogic company has constructed a typology of usage. Their ICET-model differentiates between four categories:

1. **I**nformation gathering;
2. **C**ommunication, sending messages between people;
3. **E**ntertainment, whether online or offline, alone or multi-player;
4. **T**ransactions, such as e-banking or shopping.

While conceptually useful, no one has reliable survey data building on this classification. It is a lot easier to ask 'Do you have internet access at home?' than to ask for what purposes it is used.

A study on educational achievements and home access to computers and the internet highlighted why differentiating between 'quality' of usage is important (Valentine et al., 2005). The survey results indicated that girls benefited from home access and achieved higher GCSE grades than students without home access. Surprisingly, boys with home access to the internet achieved lower GCSE grades than those without home access. The critical element was that girls tend to use the computer for homework, while boys tend to use it for gaming. This illustrates the need to look at content preferences, rather than solely looking at media access.

Digital bridges

There is a digital divide when exclusion from internet access coincides with exclusion from other resources such as education or income. Fortunately, access to technology can also be a compensation for exclusion elsewhere. Here it can form a 'digital bridge'.

Two examples illustrate technology's liberating potential. The first is where technology helps to compensate for exclusion resulting from mobility impairment. With the lack of 'access for all', people with impaired mobility can benefit from online services. These can be for work (dispersed call centres, translation work), shopping (e-commerce) or for education (off-campus e-learning). Naturally, this requires a focus on the accessibility of online services. Far too often, as with physical access issues, online services are not designed to cope with users with functional impairments, needing to use screen readers for example. There is an inclusion-exclusion paradox here, with technology having the potential to include those with functional impairments, but current use often not capitalising on this (Steyaert, 2005).

The second example is where people reduce loneliness through technology. The literature discusses whether usage of the internet reduces or increases loneliness. While Kraut and his colleagues initially said that engaging with the internet increases loneliness, their later results showed mixed effects: those rich in social contacts benefit from technology; those with poor social networks see little benefit when using the internet; those who tend to be extrovert gain from using the internet; those who tend to be introvert do not (Kraut et al., 1998 and 2002). There are, however, certain groups of people who are extroverts but still face loneliness. In Eindhoven, in the Netherlands, an experiment was carried out with older people experiencing loneliness because of chronic illness. By providing them with computers, broadband internet access and training and support, feelings of loneliness dropped. This was because, for some participants, it was lack of mobility rather than being introverted that was causing weak social networks. This illustrates when technology can play an important role and is one reason why it is important for social workers to understand its potential for service users and carers.

Digital literacy

The digital revolution has reached the stage where people need technological literacy to participate fully in society. The range of possibilities for engaging electronically with society continues to grow whether in social interactions such as keeping in touch with friends through e-mails and text messaging, accessing formal or informal learning opportunities, working in the office (word-processing, presentations) or consuming goods and services (e-tourism, e-banking, e-shopping).

The need for updated skills in the wake of the diffusion of new technologies is not new and is certainly not specific to computer technology. When the bicycle was introduced, people had to learn how to cycle. Even when the telephone was introduced, Bell trained women in the USA to make short and factual calls rather than holding long social conversations (Fischer, 1992). Telephones were, after all, intended for short business communications.

Following a similar pattern, the same is happening with current waves of innovations, especially computer and internet technology. Public sector initiatives to support digital literacy include computer-technology centres and training courses organised through public libraries or community centres. Education at primary, secondary and tertiary levels has also encompassed digital literacy within its formal curriculum.

 What skills do you think you need to use ICT? Which do you already have?

Digital literacy differs in some ways from traditional literacy. In order to clarify the concept of digital literacy, we distinguish three forms of skills: instrumental, structural and strategic (Steyaert, 2000).

Instrumental

Instrumental skills refer to dealing with the technology, knowing how to use a keyboard and mouse and more complex manipulations such as sending an e-mail with an attached file, using word-processing, database and spreadsheet applications, searching the internet or downloading and installing software. Such instrumental skills can be considered equivalent to reading skills in printed media. The European Computer Driving Licence (ECDL) initiative is an example of learning and testing instrumental skills. This level of skill has been embedded into the social work degree. In England and Scotland, social work students must have passed the ECDL or its equivalent, whilst in Wales they must meet the ICT skills set out in the ECDL. This requirement is likely to be reviewed in 2006 and may be modified (Holt and Rafferty, 2005).

Structural

Structural skills refer to the ability to use the (new) structures in which information is contained. This would be analogous in traditional printed media skills to using the index in a book or knowing how to find a book in the library. In the new media, the 'old' skills are complemented by others such as making use of hyperlinks or knowing how to undertake searches. It also involves assessing information found, not relying on others' quality checks. Information on the internet can be past its 'use-by' date or of dubious origin, and the reader needs to be aware of this. A useful tool for social work educators and learners is the online tutorial *Internet for Social Workers* (at http://www.vts.rdn.ac.uk/tutorial/social worker).

Strategic

Strategic skills refer to more strategic uses of information and include the ability to proactively seek information, the ability to critically analyse available information and act on it and the continuous scanning of the environment for information relevant to work or personal life, sometimes referred to as organised serendipity. These skills become more critical in society as the information landscape permeates our daily activities, but they are not essentially digital. They are very similar for non-digital media and have a strong relationship to media literacy. They are relevant to developing a research-minded approach to social work learning and practice.

 Which skills do you need to develop?

The new information and communication environment

A schema for considering the role of ICT in relation to individuals, families, groups or communities is to consider whether the technology is being used to replace other means of doing the same thing (first wave), such as sending an e-mail instead of posting a letter, to enhance the activity by using a particular technological means (second wave), such as sending a text message to a number of people at the same time, or in a transformative fashion, by enabling people to engage in activities they could not otherwise do (third wave). For instance, communities were once defined by geographical boundaries and social interaction within those boundaries, but a good example of third-wave technology is the ability for communities of interest to come together through the internet. We can see this clearly in relation to health issues, where a diagnosis of ill health sees us going to Google to find out more information. We will find research papers that are difficult to understand, information written by professionals for lay consumption, as on 'NHS Direct', but also bulletin boards and chat rooms where we can contact others experiencing the same illness, sometimes with professionals as part of the community. Josefsson (2003) investigated health-based online communities and found that patients 'need to get informed and to interact with others in the same situation'. Josefsson (2003) cited Mittman and Cain (2001) who described this type of community-building for patients and caregivers as being one of the leading-edge applications associated with future health care use of the internet. In the UK, Hardey (1999: 820) concluded that, 'the Internet forms the site of a new struggle over expertise in health that will transform the relationship between the health professions and their clients'. If these findings are true for health care, surely they are also true for social care?

However, it is difficult in the current framework of social work education and practice to envisage the day when we can take for granted the ability to do a virtual tour of a residential home for an ageing parent with user reviews as found as on Amazon.com for books or DVDs, or for someone with a care management package to join an online user forum. Yet the rise of service user and carer involvement in social work practice may well presage just such developments.

Changing the dialogue

Are we at the beginning of the third wave of the social work technology which represents praxis for some and a nemesis for others? As technology becomes ubiquitous will it increasingly complement or replace face-to-face social work? Since the typology of skills was identified in 2000, a fourth category needs to be added: that of digital practice skills. Social workers still and increasingly unfairly are stereotyped as technophobic – they have had to engage with social work information systems and there is evidence of the beginnings of involvement with technology to enrich professional practice such as online counselling services (Rafferty and Waldman, 2006).

Digital practice will require extending the instrumental skill set as it will be difficult to undertake social work online if your typing skills are very slow, though that will probably be overtaken by the increasing simplicity of using the computer to talk to, and see, each other through audio and visual applications. More importantly, it also requires extension of practice skills.

> The method of communication can influence not only what is discussed but also how. Sentences are often sent in shorthand and SMS text language is often used. Young people are used to texting and communicating in an abbreviated form, a skill easily transferable to the computer keyboard. The loss of visual information can create uncertainty and result in rapid exchange conversations to avoid delay. This means that in this abbreviated form there is a tendency to dispense with the normal formalities of greeting. It is this 'in your face' approach that is so different to face to face work. It might take weeks of face to face work before a young person might disclose abuse whereas through the computer it might well be the opening sentence.
>
> (Waldman and Storey, 2004)

The quote is from a social worker in a National Society for the Prevention of Cruelty to Children (NSPCC) online youth-counselling service. The evaluation cites social workers being challenged in the online medium in terms of:

> building trust and expressing sympathy and understanding without the usual body language clues; dealing with asynchronous flows of communication; the shift in power and control in the relationship from the worker to the young person; the fast levels of

disclosure, managing silences and endings; managing supervision when every word is recorded on the computer.

(Waldman, 2004)

As technology-based services driven by innovators explore new ways of working, they highlight the fact that managing change requires time, resources, training and a cooperative culture. Whereas the NSPCC evaluation highlighted the need for additional practice-skills training, an Australian survey indicated that nearly half of the social workers at Centrelink, a call-centre operation providing online benefit services, had received no formal training in how to use the technologies on which they relied heavily (Humphries and Camilleri, 2002). The instrumental and even the structural skill sets are challenges that will be met as time passes. However, we are a long way from enabling students to learn e-practice skills, and achieving this requires development of both educators and the curriculum.

Social work practice

 How can you use ICT in your social work practice? What concerns you about the use of ICT in social work?

The use of ICT in social work practice arose as a consequence of the political shift in climate within social policy as public services moved into the era of accountability and monitoring (see Chapter 22 for an analysis of this). This was a greater influence than either technological determinism (albeit a major influence) or social constructivism.

Several authors argue that technology is not a politically or morally neutral factor in the implementation of social policy (see, for example, the chapters by Harlow, Gould, and Huntington and Sapey in Harlow and Webb (2003)). Lord Laming wrote in his introduction to the Inquiry Report on Victoria Climbié:

Improvements to the way information is exchanged within and between agencies are imperative if children are to be adequately safeguarded. Staff must be held accountable for the quality of the information they provide. Information systems that depend on the random passing of slips of paper have no place in modern services.

(Laming, 2003)

Along with growth in monitoring and accountability, social workers have struggled to adapt to using computerised care management and children's information systems in the UK. Many staff experienced the introduction of such systems as often less than enhancing of their practice, particularly where their perspective is that the systems are being implemented as part of new managerialism and that the 'emphasis is on the use of performance monitoring, performance indicators and outcome measures' rather than on the service user – practitioner relationship or policy intelligence-gathering (Postle, 2002; Richards et al., 2005; see also Chapter 17).

The Electronic Social Care Record implemented in 2006 is at the heart of shared information systems, storing details of every social service 'user' in a database which can be shared with all relevant professionals. This development expands our understanding of information-system records by opening up the possibility of including unstructured information, even audio and video recordings. With growing interprofessional and multidisciplinary practice across social services, health, criminal justice and education systems, issues of skills, accuracy, privacy and data protection are growing challenges. It is not just an issue of information systems talking to each other through technological interoperability. Social workers have found working with computerised information systems raises technical and ethical complexities and feel it detracts from face-to-face work.

Using the typology above, the introduction of computerised information systems equates to the first wave of social work technology, complementing or replacing paper records. Perhaps the second wave has been the use of e-mail for communicating with colleagues and with service users, usually to arrange face-to-face meetings, and use of the internet for accessing information. Even this wave generated examples of innovative service provision. For example, the Samaritans started an e-mail support service for people with mental illness. In 1999, the Samaritans received 25,000 e-mail contacts; in 2004 the number of e-mail contacts had risen to 100,000. 'The Samaritans believe that people find it easier to express their feelings using email than they do on the phone – email contacts are three times more likely to mention suicidal thoughts than phone callers. It's not entirely clear what is happening, but it seems that people find the anonymity of the medium helpful' (LASA, 2000). Yet current systems are but the first step on the virtual ladder of e-social services in a digital society, and we are just beginning to see the potential of the third, transformative wave.

Social constructivist or technological determinism

Social workers are not just routine professionals who carry out the tasks they are asked to do. Like most modern professionals, they are reflexive practitioners who perform their job while innovating. This idea applies to most social interventions, and, hence, also to those involving technology. From that perspective, any apparent reluctance of social workers to engage too optimistically with technology in daily practice can be seen as healthy when their focus is on improving the use of technology and its relevance to social work. Such an 'innovation-through-resistance' attitude is probably more suitable for the social work context than uncritical technology fascination.

Consequently, there is one specific aspect of digital literacy that needs to be highlighted here. This relates to approaching technology from a social constructivist perspective rather than technological determinism. Technological innovation is often taken for granted and approached very similarly to the weather: you can learn to understand forecasts and take appropriate measures (your umbrella!) but you can't change the weather. Given the history of technology, that is a very peculiar approach. Most innovations were not developed in laboratories by engineers but emerged from dialogue between product innovators and early users. How did popular applications such as chat or peer-to-peer networks emerge? Because some amateur had a good idea, developed a prototype and had some success then, later, professional product/technology developers expanded it. That is how Jarkko Oikarinen kick-started chat software in 1988, and how Shawn Fanning developed Napster in 1999. In other cases, the technology comes from industry, but the actual applications were not foreseen. This is how mobile phone text-messaging developed. It was originally only a tool for telephone engineers to communicate and not a service for end-users. Sending a text message was free until the telephone companies realised that people were actually willing to pay a small amount of money for sending small amounts of text.

Approaching technology from a social constructivist perspective and learning from the 'negotiations' between industry and users provides a starting point for dealing with some of the social consequences of technology. From the perspective of a social worker, it should not make a difference whether there's a computer on their desk (or a laptop for home visits), but whether the applications that run on the technology mirror the process of social work practice or are mainly driven by a managerial or accounting and actuarial rationale. Far too often, social workers have resisted technology as such and have not been partners (or have been weak ones) in the process of constructing applications. No wonder then that the social work rationale is often missing (or weak).

There are also examples of negotiated developments. Accessibility is a major concern for people with functional impairments, or for older people. Their 'negotiations' have resulted in major software developers such as Microsoft building functionality into products to enhance accessibility and launching simple-to-use technology. See §508 of the US Rehabilitation Act and http://www.microsoft.com/enable/, http://www.corel.com/ accessibility/ or http://access.adobe.com. See also, for example, http://www.simpc.nl for simple computers for older people, or Philips' new slogan on 'sense and simplicity'. Assistive technologies provide technology solutions that can support disabled people to lead more independent lives. Outside of the assistive-technology and management-information arenas, very little research is being carried out in the UK concerning how these technology tools can support service users and carers and social work practitioners, and this situation urgently needs to be remedied.

Conclusion

In this chapter we have explored some of the ways in which ICT can impact on the individual, families and communities and have provided frameworks to make sense of what is happening around us as we enter the digital society. We have argued that the level at which technology can enhance social work practice and process is not a given, and the potential benefits of the technology will not be realised unless social workers engage creatively with the tools that are already available. We need to work with the technology and its developers to ensure future developments enhance quality of life and work for service users, carers and practitioners, as well as providing data for management and policy purposes. Preparing practitioners for this role requires curriculum changes that take account of the digital age we live in and the skills required to take this agenda forward as well as developmental research on both a micro and macro scale to analyse which uses of technology are beneficial to the social care process.

Key learning points

1. We need to acquire the digital skills to make the best of the internet and ICT. This requires professional information skills.
2. The digital divide replicates existing patterns of social exclusion but is also dynamic: while gender used to be important, now it is age.
3. Technology's effect on social work practice is something we can influence. To do this, social workers must become partners in technology developments.
4. There are myriad technological applications capable of enriching social care besides monitoring and accountability.

Taking it further

Readers who want to know more about this will find the following helpful:

Harlow, E. and Webb, S.A. (eds) (2003) *Information and Communication Technologies in the Welfare Services*, London: Jessica Kingsley.

Journal of Technology in Human Services http://www2.uta.edu/cussn/jths/.

Human Services Information Technology Applications (HUSITA), an international network, at http://www.husita.org.

Centre for Human Service Technology, at http://www.chst.soton.ac.uk.

ECDL initiative, at http://ecdl.com.

Part Four

Thriving in practice

This part of the book focuses on the development of social work practice following qualification. It is therefore most appropriate for students undertaking post-qualification training or for experienced practitioners who wish to reflect on their practice and the contexts within which they work. The chapters focus on the following areas:

- the organisational context of practice;
- continuous professional development (CPD);
- professional development in the workplace;
- partnership working with service users;
- supervision;
- management and managerialism;
- value conflicts in practice.

While there are close links between several of these chapters, their focus is distinct in each case. For example, although both Chapters 18 and 19 focus on professional development, Chapter 18 concentrates particularly on the place of post-qualifying education and training, while Chapter 19 examines the ways in which practitioners can take responsibility for their own professional development through day-to-day interactions. Similarly, several of the chapters build on similar theoretical sources; for example, Kolb's cycle of experiential learning is used in Chapters 18, 19 and 21. As noted earlier, two chapters explicitly relate to material introduced elsewhere in the book. For example, there is a close link between Chapters 20 and 6, while Chapter 23 builds on the thinking first introduced in Chapter 3. In addition, the pernicious impact of managerialism outlined in Chapter 22 is implicit in the content of Chapter 17, as performance measurement is one of the key mechanisms of a managerialist approach.

17 Social work in its organisational context

Mark Lymbery

This chapter:

- explores the organisational context for social work;
- argues that an understanding of organisational priorities is a prerequisite for informed professional practice;
- considers the need for organisations and their practitioners to work in partnership with other welfare providers;
- examines the impact of performance measurement on practitioners and their organisations.

Introduction

In order to practise successfully, social workers must be aware of the pressures on the organisations within which they operate, and the political imperatives to which they are subject. As Howe (1991) observed, since most social workers are not freelance practitioners, the organisational context is a vital area for study. The purpose of this chapter is to identify key issues for social services organisations in the early years of the twenty first century. Given that the majority of social workers are employed within statutory social services, there will be a particular emphasis on issues that particularly affect this area of provision.

The chapter will commence by reviewing changes in the delivery of services both for children and adults. Drawing on a range of policy-related literature, the chapter will then explore how the twin dynamics of partnership and performance affect social services organisations, having a major impact on the nature and content of social work practice. It will then reflect on the implications of these changes for social workers and will conclude by arguing that a key requirement for practitioners, now and in the future, will be the capacity to understand and work within their organisational contexts.

Organisational change

In commencing this section, it is important first to understand the dominant organisational form within which social workers have operated since the Local Authority Social Services Act 1968 came into being in 1970, the social services department (SSD). The original intention was that there should be a single point of contact for all people who needed the support of social services, to replace the fragmentation that was held to characterise the previous arrangements. Although Satyamurti (1981) graphically illustrated the problems that the process of forming new organisations created for practitioners, the majority of social workers have been employed within SSDs since this time.

The vision that governed the establishment of SSDs was essentially optimistic, fuelled by substantial increases in resources in the early 1970s. However, the favourable conditions governing public finances did not survive beyond the mid-1970s, and rapidly the new SSDs were forced to restrict expenditure. When the Conservative government was elected in 1979, SSDs had to contend with an ideological assault on the principles that informed their creation (Lymbery, 2004). This naturally impacted upon social workers, who represented the dominant professional voice within these organisations. Indeed, while it could be argued, following Larson (1977), that SSDs provided a secure organisational base within which social work could develop, recent history would suggest that much practice in the statutory setting has been perceived by practitioners as essentially meaningless and without value (Jones, 2001). In addition, the wide-ranging changes which have been proposed appear likely to change the organisational location for social work and, therefore, represent a potential threat.

As Hudson (2005) has indicated, the origins of these shifts are located in a pair of Green Papers relating to services for both children and adults. The death of Victoria Climbié provoked a thorough review of children's services, as numerous failings had been highlighted. In particular, these focused on the lack of coordination of the agencies involved in child protection, failures of collaboration and problems in respect of management and accountability alongside individual practitioner weaknesses, resulting in what was considered to be a highly preventable tragedy. By contrast, as Hudson (2005) notes, the proposed changes in adult social care were not caused by a single dramatic incident but by a general sense that its orientation should change, ensuring that users of services maintain as much control as possible over what they receive.

Given that one of the key problems highlighted by the Climbié case was the poor level of coordination between the different agencies and professionals involved in child protection, it is scarcely surprising that organisational change was high on the government's agenda. The creation of children's trusts is intended to improve coordination of services while also enhancing levels of accountability within child care services. However, as Hudson (2005) observes, there are inherent problems in both these areas, which organisational changes will not necessarily resolve. For example, he points out that genuine integration of front-line services has proved elusive despite numerous attempts to bring this about (see also Hudson, 2002). He also suggests that while the creation of a director of children's services should help to ensure an improved level of leadership and accountability, this will be limited by the fact that other key stakeholders will retain their own channels of management and accountability and, therefore, may not share the same priorities. At the same time, there is uncertainty about the precise roles that social workers will play in these organisations, magnified by the fact that many of these directors may not themselves be qualified social workers.

A similarly uncertain picture affects social work with adults. Given the departure of all services relating to children and families, it seems unlikely that SSDs will remain constituted as they are, particularly because of the emphasis that has been given to the development of partnership working, explored below. The Green Paper on adult social care (DH, 2005a) provides some indications of a changed role for social workers, focusing particularly on their roles in acting as service brokers on behalf of adults with social care needs. However, because the Green Paper is deficient in three specific areas, it is hard to discern what its organisational implications might be. The three problem areas are as follows:

1. The emphasis on an expanded social work role appears to increase the range of tasks that will need to be performed by social workers, yet the Green Paper suggests, somewhat disingenuously, that this can be managed with no additional resources.
2. While the focus on the desires of adults to retain the maximum amount of control over their services is admirable, the Green Paper is silent about the large numbers of service users for whom – for a variety of reasons – such expectations are unlikely to be fulfilled.
3. Yet again, there is no clarity about the organisational arrangements that should govern the changed functions outlined in the White Paper. As a subsequent section will indicate, this is a matter of continuing concern.

The issues highlighted by the final point are given further emphasis by the uncertainty about the policy direction that will follow the Green Paper. The subsequent publication of the White Paper (DH, 2006) did not allay these concerns, as the place of social care in this document was clearly secondary, worked out largely in relation to the dominant requirements of primary health care and containing little that would indicate the preferred organisational shape for social care.

As this brief summary indicates, the prospects for social work with both children and adults are uncertain. It is by no means clear how the detail of the organisational changes outlined above will affect practice. However, it is likely that they will reflect the general tenor of developments on social policy that have characterised the 'New' Labour administration. It is to these developments that the chapter now turns.

 What do you think are the benefits and costs of the reorganisation of children's and adult services?

Modernisation

The social policies of the New Labour government from 1997 have been positioned between approaches associated with either the 'old left' or the 'new right' (Powell, 2000).

This approach has been labelled the 'third way', the governing principle of which is the search for a middle ground between the dominant ideological approaches to welfare that preceded it. A key word that sums up the rhetoric of much social policy is 'modernisation' – the White Paper *Modernising Social Services* (DH, 1998) being a clear example of this. Indeed, understanding the discourse of modernisation is critical to an understanding of how the New Labour government perceives welfare reform. As it is used, the term is meant to invoke much more than simply bringing services up to date; it also conveys several critical rhetorical messages:

- that services were shackled to the past;
- that the past delivery of services was flawed (see DH, 1998);
- that the proposed policy changes represent a decisive break with the past and will result in an improved service.

While it is not certain that the concept of modernisation has any meaning beyond the rhetorical, some commentators have identified themes which connect the various policies which have been launched under this banner (see, for example, Lister, 2001). For example, there has been a pragmatic orientation combined with a strong populist slant, where the government's priority has been the impact that policies might have in electoral terms; the progress of policy in respect of, for example, asylum-seekers, has all the hallmarks of this populism, reflecting an administration that appears too timid to take on a profoundly illiberal and reactionary mood within the country, fomented by key media sources.

While populism has been less directly evident in relation to social services, a number of other consistent themes can be identified. For example, in the 1998 White Paper these were clearly outlined, ranging over protection (including inspection), performance (including standards, regulation and training) and partnership (DH, 1998). For the purposes of this chapter, the themes of partnership and performance will predominate, as they suffuse every aspect of policy and practice within contemporary social services organisations.

The pull of partnership

It has been suggested that 'partnership' has become one of the defining features of New Labour's social policy in general terms (Newman, 2001), with particular reference to the development of policy between health and social care. The proposed policies governing the delivery of services for both children and adults are strongly influenced by notions of partnership. For example, children's trusts will bring together a range of professional groupings that provide services for children and families. Similarly, in respect of services to adults, the NHS Plan (DH, 2000b) emphasised the importance of partnership working between health and social care. The Green Paper on adult social care (DH, 2005a) extended this to include service users, clearly identifying that social workers will need to adopt a different way of working, focusing on their roles in helping to broker services.

In a more general sense, Clarke and Glendinning (2002) have suggested that partnership has become the dominant theme in the delivery of welfare, replacing the emphasis on markets that characterised much of the 1980s and 1990s and the preceding ascendancy of bureaucratic hierarchies. As Hudson (2005) has observed, the key policy documents governing children's and adult services both emphasise the need to improve partnership working and advocate greater degrees of professional integration between social workers and others. In some areas of service – notably mental health and learning disability – integrated professional teams have been in existence for many years; however, this has not been a typical organisational location for most social workers.

While the promotion of more effective partnership working has obvious benefits, some of the difficulties inherent in its development have been inadequately grasped in both practice and theory. For example, partnership requires a high level of cooperation between different organisations, which can be complex given the historically different roles and responsibilities of each. While the goals of organisations may be broadly compatible, each may have pressures that create divergent policy responses. This tendency has been well illustrated by Lewis (2001) in relation to services to older people; she claims that despite the apparently complementary roles of both health and social services, much recent policy can be viewed as an attempt by either side to minimise the pressure on their own budgets by seeking to transfer responsibility to the other – a duel in which the health side has been markedly more successful (for further evidence of this, see O'Hara, 2006). As the following section will demonstrate, this tendency has been exacerbated by the impact of performance measurement. It should not be readily assumed, therefore, that there is a necessary convergence of interest between organisations involved in the provision of services.

These difficulties at the organisational level will also have a direct impact upon professionals. For example, one possible response to the problem of different organisations having incompatible goals might be to merge those organisations into one. This approach was heavily trailed in relation to services to adults in the NHS Plan (DH, 2000b) and appears to underpin the establishment of children's trusts. Yet the creation of a new organisational form creates many problems. For example, an organisation charged with the provision of health and social care might reflect the concerns of health more than social care, adopting a medicalised approach. This would replace the historical problems of joint working with another set of difficulties which could be even more complex to resolve and which could have dire consequences for social workers and service users alike. Social workers would need to carve out an occupational identity within an organisation that is dominated by other priorities. Although SSDs have not been unequivocally positive for social work, they have at least provided a secure and moderately protective organisational location for social workers (Larson, 1977). There are obvious risks in shifting to alternative forms of organisation that will not assume that protective function. This is particularly important when social work remains under attack from sections of the media and where its failings are consequently given maximum attention.

> **?** Think about your own practice, or any other aspect of the delivery of social services: to what extent do principles of partnership underpin this work, and how effective are these principles in practice?

Performance measurement and social services

The inexorable growth of performance measurement has been a key feature of the New Labour approach to the development of the public services (Newman, 2001) and can be seen as a major aspect of managerialist control of such organisations (see Chapter 22). However, its genesis can be traced back to the early 1980s and the reforms instigated by the 'new right' (Carter et al., 1992). While it is accepted that performance measures can have a beneficial effect on service quality (de Bruin, 2002), establishing them within a large multi-purpose organisation is fraught with difficulty. Indeed, a central problem is that performance measurement is often presented as if it is a simple and straightforward task, whereas it is in reality both contestable and complex (Carter et al., 1992). While the Audit Commission has recognised the limitations of target-setting for the public services, it has concluded that 'targets are invaluable and are here to stay' (2003: 2).

As de Bruin (2002) has it, the central notion of performance measurement is simple: the assumption that an organisation can formulate the desired outcomes of its performance and that these can be measured by the development of a set of performance indicators. In respect of social services, the Performance Assessment Framework was centrally established by government and has subsequently been applied to all SSDs since 2002 (CSCI, 2004a). There are two basic justifications for the system that has been developed (Cutler and Waine, 2003):

- that it provides information about performance to a range of key stakeholders, particularly the general public;
- that it provides a mechanism whereby a clear distinction can be drawn between a good and a failing organisation.

The outcomes of this process – as in other parts of the public sector – lead to 'league tables'; for SSDs there has been a system of star ratings. Each organisation was ranked annually on a scale between zero and three stars. If an authority achieved the lowest ratings, it was subjected to particular scrutiny. If it climbed to the highest ratings, it was granted additional freedoms from scrutiny.[1] In general terms, therefore, a key role of the performance-measurement system in social services is to enhance the degree of public accountability.

There are obvious incentives and threats in such a system. While a number of departments have suffered for their apparent poor performance, others have flourished. It could be suggested that the framework is effective in driving up standards of performance but, due to the contested nature of the data collected, such a claim is problematic. In addition, this conclusion is dependent upon another judgement – whether the social services Performance Assessment Framework captures the essence of what social services organisations have to accomplish.

If these two issues are examined in turn, fundamental flaws that lie at the heart of the performance-measurement system in social services can be identified. If we turn to the reliability of the data first, it contains a much greater degree of ambiguity than is generally acknowledged (Cutler and Waine, 2003). For example, both quantitative and qualitative data are collected. The quantitative data derive from a set of performance indicators compiled by each separate department; these are common across all SSDs, so that a level of performance can be assessed against criteria which are applied to each. The qualitative information is derived from reports produced through routine inspections by the Commission for Social Care Inspection (CSCI) and joint reviews, which this body has produced in conjunction with the Audit Commission. A mass of data is therefore utilised in order to produce the apparently straightforward judgement that an organisation merits its star rating. While the general public may well be able to understand what the ratings are supposed to connote, it is highly unlikely to be able to grasp the detailed evidence that produced the judgement, thereby limiting the sense that the process genuinely enhances public accountability.

In a related point, it is unclear that performance indicators accurately reflect actual service, particularly since they have been supplemented by qualitative data that varies in the time it was collected, the people responsible for its collection and interpretation and changing processes whereby the data is both collected and analysed (Cutler and Waine, 2003). By its very nature, performance measurement has to focus particularly on those aspects of service that can be measured, which may not necessarily be the same as those which are most important. The publication of the criteria against which organisations are to be measured, while necessary if that organisation is to focus on steps that need to be taken to bring about improvements, can also create significant unintended consequences.

Examination of just one of the key performance indicators – the provision of practice learning opportunities for social work students (Performance Indicator MR/D59) – illustrates just how such consequences can come into being (CSCI, 2006). While one could not argue with its inclusion – certainly it has eased the life of social work courses which have been hard pressed to provide practice learning opportunities for their students – there have also been negative as well as positive effects of this change. For example, as is typical of performance measurement, only the increased *number* of placements is cited, with no consideration of their *quality*. In addition, it provides an incentive for organisations to include in their returns placements provided in the voluntary and independent sectors, on the basis that some support will be provided to those placements. This doesn't necessarily increase their number, since some were already provided but not previously accounted as part of the department's return. As can readily be seen, the headline figures which are derived from this sort of performance data are subject to various forms of interpretation. Similar calculations can be applied to all the other performance indicators.

The second problem concerns the extent to which performance data accurately reflect the totality of work with which an SSD is engaged. As de Bruin (2002) has suggested, there are a number of perverse effects of performance measurement that can come to dominate its beneficial impact. Many of the issues that de Bruin highlights in this respect are potentially problematic for professionals working within public sector organisations:

- performance measurement can act as an incentive for strategic behaviour by simply focusing on those issues which are measured rather than those which are important to the long-term development of the organisation;
- in this respect, it can also serve to block innovation – it is less likely that time will be dedicated to the enhancement of ambitious and new ways of responding to problems;

- through its focus on the measurable, performance measurement can also serve to obscure the actual performance of organisations, particularly where this has a qualitative dimension (as in the practice of social workers);
- it can also block the development of a 'professional' response to problems, serving to reduce the sense of individual responsibility for quality by emphasising an essentially bureaucratic response.

(de Bruin, 2002)

Further to this, de Bruin (2002) also suggests that there are inherent problems in introducing performance measurement into complex public sector organisations. He indicates that there may be particular problems in organisations which are characterised by high levels of variety in their nature and range of responsibilities, where there is a strong professional presence and where its work is closely intertwined with that of other organisations – all of which characterise statutory social services (see also Munro, 2004). In the latter case he suggests that the *interdependence* of such organisations makes the *independence* of performance measurement highly unfair. Indeed, the problems of inter-agency working have been a consistent theme in many of the critical reviews of social care performance (DfES, 2004), making single agency performance measures particularly problematic. The imperatives of partnership and performance therefore appear to exert contradictory pressures on social services organisations.

 What is the impact of performance measurement on the organisation that employs you?

The nature of organisational life

This section will focus on the specific issues that this generates for social workers working in organisations that experience the twin pressures of partnership and performance. It does not suggest that good practice is impossible due to the effects of these pressures: rather, it argues that an understanding of their nature and the consequent implications for professional social work practice is an essential requirement for a practitioner, however experienced, to be able to function effectively.

In respect of partnership, this chapter has shown that it is increasingly likely the organisational locations that have housed social workers since 1970 will cease to exist in the form that has become accepted. Unified SSDs have attracted numerous criticisms throughout their history, and practitioners need not necessarily mourn their passing. However, they do need to understand the implications of organisational changes for their own practice. One of the most obvious of these is the increased likelihood that social workers will be deployed in formal multidisciplinary teams, alongside a range of other professional groups. Since this has been commonplace in specific work settings for many years, the consequences of this are far from disastrous. Indeed, the clarity that social workers need to develop about their specific contribution to the pattern of services could be a beneficial consequence of such a development. However, there are also numerous potential pitfalls in partnership working of which social workers need to be aware (Hudson, 2002). For example, the impact of differential levels of power and status has bedevilled the history of social work in health care and the relationship between social workers and doctors has, historically, been fraught. In addition, it should not readily be assumed that there exists a 'cultural' compatibility between the different professions that are constrained to work together (Lymbery, 2005). There are numerous ways in which this conflict could be experienced by practitioners; in learning how to manage these conflicts, it will be worth their while to ponder on the nature of organisations as locations of conflict (Morgan, 1997).

The pressures caused by performance measurement create another type of problem for practitioners. As many of the measures that are deployed – for example, the numbers of carer's assessments that are carried out – are simplistically formulated (Munro, 2004) and dependent upon the actions of front-line practitioners, it can reasonably be expected that that these sorts of actions will be (at the very least) strongly encouraged, potentially skewing other priorities that might exist. It is easy for practitioners to become cynical about the way their work becomes dominated by priorities over which they have little direct control, but lapsing into cynicism is an inadequate response to these circumstances. The obligations that social workers have to those who need services dictate a more positive, proactive response. This will entail clarity about the professional roles and responsibilities that social workers fulfil (noted above in the context of partnership). It also requires an acceptance that the organisation has priorities which are dictated by the requirements of performance measurement, accompanied by a refusal to accept those priorities as necessarily an appropriate guide for social work practice.

Conclusion

This chapter has concentrated on the changing priorities that govern organisations that employ social workers in large numbers. It has discussed the way in which the organisational locations of social workers are in the process of change and has identified the parallel thrusts towards partnership and performance as the factors that dominate the organisational landscape. Its focus has been diagnostic in its nature, with no attempt to outline in any detail the ways in which social workers can best manage to negotiate these organisational contexts in such a way that keeps their values and integrity alive. (This will be the focus of many other chapters in this part.) However, the chapter is written from a relatively straightforward perspective: that it is possible to maintain good social work practice in the changing organisational contexts within which social workers are employed, but that to do so requires an understanding of the structure and priorities of those organisations. As noted earlier, the majority of social workers have never been independent, autonomous practitioners in the British context. This is not liable to change; as a result, the ability to understand the nature of the organisation within which one is employed and to identify strategies that can protect good-quality practice becomes an urgent priority for practitioners.

Key learning points

1. The organisational location of social workers is changing as large SSDs are gradually broken up.
2. The governance of social work has changed in line with the 'modernisation' strategy of the New Labour administration.
3. Social services organisations are affected by two parallel developments: the pull of partnership and the increase in performance measurement.
4. Both have a significant impact on social work practice, but neither should be unquestioningly accepted by practitioners.
5. To be effective, social workers have to be capable of both understanding and functioning within their organisational locations.

Taking it further

Readers who want to know more about this will find the following helpful:
de Bruin, H. (2002) *Managing Performance in the Public Sector*, London: Routledge.
Glendinning, C., Powell, M. and Rummery, K. (eds) (2002) *Partnerships, New Labour and the Governance of Welfare*, Bristol: Policy Press.
Newman, J. (2001) *Modernising Governance: New Labour, Policy and Society*, London: Sage.

Note

1. Given the changes in the organisational structures of social work, the detail of performance measurement will have changed by the time of publication. The above system applied up to and including 2005/06.

18 Continuous professional development

Helen Gorman and Mark Lymbery

This chapter will:

- explore social workers' continuous professional development (CPD);
- concentrate on formal systems of post-qualification education and training;
- examine the conceptual and practical issues that must be addressed to maximise the effectiveness of post-qualification education and training.

Introduction

This chapter explores numerous issues and dilemmas in pursuing a policy of continuous professional education for social workers in public sector organisations, using a case study approach. At the outset, definitions of key terms are given and their contested meanings explored, since differences in interpretations of terminology are critical in determining which outcomes will prevail. Then the context of post-qualifying training for social work is examined, taking into account the intentions of the GSCC in establishing this framework (GSCC, 2005a). The case study focuses on a social worker who undertakes training in interprofessional work and returns to her employer agency to implement it. Analysis in the case study integrates two perspectives:

1. that of the social worker who is keen to develop herself;
2. that of the organisation providing training opportunities for its workforce – which can be compromised by a range of factors.

As the chapter will demonstrate, these perspectives are not necessarily always compatible. The discussion centres on learning methods and approaches, the evaluation and transfer of learning and the organisation's support for training in the context of national policy directives of audit and target-setting for health and social care delivery. The chapter focuses on using formal opportunities for post-qualification training to facilitate development; in this respect it differs from Chapter 19, which takes a more general approach.

Key terms and meanings

It is important first to define and explore the meanings behind some of the terms that have become commonplace:

- *Lifelong learning* is a concept that means individual involvement in education throughout life rather than just in the period of childhood; emphasis is placed on individual adults taking control of their own learning. However, as the case study demonstrates, the practical application of such an idea can be fraught with problems.
- In a *learning organisation*, problems are seen as indicators of changes that might be needed; learning processes are linked to work and directed towards developing the potential of 'learning to learn'. The extent to which large social services organisations have moved in this direction is questionable: for example, the idea of learning from – or even acknowledging – mistakes is problematic where their existence promotes blame and public censure.
- As used in this chapter, *CPD* involves the systemic maintenance, improvement and broadening of knowledge and skill and the development of personal qualities to carry out the work role (Walsh and Woodward, 1989). The link between the personal and the professional is endorsed by Eraut (1994), who believes that CPD relates both to formally organised educational events and work-based learning, while continuing professional education relates only to the former.

Educational frameworks for social work

One key characteristic of social work and its education is the desire for change, development and improvement, at pre-qualifying, qualifying and post-qualifying levels. For example, at the pre-qualifying level, the framework of National Vocational Qualifications (NVQs) was introduced in the 1980s, with the aim of improving the standards of workers in a range of occupations. Standards were defined at five levels, each expressing a higher level of performance than the one beneath it. All were designed on the basis of a binary scale, where the practitioner was defined as competent or not yet competent (Jessup, 1991). In social care settings, it is now common for workers to possess NVQs, and the range of training available for staff without professional qualifications has increasingly reflected their influence.

More controversially, social work education at qualifying level has also emphasised the notion of competence, which was the bedrock of the Diploma in Social Work (DipSW). While the idea of competence does have its attractions – nobody would suggest that social workers should be incompetent! – it is inadequate as an organising principle for a professional occupation (Eraut, 1994). Implicitly, the limitations of this appear to be recognised in the new framework for qualifying training, introduced in 2002, with enhanced academic requirements and greater recognition of the need for practitioners to exercise autonomy and discretion (Eadie and Lymbery, forthcoming). The need for higher levels of creativity as practitioners progress through their careers is emphasised by the fact that the post-qualifying framework for social work is pitched at postgraduate level (GSCC, 2005a). Here, practitioners are expected to demonstrate higher levels of both academic and practice attainment and can receive awards at three levels – specialist, higher specialist and advanced. Academically, social workers will be expected to operate within the general framework for M-level courses (QAA, 2001), stressing the need for the exercise of autonomy, discretion and judgement. As far as practice standards are concerned, these will include the ability to demonstrate characteristics such as 'independent critical judgement', alongside the facility to work in much more creative and innovative ways, for example, through 'a fully developed capacity to take responsibility for the use of reflection and critical analysis' and through the ability 'to work creatively and effectively […] in a context of risk, uncertainty, conflict and contradiction' (GSCC, 2005a: 19–20). The framework of 'competence', first applied to NVQs and later to qualification training for social work, is clearly inadequate in relation to CPD. As a result, it is recognised that qualified social workers need to move beyond competence to capability or expertise (Eraut, 1998) and that post-qualifying educational courses in social work should support that shift.

 To what extent is your experience of training or practice consistent with the above analysis?

Taken together, the educational frameworks for pre-qualifying, qualifying and post-qualifying levels in social work imply a progression from working in accordance with prescribed routines to the assumption of greater levels of responsibility and discretion as a practitioner progresses. This can be represented as shown in Figure 18.1.

In this conception, it is assumed that the more experienced the practitioner the more he or she will be working with the unpredictable and complex, requiring a high order of skills. By contrast, practitioners at an early stage in their career are likely to work with more predictable and relatively straightforward work. The diagonal line from X to Y represents an individual practitioner's progress through social work, with educational opportunities ideally linked to practice requirements at different stages of development. As will become clear through the case study, this idealised conception of professional development can be affected by numerous factors.

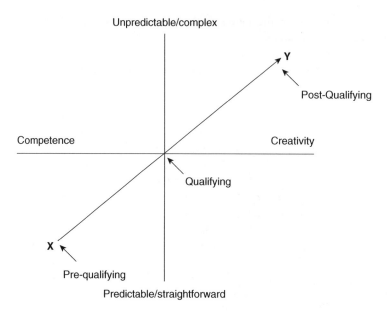

Figure 18.1 Practitioner's progress through social work education.

Source: Eadie and Lymbery, forthcoming.

Case study

Nkem is a senior practitioner within a child care team in a city area, expected to take a lead in the development of practice within her locality. She is aware of government policy that encourages more holistic child care. She would like to attend an interdisciplinary course that leads to an MA and an advanced post-qualifying award related to working interprofessionally in child care. Nkem, who is a thirty-eight-year-old Black woman, completed a degree and a DipSW eight years ago as a mature student. However, her line manager is unenthusiastic about the course, giving the reasons, first, that there are not the resources to release her on a course of this length and intensity, and, second, there is an organisational preference for shorter, specialist-level courses that more staff could attend. Nkem feels let down because at her annual performance review it was recorded on the appraisal form that she would benefit from taking advantage of post-qualifying opportunities.

Case study analysis

A difference in perspective between practitioners and their employing organisation is common. One problem is that the organisation's training strategy may not equate to the needs of an individual employee: for example, it is almost certain to be affected by considerations of cost. The impact of this can be critical; if practitioners feel that their needs are not being met by a superficially organised system of post-qualifying education, they may become demoralised and cynical about their work.

CPD and workforce issues: the organisational perspective

Traditional approaches to training within social services can be criticised for failure to link training with organisational objectives. This requires two related stages:

1. clarity about what these objectives actually are;
2. in the light of this, decisions about the forms of education and training which are required to help bring these changes about.

   As we have already observed, most social services organisations need social workers who are capable of flexibility in their practice; as a result, strategies for CPD need to focus on a collection of attributes: attitudes, behaviour, knowledge, understanding and commitment. A strategic approach to training involves activities and processes that assist in aligning training to the stated aims and objectives of the organisation. The commitment of senior management is also essential in this strategic approach, as is the capacity to take a 'long view' about the organisation's development. However, this is problematic in the volatile environment of social services, riven by frequent reorganisations, an adherence to mechanistic forms of performance management (see Chapter 17) and beset by a combination of staff shortages and high levels of sickness (Lymbery, 2004). In this context, it becomes difficult to maintain a strategic focus on staff development, with staff often sent on training programmes in an apparently random and unsystematic way. However, certain approaches – including training needs analysis, skills audits and formal training appraisals – are more likely to facilitate strategic integration of training with an organisation's objectives.

 To what extent does your own workplace take a strategic view of staff development?

Case study analysis

The case study above illustrates some of these dilemmas. Nkem has seen an opportunity to develop herself and to add value to the organisation. She is aware of the interdisciplinary nature of her work and is interested in becoming more skilled in this area. However, her employers may be paying lip-service to this agenda while in reality favouring training which is more limited in scope and job-specific – and, not at all coincidentally, less expensive. Their main concern may be immediate outcomes translated into statistical returns; in addition, they may develop an undifferentiated policy whereby all staff are offered a standardised approach, irrespective of need. While Nkem is seeking to adopt a lifelong learning approach, the agency seems to be offering training opportunities which are inconsistent with such an approach: more restricted, driven by cost, contingency and reaction to competing policy demands rather than harnessing both the personal and professional development of employees. In addition, Nkem's race and gender are factors that relate to selection for training and to support for CPD.

Lifelong learning and the learning organisation

Attempts to make identifiable links between training and education and the world of work are fraught with complexity and some wishful thinking. They are a particular challenge at levels of complex professional activity such as social work, which incorporates an intricate balance of skills, values and knowledge. If this is not managed well, there can be serious consequences for the practitioner, as Tight (1998) indicates. The notion of lifelong learning implies some flexibility, control and choice on the part of the individual learner developing him/herself through the life stages. Yet all education and training for social work – from pre-qualification to post-qualification – has been configured in a paradigm that emphasises accreditation, certification and fitness for purpose: an employer-led agenda. As a result, while employees may actively plan their own development – as Nkem has sought to do – it is ultimately the employer, through senior staff, who will manage the direction of their learning and the skills that they value. An educational process needs to be developed which is not dictated solely by employer-led outcomes but which also considers the personal development needs of employees as people who wish to contribute to the welfare project through their work capacity.

Case study (continued)

Nkem is asked to submit details of her preferred post-qualifying accredited course. However, the senior training manager also favours a child care post-qualifying course which is specifically designed to meet the organisation's needs and is at a lower level of academic attainment and, hence, less costly. He considers that her favoured course is not an effective use of resources, although he acknowledges that Nkem has a key role in developing interprofessional working.

The adult learner and CPD

As discussed in more detail in Chapter 19, Kolb and Fry's (1975) experiential learning theory places emphasis on the centrality of experience in the learning process. The four-stage experiential-learning cycle represents learning as a continuous pattern of experience based on reflection, theory-building, theory-testing and new experience (see Figure 19.1 on p. 203).

Learning can begin at any stage of the cycle: learners rely upon personal experience and reflection in order to constantly construct and modify the various concepts, rules and principles necessary to guide behaviour in new situations. This process relies on the understandings that underpin the notion of andragogy, an adult learning theory established by Knowles (1984) which is characterised by the principles of self-directedness in the learning process, the fundamental importance of experience and the need for adults to learn things of personal relevance. According to this theory, adults have a strong need to apply what they have learned and therefore learn better using problem-based rather than subject-centred approaches; this thinking has been successfully applied to social work by Burgess (1992).

Learners in a group will have differing personalities, experiences, personal orientations, motivations and learning styles. From his experiential learning theory Kolb (1984) developed the Learning Style Inventory to identify four learning styles. While most individuals will display characteristics of the four styles, one style tends to be dominant, although this preference can be affected by contextual variations – changes in work setting, promotion, etc. Honey and Mumford (1989) built on Kolb's work and developed a slightly different version of the Learning Style Inventory which reflected managerial activities. To enhance CPD, learning styles need to be considered to ensure that employees learn effectively.

Case study analysis

A key issue for Nkem – as with any applicant to a post-qualification programme – is whether the approach to learning adopted on the course suits her particular learning style and offers her the opportunities she seeks. A key reason why Nkem wishes to persuade her line manager and the senior training manager that the chosen course is both relevant to her training needs and the requirements of her job is related to this, as she understand the methods of the course to be consonant with her own preferred learning styles – founded as it is on the principles of problem-based learning.

Case study (continued)

After considerable negotiation, Nkem gets permission to attend the course. Because of the compatibility between her preferred learning style and the approach within the course, she is enabled to understand how she can improve her practice. Through systematic use of reflection, she is able to incorporate new knowledge into her thinking and to experiment with a more creative approach to practice. Through the interprofessional nature of the course, she has benefited from learning with a peer group that has expertise different from her own. In addition, the orientation of the course to problem-based learning proves an additional form of stimulation. She is concerned, however, to ensure that her learning on the course is transferred to practice and that she has some way of evaluating that this process has taken place.

Developing skills and knowledge for continuing professional development and transferring them to practice

At complex levels of practice inherent in post-qualification levels of work (as expressed in Figure 18.1) the critical element in decision-making is professional judgement. This concept underpins the work of Schön (1987), which has been heavily used by educators and training bodies in attempting to square the circle between competency-based programmes and a more fluid response recognising the significance of personal learning (Gould and Taylor, 1996; Gould and Baldwin, 2004).

As we have earlier pointed out, at post-qualification level it is expected that social workers have skills and knowledge that relate to understanding problems in context, and can exercise creativity in practice. It is the handling of non-routine matters, of complex situations involving a number of competing agendas, that test the skills of the social worker in a climate of uncertainty and change. The issue of transferability of skills is highly significant in ensuring that continuing personal and professional development becomes a reality for social workers. Professional knowledge cannot be characterised in a manner that is independent of how it is learned and used; such knowledge is constructed through experience, and its nature depends upon the cumulative acquisition, selection and interpretation of that experience.

A key issue is whether training can be evaluated to find out if it has been effective. The problem is that an evaluation is often not done, or, when it does take place, no critical approach is adopted or specific model used. The most frequent method of evaluation tends to be the 'happy sheet' handed out at the end of a training programme asking participants about their reaction to the training. The Kirkpatrick (1967) model, which proposes four levels of evaluation, is an effective tool that could be valuable in the evaluation of social work training:

1. Level 1 examines how participants felt about the training;
2. Level 2 looks at what was learned;
3. Level 3 investigates any on-the-job behaviour changes;
4. Level 4 assesses the tangible results of the training.

While this model is a realistic evaluation of training, acknowledging that information relating to Levels 1 and 2 will be generally obtainable, Level 3 and, particularly, Level 4 need to be applied within a robust system of practice development that can effectively track outcomes and take account of the many variables that can exist in determining those outcomes. The model also implies that evaluation is most effective if carried out over time, rather than as an immediate response to a training event – thereby challenging the value of the aforementioned 'happy sheet'.

 Can you think of any occasions when your practice has been changed by an educational experience? What is the most effective way of ensuring that courses can be evaluated over time?

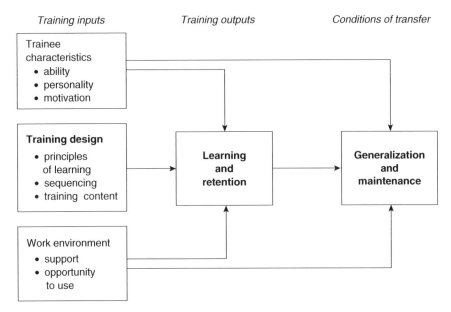

Figure 18.2   Continuous professional development in social work.

Source: adapted from Baldwin and Ford's (1988) transfer of training model.

Baldwin and Ford's (1988) model (Figure 18.2) provides a framework for understanding the transfer of learning to practice. Two key environmental factors, *social support* and *opportunity to use*, are identified as impacting on learning and retention as well as the transfer of such learning to the workplace. The utility of this model is that it places education and training within the context both of the characteristics of the learner and the environment within which that worker practises. Both of these factors impact upon training at three points: how the training is designed, what outputs it has and how its learning can be transferred into practice.

There is a limited understanding of the environmental factors that impact on the effectiveness of training. Supervisory and peer support prior to the training give a message that it is important; it is likely that trainees with supportive supervisors will be more motivated to learn. Supervisors can show support by discussing training opportunities with the employee, establishing training goals, providing release time to prepare and generally encouraging the employee. Post-training support is equally important if learning is to be transferred to the workplace. However, workgroup support, in the form of norms and group pressure, can have either a positive or a negative impact on the transfer of learning. While the positive elements of this may be self-evident, the potential for a negative effect does exist. For example, highly motivated and competent employees may actually reduce their standards if conformity with the group norms contains the message that training is a waste of time and, hence, discourages the transfer of learning. Also, constraining group norms can have an impact on *opportunity* to use training by preventing or allowing the individual to feel comfortable to perform trained tasks.

Case study (concluded)

Nkem starts to use her new knowledge and skills in practice. She offers to run a seminar for her colleagues to disseminate aspects of her learning and sets up a learning-support group with other members of the course. At first, her line manager does not appear to appreciate the value of Nkem's professional development, but gradually, through supervision sessions that focus on problem-solving related to interprofessional work, her line manager becomes aware of the value of the course and encourages another member of the team to apply for it.

Case study analysis

Nkem requires a supervisor who will support her in applying her new skills in practice (see Chapter 21). She also needs peer-group support to reinforce good practice and to talk through practice issues. It is vital to examine the organisational context within which training exists. A positive learning culture appears to encourage the application of newly trained behaviours. There are a variety of workplace factors exerting an influence on training effectiveness, such as short-term financial targets, day-to-day pressures at work and lack of time for planning. Other barriers include organisational politics and hidden agendas, the physical structure of the organisation, responsibility issues and performance criteria. In addition, the structures and priorities of social services organisations can obstruct the development of such a culture (see Chapter 17).

Gorman (2003) has described research into the experiences of learners on a post-qualification programme in social work. The research examined the narratives of care managers who were post-qualification students on a programme aimed at enhancing skills for their practice; it explored the transfer of learning to the workplace. The research supported the contention that the relationship between work and learning relies on the use of process skills as well as functional ones. Pattern recognition in the sense of developing expertise in work relates to the ability to adjust to new circumstances in a climate of uncertainty. The skills involved amount to a combination of professional knowledge, situational knowledge and judgement, in a context where it is unlikely that there is one single correct answer. However, evidence from this research endorses the view that the subtleties of the patterns of skills necessary for social work at post-qualification level are often unrecognised by employers. Attempts to adopt frameworks to create a balance between the self-development of social workers and organisational need should recognise the conflicts inherent within the systems that predominate in public sector organisations (Gorman, 2003).

The transfer of learning from the relative safety of academia to the world of practice is tricky. Crucially, it was found that the skills identified as important for the social work role are the very skills that enable such a transfer to take place (Gorman, 2003). This endorses Eraut's (1994) view that an essential element in a process of continuing personal development is 'learning to learn'. The continuous upgrading of knowledge and skills necessary to keep pace with changing demands is related to the capacity to analyse problems, negotiate issues and make predictions. Engagement in critical thinking and reasoning to make connections between familiar and new situations relates to a deeper understanding that often takes some time to evolve and may be counter-cultural in many workplaces, where increased domain knowledge has become a priority and where there is little time for CPD.

Conclusion

As indicated in Chapter 17, the organisational framework that governs social work in the public sector is in a process of reconstruction, making it essential that practitioners manage their own careers. The best way to enable this process through CPD has to be a matter of debate. The reconciling of personal development strategies with the need to meet organisational demands requires a shift of understanding about the nature of professional education and the relationship between welfare work and the wider society. A paradigm shift may be required that rejects segmentation and fixed boundaries in favour of a broader interpretation of continuous professional development, recognising a negotiated relationship between the organisation, the worker and users of the service.

In the context of learning for health and welfare service, a market model that emphasises outputs is inappropriate. It can be argued that the learning society needs to be rooted and nourished by the civil virtues of active citizenship (as outlined in Chapter 2), as opposed to consumerist rights. A knowledge base for social work that includes general principles such as empowerment needs to be constantly re-examined and reinvented in the light of the experiences of the people whose welfare it is intended to enhance. Continuous education that puts interdisciplinary effort and collaborative enterprise centre stage can add value for organisations committed to improving the quality of service outcomes. Shifting professional identities and the potential impact of the rights and responsibilities of citizens in mapping out their own futures is part of a contemporary and changing landscape that demands interdisciplinary work and collaborative effort by staff at all levels. CPD requires linkages to be established and sustained between users of services, educationalists, practitioners and managers. Such connections, while they may be espoused, need to be made real at both qualifying and post-qualifying levels of training and beyond. As skill and knowledge requirements shift and become more fluid, education and training have to keep abreast of these changes. CPD involves the systematic maintenance, improvement and broadening of knowledge and skill and the development of personal qualities to carry out the work role. The starting place is to harness the enthusiasm of employees within the inevitable confines of budgetary and organisational reality. This is no easy task but can be aided by a systematic evaluation of training needs relating to organisational mission.

This is made problematic by the recognition that the search for certainty and the avoidance of risk remain dominant within social services. As a result, employees, educational courses and social services organisations constantly have to prove their worth through audit. This cultivates a climate which can be antipathetic to CPD. However, as outlined in Chapter 4, nurturing the skills of critical reflection can help practitioners to operate in flexible and creative ways.

Key learning points

1. Training strategies should link to the organisational mission, and this process should be transparent and understood by employees.
2. Approaches to training should be evaluated for their relevance for individual employees as well as for meeting organisational needs.
3. Greater recognition is required of the ways in which educational models and methods can be devised to enable practitioners to work in complex situations.
4. Staff performance and appraisal systems should be linked to training and developmental approaches that recognise different learning styles of employees.
5. Agencies should be proactive rather than reactive in managing resources, recognising the need to improve the quality of staff.
6. A learning organisation will receive learners back into the workforce who can enhance organisational effectiveness through critical evaluation and debate.

Taking it further

Readers who want to know more about this will find the following helpful:

Burgess, H. (1992) *Problem-Led Learning for Social Work*, London: Whiting and Birch.

Eraut, M. (1994) *Developing Professional Knowledge and Competence,* London: Falmer Press.

Schön, D. (1987) *Educating the Reflective Practitioner: Towards a New Design for Teaching and Learning in the Professions,* San Francisco, CA: Jossey-Bass.

19 Professional development in the workplace

Tina Eadie

> This chapter outlines a range of models and frameworks that can contribute to a social work practitioner's professional development in the workplace. These include:
>
> - the concept of adult learning and the development of self-knowledge;
> - team role theory;
> - interpersonal conflict;
> - power in teams;
> - stress management.

Introduction

While good organisational structures for qualifying and post-qualifying education and training are an essential component of effective practice development (see Chapter 18), professional development requires social work practitioners to take responsibility for managing themselves as professionals in the work setting. This chapter discusses a range of factors that contribute towards this. It outlines frameworks and models that can assist workers in identifying the professional dimension of working with people – both as colleagues and service users – and in managing the pressures of a role.

The chapter offers what for some will be a reminder and for others additional tools to develop and retain skills required to not only survive but also to thrive in the workplace. It is based on the premise that social work practitioners who take responsibility for their own professional development – supported by sound supervisory structures (see Chapter 21) – will be better prepared for the challenges of changing organisational and policy contexts and ever-shifting operational needs and demands. It assumes an understanding and appreciation of reflective practice and its contribution to professional development (see Schön,

1991; Fook, 2002) and of the value of professional judgement alongside more 'technical' and prescribed aspects of the role.

Professional development is an ongoing process whereby individuals increase their understanding of how best to respond to situations and dilemmas presenting in the course of their work. It involves managing personal and professional tensions, such as those created when the meeting of managerial targets does not reflect the needs of individual service users (see Chapter 17), or when the more controlling and prescribed aspects of practice leave little room for creativity. Critically, it encourages the use of discretion and judgement when the particular circumstances of a case requires this, while retaining full accountability to service users, employers and the wider community for decision-making.

The ability to stand back from day-to-day policy and practice considerations and to reflect on the work in its wider context is a key aspect of professional development. Reflection outside of formal supervisory structures develops the so-called 'internal supervisor' in which the individual holds him or herself to personal account. Reflective professional practice entails the seeking out of opportunities to develop new and appropriate knowledge and skills to fit a changing practice context, while at the same time holding on to fundamental principles and values regarding work with people (see Banks, 2004; Beckett and Maynard, 2005). This requires a commitment and openness to learning. The chapter therefore starts from the perspective of learning in the workplace, including the concept of adult learning and the development of self-knowledge. In the light of this, it goes on to review a range of theories, styles and strategies that can prevent or at least help unblock factors that hinder professional development in the workplace, focusing particularly on team role theory, interpersonal conflict, power dynamics and stress management.

Learning and self-knowledge

Work and learning are inextricably linked; continuing to learn and to increase personal and professional effectiveness benefits not only the individual and his or her employing organisation but also contributes towards being a part of general education for citizenship and fuller participation in society as a whole (Boud and Garrick, 1999). Learning for the workplace takes place both formally and informally; qualifying and post-qualifying training provides a base line of knowledge, skills, values and competencies, but the extent to which practitioners continue to learn and develop throughout their careers depends on a variety of factors. Two considered here are, first, an individual's knowledge and understanding about the *process* of learning and, second, their ability to be *open* to learning and develop self-awareness.

Learning is an active process and Kolb's (1984) work is popularly used to demonstrate the cyclical nature of experiential learning. The familiar learning cycle outlined in Figure 19.1 suggests that individuals need to engage in four activities for effective learning to take place.

The cycle can be entered from any point, most often following a concrete experience – doing something – which for those open to learning leads to observations and reflections on the experience. These enhance the formation of concepts and generalisations that can

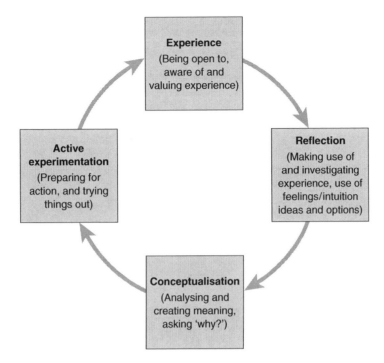

Figure 19.1   The Kolb learning cycle.

be tested in new situations and provide the building blocks of sound judgement. Honey and Mumford (1989) linked this cycle to preferences for different learning styles, the more active stages of experience and experimentation contrasting to those of reflection and conceptualisation. Morrison's analysis (1993: 50–59) can be usefully drawn upon to identify how workers preferring a certain style might become stuck in this part of the cycle and to provide a checklist of strategies to help them move on. For example, a worker blocked at reflection might be strong on ideas but feeling too anxious to translate them into actions where they can be tested. Strategies that focus more on doing than feeling are required here.

In addition to understanding the process of learning, therefore, a key part of professional development is self-knowledge or self-awareness (see Thompson, 2002: 3–11). This can be expanded by the 'Johari Window', a framework developed by two American psychologists Joseph Luft and Harry Ingham (Luft and Ingham, 1955). The model can help people to recognise differences between their self-perception and others' perception of them, thereby increasing their own awareness of the effect they have on others. The basic window is made up of four quadrants, outlined in Figure 19.2.

Quadrant 1, the 'Open' area, represents information about ourselves – such as personality, attitudes and behaviours – which are known to us and known to others because we feel

	Known to self	Unknown to self
Known to others	1 Open	2 Unaware
Unknown to others	3 Hidden	4 Unknown

Figure 19.2   Johari Window: basic model.

able to share them. There are also facets of ourselves which others see but we do not – the 'Unaware' area in Quadrant 2. Constructive feedback can usefully open up this area. There are other facets we keep 'Hidden' (Quadrant 3) until we feel more at ease with the people and situation we find ourselves in. Quadrant 4, the 'Unknown' area, represents potential skills that neither we nor others can see. Increasing Quadrant 1 develops the 'Open' area – our self-knowledge – as demonstrated in Figure 19.3.

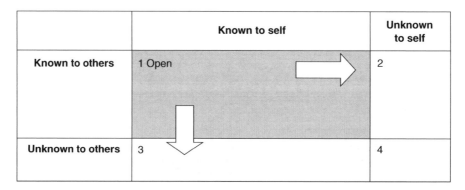

Figure 19.3   Johari Window: opening up self-knowledge.

This can be achieved through asking for feedback informally from colleagues and more formally from line managers in supervision and through being more open about ourselves in the workplace. This is not always a comfortable process but is one that encourages constant reappraisal of our approach, its appropriateness and overall effectiveness.

 Have you ever asked for feedback on your performance (from a line manager, colleague or service user), and what did this contribute to your self-knowledge?

Just as developing self-knowledge can be potentially uncomfortable at times, recognising the need for new learning leads to another cyclical process which can have an initially deskilling effect. This is outlined in Box 19.1.

Box 19.1   Developing competence.

Stage 1   **Unconscious incompetence**: we do not know what it is we do not know.

Stage 2   **Conscious incompetence**: we begin to realise what and how much we do not know.

Stage 3   **Conscious competence**: we learn something new and think through each step consciously.

Stage 4   **Unconscious competence**: we know something so well that the steps of reasoning are internalised.

Stage 1 equates to the phrase 'ignorance is bliss': we are unaware of how much we do not know and need to learn before the new theoretical understandings can be assimilated into our practice. Stage 2 can occur at any time when new learning takes place but is most likely to occur in qualifying training – especially for those who have been in paid employment for some time and start the training feeling reasonably confident. The challenge for professional development is to regularly undertake new experiences and learning for which one's existing knowledge base is inadequate in order to expand and develop knowledge and skills. Taking time to reflect after new learning will help to both highlight and fill gaps in knowledge uncovered by new experiences. In this way, Stage 3 draws on Schön's (1991) concept of 'reflection-on-action' as individuals begin to learn what to look for and how to respond to what they find, to develop theories, and to test them out. Schön's concept of 'reflection-*in*-action' links Stages 3 and 4: individuals reflect on the best way of doing something while doing it and make any necessary adjustments. This can be illustrated with the following example: 'When good jazz musicians improvise together, they also manifest a 'feel for' their material and they make on-the-spot adjustments to the sounds they hear. Listening to one another and to themselves, they feel where the music is going and adjust their playing accordingly' (Schön, 1991: 54).

While the third stage is conscious, reflection at the fourth stage is increasingly unconscious as practitioners internalise the learning that has taken place and begin to 'improvise' automatically on their practice. Although this 'speeds up' the reflective process and is therefore important for busy workers, it makes theoretical knowledge less immediately accessible and, as a result, less available to explain or justify decision-making. A valuable way for experienced practitioners to avoid this is to supervise students regularly or to mentor newly qualified staff (acknowledging the impositions on time and team resources that this entails).

Can you identify the above stages in relation to your own practice development and place yourself at one of the stages currently?

Team learning

Just as Schön's jazz musicians adjust the direction of the music that is developing out of their interwoven contributions, individuals in teams can work together in ways that will ensure the collective effort. Jonny Wilkinson, fly-half star of the England rugby union team, is quoted as saying, 'I may be the person who puts the points on the board but all those points are the product of hard work by others' (cited in Kakabadse et al., 2004: 76). The professional development of individuals then can be enhanced by team development. Teams can achieve a synergy in which output exceeds the sum total of each member's capabilities, and a high-functioning team in which members are playing to their strengths will provide them with 'added value' in terms of increased job satisfaction and reduced stress.

Research into team behaviour suggests that the success of a team depends upon its balance of specific roles and members' ability and willingness to transfer between them (Belbin, 1993). Improvisation in a team, therefore, requires its members to be able to identify their own preferred role, to understand how that fits with other roles, and to find ways in which gaps can be filled. Belbin's team role theory originally proposed that successful teams are composed of people who collectively share a capacity to work in eight different roles. Box 19.2 identifies these (adapted from Kakabadse et al., 2004: 84–5). Although these roles may not be as fixed as implied here, Belbin's theory has continuing relevance, particularly as – increasingly – social workers are located in multidisciplinary teams.

Box 19.2   Belbin team roles.

Shapers   High achievers, demonstrating drive and creativity. Able to unite a group's effort but can be abrasive and prone to fall out with people.

Coordinators   Also known as 'Chairperson', coordinators can bond and energise a newly formed team by establishing a sense of purpose and ensuring that all members are involved. Good team managers, able to bring out the best in people, often take this role.

Plants   Contribute original and creative thinking to a team with their breadth of vision and ability to solve difficult problems. Despite good ideas, they can be poor at following them through and careless with detail.

(Continued)

Resource Investigators   Keeps the team in touch with the 'outside world' through taking a lively interest in things that are taking place outside of the team. They are rarely in the office and, when they are, are likely to be on the phone or surfing the internet. They quickly lose interest in projects, preferring to work up new ideas.

Monitor Evaluators   Can be critical and ready to find fault in the behaviour of others. More positively, they bring an objective approach which can prevent the team from making bad decisions or committing itself to unworkable projects.

Implementers   Also called 'Company Workers', implementers are practical and organised, methodical and systematic, reliable, responsible and hard-working. They can be somewhat inflexible and can be thrown by sudden changes, but they take ideas generated by other team members and turn them into manageable tasks.

Team Workers   The glue that binds members together by bringing friendliness, sensitivity and caring to the team. Although tending to be indecisive in 'crunch' situations, team workers bring harmony as they listen to others and help smooth over friction between other members.

Completers   Also known as 'Finishers', every team needs at least one for follow-through, reliability and completion of tasks. They bring a conscientious approach to quality and standards of performance. Their attention to detail and inclination to worry unduly can create problems for them personally.

The brief descriptions demonstrate the variety of roles which, together, can help a team succeed in the workplace. No one role is 'better' than another – it is the mix and balance of roles that ensures success. Team members' awareness of their 'most preferred' team role can highlight individual contributions to the team and help explain team dynamics. For example, Shapers are likely to challenge the ideas of others but can benefit from the assertive 'steer' of a Coordinator manager, can appreciate dynamic colleagues who will not be offended by their somewhat 'pushy' style (such as the Resource Investigator), nor feel threatened by their creativity and generation of ideas (for example, the Team Worker). The originality and creativity of the Plant, on the other hand, is likely to be ignored or 'squeezed out' by the powerful Shaper role.

 Are you aware of your preferred 'team role' and those of your colleagues and how these impact on the distribution and completion of tasks within your team?

Team role theory can also contribute towards professional development by highlighting an individual's second 'preferred' role and 'least preferred' team role. For example, if there is no Implementer in the team and a routine task is not being done, it is useful to be able to identify a person who scores fairly high on Implementer or Completer/Finisher to follow through on a task. Conversely, as part of an individual's professional development, he or she could take on a 'least preferred' role: for example, a strong Shaper could take responsibility for seeing through a particular team task and for ensuring all the team are in agreement with its implementation. Such exercises encourage openness about preferences and strengths and highlight for individuals what they and others bring to the team, and why certain team members feel less tolerant of some colleagues and work better with others. However useful these might be for professional development purposes, team role theory focuses on the *balance* between roles rather than the power distributed between the role-holders or the conflicts that this can produce. Power and conflict are therefore two further areas that need to be considered.

Power and conflict

Power in teams, as with organisations, is likely to reflect the distribution of power within society: those with more have the ability to influence or control people, events, processes or resources to a greater extent than those with less. Power, while acknowledged as a complex concept (Foucault, 1984), is a central feature of the struggle to promote equality (Thompson, 2003: 45) with the way it operates tending to follow recognizable patterns. Being part of the dominant organisational culture – most often white, middle-class, able-bodied and heterosexual – means having control over its terminology, language, humour and dress code and having an inherent understanding of 'the way things are done'. This bestows power, which can be shared and used constructively, used destructively to oppress and bully, or – most often – used unconsciously in ways that disadvantage those outside of the dominant group. The following case study offers an example of this form of disadvantage, demonstrating how it can impact negatively on an individual's professional development and wider career progression.

Case study

Sally is a white woman with a hearing impairment. The department arranged for her to have a work-based assessment, and she is broadly satisfied that the provision of special equipment enables her to work as a qualified social worker. Sally, however, is increasingly irritated by the tendency of some colleagues – and managers – to regard her as a disability expert. For example, she was recently asked for advice about a child with a learning disability and is regularly asked to attend inter-agency meetings regarding access to buildings. Not only does she feel that this prevents all employees from developing an understanding of disability, but there is no weighting for the additional tasks. Sally has just been asked to take a case from outside of the area. The young person involved has a hearing impairment. Sally is interested in the case but does not feel she should accept it while her workload remains disproportionately higher than others in the team.

What might Sally do to address this situation?

Parallels can be made from the experience in the case study to that of others; for example, multilingual staff are sometimes asked to act as interpreters – both formally by the organisation and informally by reception or other staff – and staff from minority groups are often asked to become members of working parties and interview panels to ensure a diverse representation, without workload relief being formally arranged. A key part of professional development, therefore, is to understand ways in which organisational and team expectations of colleagues from minority groups can serve to further disadvantage them.

 What sorts of norms operate in your team? Are there any individuals who could be disadvantaged by them?

Power imbalances between groups and individuals in the workplace represent one of many ways in which interpersonal conflict between individuals, within teams and across organisations is created. While conflict tends to be viewed as a dysfunctional force (Morgan, 1997), research suggests that disagreement and a desire to debate issues can be a sign of organisational health (Eisenhardt et al., 1997). Many of the achievements over past decades in relation to diversity and anti-discriminatory practice have developed through a critical and questioning approach, for example, understandings of disability. Methods used to manage conflict on an individual basis tend to depend on temperament and strategies learnt in childhood. By the time adulthood is reached, reactions to conflict are usually instinctive, with a tendency to 'prefer' one style over another. The Thomas–Kilmann conflict mode instrument (Thomas and Kilmann, 1974) can help identify preferred styles for dealing with conflict. Individuals are presented with a series of conflict situations and asked to choose a course of action between two seemingly incompatible concerns. The 'solutions' are measured along two axes, one representing the extent to which the individual attempts to satisfy his or her *own* concerns (assertiveness), the other the extent to which the individual attempts to satisfy the *other's* concerns (cooperativeness). This results in scores for five main styles, set out in Figure 19.4.

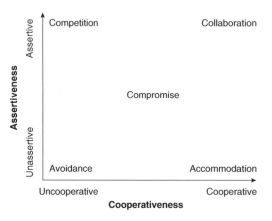

Figure 19.4   Dimensions of handling conflict.

Source: Morgan, 1997: 206.

As with team roles, no one style is 'best', and an experienced practitioner will identify and use those most appropriate to each situation. Examples are set out in Box 19.3 (adapted from Morgan, 1997: 207).

Box 19.3   Conflict styles.

Competing   The 'I know best' position in which individuals believe theirs is the most rational and only possible way forward. Useful in emergencies when quick decisive action is required (and can be justified if necessary at a later time) but can also feel oppressive.

Collaborating   Working with others to identify areas of disagreement, find common ground and jointly solve problems. Useful when both sets of concerns are too important to be compromised. The most time-consuming but potentially most rewarding style.

Compromising   Adopting a 'give-and-take' approach which will achieve a quick solution and ensure that both parties come away with something. Can be used to achieve a temporary or expedient settlement to a complex issue when there is no time for a longer-term strategy.

Avoiding   The 'head-in-the-sand' position of not wanting to get involved or take responsibility. Can be useful when a 'breathing space' is needed or when the situation is best addressed without an individual's personal involvement.

Accommodating   Willing to concede and agree a solution, accepting the other's point of view. Conceding can be like money in the bank – there to spend another time.

Think about some conflict situations you have witnessed or have been involved in recently. Did the conflict styles used contribute positively or negatively to a satisfactory outcome?

Whether or not engaging with conflict results in a positive outcome, ignoring it is one of the factors that can increase pressure on individuals. Pressure can lead to stress and ultimately burnout (see Cherniss, 1995).

Pressure, stress and burnout

When the daily demands of the job result in unsustainably high levels of pressure, the result is stress. Arroba and James (cited in Thompson et al., 1994: 2) make the point that stress and pressure are not the same; a certain amount of pressure is actually beneficial – it enables us to feel energised and ready to face the day's challenges. Stress results from an *inappropriate* level of pressure, usually too much but occasionally too little, as shown in Figure 19.5.

Wainwright and Calnan (2002) highlight the contested nature of workplace stress, as evidenced in social work by Balloch et al. (1999). It can be perceived as 'a product of the unsustainable pressures and demands placed on the worker by late capitalism' or as 'claims making' by 'disgruntled or feckless workers backed by woolly and imprecise science' (Wainwright and Calnan, 2002: v). Whatever the cause, the consequence for those experiencing it can be long-term incapacity: physiological, behavioural or psychological. Prevention, therefore, is better than cure.

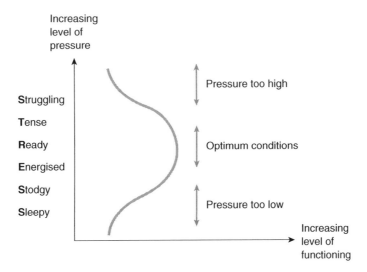

Figure 19.5 The stress continuum.

The potential for stress in social work is high; practitioners work with some of society's most disadvantaged, damaged and, occasionally, dangerous individuals. They are under constant pressure to maintain procedural efficiency through form-filling and record-keeping while managing rising caseloads. While it is the duty of an organisation to ensure that staff are supported appropriately, line managers are themselves under increasing pressure to meet targets, and some may focus more on which boxes have been ticked than on how staff are experiencing the job. This is a practice reality and, while not condoning this, individuals are advised to know how best to help themselves manage these pressures. This might be through strategies known to reduce stress, such as taking regular exercise or maintaining interests and hobbies outside of work. Additionally, there are a range of books on stress management – for example, Cooper and Palmer (2000) offer an excellent analysis of 'thinking errors' that hinder successful problem-solving and suggest how best to challenge and positively reframe these.

The results of a longitudinal study into stress and burnout in the US public sector usefully highlight ways of preventing this (Cherniss, 1995). First, professionals who continued to feel that they were making a positive difference to people's lives maintained their enthusiasm for the work. Many of these had developed expertise through cultivating a specialism. Second, feeling supported within the organisation and finding ways of using a high degree of autonomy were identified as important in avoiding the disengagement and disillusionment that can result in burnout. Finally, a list of personal factors linked to career satisfaction was developed from the interviews with employees. These included making opportunities for further training, maintaining realistic expectations of oneself, others and the job, career-planning and balancing work, family and leisure. Importantly amongst these was developing 'organisational negotiation skill', defined as an ability to get the most out of a job. For example, increasing the variety of one's work, finding ways of getting round organisational barriers in order to obtain a better deal for service users and, generally, developing a problem-solving attitude towards difficulties that arise at work (Cherniss, 1995: 159).

While factors such as 'developing a specialism' and 'using autonomy' might appear to be unattainable in statutory social service organisations, developing expertise in a specific area and using professional judgement where possible might help retain enthusiasm and manage the pressures of the job. Perhaps of greater relevance are the personal factors that contributed towards a sustainable and satisfying work experience – some of which might be useful pointers for staff under pressure.

 How do you manage the pressures of the job and how many of Cherniss's 'antidotes to burnout', as he called the protective factors, can you identify for yourself?

Conclusion

This chapter has focused on the team and personal environments of the practitioner rather than on the external or internal environments of the wider organisation. It has outlined ways in which social work professionals can draw on a 'lifelong learning' approach to managing the competing demands, tension and priorities of the job. This approach assists individuals to practice in a way that contributes to fully professional and accountable provision to service users, employers and the wider political and public stakeholders. It entails understanding the process of learning and being open to new learning experiences. It also encourages the development of self-knowledge through self-awareness and feedback from colleagues.

In the wider context of the team, the approach draws on an understanding of team role theory to help individual members to maximise a team's overall performance. Understanding how power operates helps ensure that those with particular expertise or from minority groups are not further disadvantaged by higher workloads due to additional demands being placed on their time. A theoretical model of conflict styles highlights how conflict can be used constructively, and strategies that work to manage the stresses of the job and to prevent burnout are outlined.

Working in an organisational environment that prioritises quantitative over more qualitative measures of success and in which professional judgement at times feels constrained by prescriptive measures and instructions can have a deskilling impact on professional staff. As this chapter has demonstrated, there are ways in which practitioners themselves can develop an armoury of knowledge, skills and techniques that will help them retain their resilience to the external forces that threaten the professional role.

Key learning points

Professional development can enable practitioners to:

1. be more responsive and open towards people and ideas;
2. actively seek feedback to improve performance;
3. reflect on past practice to develop future practice;
4. become more team-focused and sensitive to colleagues;
5. seek to expand knowledge of diversity, power and anti-discriminatory practice;
6. identify and manage responses to conflict;
7. develop a personal strategy to avoid stress and burnout;
8. use career planning to sustain enthusiasm and commitment.

Taking it further

Readers who want to know more about this will find the following helpful:

Cherniss, C. (1995) *Beyond Burnout: Helping Teachers, Nurses, Therapists and Lawyers Recover from Stress and Disillusionment,* New York: Routledge.

Schön, D.A. (1991) *The Reflective Practitioner: How Professionals Think in Action,* Avebury: Ashgate.

Thompson, N. (2003) *Promoting Equality: Challenging Discrimination and Oppression* (2nd edn), Basingstoke: Palgrave. (See, especially, Chapter 4, 'Power', and Chapter 7, 'Working in Organisations'.)

Partnership working
20 *Service users and social workers learning and working together*

Peter Beresford, Fran Branfield, Brian Maslen, Anna Sartori and Jenny, Maggie and Manny,[1] all service users from Shaping Our Lives

This chapter will:

This chapter has been written by people who all have experience of using health or social care services. It will:

- present models of partnership working and explain what this entails;
- give examples of obstacles to partnership working;
- explain the importance of equality and agreed principles for partnership.

Introduction

For many service users, the word 'partnership' has negative associations. This has sometimes been true for us. Partnership is one of those words like 'empowerment', 'care' and 'involvement' now used a lot in public policy but frequently not thought through carefully. Services talk about partnership with service users without always acknowledging what it might mean. The result, perhaps not surprisingly, is often disillusionment all round. When we talked with each other about partnership before writing this, it was clear it is an idea that has to be thought about carefully. These are some things we said:

There is no point in deciding high up that there should be an equal partnership if the people who are working with you don't know about the partnership – it's not going to make any difference.

There is still a lot of bullying going on between workers and service users. This is a particularly common problem for people with learning difficulties. You can't talk about equal partnerships when the reality of people's lives is shaped by being bullied.

If you think that you are better than someone else because of who they are seen to be, then you cannot have equality. Service users are generally not seen in a positive light. And then, if you add other issues such as being gay or lesbian, Black, or old, people feel superior or inferior and not equal.

Ours is not an equal society, so you are not likely to get equal partnerships.

The service users who agree to join a partnership want to improve things and will do their utmost to make it work but are not fooled by good words. They know they have not got a chance of being equal, but will try.

You can't just say 'let's have a partnership'. You have to change the structural things, the way services are managed and organised and look at why people don't always work in a respectful way; otherwise it is just more empty words.

Partnerships can only work if the user feels valued, and their access needs are met as a matter of routine.

If things like these go unrecognised, partnership is likely either to be a meaningless or actually unhelpful idea. All of us writing this are involved in the independent national user-controlled organisation Shaping Our Lives. Shaping Our Lives is made up of and works across a wide range of service user groups, including older people, people with physical and sensory impairments, mental-health service users/survivors, people with learning difficulties, people living with HIV/AIDS and so on. Most of us are also involved in local service user organisations and groups. Shaping Our Lives has been involved in formal and informal partnerships, official signed partnerships and unwritten partnerships, good and bad partnerships, partnerships that have become a burden and others which have been exciting, encouraging and productive. These have included partnerships between us as service users and other stakeholders, including research, government, voluntary, service-provider, policy and educational organisations. We have also been involved in partnerships with other service user-controlled organisations.

We are not all used to writing, so to ensure we can all contribute, we had discussions and worked out what we wanted to say and had the support we needed for this. This chapter includes the views of us all, including people's individual comments. We agreed it together. To include the contributions of people with learning difficulties, a skilled supporter helped them work out what they wanted to have included and agreed this with them. Other people contributed through telephone interviews. These contributions have then all been written out and agreed and formed the basis for putting the chapter together. Clearly, this process takes time, because we had to exchange our views and build them up into one chapter.

However, we believe it can work and makes for a much more inclusive and fully informed discussion than would otherwise be possible.

Inequality: a problem for partnership

There is a significant difference between partnerships with other service users and non-service user organisations and workers. This is because of the general inequality of power existing between the two. It is crucial to raise issues of power and powerlessness in relation to the idea of partnership with service users and their organisations. Historically, discussions and writings of service users have started with and focused on their powerlessness and disempowerment. That is, of course, why their empowerment (alongside participation, inclusion, integration and independence) has been a key concern of service users' movements. People included as service users have been routinely and institutionally devalued, discriminated against, pauperised and denied their human and civil rights. Their organisations have reflected this inequality, generally being under-resourced, fragile and insecure. Thus, any consideration of partnership, for both service users and their organisations, must begin with an appreciation of their relative powerlessness in relation to the service system and institutions which have traditionally been part of the process of their disempowerment. This must be acknowledged. Any discussion of partnership which does not do this is unlikely to be helpful. Service users generally come to partnerships with other stakeholders from a position of inferior power and formal legitimacy.

> There is a power imbalance. No matter what you go to, no matter what it's for, it is always overpowering by professionals. We should be working together in an equal partnership. But it never is. How can it be equal? The user lives with the illness or condition every day. The professional does not.

Because of this, we particularly focus on partnerships with non-service user organisations, although we discuss both, and partnerships with service users and service user organisations also encounter problems, for example, 'The worst kind of abuse is by one user over another user, if the worker has been a user before and colludes in the abuse by turning a "blind eye" to the abuse'.

Here we write about some of the issues that concern service users about partnership, offer an example of a positive partnership involving us and look at what helps and hinders partnerships with service users to work well.

Some positive experiences

When we first wrote this, the editors thought what we had said about our experience of social work and partnership was rather negative and might put off people who were thinking of becoming social workers. Perhaps this is because you often think first of your most difficult experiences. We wouldn't want to discourage people who could be good social workers. So we tried to think also of more positive experiences and included some. As you will see, even positive experiences are quite complicated, and it does look as though service users have to be quite assertive to get the kind of social work and social worker that we might all like. This of course can be difficult if you are having a difficult time or do not feel empowered, and that is something for all social care workers to remember. Another problem is that who you get as a social worker can still be rather a lottery, when you need to be able to rely on having a good one. We did find it difficult to think of good things, but these are the additional comments that three of us made:

> Social workers wanted me to leave where I'm living now. I said to them, 'Don't be silly I can't live on my own, I don't want to live on my own.' They asked me to live on my own and I can't live on my own in a flat. My family came here to say I had to live with people. I like living with people [rather] than living on my own. I like the social workers I have got now. They let me stay where I am. They let me feel settled. It's alright where I am now. People get on well with me where I live. I am pleased to stay where I am. Social workers ask me if I want to live there. I said, yes I will stay there. It's great that they understand what we want.

> (Man with learning difficulties)

> Social workers could have talked to me about why I went into a mental health home. They didn't give me a choice. I went to visit there and they said that's the only place available for you and I didn't have a mental health problem. I was low but I wasn't mentally ill. I didn't have to take tablets or anything. They should have asked me first where do you want to move to because I had nowhere to live. I had to move out of a place – a family. I wasn't happy in the mental health home. I went to visit a duty social worker and they found me a new social worker. His job was to help me move out of there, to see what kind of place I wanted to live in. He was very good because he didn't like me being in that home. He made me feel comfortable. He phoned up to put me on the waiting list and I went to visit a lady from Lifeways to talk to me if I wanted to live with a family, just to get on my two feet, to feel confident. I said that would be a good idea. I really enjoyed living there. It gave me more confidence because living in the home made me feel a bit unconfident.

> (A woman with learning difficulties)

> One of our lads with a learning difficulty had a social worker who used to visit him irregularly, always kept the appointment if he confirmed it, but whenever he turned up, without exception, every single time he took and made endless calls on his mobile phone when he was supposed to be with Daniel [not his real name]. Time and time again. It didn't matter what was going on, he never even said, 'Oh excuse me' or turned it off – it was half a sentence to Daniel and then back to his mobile phone. So Daniel was never given any one-to-one private attention. He was never listened to. He is now, having got a new case worker, working at a local supermarket and says he is very, very happy.
>   He came to us and said he didn't want to complain but that he was fed up. So I made a phone call on his behalf and said that the social worker's behaviour was inappropriate … the person I was speaking to obviously didn't think this was too serious … but they looked into it and it was addressed. Apparently once Daniel had asked us to tell

someone, other people got up the courage to complain as well and it had not only been Daniel who had been treated this way. So I think people have to be encouraged to speak up and try not to be afraid, and I think that is the social worker's responsibility to listen to the service user and to hear what is being told them and to do something about it if it is not good. This was a good outcome for Daniel and for others who had the same social worker.

(A service user advocate)

A positive example with difficult beginnings

The example of partnership between service users and professionals we want to draw on is about service user involvement in social work education. We know such involvement is patchy (Levin, 2004). However, service users argued, and it is now embodied in the social work qualification which was introduced in 2003, that involving service users in education and training is a vital way of improving the culture of social care practice to make it more user-centred (Beresford, 1994). Shaping Our Lives has a long-standing involvement in social care training and education. It organised the first national user-led seminar on user involvement in social work training and education. It had a representative on the external committee established by the DH leading up to the reform of social work education.

We chose this example because it is ultimately positive. While its focus is social work education, we think the process it followed is one that could work equally well in other areas of social work activity, including, for example, the development of social work practice, management and research. We think this because this example was based on service users working together and service users and workers getting to know and trust each other on equal terms in safe settings. This can apply in a case like this where people are working at a broader level to achieve change and improvement. But we also think it is at the heart of good social work between practitioners and service users, where the same priorities of getting to know each other, of building trust and working on equal terms are equally important. So while we describe a specific example from social work education, we think it has much wider application in social work and social care.

Shaping Our Lives' recommendations at the external committee, for systematic user involvement in the social work qualification and funding for colleges to do it properly, were agreed and introduced. As a result, a specific budget was made available annually to support service user involvement on all courses. This money has been used in very different ways. Some colleges have worked hard to involve service users. Others seem to have done little or nothing. Yet what could have more importance in developing effective involvement and partnership in practice and among practitioners than through building such experience and expectations into social workers' education and learning?

Being asked and ignored

In 2004 the DH asked Shaping Our Lives to organise a national consultation with a wide range of social work/care service users to find out what they thought was needed to help to improve user involvement in the social work degree. Shaping Our Lives successfully involved a diverse range of service users in this. Participants emphasised that service users and their organisations needed to have support to develop their capacity to be effectively involved in the qualification and that some of the funding now being made available for user involvement should go directly to service user organisations to help make this possible. This was the clear and agreed message from the consultation, but the DH did not take it forward, and service users expressed their regret to them. Participants were bitterly disappointed, making this clear in the comments they fed back to the government. For example:

> I was pretty shocked (at the decision). It makes a nonsense of the whole process.

> I think this is appalling!!! It makes an absolute mockery of consulting user organisations if they then go and do exactly the opposite of what was recommended.

> I am totally disgusted by this decision. This means that grass-roots groups, especially Black and minority ethnic [groups], don't stand a cat's chance in hell of involving more service users.

> How can a user group supposed to consult and empower other users to get involved, [do so] without having the finances to do this, and capacity build, so more grass roots users can get involved? This is [the] worst form of tokenism.

> What a disappointment. I expect these organisations will now look to service users and our organisations for help in trying to do the job asked of them. But we should be involved at the start in this. We should be directly involved. This looks like setting things back and being a really lost opportunity.

> What a blow, yet another way to show us that we are all equal but some are more equal than others.

Being asked and listened to

Some money (£60,000 from the well-over £1 million allocated) was made available to the Social Care Institute for Excellence (SCIE) to develop strategy for user involvement in social work education for the future, and Shaping Our Lives was commissioned to lead this work in association with SCIE. It is this partnership project we are focusing on. It was shaped and led by service users working in collaboration with social care professionals. It demonstrated both the feasibility of service users taking a lead and the possibility of effective negotiation on equal terms between service user and provider stakeholders at national policy level. Shaping Our Lives identified service users nationally with relevant skills and experience to make up a 'reference group', drawing on people involved in the earlier consultation, as well as identifying additional perspectives. The group fully included Black and minority-ethnic service users and a wide range of service users including people with experience of children and family as well as adult services. It also included people with experience of a wide range of disabling barriers, for example, people with learning difficulties, a visual impairment or living with HIV/AIDS.

This group held a series of meetings, with service user members meeting in the mornings and then being joined by representatives of key social care organisations in the afternoons to share views, take forward discussion and agree action. These organisations include the GSCC, Skills for Care (formerly TOPSS), Joint University Council Social Work Education Committee (JUCSWEC), the Practice Learning Taskforce and SCIE. In this way, positive and equal collaboration developed rather than different stakeholders remaining wary of each other. A lot of understanding and common ground were established. It meant that for the first-time service users were involved strategically at national level in influencing social work education. This project not only led to effective collaborative and partnership working. It also had some practical outcomes.

A key outcome was a national consultation with service users on developing a strategy for user involvement in social work education. This was undertaken through four regional consultations with service users organised by local service user organisations. This has extended the knowledge base for building capacity among service users to get involved in social work education. There was a high level of consistency in what service users said. They valued user involvement in social work education but identified common barriers inhibiting effective involvement, as well as proposing actions to be taken by government, universities and user-controlled organisations. Barriers identified included:

- academics attaching a low value to service users' knowledge;
- the need for change in universities' culture;
- the need to address access issues;
- service user organisations' own lack of capacity to get involved in social work education;
- lack of training for service users and their organisations;
- incompatibility between user involvement and benefits policy and practice.

(Branfield et al., 2006)

The project also led to a positive change in JUCSWEC policy on user involvement in social work education. JUCSWEC agreed to support some government funding going directly to service users' organisations instead of universities, to build capacity and infrastructure for effective involvement in social work education. The project also resulted in a place being gained for a user representative on the GSCC Overview Group, which includes representation from the DH as well as social care bodies, to take forward user involvement in social work education.

The strategy document's key recommendation, agreed unanimously by the group, was to establish a national forum of service users in social work education to ensure service users a stronger voice in national, regional and local developments. This national structure would provide a focus for service users and their organisations to increase their capacity to be involved in social work education effectively. This structure would be developed by user-controlled organisations and committed to ensuring diversity in its membership (SOL/SCIE, 2005). The group heard in March 2006 that the DH was making £90,000 available to take forward this initiative.

This has been a positive project to be involved in which feels as though it has made some real progress. Its success seems linked to its being based on a series of helpful characteristics and qualities including:

- service users being treated with equal value;
- being co-chaired by a service user;
- the project having the support of a committed and experienced champion for user involvement within SCIE (Enid Levin);
- the project being adequately resourced, making it possible to meet participants' access and support costs and to pay service users appropriately for their expertise and experience;
- working explicitly to address issues of equality and inclusion in its process and objectives;
- learning to respect each other and treat each other accordingly;
- taking broadly defined issues of access seriously;
- being an ongoing project, thus enabling different stakeholders to:
  - get to know each other;
  - gain skills;
  - learn more about each other's perspectives;
  - gain trust and confidence;
  - have time to negotiate and reach agreement;
  - have a safe space and forum.

What partnership means to us

These are some of the things we said to each other about what partnership should mean when we were preparing to write this chapter:

Making sure that the services are better for people with learning difficulties.

Social workers should work as a team with you but they don't because they don't listen …

Sometimes they don't listen to us, [to] what we want.

They do what *they* want but they don't do what we want.

They should do what we want.

Because we are the ones that got them into the job in the first place. If it wasn't for us they wouldn't be in a job. They should think about that, take that on board, because what they are good at is taking people's kids away.

One of my friends had her kids taken away yesterday. That's what they do. She came to me. She was very upset and emotional. She has a learning difficulty.

I haven't forgiven them since they took away my two boys.

They need training.

We should train them up, never mind them training us.

The importance of equality and agreed principles for partnership

The importance of equality in any partnership between service providers and service users was a theme to which we were repeatedly drawn back in thinking about this writing –

perhaps because it is so often lacking. As one of the writing team said: 'My idea is that it should be a partnership of equals, in that the social worker accepts that the client is the expert, as far as [s]he is in charge of his or her body, mind and soul.' The most important partnerships for most service users, between them and workers, are the ones that they have with individual practitioners. A helpful starting point for thinking about partnership is offered by the conventional idea of it being based on a contract between people engaged in business. Service users and social care workers need to negotiate how it will work for both of them. A set of rules or common values needs to underpin the partnership, which both sign up to.

We believe that any partnership between service users and social care workers has to be built on a basis of mutual cooperation, openness and equality. This does not mean that either side has to agree with, or endorse, all the other's choices, beliefs or opinions, but it should mean that both sides respect the other's rights to make their own choices, decisions and beliefs. This was the situation in our strategy group. A partnership between service users and social care workers should commit both parties to an agreed approach to working together, based on shared values.

A partnership between service users and social care workers could be about:

- sharing and promoting the idea of service user independence, choice and equality: a social model perspective;
- making working together easier, avoiding misunderstandings, by having planned processes and written agreements;
- providing a framework for negotiating arrangements for individual service users.

For any partnership to work, social care workers need to have an understanding of and a commitment to opportunities for redress, bearing in mind:

- the unequal position of service users and the barriers excluding them from participating fully in all aspects of society;
- the lack of power and control that service users commonly experience.

If any partnership is to be successful, then service users need to understand:

- the social care worker's role;
- what is and what is not their job;
- the boundaries of their social care worker's role.

For partnership to work, service users and social care workers both need to understand equality issues in terms of race, ethnicity and culture, gender, sexuality, age, class, belief systems and impairment.

Broader problems for partnership

So far, we have examined and discussed individual and collective partnerships between service users and service providers/professionals. Both are clearly important and both demand further development. To some extent, it is likely that the quality of individual personal partnerships between service users and workers will depend on how successful organised service users are in bringing about change in social work and social care that ensures it is more 'person centred' and 'user-led'. Some helpful insights into the difficulties facing service users and service user organisations seeking to get together and do things with others comes from a study of service user networking and knowledge. This was undertaken by Shaping Our Lives and supported by the Joseph Rowntree Foundation (Branfield and Beresford, 2006). There is clearly a relationship between service users' capacity to enter into equal and successful partnerships and their capacity to link up more generally.

In the study, service users highlighted the importance and benefits they attached to being able to network with each other, as individuals and in user-controlled organisations, both in terms of improving their quality of life and in sustaining a more effective voice and presence to make a difference. However, both service user organisations and individual service users emerged as frequently isolated with little knowledge of or contact with other service-user organisations, locally, regionally or nationally.

Service users identified a range of obstacles in the way of networking as individuals, including:

- problems of mobility in rural areas;
- the fragility of user-controlled organisations;
- the effort of being actively involved.

For service user organisations, problems undermining networking included the following:

- Inadequate and insecure funding and resources. Service user organisations generally do not have secure or reliable funding. Because of this, many service user organisations are liable to become funding-led rather than led by their own concerns, priorities and principles, undermining their independence.
- Lack of adequate and secure funding can also be divisive as service user-controlled organisations are put under strong pressure to compete with each other for the same inadequate funding sources.
- The unequal position of service user organisations in competition with big charitable organisations.
- Inadequate resources leaving user-controlled organisations dependent on a small core of activists as they are unable to reach out, engage and maintain the involvement of more people.
- The limited profile of most user-controlled organisations.
- Lack of resources to ensure full and equal access for all service users.
- The lack of local user-controlled organisations generally and, for particular user groups, for example, young disabled people, people living with HIV/AIDS, disabled parents, etc. There are major gaps in types of user-controlled organisations existing in most areas.
- Inadequate provision for Black and minority-ethnic involvement because of restricted funding.
- There is a strong perception among some service users that, in practice, not all organisations claiming to be user-controlled are actually controlled by service users.

The importance of funding

This project's findings highlighted that service users saw the issue of inadequate resources, particularly funding, as crucial in inhibiting service user networking. This was mirrored in our discussions prior to writing this. For example:

> They are making so many cutbacks on everything. If services are not adequately funded then they are not going to work well and cutbacks won't only be financial. Standards fall and there will be a knock-on effect on equal partnerships.

> There are cutbacks on everything. Services haven't got the means to make sure that there are equal partnerships.

> Equal partnerships between service users and social work staff all sounds great, but we have so many agency staff, or temporary staff, because there isn't the money, and then partnership agreements don't mean anything.

> Many service users have spent a lot of their lives learning to be grateful for what they get. Then you get worried in case you might lose it. I am not sure how real an equal partnership can ever be.

> On the issue of money, users get same old excuse, 'We would love to pay you, but you might lose your benefits – do you want to take the risk of that happening to you?' In other words, be grateful for sandwiches and bus fares home (see also Chapter 6).

It is not just that the *lack* of money can undermine partnerships between service users and providers. Having some *control* over money is also key to successful partnerships and, as we have seen, was an underpinning objective of the positive partnership we have described here. As one member of our writing team put it:

> Service users should be a partner in dishing out the resources … In other words users must control the levers of finance as equals … This will result in more users staying involved and thus you will have a resource that can be used to train the next generation of service users. Instead of going to a group of service users and then to another group and then another group and there is a lack of continuity and nothing gets achieved and the same questions are asked time and time again!

An infrastructure for effective partnership

Clearly good partnership working between service users and providers/workers benefits greatly from being based on positive human qualities. As we have seen, it needs good personal relationships and the development of skills and understanding. But the findings of the networking project highlight that such partnership also requires broader, infrastructural support in order to work well, consistently and in an inclusive way, reflecting diversity. In the study, service users identified two closely interrelated issues for helping make this possible; first, strengthening service user networking at individual and organisational levels; and, second, promoting effective user involvement by service users.

Service users suggested a wide range of ways of improving their contact with each other individually and collectively, highlighting the importance of involving Black and minority-ethnic service users in such networking. They saw a properly resourced national database of service user organisations owned and controlled by service users as being helpful here. They also saw an adequately and securely funded user-led national user network as valuable, which could offer support, information exchange, improved communication, contacts, advice on good practice and a national voice for service users.

Service users saw two routes to effective involvement: campaigning and negotiation. Negotiation approaches clearly connect with the idea of partnership, while campaigning suggests a more independent approach. Service users repeatedly stated that the best way for them to have more say in the services they used and for their knowledge to become valid in the eyes of service providers was through better and sustained involvement, as opposed to 'tick-box' exercises. This may sometimes mean involvement in collaborative partnership arrangements with services and workers. On other occasions, it might mean working separately from outside in developmental ways. Each has something to offer. Both are likely to have something helpful to contribute to different situations and both have their particular strengths and weaknesses.

As we saw in the social work education example focused on earlier, partnerships from positions of strength and choice are much more likely to feel positive and effective than those growing from inequality and powerlessness. This offers social care an important lesson, whether it relates to individual relationships between service users and practitioners or to collective relationships between user-controlled organisations and the service system. It offers hope for the future as well as highlighting some principles for good practice more generally.

Key learning points

Working and learning in partnership with service users means:

1. acknowledging service users' expertise;
2. recognising and addressing the barriers to service users' involvement in education;
3. recognising service users' positions of inequality and powerlessness;
4. allowing enough time and resources and making sure people have the support they need to participate fully;
5. listening to people and not ignoring their views;
6. working to a set of rules or common values which everyone agrees to;
7. addressing access issues in their broadest sense.

Taking it further

Readers who want to know more about this will find the following helpful:

Branfield, F. Beresford, P. and Levin, E. (2006) *Common Aims: Strategies to Support Service User and Carer Involvement in Social Work Education*, London: Shaping Our Lives/SCIE.

Levin, E. (2004) *Involving Service Users and Carers in Social Work Education, Resource Guide No. 2*, London: SCIE.

Shaping Our Lives and SCIE (2005), *A Strategy to Support Service User and Carer Participation in Social Work Education: Proposal to the Department of Health*, London: Shaping Our Lives/SCIE.

Note

1 Some of the authors have only used first names as they fear recriminations from services if their full names are known.

21 Using supervision
Support or surveillance?

Jeremy Peach and Nigel Horner

This chapter will:

- analyse supervision of staff in relation to developmental and managerial functions;
- argue that pressures on social work organisations have resulted in the need for agency accountability outweighing the developmental function of supervision;
- suggest that the need for professional supervision is greatly enhanced given the development of interprofessional working arrangements;
- propose that approaches to supervision can be applied to social work that have first been developed in the health service.

Introduction

A belief in the importance of the supervision of social workers has a lengthy history within the personal human services. Practitioners within the sector talk about 'good, effective or supportive supervision', implying there are agreed notions as to the positive qualities inherent in this relationship between supervisor and supervisee. Furthermore, there has been an axiomatic assumption that 'quality' supervision has fulfilled a number of functions within social work (guiding, supportive, educative, developmental and quality management) in equal measure. Examples of this can be seen in the work of Hawkins and Shohet (1989) and Kadushin (1992) and, indeed, this concept relates back to the early work of John Dawson (1926).

'Good' supervision has come to be seen as a precondition for effective managerial practice in social work. A cursory glance at the fatal child abuse inquiries from the mid-1980s onwards, such as those concerning Tyra Henry (London Borough of Lambeth, 1987) and Kimberley Carlisle (London Borough of Greenwich, 1987), through to the Victoria Climbié report (Laming, 2003) and parallel inquiries such as the Allitt Inquiry (Clothier, 1994), demonstrates the importance that is placed upon practitioners' supervision, and the reports collectively endorse the notion that practice is made 'safe' by effective supervision (and that, conversely, inadequate supervision results in 'unsafe' practice).

Indeed, Recommendation 45 of the Laming Report (2003) states that: 'Directors of social services must ensure that the work of staff working directly with children is regularly supervised. This must include the supervisor reading, reviewing and signing the case file at regular intervals.'

Furthermore, the GSCC Code of Practice (2002a), and the Leadership and Management Standards for Social Care developed for post-qualifying programmes (Skills for Care, 2005) both reinforce the centrality of supervision for effective practice.

However, the practice of supervision is not without tensions. The concept has contested meaning, and the functions that it serves are determined by myriad factors, which include the values and beliefs of those who manage and influence the process. The move toward greater levels of partnership working and new administrative arrangements within and between departments of adult care services, children's services, and health and education all provide unique contexts for emerging and revised supervision practices. The process of supervision per se is a relatively new construct within health, particularly in mental health practice (Bernard and Goodyear, 2003), and those who provide *clinical* supervision may not necessarily be the line manager of the supervisee. Furthermore, supervision for newly qualified staff is not an intrinsic element of practice within the arena of education (at primary, secondary and tertiary levels). Additionally, tensions have arisen from the emergence of New Right ideologies, introducing market relations into the public sector and advancing the process of managerialisation and the new public manager role (see Chapter 22). Such factors have led to greater levels of accountability and managerial control within social work practice; as Briskman (2005: 208) asserts, 'social work is increasingly working within a managerialist framework'.

Given this set of conditions, it is the aim of this chapter to critically reflect upon the purpose of supervision within these structures. We argue that there is a danger that the essentially supportive elements of classical supervision may be compromised at the expense of managerial surveillance. We also argue that an essential element of professional responsibility is the obligation to be clear about one's support and developmental needs and that competent workplaces need to construct processes that ensure the needs of practitioners and their managers are met in equal measure.

According to Argyris and Schön (1996: 215), flexible, developmental organisations are characterised as 'responsible, productive and creative, and where errors are seen as the vehicle for learning'. Unfortunately, 'modern' social work organisations suffer from the convictions that no mistakes are tolerable and, therefore, that the sole goal of supervision is in danger of becoming the elimination of risk through the micro-management and surveillance of practitioners and their outcomes. If the paramount discourse in the supervisor–supervisee relationship has indeed become one of corporate surveillance of the practitioner, then it is hardly surprising that research by Jones (2001: 552) has found that 'social workers felt they were no longer trusted or acknowledged for their skill and abilities', pointing to 'anguish over the growing intensity of bureaucracy and paperwork' and the 'speed up of work and the prevalence of poor and sometimes aggressive management'. Apparently social workers feel managed, but are they supervised?

What is supervision?

While the term has many interpretations, we begin with the perceptions of classical management theory, which imply that supervision is a management activity singularly concerned with overseeing the productivity and progress of staff. As such, the term has connotations with direct control, discipline and surveillance and is axiomatic within Max Weber's concept of heteronymous professional organisations (Weber, 1947), in which staff who hold professional qualifications are progressively subordinated to administrative control. It may be argued that it is this hierarchical and bureaucratic conception of the managerial function that dominates contemporary social work practice and, thus, influences the prevailing constructions of functional supervision.

However, the Advisory, Conciliation and Arbitration Service (ACAS, 2003) identify the role of supervision as 'supporting, developing and motivating'. This relates to the concept of a 'learning organisation', which is defined as: 'organisations where people continually expand their capacity to create the results they truly desire, where new and expansive patterns of thinking are nurtured, where collective aspiration is set free, and where people are continually learning to see the whole together' (Senge, 1990: 3; see also Chapter 18).

However laudable these sentiments may be, Senge et al. (2005) recognise that this is an aspirational vision – rather than an independent reality – of an organisation to which people may wish to belong (expressed in the current populist truism of organisations aspiring to be an *employer of choice*). Research by the Chartered Institute of Personnel and Development (CIPD, 2005) highlights the importance that employees place on developmental opportunities, which they directly link to greater levels of job satisfaction and, consequently, better staff retention.

ACAS's humanistic views are congruent with the language of CPD, which is an ongoing, planned learning process that enables practitioners to update professional knowledge and skills, with the presumed outcomes of improved competence and enhanced outcomes for service users – including better protection in the case of vulnerable persons. Engaging in CPD activities is highlighted in the GSCC's code of practice for social care workers and employers (GSCC, 2002a), and undertaking post-qualifying learning has become a precondition for practitioners to maintain their professional registration. In this sense, social work has 'caught up' with the CPD arrangements for nurses, doctors, lawyers and other professions. Indeed, as social workers are *knowledge* workers – people who are typically defined as being well-educated, highly skilled and people who work with knowledge – then they will have to be individually and collectively proactive in addressing their competency needs, which enable them to remain relevant and up to date in an ever changing dynamic environment where the management of information and knowledge is crucial to individual and organisational effectiveness.

This illustrates the duality at play: one school of thought regards supervision as having concern for *production* (and the associated requirements for target-setting, performance management, quality control and monitoring) while the other focuses on *people* (and the associated language of leadership, coaching, lifelong learning and developing potential). To some, such an apparent dichotomy might illustrate the diversity and flexibility of post-modernism, in which concerns for both performance outcomes *and* resources development are seen as being of equal importance as complementary managerial responsibilities.

These elements can be seen in the work of different writers such as Proctor (1987, 1991), Hawkins and Shohet (1989) Brown and Bourne (1996) and Kadushin (1992), who highlight three main functions of supervision:

- **Educational** This concerns the educational development of practitioners and the fulfilment of their potential. The primary focuses of attention concern their lack of competence regarding understanding, knowledge, skills and, importantly, their attitude toward their role. The goals of supervision are to encourage reflection and exploration of the work and to develop new insights, perceptions and ways of working.
- **Supportive** This involves supervisors providing support for both the practical and psychological elements of a practitioner's role. Primary issues of concern in this area are stress levels, morale and job satisfaction.
- **Administrative** This concerns the promotion and maintenance of good standards of work and the adherence to organisational policies and those of other key stakeholders, such as the GSCC, CSI and the Office for Standards in Education (OfSTED). In essence, this is the quality assurance dimension within supervision.

In a similar vein, Proctor (1991) has described the three functions of supervision as formative, restorative and normative. By focusing on process models, Hawkins and Shohet (1989) list ten separate areas in relation to Kadushin's (1992) functions (see Box 21.1).

Box 21.1   Primary focuses of supervision.

Purpose	Focus
To provide a regular space for the supervisees to reflect upon the content and process of their work	Educational
To develop understanding and skills within the work	Educational

(Continued)

(Continued)	
To receive information and another perspective concerning one's work	Educational/Supportive
To receive both content and process feedback	Educational/Supportive
To be validated and supported both as a person and as a worker	Supportive
To ensure that as a person and as a worker one is not left to carry unnecessarily difficulties, problems and projections alone	Supportive
To have space to explore and express personal distress, re-stimulation, transference or counter-transference that may be brought up by the work	Administrative
To plan and utilize their personal and professional resources better	Administrative
To be pro-active rather than re-active	Administrative
To ensure quality of work	Administrative/ Supportive

Source: adapted from Hawkins and Shohet (1989: 43).

Whist Kadushin's (1992) work has been found to be helpful within social work, it nevertheless emphasises a *deficit* model, whereby the worker is deemed to be lacking in some area. Aligned to this is the notion of dependence. Many models of supervision put the emphasis on the supervisor to take some form of action. Rather than creating independent, self-regulating practitioners, this form of managerialist leadership can engender a relationship of reliance and dependency – in itself somewhat antithetical to social work values. Nevertheless, this mode of supervision may promote reflexivity, and critical reflection, which sits at the heart of effective assessments and interventions.

 To what extent has your experience of supervision promoted reflexivity and critical reflection?

The reflective practitioner

> Our perceptions, appreciations, and beliefs are rooted in worlds of our own making which we come to accept as reality.
>
> (Schön, 1987: 36)

Schön (1987) highlights two aspects of reflection: *reflection in action* and *reflection on action.* The latter occurs *post hoc,* within the supervision session, and enables the worker to spend time exploring practice, such as why they may have acted in a particular way, the results of their actions, and how different actions may have produced different outcomes. In doing this, a set of questions and ideas about activities and practice are developed. The former draws upon reflexivity *in situ* (and may draw upon the supervisory relationship via coached responses to difficult situations) and gives greater coherence and structure to the function of 'conceptualisation' in Kolb's (1984) concept of experiential learning (see Figure 19.1 on page 203).

The concept of experiential learning aids our understanding of reflexive activity. Supervisors may begin by asking supervisees to return to a situation and to attend to their feelings. They may then encourage the practitioner to draw relationships with other situations. The next stage may be to help supervisees to make judgements and to build theories about why they acted in a particular way and to think about what they may do differently in a similar situation. Supervisees may then take that plan into a future scenario which, in turn, may stimulate further reflection.

Kolb's and Schön's work have both been subject to criticism, in that they require the practitioner's commitment and competence to fully engage with the process. Argyris and Schön (1996) argue that our actions are guided by *theories in use*, which are based on implicit assumptions and values. When we attempt to solve problems, we correct perceived errors in such a way as to maintain the assumptions and values that lie behind our theory in use, and we learn how to do better by improving performance within our current paradigms, a process associated with single-loop learning. For double-loop or transformative learning (Mezirow, 2000) to occur – which is concerned with breaking out of our current mindset – we need to move beyond our theories in use (as shown in Figure 21.1) by opening them up to questioning and challenge. We can then understand why we think and do certain things, leading to potentially radical changes in our way of seeing and understanding the world.

Such a process is a hallmark of 'quality' supervision that moves beyond organisational concerns (the managerial agenda of the supervisor) and engenders transformative learning. It may also lead to greater levels of empowerment, albeit within existing power structures.

Line management supervisory relationship

An environment of mutual trust is required to engender this mutual questioning of theories in use. However, a study in the mid-1990s illustrated the depth of the potential discord

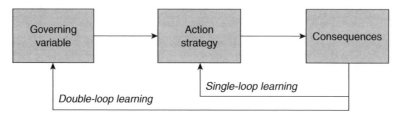

Figure 21.1   Single- and double-loop learning.

Source: Argyris and Schön, 1996.

between the agendas of the supervisors (on behalf of the department) and the supervisees (in terms of their professional objectives). In this study, 44 per cent of those interviewed agreed with the statement 'I feel my values are different from the Department's values' (Balloch et al., 1995: 93). For the person being supervised, such an affective and cognitive dissonance between the professional self–concept and the managed 'employee self' can result in various ways of 'making out', such as operating defensive routines, that result in ineffectual supervision.

It is common in social work for those who conduct supervision to be the line managers of the supervisee. Those who occupy managerial roles have a level of *power* (the actual ability to control others) and *authority* (the perceived and ascribed right to do so). French and Raven (1960) identified five sources of social power (see Box 21.2). The first three types of power arise from the supervisor's position; the last two (referent and expert) are a result of the supervisor's personal and professional qualities. Aspects of power are socially constructed in the relationship between the supervisor and the supervisee, and the perception each has of the other's competence will impact on the process. If, for example, the supervisor has little confidence in the knowledge, understanding or ability of the supervisee, then they may feel the need to adopt greater levels of surveillance, albeit complemented by higher levels of support. Indeed, a worker new to their role may welcome higher levels of surveillance and support, and the supervisor may feel it is a necessary part of ensuring service user protection.

Box 21.2   Perceived sources of power.

1. **Reward power**   A person may give or take away a reward.
2. **Coercive power**   A person is in a position to administer a punishment.

(Continued)

3. **Legitimate power**   A person has the organisational right to prescribe actions and or make decisions.
4. **Referent power**   The identification someone has with another person and their feeling of similarity and understanding or desire to be similar to them.
5. **Expert power**   A person has specific knowledge and understanding, which is greater than their own.

Source: French and Raven, 1960.

 Is your experience of supervision more oriented to support or surveillance functions? What have been the consequences of the approach adopted?

Hawkins and Shohet (1989: 49–51) highlight a four-stage development model that suggests supervisors may adopt a different approach depending on the supervisee's stage of competence:

1. Level 1 signifies a high level of dependency by the supervisee on their supervisor.
2. Level 2 is characterised by supervisees who, having overcome their initial concern, fluctuate between dependence and autonomy and between overconfidence and being overwhelmed.
3. Level 3 supervisees have increased self-confidence and only conditional dependency on the supervisor.
4. At level 4, supervisees have reached proficiency in their profession and require personal autonomy.

However, the 'halo and horns' effect influences these levels. In the halo effect, workers are perceived as being highly competent, because they exhibit desired qualities that mirror and match the supervisor's self-concept ('I'm OK, so therefore he or she is') and, thus, surveillance is low, autonomy high. In the horns effect, the reverse is true: the practitioner exhibits behaviours that are anathema to the supervisor and, thus, surveillance is high, and autonomy low. *Recency bias* causes another skewing dynamic, whereby recent performance (positive or negative) overshadows an objective perception of performance.

Other factors may create circumstances that tend towards *supervision as surveillance*. When a supervisor takes over a well-established team, he or she may feel outside of the group, causing the adoption of autocratic behaviours while attempting to establish her or his presence. The dynamics engendered through gender, race, ethnicity, sexuality, age, ideology and personality orientations may cause significant differences of understanding. Transference may occur, with supervisor, or supervisee, or both, replaying the past within the current relationship, or there may be a confusion of relationship. Tsui (2004) identifies three kinds of relationship, each having implications for the way supervision is enacted:

1. The relationship is based upon subordination, which may cause the process to be more hierarchical, autocratic and administratively orientated and may lead to reduced willingness to share problems in an honest and open way.
2. There is a perceived professional peer relationship, which may lead to greater levels of personal development and growth orientation.
3. The relationship is based on friendship, which may be more supportive, but within which it may be difficult to address highly sensitive and problematic areas.

However, supervision has a wider context and involves more people than those participating in the supervision session (O'Donoghue, 2003).

The wider context of supervision

Supervision takes place in a context that may be summarised as the interaction of four systems: political, service, professional and practice. Research suggests that organisational climate and associated perceptions of the work environment have a profound and direct influence on a number of important outcomes including leader behaviour and job satisfaction (James et al., 1990).

Additionally, organisations have cultures, which guide decision-making and shape the way that people behave, feel, contribute, interact and perform. The culture within many social work organisations has been increasingly shaped by successive governments, which set out a legislative framework, establish national targets and require inspection agencies to ensure that quality standards are being met. This has engendered significant changes in the management of all public sector organisations. Neo-Taylorist managerialism requires managers to achieve public sector reform through an integrated model of mission statements, target-setting, performance management, outcome measures and service review (see Chapters 17 and 22). The resultant effect has been a diminution of professional autonomy and accountability, as the practitioner's performance becomes increasingly accountable to managers, often exhibiting aggressive and macho management styles (Hadley and Clough, 1996). Clarke et al. (2000) noted that the most visible shift might be witnessed in the growth in the number of public sector managers and their power relative to other organisational groups.

Nevertheless, alternative models of transformational- and transactional-leadership approaches have been recommended as good practice by academics such as Alimo-Metcalfe (2000). While transactional leadership is concerned with day-to-day operational needs, such as planning, budgeting, staffing and the working environment, transformational leadership is aimed at the process of engendering higher levels of motivation and commitment among followers.

Furthermore, Adams et al. (2005: 13) define transformational practice as one that 'moves beyond managerialism and accountability primarily to the organisation, and asserts account-ability to professional values, principles and approaches as well'. This recognises that leaders are required to adopt a supportive and facilitative approach to achieve optimum working conditions for practitioners and, therefore, optimum outcomes for service users.

In supervision, this transformational practice, which has an inextricable relationship with double-loop learning, may be achieved through the facilitation of learning that explores and understands organisational systems. This form of transformation is characterised by total employee involvement in a process of collaboratively conducted, collectively accountable change directed towards shared values and principles. Crucial to this process is that the super-visor is not the teacher but part of this collaborative learning and relearning process.

Interprofessional supervision – learning from health models

As we have seen, the tensions between the use of supervision as a tool of surveillance and as a mechanism for support are well documented. The solution within the health arena has been to distinguish between *management supervision* (to perform the necessary normative and some formative functions, often referred to as *clinical governance*) and *practice super-vision* (with more focus on formative and restorative functions).

Management supervision/clinical governance sets work objectives, ensures agency compli-ance and assures the quality of service received by patients and service users. Because of the fears that singular supervision frameworks would lead to the predominance of appraisal, censure and managerial control – linked with a concomitant erosion of professional autonomy (see Butterworth and Faugier, 1992) – the need was perceived for a professional supervisory rela-tionship alongside but explicitly separate from the managerial relationship. Accordingly, the NHS management executive defined clinical (or practice) supervision as: 'a formal process of professional support and learning which enables individual practitioners to develop knowledge and competence, assume responsibility for their own practice, and enhance consumer protec-tion and safety of care in complex situations' (NHS Management Executive, 1993).

In health settings, it is the responsibility of the practitioner to ensure practice supervi-sion takes place by negotiating a supervisory relationship with an appropriate individual, in accordance with specified guidance about contact, frequency and duration. The United Kingdom Central Council for Nursing, Midwifery and Health Visiting (1995) makes it clear that managerial supervision is not part of clinical supervision, which is designed to meet the support needs of practitioners. Indeed, an evaluative study by Butterworth et al. (1997) concluded that it was the restorative function of the clinical supervision process that was the most valued by nurses.

Clinical supervision in a social work context could therefore take the form of a tripartite arrangement, where the supervisee is part of two separate processes. The first would aim to provide professional support and development and would be conducted with an agreed supervisor, such as a peer, while the second would aim to satisfy demands of accountabil-ity with the worker's line manager taking a key role. However, although these processes have different objectives, both should be undertaken in an environment that values collab-oration and agreement.

Drawing on your own experiences of work and supervision, to what extent do you consider this tripartite arrangement to be an achievable aspiration?

Conclusion

So, what of the future for social work practice and supervision within emerging and developing interprofessional practice? As Jones states (1999: 42), 'clinical supervision is concerned neither with management authority nor a therapeutic relationship', and it is precisely this focus on reflection, on professional support and on development that is potentially absent in the supervision model historically associated with social work and social care. We do not dispute the necessity for managerial surveillance, but the lack of professional support and development as experienced by practitioners is well documented. The four modes of supervision in Figure 21.2 are recognised in social work practice, with Type C being most evident in settings ruled by fear but without the capacity, or will, to engage in effective support processes.

	High Levels of surveillance Low	
High **Levels** **of** **support** **Low**	**Type A** High support and high surveillance/guidance standards, often seen as desirable for newly qualified workers.	**Type B** The experienced practitioner has autonomy in decision-making, but the supervisor maintains a supportive/developmental role.
	Type C Defensive managerialist mode where the supervisor maintains high levels of control, but provides low levels of surveillance	**Type D** Where little support or surveillance is provided and which may result in dangerous and destructive managerial practice.

Figure 21.2   Four modes of supervision

The need for professional supervision will be significantly increased with the development of interprofessional working arrangements. One of the emerging challenges of interprofessional practice will be to ensure that practice governance and practitioner support feature equally in the supervision models that are developed for social workers in the new settings. The nursing model – separating out clinical governance from clinical/practice supervision – may offer a viable vision for social work. Without doubt, social workers must be collectively clear about their support and supervisory needs, and employing organisations should construct frameworks so that these needs can properly addressed. Finally, this chapter also raised the issue of supervision having countless interpretations. Definitions in contemporary social work and human-services organisations are inseparable from and made more complex by cultural, socio-economic environments at the macro, meso and micro level, in addition to actors' own beliefs and perceptions.

Key learning points

1. Supervision is mediated by a social, economical, cultural, political and technological context.
2. Regular, reliable and assured supervision is essential for all practitioners, in particular those newly qualified or entering new posts and roles.
3. Developmental and supportive supervision is the cornerstone of improving and assuring practice.
4. Supervision without the core ingredients of support, development and professional enhancement is little more than performance management and outcome surveillance.
5. Supervision is the pathway to reflective practice, the identification of staff training and development needs, and the vehicle for service enhancement.
6. Within interprofessional contexts, the need for professional social work supervision will both be challenging to achieve and increasingly important.

Taking it further

Readers who want to know more about this will find the following helpful:

Hawkins, P. and Shohet, R. (2000) *Supervision in the Helping Professions: An Individual, Group and Organizational Approach* (2nd edn), Buckingham: Open University Press.

Kadushin, A. and Harkness, D. (2002) *Staff Supervision in Social Work* (4th edn), New York: Columbia University Press.

Morrison, T. (2001) *Staff Supervision in Social Care* (2nd edn), London: Pavilion.

22 Management

Vicky White and John Harris

This chapter will:

- highlight the absence of a discussion of managerialism from much of the social work literature;
- provide a critique of managerialism, identifying its origins and current manifestations;
- explore how managerialism is encountered in social work and ways in which social workers can mitigate its impact.

Introduction

Can you work out what is being discussed in these two extracts?

Mapping supply will involve an analysis of the market within which the service is operating. Within this analysis there will be four key areas for enquiry:

- an analysis of the existing stock;
- an analysis of the various elements of service;
- an analysis of services from other providers;
- an analysis of alternatives that can be spot-contracted.

This is an extract from a paper on a local authority's foster parent 'market' by a social work manager. The 'stock' mentioned is foster parents.

How about this statement? What do you think is being discussed here?

Our interest is in best practice in terms of what works, why and how at the business level, when customer-facing technologies are introduced. We have a services transformation practice and want to learn more about the art of the possible in order to help our clients solve their problems.

This is from a consultancy firm's promotional literature, explaining how it wants to assist social work agencies to introduce commercial-style call centres as the first point of contact for potential service users.

The use of this kind of language - in the past, exclusively associated with private businesses – is now common in social work. The language of 'strategies', 'visions', 'missions', 'business plans', 'performance indicators' and 'devolved budgets' stems from managerialism: the belief that management knowledge and practices are essential ingredients in social work. In this chapter, we explore the emergence and characteristics of managerialism and some of the aspects of it that social work students encounter during their periods of practice learning. Before doing so, we note the lack of attention paid to management in much of the social work literature and consider briefly the professional bureaucracy that existed prior to the arrival of managerialism.

The mystery of missing management

Management is rarely mentioned in social work textbooks and often not mentioned on social work courses. It seems to be seen as a topic which is not relevant to being a social work student; it might be acknowledged as being important later on, in the careers of those students who decide subsequently that management is for them, at which point they will discover the business literature about 'how to be a manager'. Yet, when a student goes into a period of practice learning, it is usually only a short time before comments are heard about 'management', as a kind of amorphous presence. Complaints are probably heard about what 'management' is or isn't doing or what 'management' should or shouldn't be doing, ranging on a scale from mild rebuke to carping criticism. In contrast, sometimes students will be told that 'management' in a particular work setting is 'good' or 'supportive' and that this is one of the reasons why people have stuck around.

Given these kinds of day-to-day experiences of 'management', the dearth of references to it in many social work textbooks seems odd, especially as frequent references are made to legislation and policy, along the lines of: 'here are the statutory duties and policies that social work students need to know about - now go and put them into practice'. Statutory duties and policies do sanction social workers' intervention in what are identified by the state as problematic areas of service users' lives (White, 2006: Chapter 3), but legislation and policy are mediated by organisations. When a student goes to work in what is often referred to as a 'social work agency', it *is* the *agency* of social work – the organisational location in which the roles and tasks of social workers are managed, resulting in what is regarded as 'social work'.

Of course, the day-to-day running of any organisation has to be managed, and thought has to be given to the challenges it faces. For some years, the necessity for such short- and long-term management has been seen as synonymous in public (and increasingly in voluntary) social work agencies with management of a particular type – often referred to as 'managerialism'. The existence of this form of management marks indelibly students' experiences in practice, and a critical appreciation of its impact needs to be included in the curriculum of social work courses. Before considering managerialism further, we note that this has not always been the dominant approach to managing social services organisations by examining a previous approach that we have termed 'professional bureaucracy'.

Professional bureaucracy

In the organisations established by the post-war welfare state, the term 'management' was rarely heard. 'Management' was associated with private businesses: public sector services were seen as needing 'administration'. The assumption that public services should be run differently enjoyed a broad measure of support across the political spectrum in Britain from 1945 until the late 1970s, and social work was regarded as unsuited to being organised in ways that were derived from the business sector (Marshall, 1981). The form of administration employed in social services in this era drew on professionalism and bureaucracy as sources for what were seen as relevant knowledge and acceptable practice. Bureaucracy was seen as embodying the ideals of efficiency and impartiality, with organisational structures rooted in and routed through rules and procedures. Within this bureaucratic framework, services involving roles and tasks which were seen as unsuited to the straightforward application of rules, such as social work, were assigned to professional staff, who were given areas of considerable discretion within which to operate (Parry and Parry, 1979: 42–3).

The professional bureaucracy approach to management was the taken-for-granted way of doing things in local authorities as the primary location of social work, with acknowledgement of a 'proper place' for social workers' use of discretion. This involved a form of supervision that emphasised a supervisor and a social worker meeting as colleagues, with social workers being accorded a high degree of autonomy in their work. A front-line manager, speaking in 1981, captured the spirit of professional bureaucracy: 'I see social workers as autonomous. They should accept the responsibilities they have and supervision should be sharing those situations that they feel they need to talk over [...] You have to allow social workers their autonomy' (Harris, 1998: 855–6). However, professional bureaucracy began to fade in significance under the glare of managerialism.

Managerialism

Managerialism is a term which has been used to describe changes that have taken place in social work and other public (and also, increasingly, voluntary sector) services in recent years in many parts of the world. The core concern of managerialism in the UK, from the early 1980s onwards, was the application of business management structures, systems and techniques to public services, with the objective of getting more for less (Waine and Henderson, 2003: 54).

Some of the key features of managerialism are:

- 'management' is a separate and distinct organisational function;
- progress is seen in terms of increasing productivity;
- increased productivity will come from the application of information and organisational technologies;
- there must be a shift from a focus on inputs and processes to outputs and outcomes;
- measurement and quantification need to increase;
- markets or market-type mechanisms should be used to deliver services;
- contractual relationships should be introduced;
- customer orientation should be central;
- the boundaries between the public, private and voluntary sectors should be blurred;

(Adapted from Pollitt, 1990: 2–3, 2003: 27–8)

Underpinning all of these features of managerialism is the advocacy of greater power for managers; managers have the 'right to manage'. Their role is seen as central to the improvement of organisational performance, which is to be achieved by limiting the discretion of professionals, ostensibly in the interests of empowering the 'customer'.

Moves to strengthen the role of management began with the coming to power, from 1979 onwards, of Conservative governments influenced by New Right ideas. The New Right belief that the market was superior to the state undermined the position accorded to social workers in professional bureaucracies. The New Right saw the professions as needing to be immersed in 'the bracing competitive stimulus of market forces [...] Professions were seen as very much secondary to management as an instrument of effective social policy' (Foster and Wilding, 2000: 146). Accordingly, the New Right asserted, public services such as social work needed to become more like businesses and managed in ways which were drawn from the private sector. The power relations between professionals and managers shifted, as managers were given responsibility for achieving economy, efficiency and effectiveness (Audit Commission, 1983) and bringing professionals under control. The increased power for managers was seen as sounding the death knell for the much caricatured professional bureaucracy: 'Bureaucracy is pictured [...] like a dinosaur [...] it was too big, too slow-moving, too insensitive, insufficiently adaptable and seriously underpowered as far as brains were concerned' (Pollitt, 2003: 32–3).

From the outset, managerialism was presented as having a mission to transform, drawing on texts that presented the work of the manager in urgent and dynamic terms:

Ask yourself at the end of the day, every day, 'what exactly and precisely and explicitly is being done in my work area differently from the way it was done when I came to work this morning?' [...] If you can't put your hands on something [...] that's being done differently in the afternoon from the way it was done in the morning, then you haven't been alive [...] The manager, in today's world, doesn't get paid to be a 'steward of resources', a favoured term not so many years ago. He or she gets paid for one and only one thing [...] to change things, to act – today.

(Peters, 1988: 469)

The certainties of such texts encouraged the belief that managerialism is technical, objective and neutral, claiming to reveal the self-evident best way to do things and removing political and ethical difficulties. However, as Banks points out through two examples, this is impossible:

> To regard child protection purely as a technical exercise is misguided and ignores the ethical questions which are really about how much 'abuse' is society prepared to tolerate, balanced against how much interference in family life is thought to be justified [...]
>
> In the field of community care [...] the language is largely technical and standardised forms are often used [...] Ultimately the decision regarding what services to provide and how will depend on the availability of resources and political and ethical decisions about priorities [...]

(Banks, 1995: 136)

Given that the origins of managerialism lay in the agenda of the Conservative governments from the early 1980s onwards, when New Labour came into office in 1997 it inherited social services in which managerialism was firmly entrenched. New Labour took over the language and practices of managerialism and continued to support its key ideas, such as the setting of explicit targets for services, performance monitoring and the use of market-type mechanisms. However, the Labour government has also developed its own twists to managerialism, involving the use of more performance measures, an emphasis on partnership, using management to achieve policy goals, rather than as an end in itself, and the use of new concepts derived from business practice such as 'stakeholders' (Newman, 2001).

Perhaps the most significant development in managerialism has been New Labour's intensification of performance management (see Chapter 17). It defines social work's objectives at national level, sets outcomes to be achieved locally and monitors the results. Its emphasis on local management and a strong performance culture is directed unequivocally towards the achievement of targets it has set, and it has strong expectations that its agendas will be delivered by social workers. These demands are reinforced by the publication of 'naming and shaming' reports, when social work agencies are considered not to be up to scratch on performance against centrally set indicators, and comparative data appears in star rankings and league tables, indicating agencies' relative success in reaching New Labour's requirements. Exposing performance in this way is assumed to stimulate continuous improvement.

Encountering managerialism

Given that we have argued that managerialism has been consolidated across the political spectrum and is firmly embedded in social services, in what ways might social work students run into it? Given its all-pervasive character, almost everything that students do during periods of practice learning will be imbued with some facet of managerialism, emphasising the importance of considering managerialism on social work courses. We have selected five aspects of managerialism for particular attention:

1. management culture;
2. core business;
3. performance management;
4. audit;
5. work organisation.

Management culture

Part of the ethos of managerialism is to suggest that the worst excesses of discrimination have been overcome and that this has opened up opportunities for advancement through management jobs to anyone who is suitably qualified. Rather than managerialism being seen as having achieved a new, fair, harmonious organisational order, it could be regarded as masking the continuing impact of social divisions within social work organisations. For example, there is a long-standing pattern of such organisations being 'gendered' (White, 2006), with the social work workforce composed largely of women and management positions occupied overwhelmingly by men (SSI, 1991; Ginn and Fisher, 1999). There is also a paucity of Black or Asian senior managers (Mullender and Coulshed, 2001: 222). Any work organisation tends to reflect the social relations in the wider society so that in social work, 'The work which people undertake, whether or not they are professionally qualified, the hierarchical positions they occupy and so on are all linked, and all these factors are related to whether the person is black or white, female or male' (Hugman, 1991: 204).

Not only are organisational structures (white) male-dominated but also, as Grey notes more generally, the dominant management culture is 'masculinist' in its preoccupation with order, control, instrumental rationality and domination (Grey, 2005: 127–8). This masculinist management culture, whether reproduced by men or women, affects who gets heard, who gets the credit, what gets done (Tannen, 1995) and how managers are trained (Sinclair, 1995). Mainstream management culture also reflects the multifaceted nature of patterns of domination in social work organisations along the lines of age, class background, (dis)ability, 'race' and sexuality:

> There is still a long way to go before 'management', instead of being synonymous with white men, is opened up the rich range of interpretations and debates generated by the diverse experiences and potential contributions of women (lesbian and heterosexual), gay men, Black people and people of different ages and class backgrounds.
>
> (Kelly and Harris, 1996: 14)

Social work students encounter managerialist culture at every turn. They are positioned within it in particular ways and can see how other people are positioned. They can become aware of whose voices are amplified by the culture and whose are marginalised.

Core business

The notion of focusing on the 'core business' of social work involves managers in setting clear organisational goals and dispensing with activities that do not contribute to their achievement, thus narrowing the range and amount of services to those seen as absolutely essential to the fulfilment of statutory requirements or to the implementation of central government's priorities. This is often achieved through tightening eligibility criteria, thus masking difficult issues about inadequate budgets and service priorities. Some of these issues are revealed by this hospital social worker:

> Well we've had to tighten up. We used to cover three levels, priority 1, 2 and 3 [... Now] we're not supposed to get involved with priority 3s. So what we have to do is go back to the ward staff and tell them to either direct the referral to the local Social Services office for home care or to CAB [Citizens' Advice Bureau] for benefits ... we've got so much work coming in that we're supposed to bring all the referrals back here and then [the manager] prioritises them, so, we're a bit restricted. I'm very reluctant to go in to talk to anybody because you often start something off, that you can't really finish. So I feel restricted in that sense.

> (White, 2006: 211)

For any student, during a period of practice learning, the issue of what is considered to constitute core business and how it is enforced through the use of eligibility criteria or access thresholds can be a central, and often emotionally taxing, experience.

Performance management

As we have seen, managerialism has imported the idea of performance management from the business world. Effective organisations are seen as needing clear objectives resulting in quantifiable outcomes, requiring performance indicators and monitoring of performance against them, in order to decide whether they have been successful. Accordingly, New Labour has defined social work's objectives at national level, has set outcomes to be achieved locally and has monitored the results. This emphasis on a strong performance culture has been highlighted through publicising the results in terms of successful and unsuccessful organisations, for example through the award of star ratings. Social work students will encounter ways in which performance indicators set the priorities and shape the form of social work that is carried out in the settings in which they work. This is because the indicators identify which aspects of practice are to be encouraged, within the framework of accountability to government.

A common practice is the use of output measures as proxies for performance outcomes. For example, one SSD decided on four such measures of the quality of asessments with adults:

1. all people who receive a formal assessment of their needs will be offered a copy of their assessment;

2. for all people who receive a service provided or arranged by the department, a written statement or care plan, describing the service they are to get, will be produced and they will be given a copy of it;
3. all written statements (care plans) will indicate when and how the plan is to be monitored and reviewed;
4. all written care plans will show in measurable terms the outcomes which the service is designed to achieve.

If social workers indicate on the computerised record that they have given service users copies of assessments and care plans, this is taken as a proxy measure of the (high) quality of the service. A service user could have experienced the worst possible assessment but, provided this output measure was satisfied, a high quality outcome would be assumed to have taken place and it would be recorded as such.

Audit

A key means of implementing performance management is the use of audit: the practice of external (for example, the CSCI) and internal reviews of performance. There has been a huge increase in social worker activity geared to feeding information to monitoring systems in anticipation of future audits. Students may experience an audit during a period of practice learning. They will certainly experience having to meet demands to create trails of information and will have to perform to targets designed to satisfy audits of organisational performance. One example of this we have come across is of social workers having to meet managerial demands for core assessments to be 'completed' on children and their families before the social workers have had time to gather comprehensive information, in order to comply with timescales that will be subject to audit at some point.

Work organisation

Across social work, managerialism has resulted in tighter managerial control of practice (Harris, 2003). In services for children, there are procedures that regulate decision-making and require standardised approaches to assessment (Garrett 2003). In adult services, there have been parallel moves to standardise through the use of care management systems (Lymbery, 1998; Postle, 2002). Many social workers identify increased workloads and increased scrutiny of their work as stressful aspects of these developments (Jones, 2001). A significant development has been the impact of information technology (Harris, 2003; Garrett, 2005). This can be used to monitor social workers' rationing of resources and to prioritise budgetary considerations in the allocation of services. In addition, social workers' recording is constrained by standardised procedures for information-processing and codification, with many IT systems introducing tick-lists and pick-lists. Around the time New Labour came to power, Sapey commented prophetically:

> The use of computers therefore reduces the scope for interpretation of data and [...] is transforming organisations from professionalised bureaucracies to centrally controlled

administrative activities. While the rules and regulations of agencies will increase, adding controlling bureaucratic features, their flexibility and responsiveness to individuals in need will decrease. The primary task of the organisation may also be changed [...] from one of welfare provision to the collection of data to regulate and determine eligibility for such provision [...] Social workers will find themselves [...] part of a machine that has achieved an objective reality [...] Such systems will inevitably result in greater control over the interpretation of data and consequently over the activities of practitioners.

(Sapey, 1997: 809)

Students experience this kind of control during practice learning. It is now so entrenched in social work that when a student encounters some aspect of their practice being controlled in this way, they are likely to see it as simply a computer request for data. Rather than experiencing this in straightforward managerial terms, as being coerced to undertake work in a particular way, it is more likely to feel like a 'neutral', 'technical' requirement of the software.

Surviving managerialism

Managerialism has reshaped social work and changed what it means to be a social worker. Taken together, the five aspects of managerialism which we have envisaged students encountering during periods of practice learning could be seen as painting a depressing picture of what lies in store for students in the contemporary experience of social work. While acknowledging that managerialism does run through the experience of being a social work student, and later on of being a qualified social worker, it would be unfortunate if we left the impression that present-day social work only offers the possibility of instrumental and uncreative practice, subject to the dictates of managerialism. Our experience of working with social workers and managers has been that not everything that happens is the outcome of managerialism. People with whom we have worked have found ways to collaborate with others, including service users, in maintaining what they see as good practice and have gone beyond that in introducing innovations (White and Harris, 2001, 2004). Accordingly, there are three points that need to be emphasised in order to even up the account given in the previous sections.

First, given the way in which managerialism has grown in significance, it is all too easy to assume that managers have reached the stage of being all-powerful, of wanting and being able to completely dominate and direct the detail of social workers' day-to-day practice. Even if they wanted to do so, and that is by no means necessarily the case, there are limitations on the extent to which managers can control day-to-day practice. Given that social work is an 'invisible trade' (Pithouse, 1987), even tight procedures offer some scope for interpretation and the use of discretion by social workers (Evans and Harris, 2004). For example, social workers have been found either not to have completed or to have adapted documentation with which they were unhappy (SSI, 1994, 1997) or to have manipulated eligibility requirements in what they saw as service users' interests (SSI, 1999). In other words, social workers may be *subject to* managerialism, but they are not necessarily always *subjected by* it, with experiences of divided loyalties (Postle, 2002), the use of strategies such as overt compliance/covert subversion and engagement in active resistance.

Second, management is not an amorphous presence, even though it is often castigated for being so. Organisations, as we all know from our experience of them, are never completely integrated and consensual wholes, as envisaged in their mission statements. This is partly because they are stratified on a number of levels (Harris, 1998) and, as a consequence, the goals of senior managers and local front-line managers may be very different, with the possibility of overlapping interests between local managers and social workers.

Third, managerialism is not a homogeneous phenomenon. There are many different versions of it in different organisations – even within different work settings within the same organisation – and there is evidence of variations in its impact (Kirkpatrick et al., 2005: 161–3 and 170–2). For example, although the dominant culture encouraged by managerialism is 'macho', there are elements within some of its variants that stress 'softer', more relational approaches to facilitating communication, building partnerships and working through networks. Such approaches could be seen as more 'feminised' and generally more inclusive alternatives to managerialism's masculinism.

These three points suggest a final thought; students might benefit from regarding managerialism not as monolithic and omnipotent but as a loose, messy and complex set of dominant ideas and practices (in the wider organisational context and in specific local circumstances) which vary in different social work settings and which contain some room for manoeuvre in seeking to develop social work practice.

Key learning points

1. Legislation and policy are implemented through social work organisations; the way these are managed shapes the nature of practice.
2. 'Professional bureaucracy' was the main approach to managing social work until the late 1970s. It accorded social workers a high degree of discretion compared to today.
3. 'Managerialism', advocating the use of business-style management in public services, was introduced by the New Right from the early 1980s onwards.
4. From 1997 onwards, the New Labour governments have continued to promote managerialism and have intensified its emphasis on performance management.
5. Students encounter the impact of several facets of managerialism during periods of practice learning including management culture, core business, performance management, audit and work organisation.
6. Management takes on different forms in different places. The impact of managerialism on the forms management takes is uneven.

Taking it further

Readers who want to know more about this will find the following helpful:

Clarke, J., Gerwitz, S. and McLaughlin, E. (2000) *New Managerialism New Welfare?* London: Sage.

Harris, J. (2003) *The Social Work Business*, London: Routledge.

McLaughlin, K., Osborne, S.P. and Ferlie, E. (2002) *New Public Management: Current Trends and Future Prospects*, London: Routledge.

White, V. (2006) *The State of Feminist Social Work*, London: Routledge.

23 Value conflicts in practice

Karen Postle

This chapter will:

- explain that there are dilemmas to be encountered and addressed by practitioners seeking a value-based approach to practice.
- draw on themes developed through the book to suggest that social workers need understanding of the self, an ability to undertake critical reflection; the capacity to use supervision effectively and an ability to apply research findings creatively and selectively.
- argue that the ability to manage value conflicts in practice is a critical determinant of an individual's ability to thrive in social work practice. It suggests key means to achieve this.

Introduction

As registered practitioners, social work students receive the GSCC codes of practice at the outset of their training. This includes a credit card-sized fold-out version which, presumably, practitioners can use as a handy reminder of the codes. These codes embody social work values and are therefore a yardstick by which to measure competent practice. Similarly, the National Occupational Standards for social work outline six key roles for practice (TOPSS, 2002). These helped to shape the social work curriculum and students' progress is assessed against them. The sixth key role is a 'catch-all' one, stating social workers will 'Demonstrate professional competence in social work practice'. Key roles are further broken down, like *matryoshka* dolls, into smaller units. For example, Unit 20 of Key Role 6 states that social workers will 'Manage complex ethical issues, dilemmas and conflicts'. Units are broken down again, and Point 20.1 states staff will 'Identify and assess issues, dilemmas and conflicts that might affect your practice'. The introduction to the National Occupational Standards has a diagram showing values and ethics in the centre of the key roles to demonstrate that 'Values and ethics are core to competent social work practice' (TOPSS, 2002: 4).

Hence as Hugman, in Chapter 3, shows, understanding social work values is core to good practice and underpins social workers' education. There is an immediate difficulty here because, as Banks (2001) argues, solidifying values into codes robs them of complexity and ignores inherent contradictions. For example, the first code states that social workers must 'Protect the rights and promote the interests of service users and carers'. In situations where people giving care or support are exhausted and desperate for a break, while the person for whom they provide support or care dreads leaving familiar surroundings and people dear to her or him, social workers trying to consider appropriate solutions will know how over-simplified that statement is!

Hugman has fully explored the values needed for social work practice and has introduced the issue of conflicting values. This chapter will explore further the messy terrain of what happens when values conflict. The complexity of this means that there will not be a handy credit card-sized version to take away, but readers may begin to grasp ways to develop the 'moral fluency' that Hugman describes to help them to deal with complex situations.

This chapter considers three main areas in which values can conflict, giving examples of conflicts and suggesting ways to address them. There is inevitable overlap between these three areas (especially points 1 and 2 below), both in how conflicts arise and in potential remedies, but the division is made for ease of reading. In essence, this chapter endorses the view of social work as a 'practical–moral' rather than a 'rational–technical' activity (Parton and O'Byrne, 2000: 30). Hence, while codes of practice and National Occupational Standards provide useful guidance, they are not a road map for negotiating difficult routes through practice. The three areas are where practitioners' own values conflict with:

1. the context in which they work;
2. the values of the organisation for which they work;
3. the values of the person/family with whom they are working.

For each there will be practice examples and a discussion of likely contributing factors. Finally, there will be a discussion of practice issues which can help practitioners to deal with value conflicts.

Two important points to note:

1. Unfortunately there are people who, for whatever reason, do not hold the values required to practise as a social worker. They may be racist or homophobic, for example, or may lack integrity. Strongly held views and beliefs, at odds with values needed for social work practice, cannot be ignored. Mindful of this, the GSCC introduced assessed preparation for practice (DH, 2002: 3) requiring that all education programmes must assess students' suitability before they commence practice placements. This should not be a 'one off', however, and students should expect that their behaviour throughout their education will be scrutinised. Instances such as repeatedly missing teaching sessions without adequate

explanation would call into question whether someone will let down the people with whom they work by not turning up for appointments (see Chapter 5). Will students whose essays have been copied from someone/somewhere else or bought from a website have the integrity required to be trustworthy social workers? Once in practice, supervisors should be alert to the potential for values which are inconsistent with those of social work.

2. Social work students and staff sometimes claim that social work values clash with those of other professions. As social work is increasingly located in multidisciplinary teams and settings, this issue becomes increasingly important. Differences in values can be overstated, though, and it is worth making comparisons, as Payne (2000a) does, between different professions to see whether other issues contribute more to interprofessional clashes. For example, doctors may well seek predominantly physical explanations for someone's condition while social workers favour broader, social and psychological explanations. In many respects, espoused values are similar. See, for example, the Nursing and Midwifery Council (2004), which has very similar wording to the social work codes of practice. Often it is values of managerialism and consumerism (see, for example, Payne (2000b) and White and Harris in Chapter 22 of this volume) which, when translated into policies, cause greatest conflicts as practitioners from all professions struggle to deliver a professional service against seemingly overwhelming odds of financial and bureaucratic constraints. Social workers, like other professionals, will inevitably find dissonance between their value base and the policy context for their work (Braye and Preston-Shoot, 1995).

 As you read these three sections, can you think of similar examples from your practice?

Practitioners' own values conflicting with the context in which they work

In my research into care managers' work (Postle, 1999b), I was shocked when hearing a member of staff on a training course I observed say, 'Some people in our office are saying, "If we haven't got it [money], they can't bloody have it"'. The speaker expressed concern, saying she found such sentiments worrying because of their apparent distancing from people and their difficulties. This comment epitomised the level of routinisation resulting from trying to cope with high workloads and reduced resources. Similarly, students sometimes comment that families with whom they work 'know how to work the system', as if the resilience and determination needed to tackle poverty and abuse was something to be criticised. The impression gained from such statements is of a profession perceiving itself to be under siege, not just from policy-makers, legislators and accountants but, crucially, from people receiving (or attempting to receive) services themselves. Values conflict where the context for social work appears to privilege the need to process work as fast as possible, constantly aware there are always far more people needing services than there are staff to work with them or resources to meet their needs.

Social workers, whose values tell them to treat people as individuals, can nonetheless find themselves adopting what Lipsky (1980: 140-56) termed a 'client processing mentality'. People can no longer be seen as individuals for fear that the claims they make on one will be too great and, instead, as in the examples given above, processes such as routinising and stereotyping help workers to distance themselves to the point of 'othering' people with whom they work. People who use services are easily labelled 'manipulative', whereas staff, faced with needing to achieve something they want, might consider themselves 'creative'. Such tactics become a survival mechanism for staff, which can be summarised as, 'When the going gets tough, the tough get going!'

We need to understand why this happens. It seems to occur in work contexts where, as Thompson (2005) identifies, there is work overload, an organisational culture encouraging such approaches (or at least not discouraging them), where workers lack confidence or where these factors combine. There is little room for empathy and understanding, let alone genuine regard in such climates because there is constant fear that such feelings might herald the slippery slope into burnout (see Chapter 19). Research into the social work workforce has indicated that these are very real concerns and that stress results when social workers fear loss of control over their work (McLean, 1999). Apparently ignoring, or at least not examining, clashes of values inherent in routinising and stereotyping becomes, in effect, a survival mechanism for some staff and, indeed, part of some teams' and organisations' cultures.

Practitioners' own values conflicting with those of the organisation for which they work

Social work educators are afforded a privileged position for hearing practice 'horror stories' which at best represent bad practice and at worst leave agencies open to censure and even litigation. Examples include:

- A fourteen-year old boy placed in bed and breakfast accommodation of very poor quality where the landlord asked that he share a bed with an older man. This happened because the local authority had a policy of not accommodating teenagers under Section 20 of the Children Act 1989.
- Older people being refused services to meet relatively low needs which might prevent/delay their situation worsening, while others, with heavy care packages, are encouraged to accept increases. This was being done because there was a 'performance indicator' (the measure of local authorities' performance against set targets, see http://www.bvpi.gov.uk/pages/glossary.asp, Clarke et al. (2000) and Chapter 17 in this volume) attached to the number of high packages of care that the local authority achieved.
- Not telling people about services to which they might be entitled or giving information in such a way that deters take-up. For example, one local authority sent out very lengthy and complex carer's assessments by post. This begs the question of how someone might explain on a form how they feel about meeting another person's support needs, how acceptable this is to the person receiving care/support and how the relationship between them is affected by this role.

These examples are invariably greeted with dismay by other students but have inevitably been seen as organisational policy and practice and often something increasingly difficult for practitioners to question. It is to their credit that the students relating these examples have been able to describe what they did or tried to do to challenge these policies and practices.

Hugman explains the root of the conflict of values that can lead to the kind of practice described here. As he explains, the bureaucratic or economic goals which all too often now predominate seem to be on a collision course with professional values. Additionally, as Braye and Preston-Shoot (1995) demonstrate, practice is often constructed as surveillance, monitoring and control, with antagonism and mistrust displacing empowerment.

Managerialist imperatives, intended to address areas where social services were seen as failing (Langan 2000), and resource constraints have led to policies and practices resulting in tensions and dilemmas for practitioners in all spheres of work (Lloyd, 2002; Postle, 2002). Here are some examples:

- social workers in child protection teams finding they have such tight deadlines to complete enquiries under Section 47 of the Children Act 1989 regarding a child who may be at risk that they hardly have time to get to know the child;
- hospital social workers trying to complete assessments and arrange suitable discharges for older people in order to avoid agencies being subjected to 'reimbursement' charges under Section 6 of the Community Care (Delayed Discharges etc.) Act 2003 having very little time to discuss people's wishes with them;
- social workers in youth offending teams trying to complete assessments to very tight timescales and finding that young people have considerable social problems which cannot begin to be addressed in the time available.

Research (Coffey et al., 2004) indicates that staff in a large survey found lack of time and rigid timescales for completing work the most stressful aspect of their jobs, consistently rating these aspects more stressful than issues of difficulty in face-to-face work, such as aggression or considerable risk.

A real danger here is that 'Groupthink' (Irving, 1972) occurs where, typically, agencies and teams within them will not consider alternative ways of working, fail to be critical of actions taken, fail to seek expert opinion (such as legal advice) and rationalise their behaviour. Like Lipsky's 'client processing mentality', this can be all-pervasive, and it becomes very hard for practitioners who are trying to operate according to their value base to swim against the tide and challenge inappropriate policies and practices or work in ways that do not compromise social work's value base.

Practitioners' own values conflicting with those of the person/family with whom they are working

Social workers' values may conflict with those of people with whom they are working in three main ways:

1. Where they are working with someone whose actions demonstrate that their values differ considerably. This happens, for example, where practitioners are required to work with people who have perpetrated child abuse or have committed offences which workers may find inexplicable and unacceptable. To a different degree, this can happen where people demonstrate very different values from those core to social work, such as by telling the worker who has arranged home care support, 'Don't send me anyone Black or I'll soon send them packing'.

2. Where conflict exists about rights and risk or autonomy and protection. This may involve weighing up one person's rights against the risk to themselves or someone else or against another person's rights. An example would be where the parents of a young person with learning difficulty want them to enter residential care, yet the worker knows from careful assessment and ascertaining the young person's wishes that they are capable of living in supported accommodation and going out to work.

3. Sometimes workers have strongly held views, perhaps faith-based, which mean they view a course of action as morally wrong. For example, a social worker might consider that abortion is wrong. They will probably have chosen a career option which means they are unlikely to face the dilemma of giving support/advice to a woman seeking a termination but could find that they are working with an older person who wants to discuss their feelings about having an abortion many years previously.

As Shardlow (2002) has noted, generalised professional codes of ethics have limited use in specific situations.

Dealing with the conflicts

Having identified three areas of value conflicts, I now consider ways in which practitioners can begin to address them. Clearly, social workers need a good understanding of social work values, as outlined by Hugman. They also need a real sense of their own value base and an understanding of what has informed it (Dalrymple and Burke, 1995). They need to be aware, from the outset of their learning, that the values they bring to their work were shaped by a complex mixture of influences in their lives and experiences, that people's values and ideas shape ideologies but that individual's values will, in turn, have been influenced by dominant ideologies (George and Wilding, 1993; Denney, 1998). What follows can inform students and practice teachers/assessors as well as practitioners and managers, but the complexity inherent in all discussions of values and value conflicts cannot be minimised, and acquiring the 'moral fluency' of which Hugman writes requires continual effort. Suggestions can easily be conflated with 'answers' and the following is in the spirit of the former, not the latter.

 Reading the following, how can you work differently?

Knowledge of the law and forms of legal redress

When social workers feel they are under siege, knowledge of the law becomes viewed largely or solely as a defence mechanism. For example, Ellis (2004) succinctly highlights the risk that SSDs will use the Human Rights Act 1998 to promote defensive practice in order to avoid litigation. She highlights front-line staff's lack of awareness of the Human Rights Act's provisions and notes that most local authorities have not reviewed policies and practices to ensure compliance. There are implications for learning and teaching about legislation relevant to social work practice so that it can be used from a perspective of justice and rights rather than justifying the limitations of defensive practice (see Chapter 10 and Braye et al. (2005)).

Rather than following local policies and practices which do not encapsulate social work values and, perversely, leaving themselves further open to legal challenge, practitioners should understand how to use the law to counter policies that are not acting in people's interests and, crucially, how to help people to challenge decisions which appear unjust (Dalrymple and Burke, 1995; McDonald, 1997).

Alliances with service users and their organisations

Beresford and Croft (2004) have shown that movements and organisations of service users have changed over time. Increasingly they are a force for change in legislation, policy and service provision and challenge patronising and paternalistic forms of practice. These authors view progressive social workers as a key positive force for change, seeing liberatory forms of social work as challenging problems like homophobia, domestic violence and racial violence.

Braye and Preston-Shoot (1995) demonstrate how ways of working in partnership with service users can address issues of power imbalance, discrimination and oppression, and Postle and Beresford (2005) suggest that, through alliances with people using services and their organisations, social workers can, as appropriate, contribute to supporting capacity building within groups. They can do this by, for example, giving information and providing opportunities for people to develop skills where needed, thus increasing people's confidence and abilities. The chapters by Advocacy in Action and Shaping Our Lives (Chapters 6 and 20) explain how partnership can work successfully. Freire (1996) described the concept of transforming action as a means for liberating oppressed people. It indicates a very different role for practitioners from one that concentrates solely or largely on individualistic practice and resonates much more with ways of working that encompass work with and within communities to effect change (Holman, 2000; Smale et al., 2000; see also Chapter 9).

Use of supervision

Chapter 21 addresses supervision in detail, so this is a brief comment. In McLean's (1999) research, only one in ten staff surveyed used their manager as the most important source of support for dealing with job-related stress, although this was the person specifically paid to do this. Banks (2002) sees the supervisory role as being crucial in providing opportunities for social workers to give reflective accounts of practice yet, all too often, supervision focuses upon managerialist imperatives concerned with workload management and budgetary concerns rather than practitioners' reflections, including those concerning value conflicts. It is questionable how and where, if at all, practice issues such as those described above can be safely aired and discussed if supervision does not provide that forum (Thompson, 2005).

Advocacy

Writers including Brandon and Brandon (2001), Braye and Preston-Shoot (1995) and Payne (2000b) argue strongly for social workers' advocacy role, countering arguments that it necessarily or invariably involves conflicts of interest and suggesting routes for when such conflicts occur. Whether social workers themselves act as advocates or facilitate people's contact with one another to act in an advocacy capacity, advocacy is a crucial part of social work, consistent with building capacity within groups of people using services and thus enabling them to work autonomously.

Advocacy is a complex and contested area which, as Brandon and Brandon exemplify, can result in social workers being in conflict with their employing agencies. However, Beresford (1994) gives a timely reminder that, even if there are apparent conflicts of interest, the social worker's role is to try to protect the service user's interests. At best, advocacy can counter practice which, whether inadvertently or not, pathologises the people it should seek to support (Brandon and Brandon 2001).

Critical use of research

There is a risk that social workers use research like the adage about misuse of statistics. That is, they use it as someone who is drunk uses a lamp-post: for support rather than illumination! For example, practitioners are sometimes encouraged to find research to support actions which agencies have already decided to take. In recent years there has been a considerable drive to encourage social workers to ensure their practice is 'evidence-based', with an emphasis on 'what works' in given situations (Parton and O'Byrne, 2000). As these authors clearly show, there is a danger in simplifying the nature of the social work task and ignoring the uncertainty and doubt often characterising practice.

Humphries, in Chapter 7, shows that what is required is, instead, a critical approach to research that may actually raise more questions than it poses answers. It requires openness to considering a range of research approaches and preparedness to use research findings to challenge policy and practice. Hence, the processes of evaluation, reflection and research become woven together in a critical process (Fook, 2002). When practitioners are encouraged to do this, from training onwards, they are better placed to offer a reasoned critique of the kind of practice examples described above where managerialist imperatives appear to dictate practice. For example, there is a growing body of research concerning both the difficulties inherent in operating the Community Care (Delayed Discharges) Act 2003 (see, for example, CSCI, 2004b; Rowland and Pollock, 2004; CSCI, 2005) and in developing viable forms of intermediate care options (see, for example, the research publications of the King's Fund, http://www.kingsfund.org.uk).

Knowledge and use of oneself

Harrison and Ruch addressed this extensively in Chapter 5. Hence this simply serves as a reminder that it is essential for practitioners to explore their values and to find the interconnectedness between these and social work values and also to consider possibilities for value conflicts with people with whom they work. As Banks (2001) argues, social workers should consider which values have primacy when personal values clash with those of someone with whom they are working. She gives an example of someone viewing abortion as wrong but accepting that an individual's right to self-determination and the importance of a non-judgemental approach (Biestek, 1961) should predominate. Biestek's work reminds us that holding a non-judgemental attitude does not mean sliding into moral relativism where one cannot judge right from wrong but, rather, understanding and acknowledging that people needing help and support do not need to be judged. It is possible, as Biestek argues, to hate someone's actions, without extending judgment to the person.

Fook (2002) gives helpful pointers for developing a reflective climate where challenge is acceptable and the norm in social work education so that students can be encouraged to explore their views rather than simply hearing disagreement. A similar approach could easily apply to supervision conducted with a group of staff instead of solely individually. By doing this, as Parton and O'Byrne (2000: 24) suggest, practitioners develop 'a critical stance towards our taken-for-granted ways of understanding the world including ourselves'.

Avoiding defensive practice

Avoiding defensive practice has been core throughout this chapter. Thompson (2005) sees this as a result of criticism in the media and elsewhere as well as a fear of something going wrong. In my care management research (Postle, 2002), I found widespread concern about litigation, resulting in apparently excessive defensive practice, such as ensuring a record was made that someone had refused services, at the cost of thorough risk assessment, undertaken within the context of a trusting relationship. The irony here, as Thompson highlights, is that such practices actually increase the chances of difficulty for the worker and, possibly, of litigation.

In place of defensive practice, Banks (2001) proposes reflective practice, recognising the complexity of ethical dilemmas and value conflicts rather than slavishly following bureaucratic procedures. In considering the three examples on page 254, for each, fulfilling bureaucratic requirements obscured the need for morally right action. Bureaucratic procedures are essential, and it would be culpable neglect for social workers not to record actions taken and decisions made. However, when, for example, forms for recording assessment become conflated with the skilled process of assessment itself, practice is impoverished. Practitioners and their managers need to continually consider whether bureaucracy, often instigated by defensive imperatives, is driving practice rather than complementing it. If it has supplanted, rather than supplemented, the tacit process of critical reflection, something is wrong and the task is not social work.

Conclusion

As Hugman states, social workers need to be able to work with the incompatibilities and incommensurabilities that are the reality of value conflicts in their practice. They cannot assume that unquestioning adherence to policies and procedures or solely 'plumbing' (see Chapter 10, pp. 104–5) approaches to legislation will help them steer a straight course through the dilemmas encountered in practice. They need to develop and be helped to develop skills of critical reflective practice.

This chapter has outlined the main ways in which social workers are likely to encounter value conflicts in their practice and has posed suggestions for how practitioners, in training and beyond, can be helped to work in ways that enable them to address these conflicts.

Key learning points

1. Value conflicts are an inevitable part of social work practice and are best addressed by critical, reflective practice.
2. Value conflicts can arise because practitioners' values conflict with the context of managerialism and of reduced resources within which they work. This context may shape agency policies and practices, causing, contributing to or exacerbating value conflicts.
3. Social workers need to consider which values have primacy when they experience conflict between their own values and those of people with whom they work.
4. Suggestions for areas to consider in order to resolve or minimise value conflicts include:

   - knowledge of legislation and forms of legal redress;
   - alliances with service users and their organisations;
   - supervision;
   - advocacy;
   - critical use of research;
   - knowledge and use of oneself;
   - avoiding defensive practice.

Taking it further

Readers who want to know more about this will find the following helpful:

Balloch, S., McLean, J. and Fisher, M. (eds) *Social Services: Working under Pressure*, Bristol: Policy Press.

Banks, S. (2004) *Ethics, Accountability and the Social Professions*, Basingstoke: Palgrave.

Brandon, D. and Brandon, T. (2001) *Advocacy in Social Work*, Birmingham: Venture Press.

Smale, G., Tuson, G. and Statham, D. (2000) *Social Work and Social Problems: Working towards Social Inclusion and Social Change*, Basingstoke: Macmillan.

Part Five

Conclusion

Opportunities and threats

24 *Social work in the twenty first century*

Karen Postle and Mark Lymbery

Introduction: a profession to be proud of

It is nearly impossible, without diminishing immensely valuable contributions, to attempt to summarise authors' work from preceding chapters. Instead, we elicit themes derived from all chapters to briefly explore threats and opportunities facing social work and social work education and to look to the future.

A student on a post-qualifying social work course told a seminar group that she had puzzled about how to represent her work with an elderly couple. The situation was complex, involving months of skilled, careful work, and she drew it in cartoon strip form, detailing the couple's life events and her involvement. She described her input, referring to her drawing, and the group discussed this. In facilitating and summarising the discussion, something about the cartoon strip became apparent; the couple became bigger as the story progressed until, at the bottom of the page, they were about three times the size from the top. Over time, this student, a skilled, experienced and reflective practitioner, used a range of social work skills, drew on a body of knowledge, informed her work from a strong value base and used herself as a tool in building a relationship with the couple and with other professionals and people in their network. It had not been easy. Like others in the group, she described appropriately challenging other professionals, advocating on the couple's behalf, working at the right pace for them despite pressure to close their case and needing to engage with them at an emotional level, which could prove exhausting. What she had done, as her drawing seemingly unconsciously showed, was enable the couple to 'grow', finding ways to ensure that, at the end of their lives and in very difficult circumstances, they maximised and retained independence and autonomy.

In its simplest expression, yet entailing detailed and complex work, social work can be seen as, essentially, about 'growing' people. As this volume's authors demonstrate, this entails work at micro level, where key skills of communication and assessment and use of oneself are exercised. Micro-level work requires clear values, constantly open to examination, challenge and reflection, understanding the life course and its impact on people and an ability to appreciate and work alongside other professions. Such work does not happen in a theoretical vacuum but within a legal context and informed by research and theory. Despite its theoretical base, it does not mouth mantras of uncritically accepted wisdom but remains open to questioning, recognising strength in living and working with uncertainty. Rather than happening in isolation, it is guided by insights opened to scrutiny, reflection and discussion in supervision. Where relevant, it is informed and supported by appropriate use of ICT. This is good social work.

Social work is distinguished from other professions in its ability, as this volume's authors clearly identify, also to operate at macro level. This entails an awareness of social work's wider social and political context and a desire to effect wider change, appreciating and acknowledging inequalities and injustices impacting upon the lives of many people with whom practitioners work. Crucially, as service user authors have shown, practitioners must be prepared to learn not solely from lectures and textbooks but also from the lived experiences of people receiving social care.

Further, as authors identify, social work operates at a meso level (Lymbery and Butler, 2004) within organisations where there is responsibility for professional supervision and development. This level has been endorsed by the requirement that all registered social workers will need to demonstrate their continuing professional development.

Yet social work is a profession continuing to struggle with its identity and even its belief in itself. Frequently it regards as weakness its inability to clearly identify what it actually does when compared to professions who arbitrate between, mend or educate people. It fears being swallowed up, subsumed within multidisciplinary teams where it cannot exert an identity and residualised to picking up the pieces of what other professions cannot or choose not to do. At its most pessimistic, it fears disappearance, becoming something that can be done by other professionals or by people lacking social work education and qualification.

Social work seems, in many respects, an adolescent profession. It lacks both the history and gravity of professions such as medicine or law which have come of age, so, like the adolescent demanding to be heard, it struggles to be taken seriously. Sometimes, like adolescents who cannot see why they cannot stay out late, have bigger allowances or do what everyone else does, social work whinges 'it's not fair' when it receives bad press, when no one appears to understand what it does, when it seems 'damned if it does and damned if it doesn't' or when no one likes it as much as other professions. In contrast, adolescence's positives are its commitment, passion and ideals. Social work has those and, as this volume's authors demonstrate, it is a profession that can and should be driven by ideals of equality and social justice. Strength and tenacity to keep these ideals in mind and to work at macro, meso and micro levels are defining features of social work. They make it a profession to be proud of.

Social work under threat

Just before writing this chapter, I (Postle) had two experiences within one day which epitomised dissonance and distance between research, academia and practice. In the morning, social work students presented research findings relevant to work with older people. They analysed and summarised these and, importantly, drew conclusions for practice and for challenging endemic ageism. They related the research to their work placements, drawing lessons for future practice. Hearing this gave me cause for optimism that, in practice, students will remember lessons learned from theory and research and will synthesise and translate these into effective practice.

Later that day I spoke with a senior manager in a Social Services Department who explained why our bid for an evaluation project was unsuccessful. She explained that, although we had demonstrated considerable relevant knowledge, we were, bluntly, 'too academic', and they did not want this approach. The manager explained that our proposal contained several pages detailing our understanding of the research and policy background to the project, whereas what they really wanted was a couple of pages saying, 'This is your question. Here is how we will answer it.' The tender was given to a consultancy who did this and whose website contains statements resonating with managerialist language quoted by White and Harris (Chapter 22). While my response to this news could simply be seen as the grumbles of a bad loser, there is an important issue here. This senior manager, who clearly needed a quick answer, not burdened by theory, research or policy critiques, could soon be employing some of the students I'd worked with earlier. How will they be able to sustain what they have learned or be encouraged to continue in their professional development if these attitudes prevail at senior levels?

The history of the probation service in the UK since the 1980s provides a helpful, if worrying, lesson. Over two decades we have witnessed erosion and decline of the important social work elements of probation. Under successive governments of Margaret Thatcher and John Major, probation (originally 'court missioners' whose role was to assist, advise and befriend) became divorced from social work training, becoming a regulatory and punitive service, epitomising Major's 1992 comment that what society needed to do was 'condemn a little more and understand a little less'. In 2006, there were several examples of the probation service apparently failing to carry out its duties properly, resulting in seemingly avoidable tragedies (see, for example, Travis, 2006). Reporting of these cases contains two familiar elements: an understaffed workforce, seemingly stretched to its limits, and absence of senior management's support. The writing is now on the wall for the probation service in anything resembling its previous form and it appears ripe for privatisation (Community Care, 2006b). It is deeply worrying to see senior management appearing to collude in this.

In 1999 I documented my concerns about an apparently widening gulf between academia and practice in social work (Postle, 1999a). Several authors, some contributing to this volume, have commented here and elsewhere on the worrying state of social work at the beginning of the twenty first century (see, for example, Jordan, 2001; Lymbery, 2001; Harris, 2003). The senior manager's approach referred to above seems very similar to a team manager I interviewed who saw her role as a 'gatekeeper' of resources. This person was clear that her staff:

> need to get their job satisfaction from quantity rather than quality and perhaps you need to think, 'Wow! I helped x number of people' rather than, 'I have helped Mrs. so and so over the last six months'. (Postle, 1999b: 117)

She further explained:

> I don't think it's any accident that the duty team is being built partially of new staff …
> I think that's an awareness from the service manager level that I'm coming at it from a
> slightly different angle and that, for everybody's peace of mind, it may be better if new
> members of staff come in and are familiar with the way that I prefer to work.

(Postle, 1999b: 124)

The 'new members of staff' were unqualified. The practice of employing unqualified staff to undertake work formerly done by qualified staff has continued and has been extended in almost all areas of social work practice. It clearly threatens the continuation of a qualified workforce and is potentially harmful for people using services.

Authors in this volume identify a number of threats to social work practice including, for example:

- the conflict of individualistic 'choice' and collective 'community cohesion' agendas polarising social work aims and objectives (Jordan);
- managerialist practices, originating from New Right ideology but perpetuated by New Labour (White and Harris);
- diminishing value placed upon skills of assessment and communication and on skilful use of self (Parker, Koprowska, Harrison and Ruch);
- rapidly changing organisational contexts, often little understood by practitioners (Lymbery);
- simplistic models of practice teaching and assessing (Harris and Gill).

Social work and social work education face difficult times in countering these threats. Thankfully, this is not the whole story.

Tipping points and opportunities

Rumblings of discontent about social work and social work education are gathering momentum. In 2006 several events and activities taking place within a short time exemplified this. They include:

- a conference, 'Affirming Our Value Base in Social Work and Allied Professions', held in Nottingham on 1 March 2006, drawing over 1,500 participants to hear speakers reasserting social work's value base;
- the launch of 'Social Work and Social Justice: A Manifesto for a New Engaged Practice', http://www.liv.ac.uk/sspsw/Social_Work_Manifesto.html;
- a conference, 'Social Work in the 21st Century', held at the University of Liverpool, 7–8 April 2006, reasserting social work's social justice agenda;
- the ESRC-funded seminar series: Social Work and Health Inequalities Research, http://www2.warwick.ac.uk/fac/cross_fac/healthatwarwick/research/devgroups/social-work/swhin/esrc_seminar_series;
- publication of *Changing Lives: Report of the 21st Century Social Work Review* in Scotland, highlighting the importance of social work skills while being realistic about challenges to the profession, http://www.scotland.gov.uk/Publications/2006/02/02094408/0;

- the launch of Community Care's campaign to 'Stand up for Social Work', http://www. communitycare.co.uk/OnlineTeam/StandUp/Home.htm.

These events indicate a changing mood within social work and a realisation that, simply, 'enough is enough!' Within this volume, authors have demonstrated ways the profession can be effective and develop and have outlined the role of social work education in this. These include:

- working in partnership with service users in practice and education (Advocacy in Action, Shaping Our Lives);
- continuing professional development (Gorman and Lymbery, Eadie);
- appropriate support and supervision (Peach and Horner, Harrison and Ruch);
- working in partnership with other professions (Payne, Whittington);
- being alert to the work's dilemmas and difficulties and the need for a clear value base (Hugman, Fook, Postle);
- practice underpinned by research and legal knowledge (Humphries, Johns);
- appropriate and proactive use of ICT(Rafferty and Steyaert);
- awareness of the social and political context for practice, the impact of injustice and inequality and the importance of understanding how social work operates internationally and what can be learned from other cultures (Jordan, Bywaters, Shardlow).

The authors all take critical approaches to social work and social work education, asserting the need for learning and teaching that equips practitioners to understand the wider context of their work and to carry out their work skilfully and well. This is amply demonstrated in guidance given, for example, by Parker concerning assessment processes and by Koprowska concerning communication.

Into the future

It is increasingly apparent that in social work education, as in social work, 'Doing more of the same won't work' (Scottish Executive 2006: Executive Summary). This echoes calls to reconstitute and remake social work and social work education (Postle, 1999a; Statham, 2003). Langan (2003) rightly describes social work as a resilient profession. Hopefully its educators and practitioners can find support, encouragement and guidance in this volume.

One of the greatest changes in social work and social work education has been understanding how much must be learned from people who use services. We therefore end this book by acknowledging its inception. Its genesis was a Joint Social Work Education Conference (Warwick, 2003). Presentations by Advocacy in Action and Shaping Our Lives moved, enthused and inspired us, and we are delighted that people from both organisations have written chapters. Partnership with and involvement of people using services in their design and delivery and in all stages of social work education is one of the most positive grounds for optimism about the future of social work. In the task of 'growing' social workers, the focus must remain the people who will use services.

Taking it further

Readers wanting to further their understanding of issues raised in this chapter will find the following helpful:

England, H. (1986) *Social Work as Art: Making Sense for Good Practice*, London: Allen and Unwin.

Parton, N. (ed.) (1996) *Social Theory, Social Change and Social Work*, London: Routledge.

Smale, G., Tuson, G. and Statham, D. (2000) *Social Work and Social Problems: Working towards Social Inclusion and Social Change*, Basingstoke: Macmillan.

Report of the 21st Century Social Work Review in Scotland, http://www.scotland.gov.uk/Publications/2006/02/02094408/0.

Bibliography

Abrahamson, P. (1992) 'Welfare Pluralism: Towards a New Consensus for a European Social Policy', in L. Hantrais, M. O'Brien and S. Mangen (eds) *Cross National Research Papers 6: The Mixed Economy of Welfare*, Leicester: European Research Centre, Loughborough University.

Adams, A., Erath, P. and Shardlow, S.M. (eds) (2000) *Fundamentals of Social Work in Selected European Countries: Present Theory, Practice, Perspectives, Historical and Practice Contexts*, Lyme Regis: Russell House.

—— (eds) (2001) *Key Themes in European Social Work: Theory, Practice Perspectives*, Lyme Regis: Russell House.

Adams, R., Dominelli, L. and Payne, M. (2005) 'Transformational Social Work', in R. Adams, L. Dominelli and M. Payne (eds) *Social Work Futures*, Basingstoke: Palgrave.

Addams, J. ([1907] 2002) *Democracy and Social Ethics*, Introduction by C.H. Seigfried, Chicago, IL: University of Illinois Press.

Advisory, Conciliation and Arbitration Service (ACAS) (2003) *ACAS Advisory Booklet: Supervision*, London: ACAS.

Aldgate, J., Jones, D., Rose, W. and Jeffery, C. (eds) (2005) *The Developing World of the Child*, London: Jessica Kingsley.

Ali, Z. (2005) 'Negotiating Identity: The Perspectives and Experiences of Pakistani and Bangladeshi Disabled Young People in the UK', Coventry: Coventry University, unpublished PhD thesis.

Alimo-Metcalfe, B. and Alban-Metcalfe, R.J. (2000) 'Heaven Can Wait', *Health Service Journal*, 12 October, 26–29.

Alston, M. and Bowles, W. (2003) *Research for Social Workers: An Introduction to Methods* (2nd edn), London: Routledge.

Arber, S., Davidson, K. and Ginn, J. (eds) (2003) *Gender and Ageing*, Maidenhead: Open University Press.

Argyle, M. (1999) 'Causes and Correlates of Happiness', in D. Kahneman, E. Diener and N. Schwartz (eds) *Well-Being: Foundations of Hedonic Psychology*, New York: Russell Sage Foundation.

Argyris, C. and Schön, D. (1976) *Theory in Practice: Increasing Professional Effectiveness*, San Francisco, CA: Jossey Bass.

—— (1996) *Organisational Learning II: Theory, Method and Practice*, Reading, MA: Addison-Wesley.

Ash, E. (1992) 'The Personal–Professional Interface in Learning: Towards Reflective Education', *Journal of Interprofessional Care*, 6 (3): 61–71.

—— (1995) 'Taking Account of Feelings', in J. Pritchard (ed.) *Good Practice in Supervision*, London: Jessica Kingsley.

Audit Commission (1983) *Performance Review in Local Government: A Handbook for Auditors and Local Authorities*, London: HMSO.

—— (1993) *Their Health, Your Business: The Role of the District Health Authority*, London: HMSO.

—— (2003) *Targets in the Public Sector*, London: Audit Commission.

Australian Association of Social Workers (AASW) (2000) *Policy and Procedures for Establishing Eligibility for Membership of AASW*, Barton, ACT: AASW.

Baldwin, M. (2000) *Care Management and Community Care*, Aldershot: Avebury.

Baldwin, T.T. and Ford, J.K. (1988) 'Transfer of Training: A Review and Directions for Future Research', *Personnel Psychology*, 41 (1): 63–105.

Ball, C., Harris, R., Roberts, G. and Vernon, S. (1988) *The Law Report: Teaching and Assessment of Law in Social Work Education*, London, CCETSW.

Ball, C., Preston-Shoot, M., Roberts, G. and Vernon, S. (1995) *Law for Social Workers in England and Wales*, London: Central Council for Education and Training in Social Work (CCETSW).

Balloch, S., Andrew, T., Ginn, J., McLean, J., Pahl, J. and Williams, J. (1995) *Working in the Social Services*, London: National Institute for Social Work.

Balloch, S., McLean, J. and Fisher, M. (1999) *Social Services: Working under Pressure*, Bristol: Policy Press.

Banks, S. (1995) *Ethics and Values in Social Work*, Basingstoke: Macmillan.

—— (2001) *Ethics and Values in Social Work* (2nd edn), Basingstoke, Palgrave.

—— (2002) 'Professional Values and Accountabilities', in R. Adams, L. Dominelli, and M. Payne (eds) *Critical Practice in Social Work*, Basingstoke: Palgrave.

—— (2004) *Ethics, Accountability and the Social Professions*, Basingstoke: Palgrave.

—— (2006) *Ethics and Values in Social Work* (3rd edn), Basingstoke: Palgrave.

Barn, R., Andrew, L. and Mantovani, N. (2005) *Life after Care: The Experiences of Young People from Different Ethnic Groups*, York: Joseph Rowntree Foundation.

Barnes, M., Davis, A. and Tew, J. (2000) 'Valuing Experience: Users' Experiences of Compulsion under the Mental Health Act 1983', *The Mental Health Review,* 5 (3): 11–14.

Barr, H., Koppel, I., Reeves, S., Hammick, M. and Freeth, D. (2005) *Effective Interprofessional Education: Argument, Assumption and Evidence*, Oxford, Blackwell.

Barron, C. (2004) 'Fair Play: Creating a Better Learning Environment for Social Work Students in Social Care Settings', *Social Work Education*, 23 (1): 25–38.

BBC Radio 4 (2004) *Business News*, 3 August.

Bean, P. and Melville, J. (1989) *Lost Children of the Empire*, London: Unwin.

Beck, U. (1992) *Risk Society: Towards a New Modernity*, London: Sage.

Beckett, C. and Maynard, A. (2005) *Values & Ethics in Social Work: An Introduction*, London: Sage.

Beckford Report (1985) *A Child in Trust*, London: London Borough of Brent.

Belbin, R.M. (1993) *Team Roles at Work*, Oxford: Butterworth–Heinemann.

Ben-Shlomo, Y. and Kuh, D. (2002) 'A Lifecourse Approach to Chronic Disease Epidemiology: Conceptual Models, Empirical Challenges and Interdisciplinary Perspectives', *International Journal of Epidemiology*, 31 (2): 285–293.

Beresford, B., Sloper, P., Baldwin, S. and Newman, T. (1996) *What Works in Services for Families With a Disabled Child?*, Ilford: Barnados.

Beresford, P. (1994a) 'Advocacy', in *Speaking Out for Advocacy: A Report of the National Conference*, Haworth: Labyrinth.

Beresford, P. (1994b), *Changing the Culture: Involving Service Users in Social Work Education*, London: CCETSW, Paper 32.2.

Beresford, P. and Croft, S. (2004) 'Service Users and Practitioners Reunited', *British Journal of Social Work*, 34 (1): 53–68.

Beresford, P. and Evans, C. (1999) 'Research Note: Research and Empowerment', *British Journal of Social Work*, 29 (5): 671–7.

Bernard, J.M. and Goodyear, R.K. (2003) *Fundamentals of Clinical Supervision* (3rd edn), New York: Allyn & Bacon.

Beverley, A. and Coleman, A. (2005) *Workbook for Assessors*, Salford: University of Salford.

Biestek, F. (1961) *The Casework Relationship*, London: George Allen and Unwin.

Bion, W. (1962) *Learning from Experience*, London: Heinemann.

Blair, T. (2005) Speech at Leeds, *Guardian*, 2 February.

Blanden, J., Gregg, P. and Machin, S. (2005) *Intergenerational Mobility in Europe and North America*, London, London: School of Economics.

Blunkett, D. (2003) 'Active Citizens, Strong Communities; Progressing Civil Renewal', Scarman Lecture to the Citizen Convention, London, Home Office, 11 December.

—— (2004) 'New Challenges to Race Equality and Community Cohesion in the 21st Century', speech to the Institute for Public Policy Research, London, 7 July.

Blyth, E., Dunkley, A., Hodgson, A., Milner, J., Platt, C. and Wilson, J. (1995) *Education, Social Work and the Law: Preparing for Professional Practice*, London: CCETSW.

Bonfadelli, H. (2002) 'The Internet and Knowledge Gaps: A Theoretical and Empirical Investigation', *European Journal of Communication*, 7 (1): 65–84.

Borrill, C.S., Carletta, J., Carter, C.S., Dawson, J.F., Garrod, S., Rees, A., Richards, A., Shapiro, D. and West, M.A. (2001) *The Effectiveness of Health Care Teams in the Nationa Healt Service*, retrieved on 2 October 2006 at http://homepages.inf.ed.ac.uk/jeanc/DOH-final-report.pdf.

Boud, D. and Garrick, J. (1999) *Understanding Learning at Work*, London: Routledge.

Bowpitt, G. (1998) 'Evangelical Christianity, Secular Humanism, and the Genesis of British Social Work', *British Journal of Social Work*, 28 (5): 675–693.

Bradshaw, J. (2001) 'Complexity of Staff Communication and Reported Level of Understanding Skills in Adults with Intellectual Disabilities', *Journal of Intellectual Disability Research*, 24 (3): 233–243.

Brandon, D. and Brandon, T. (2001) *Advocacy in Social Work*, Birmingham: Venture Press.

Branfield, F. and Beresford, P. with others (2006) *Making User Involvement Work: Supporting Service User Networking and Knowledge*, York: Joseph Rowntree Foundation.

Branfield, F., Beresford, P. and Levin, E. (2006) *Common Aims: Strategies to Support Service User and Carer Involvement in Social Work Education*, London: Shaping Our Lives/Social Care Institute for Excellence.

Braye, S. and Preston-Shoot, M. (1995) *Empowering Practice in Social Care*, Buckingham: Open University Press.

Braye, S., Lebacq, M., Mann, F. and Midwinter, E. (2003) 'Learning Social Work Law: An Enquiry Based Approach to Developing Knowledge and Skills', *Social Work Education*, 22 (5): 479–492.

Braye, S., Preston-Shoot, M., Cull, L.-A., Johns, R. and Roche, J. (2005) *Teaching, Learning and Assessment of Law in Social Work Education*, London: Social Care Institute for Excellence.

Brindle, D. (2005) 'Opinion: Long Neglected, Mental Health Might Yet Become the Government's Highest Priority', *Guardian Society*, 11 May, p. 5.

Briskman, L. (2005) 'Pushing Ethical Boundaries for Children and Families: Confidentiality, Transparency and Transformation', in R. Adams, L. Dominelli and M. Payne (eds) *Social Work Futures*, Basingstoke: Palgrave.

British Agencies for Adoption and Fostering (BAAF) (ed.) (1986) *Working with Children*, London: BAAF.

Bronfenbrenner, U. (1979) *The Ecology of Human Development: Experiments by Nature and Design*, Cambridge, MA: Harvard University Press.

Brookfield, S. (1995) *Becoming a Critically Reflective Teacher*, San Francisco, CA: Jossey-Bass.

Browne, J. (1995) 'The Meaning of Respect: A First Nations perspective', *The Canadian Journal of Nursing Research*, 27 (4): 95–110.

Bunting, M. (2004) *Willing Slaves: How the Overwork Culture Is Ruling Our Lives*, London: HarperCollins.

—— (2005) 'Threats, Fear and Control', *Guardian*, 23 May, p. 17.

Burgess, H. (1992) *Problem-Led Learning for Social Work*, London: Whiting and Birch.

—— (2004) *Matrix Showing the Variations of Requirements for the Social Work Degree for the Four UK Countries*, The Higher Education Academy, Social Policy and Social Work (SWAP), http://www.swap.ac.uk/quality/swreform.asp.

Burholt, V. and Wenger, G.C. (2004) 'Migration from South Asia to the UK and the Maintenance of Transnational Intergenerational Relationships', in M. Silverstein, R. Giarrusso and V.L. Bengtson (eds) *Intergenerational Relations across Time and Place: Springer Annual Review of Gerontology and Geriatrics*, New York: Springer Publishing.

Burke, B. and Dalrymple, J. (2002) 'Intervention and Empowerment', in R. Adams, L. Dominelli and M. Payne (eds) *Critical Practice in Social Work*, Basingstoke: Palgrave.

Butler, I. and Pugh, R. (2004) 'The Politics of Social Work Research', in R. Lovelock, K. Lyons and J. Powell (eds) *Reflecting on Social Work: Discipline and Profession*, Aldershot: Ashgate.

Butterworth, T. and Faugier, J. (1992) *Clinical Supervision and Mentorship in Nursing*, London: Chapman and Hall.

Butterworth, T., Carson, J., White, E., Jeacock, J., Clements, A. and Bishop, V. (1997) *It's Good to Talk: An Evaluation Study in England and Scotland*, Manchester: University of Manchester.

Bynner, J. and Parsons. S, (2003) 'Social Participation, Values and Crime', in E. Ferri J. Bynner and M. Wadsworth (eds) *Changing Britain, Changing Lives; Three Generations at the Turn of the Century*, London: Institute of Education.

Calman, R., Cox, A., Glasgow, D., Jimmieson, P. and Larsen, S.G. (2005) *In My Shoes: A Computer Assisted Interview for Communicating with Children and Vulnerable Adults*. Supported by Child and Family Training, Department for Education and Skills, University of Liverpool, University of Manchester, and Instone Bloomfield Charitable Trust.

Care Council for Wales (2004) *Approval and Visiting of Degree Courses in Social Work (Wales) Rules 2004*, Cardiff: Care Council for Wales.

Carlile Report (1987) *A Child in Mind*, London: London Borough of Greenwich.

Carr, S. (2004) *Has Service User Participation Made a Difference to Social Care Services?*, London: Social Care Institute for Excellence.

Carrese, J.A. and Rhodes, L.A. (1995) 'Western Ethics on the Navajo Reservation: Benefit or Harm?', *Journal of the American Medical Association*, 274 (10): 826–829.

Carter, N., Klein, R. and Day, P. (1992) *How Organisations Measure Success: The Use of Performance Indicators in Government*, London: Routledge.

Central Council for Education and Training in Social Work (CCETSW) (1995) *Assuring Quality in the Diploma in Social Work: 1. Rules and Requirements for the Diploma in Social Work*, London: CCETSW.

—— (2000) *Requirements for the Training of Approved Social Workers in England, Wales and Northern Ireland and of Mental Health Officers in Scotland*, London: CCETSW.

Channel 4 TV (2005) *Jamie's School Dinners*, 24 February, 2 and 9 March.

Charles, C. (2001) 'The Meaning of Uncertainty in Treatment Decision-Making', in J. Higgs and C. Titchen (eds) *Professional Practice in Health, Education and the Creative Arts*, Oxford: Blackwell Science.

Charles, C.A., Redko, C., Gafni, A., Whelan, T. and Renyo, L. (1998) 'Doing Nothing is No Choice: Lay Constructions of Treatment Decision-making among Women in Early Stage Breast Cancer', *Journal of Sociology and Health*, 20, 1: 71–95.

Charles, M. and Butler, S. (2004) 'Social Workers' Management of Organisational Change', in M. Lymbery and S. Butler (eds) *Social Work Ideals and Practice Realities*, Basingstoke: Palgrave.

Chartered An Institute of Personnel and Development (CIPD) (2005) 'Employee Turnover and Retention', London: CIPD, retrieved 1 October 2005 at: http://www.cipd.co.uk/ subjects/ hrpract/turnover/empturnretent.htm?IsSrchRes=1.

Cherniss, C. (1995) *Beyond Burnout: Helping Teachers, Nurses, Therapists & Lawyers Recover from Stress & Disillusionment*, New York: Routledge.

Clapton, G. (2001) 'In Praise of the Process Recording', in V. Cree and C. McCauley (eds) *Transfer of Learning in Professional and Vocational Education*, London: Routledge.

Clarke, J. (ed.) (1993) *A Crisis in Care*, London Sage.

Clarke, J. and Glendinning, C. (2002) 'Partnership and the Remaking of Welfare Provision', in C. Glendinning, M. Powell and K. Rummery (eds) (2002) *Partnerships, New Labour and the Governance of Welfare*, Bristol: Policy Press.

Clarke, J., Gewirtz, S. and McLaughlin, E. (eds) (2000) *New Managerialism New Welfare?*, London: Sage.

Clothier, C. (1994) *Allitt Inquiry: Independent Inquiry Relating to Deaths and Injuries on the Children's Ward at Grantham and Kesteven General Hospital during the Period February to April 1991*, London: HMSO.

Coffey, M., Dugdill, L. and Tattersall, A. (2004) 'Research Note: Stress in Social Services: Mental Well-being, Constraints and Job Satisfaction', *British Journal of Social Work*, 34 (5): 735–46.

Colton, M., Sanders, R. and Williams, M. (2001) *An Introduction to Working with Children: A Guide for Social Workers*, Basingstoke: Palgrave.

Commission for Social Care Inspection (CSCI) (2004a) *Understanding the Performance Assessment Framework*, retrieved 8 March 2006 at http://www.csci.org.uk/council_ performance/paf/understanding_paf.htm.

—— (2004b) *Leaving Hospital: The Price of Delays*, London: CSCI.

—— (2005) *Leaving Hospital: Revisited: A Follow-Up Study of a Group of Older People who Were Discharged from Hospital in March 2004*, London: CSCI.

—— (2006) *Performance Indicator Definitions 2005–06*, retrieved 8 March 2006 at http://www.csci.org.uk/council_performance/paf/performance_indicators.htm#1.

Community Care (2004) 'Increase in Overseas Social Workers Poses Ethical Questions for Councils', 5 February. Retrieved 31 March 2006, at http://www.communitycare.co.uk/ Articles/2004/02/05/43656/Increase+in+overseas+social+workers+poses+ethical+ questions+for.html?key=DOLMA.

—— (2006a) 'One Suspension and One Removal from Social Care Register', Community Care, 20 June.

—— (2006b) 'Failing Services Face Privatisation', 3 April, retrieved on 7 April 2006 at http://www.communitycare.co.uk/Articles/2006/04/06/53477/Failing+services+face+ private+competition.html?key=PROBATION+AND+SERVICE.

Cooper, A. and Lousada, J. (2005) *Borderline Welfare: Feeling and Fear of Feeling in Modern Welfare*, London: Karnac.

Cooper, C. (1986) 'The Growing Child', in British Agencies for Adoption and Fostering (BAAF) (ed.) *Working with Children*, London: BAAF.

Cooper, C.L. and Palmer, S. (2000) *Conquer Your Stress*, London: Institute of Personnel Development.

Cooper, H., Braye, S. and Geyer, R. (2004) 'Complexity and Interprofessional Education', *Learning in Health and Social Care*, 3 (4): 179–89.

Crawford, K. and Walker, J. (2003) *Social Work and Human Development*, Exeter: Learning Matters.

Creating An Interprofessional Workforce (2005) 'Creating an Interprofessional Workforce', retrieved 4 December 2005 at: http://www.cipw.org.uk/.

Cree, V. and Davidson, R. (2000) 'Enquiry and Action Learning', in V. Cree and C. McCauley (eds) *Transfer of Learning in Professional and Vocational Education*, London: Routledge.

Cross, M. (2004) *Children with Emotional and Behavioural Difficulties and Communication Problems: There is Always a Reason*, London: Jessica Kingsley.

Cruikshank, B. (1994) 'The Will to Empower: Technologies of Citizenship and the War on Poverty', *Socialist Review*, 23 (4): 29–55.

Cull, L.-A. and Roche, J. (eds) (2001) *The Law and Social Work*, Basingstoke: Palgrave.

Cupach, W.R. and Spitzberg, B.H. (eds) (1994) *The Dark Side of Interpersonal Communication*, Hillside, NJ: Lawrence Erlbaum.

Cutler, T. and Waine, B. (2003) 'Advancing Public Accountability? The Social Services "Star" Ratings', *Public Money and Management*, 23 (2): 125–8.

Dalrymple, J. and Burke, B. (1995) *Anti-Oppressive Practice: Social Care and the Law*, Buckingham: Open University Press.

Darwin, C. (1998) *The Expression of Emotions in Man and Animals*, Oxford: Oxford University Press.

Davey Smith, G. (ed.) (2003) *Health Inequalities: Lifecourse Approaches*, Bristol: Policy Press.

Davies, M. (1994) *The Essential Social Worker* (3rd edn), Aldershot: Arena.

Dawson, J.B. (1926) 'The Casework Supervisor in a Family Agency', *Family*, 6: 293–5.

de Bruin, H. (2002) *Managing Performance in the Public Sector*, London: Routledge.

de Koning, K and Martin, M. (eds) (1996) *Participatory Research in Health*, London: Zed Books.

de Winter, M. and Noom, M. (2003) 'Someone who Treats You as an Ordinary Human Being … Homeless Youth Examine the Quality of Professional Care', *British Journal of Social Work*, 33 (3): 325–38.

Dean, H. (ed.) (2004) *The Ethics of Welfare: Human Rights, Dependency and Responsibility*, Bristol: Policy Press.

Dempsey, M., Halton C. and Murphy M. (2001) 'Reflective Learning in Social Work Education: Scaffolding the Process', *Social Work Education*, 20 (3): 631–42.

Denney, D. (1998) *Social Policy and Social Work*, Oxford: Oxford University Press.

Department for Education and Skills (DfES) (2004) *Every Child Matters*, Nottingham: DFES.

—— (2005) *Common Core of Skills and Knowledge for the Children's Workforce*, Nottingham: DFES.

Department of Health (DH) (1998) *Modernising Social Services Cm 4169*, London: The Stationery Office.

—— (2000a) *Framework for the Assessment of Children in Need and their Families*, London: The Stationery Office.

—— (2000b) *The NHS Plan Cm 4818–1*, London: The Stationery Office.

—— (2000c) *A Health Service of All the Talents: Developing the NHS Workforce*, London: DH.

—— (2000d) *A Quality Strategy for Social Care*, London: DH.

—— (2002a) *Requirements for Social Work Training*, London: DH.

—— (2002b) *The Single Assessment Process Guidance for Local Implementation*, retrieved 2 June 2005 at http://www.doh.gov.uk/scg/sap/locimp/htm.

—— (2002c) *Focus on the Future: Key Messages from Focus Groups about the Future of Social Work Training*, London: DH.

—— (2002d) *Fair Access to Care Services: Guidance on Eligibility Criteria for Adult Social Care,* LAC 13, London: DH.

—— (2004) *Choosing Health*, London: DH.

—— (2005a) *Independence, Well-being and Choice: Our Vision for the Future of Social Care for Adults in England Cm 6499*, London: The Stationery Office.

—— (2005b) *Health Reform in England: Update and Next Steps*, London: DH.

—— (2005c) *The National Service Framework for Long-Term Conditions: Information Leaflet*, London: DH.

—— (2006) *Our Health, Our Care, Our Say: A New Direction for Community Services* Cm 6737, London: The Stationery Office.

Department of Social Security (1998) *A New Contract for Welfare* Cm 3805, London: Stationery Office.

Dickens, J. (2004) 'Teaching Childcare Law: Key Principles, New Priorities', *Social Work Education*, 23 (2): 217–230.

Doel, M. (2005) *New Approaches to Practice Learning*, Practice Learning Taskforce, London: DH.

Doel, M. and Shardlow, S.M. (2005) *Modern Social Work Practice*, Aldershot: Ashgate.

Doel, M. and Shardlow, S.M. (2006) *Gulliver's Travels.* Retrieved 30 March, at http://www. shu.ac.uk/research/hsc/mswp.html.

Doel, M., Deacon L. and Sawdon, C. (2004) *An Audit of Models of Practice Teaching in the New Social Work Award*, National Association of Practice Teachers and Practice Learning Taskforce, London: DH.

Dominelli, L. (2002) 'Anti-Oppressive Practice in Context', in R. Adams, L. Dominelli and M. Payne (eds) Social Work: *Themes Issues and Critical Debates* (2nd edn), Basingstoke: Palgrave.

Douglas, M. (1987) *How Institutions Think*, London: Routledge and Kegan Paul.

Doyal, L. and Gough, I. (1991) *A Theory of Human Need*, Basingstoke: Macmillan.

Eadie, T. and Lymbery, M. (2002) 'Understanding and Working in Welfare Organisations', *Social Work Education*, 21 (5): 515–528.

—— (forthcoming) 'Promoting Creative Practice through Social Work Education', *Social Work Education.*

Eisenhardt, K.M., Kahwajy, J.L. and Bourgeois III, L.J. (1997) 'How Management Teams Can have a Good Fight', *Harvard Business Review*, 75 (4): 77–85.

Ekman, P. (2004) *Emotions Revealed: Recognizing Faces and Feelings to Improve Communication and Emotional Life*, New York: Owl Books.

Ellesworth, E. (1989) 'Why Doesn't this Feel Empowering? Working through the Repressive Myths of Critical Pedagogy', *Harvard Educational Review*, 59 (3): 297–323.

Ellis, K. (2004) 'Promoting Rights or Avoiding Litigation? The Introduction of the Human Rights Act 1998 into Adult Social Care in England', *European Journal of Social Work*, 7 (3): 321–340.

Eraut, M. (1994) *Developing Professional Knowledge and Competence*, London: Falmer Press.

Ekman, P. (2004) *Emotions Revealed: Recognizing Faces and Feelings to Improve Communication and Emotional Life*, New York: Owl Books.

—— (1998) 'Concepts of Competence', *Journal of Interprofessional Care*, 12 (2): 127–39.

Erikson, E.H. (1965) *Childhood and Society*, Harmondsworth, Penguin.

Escher, S., Morris, M., Buiks, A., Delespaul, P., van Os, J. and Romme, M. (2004) 'Determinants of Outcome in the Pathways through Care for Children Hearing Voices', *International Journal of Social Welfare*, 30 (3): 208–222.

Esping-Andersen, G. (1990) *The Three Worlds of Welfare Capitalism*, Cambridge, Polity Press.

—— (1996) *Welfare States in Transition*, London: Polity.

Evans, T. and Harris, J. (2004) 'Street-Level Bureaucracy, Social Work and the (Exaggerated) Death of Discretion', *British Journal of Social Work*, 34 (6): 871–95.

Fahlberg, V. (1982) *Child Development*, London: British Association for Adoption and Fostering.

Featherstone, M. and Hepworth, M. (1989) 'Ageing and Old Age: Reflections on the Post-Modern Lifecourse', in B. Bytheway, T. Keil, P. Allat and A. Bryman (eds) *Becoming and Being Old: Sociological Approaches to Later Life*, London: Sage.

—— (1991) 'The Mask of Ageing and the Postmodern Lifecourse', in M. Featherstone, M. Hepworth and B.S.Turner (eds) *The Body, Social Process and Cultural Theory*, London: Sage.

Ferguson, H. (2001) 'Social Work, Individualization and Life Politics', *British Journal of Social Work*, 31, (1): 41–55.

—— (2005) 'Working with Violence, the Emotions and the Psycho-Social Dynamics of Child Protection: Reflections on the Victoria Climbié case', *Social Work Education*, 24 (7): 781–96.

Ferguson, I. and Lavalette, M. (2004) 'Alienation and Social Work', *British Journal of Social Work*, 34 (3): 297–312.

Ferri, F. and Smith, K. (2003) 'Partnership and Parenthood', in E. Ferri, J. Bynner and M. Wadsworth (eds), Changing Britain, Changing Lives: *Three Generations at the Turn of the Century*, London: Institute of Education.

Fischer, C. (1992) *America Calling, a Social History of the Telephone to 1940*, Berkeley, CA: University of California Press.

Fook, J. (2001) 'What is the Aim of the Bachelor of Social Work?', *Australian Social Work*, 54 (1): 20–22.

—— (2002) *Social Work: Critical Theory and Practice*, London: Sage.

—— (2004a) 'What Professionals Need from Research', in D. Smith (ed.) *Evidence Based Practice*, London: Jessica Kingsley.

—— (2004b) 'Critical Reflection and Transformative Possibilities', in L. Davies and P. Leonard (eds) *Scepticism/Emancipation: Social Work in a Corporate Era*, Aldershot: Ashgate.

—— (2004c) 'Critical Reflection and Organisational Learning and Change: A Case Study', in N. Gould and M. Baldwin (eds) *Social Work, Critical Reflection and the Learning Organisation*, Aldershot: Ashgate.

—— (in press) 'Reflective Practice and Critical Reflection', in J. Lishman (ed.) *Handbook of Theory for Practice Teachers: A New Updated Edition*, London: Jessica Kingsley.

Fook, J. and Askeland, G.A. (2006) 'The "Critical" in Critical Reflection', in S. White, J. Fook and F. Gardner (eds) *Critical Reflection in Health and Social Care*, Maidenhead: Open University Press, pp. 40–53.

Fook, J., Ryan, M. and Hawkins, L. (2000) *Professional Expertise: Practice, Theory and Education for Working in Uncertainty*, London: Whiting and Birch.

Fook, J., White, S. and Gardner, F. (in press) 'Critical Reflection: A Review of Current Understandings and Literature', in S. White, J. Fook and F. Gardner (eds) *Critical Reflection in Health and Welfare*, Buckingham: Open University Press.

Forsythe, B. and Jordan, B. (2002) 'The Victorian Ethical Foundations of Social Work in England: Continuity and Contradiction', *British Journal of Social Work*, 32 (7): 847–862.

Foster P. and Wilding P. (2000) 'Whither Welfare Professionalism?', *Social Policy and Administration*, 34 (2): 143–159.

Foucault, M. (1984) 'Truth and Power (from: Power/Knowledge)', in P. Rabinow (ed.) *The Foucault Reader: An Introduction to Foucault's Thought*, London: Penguin.

—— (1988) 'Technologies of the Self', in L. Martin (ed.) *Technologies of the Self*, London: Tavistock.

Freeden, M. (1990) *Rights*, Milton Keynes: Open University Press.

Freire, P. (1996) *Pedagogy of the Oppressed*, London: Penguin.

French, J.R.P. and Raven, B. (1960) 'The Bases of Social Power', in D. Cartwright and A. Zander (eds) *Group Dynamics*, Evanston, IL: Row Peterson.

Frey, B. and Stutzer, A. (2002) *Happiness and Economics: How the Economy and Institutions Affect Well-Being*, Princeton, NJ: Princeton University Press.

Fuller, R. and Petch, A. (1995) *Practitioner Research: The Reflexive Social Worker*, Buckingham: Open University Press.

Furness, S. and Gilligan, P. (2004) 'Fit for Purpose: Issues from Practice Placements, Practice Teaching and the Assessment of Students' Practice', *Social Work Education*, 23 (4): 465–479.

Gallagher, A. (2005) 'Too Clever to Care? Nurses Are Not Best Served by Being Precious about Professionalism', *Nursing Standard*, 12 (8): 14.

Garrett P.M. (2003) *Remaking Social Work with Children and Families: A Critical Discussion on the 'Modernisation' of Social Care*, London: Routledge.

—— (2005) 'Social Work's "Electronic Turn": Notes on the Deployment of Information and Communication Technologies in Social Work with Children and Families', *Critical Social Policy*, 25 (4): 529–553.

General Social Care Council (GSCC) (2002a) *Codes of Practice for Social Care Workers and Employers*, London: GSCC.

—— (2002b) *Guidance on the Asssessment of Practice in the Work Place*, London: GSCC.

—— (2004) *'Living and Learning' Conference Report*, London: GSCC.

—— (2005a) *Post-Qualifying Framework for Social Work Education and Training*, London: GSCC.

—— (2005b) *Working towards Full Participation*, London: GSCC.

George, V. and Wilding, P. (1993) *Welfare and Ideology*, London: Prentice Hall.

Gibbons, J. and Gray, M. (2002) 'An Integrated and Experience-Based Approach to Social Work Education: The Newcastle Model', *Social Work Education*, 21 (5): 529–550.

Gibbs, J. (2002) 'Sink or Swim: Changing the Story in Child Protection. A Study of the Crisis in Recruitment and Retention of Staff in Rural Victoria', unpublished PhD thesis, La Trobe University.

Giddens, A. (1991) *Modernity and Self-Identity*, Oxford: Polity Press.

Ginn J. and Fisher M. (1999) 'Gender and Career Progression', in S. Balloch, J. McLean and M. Fisher (eds) *Social Workers under Pressure*, Bristol: Policy Press.

Glasby, J. and Littlechild, R. (2004) *The Health and Social Care Divide: The Experiences of Older People* (2nd edn), Bristol: Policy Press.

Gorman, H. (2003) 'Which Skills do Care Managers Need? A Research Project on Skills, Competency and Continuing Professional Development', *Social Work Education*, 22 (3): 245–259.

Gould, N. and Baldwin M. (eds) (2004) *Social Work, Critical Reflection and the Learning Organization*, Aldershot: Ashgate.

Gould, N. and Taylor, I. (eds) (1996) *Reflective Learning for Social Work*, Aldershot: Arena.

Grace, C. and Wilkinson, P. (1978) *Negotiating the Law: Social Work and Legal Services*, London: Routledge & Kegan Paul.

Graham, H. (ed.) (2000) *Understanding Health Inequalities*, Maidenhead: Open University Press.

—— (2002) 'Building an Inter-Disciplinary Science of Health Inequalities: The Example of Lifecourse Research', *Social Science and Medicine*, 55 (11): 2005–2016.

Graham, H. and Power, C. (2004) *Childhood Disadvantage and Adult Health: A Lifecourse Framework*, London: Health Development Agency.

Granovetter, M. (1983) 'The Strength of Weak Ties: A Network Theory Revisited', *Sociological Theory*, 1: 201–233.

Grey, C. (2005) *A Very Short, Fairly Interesting and Reasonably Cheap Book about Studying Organizations*, London: Sage.

Guardian (2005a) 'Inequality Persists Under New Labour', 7 May.

—— (2005b) 'UK Low in Social Mobility League, Says Charity', 25 April.

Gustafson, J.M. (1982) 'Professions as "Callings"', *Social Service Review*, 56 (4): 501–515.

Hadley, R. and Clough, R. (1996) *Care in Chaos*, London: Cassell.

Hallett, C. (1995) *Interagency Cooperation in Child Protection*, London: HMSO.

Hämäläinen, J. (2003) 'The Concept of Social Pedagogy in the Field of Social Work', *Journal of Social Work*, 3 (1): 69–80.

Hammersley, M. (1995) *Ethnography: Principles in Practice*, London: Routledge.

Hammersley, M. (2003) 'Social Research Today: Some Dilemmas and Distinctions', *Qualitative Social Work*, 2 (1): 25–44.

Hardey, M. (1999) 'Doctor in the House: The Internet as a Source of Lay Health Knowledge and the Challenge to Expertise', *Sociology of Health and Illness*, 21 (6): 820–835.

Hargie, O. and Dickson, D. (2004) *Skilled Interpersonal Communication: Research, Theory and Practice* (4th edn), London: Routledge.

Harlow, E. and Webb, S.A. (eds) (2003) *Information and Communication Technologies in the Welfare Services*, London: Jessica Kingsley.

Harris, J. (1998) 'Scientific Management, Bureau-Professionalism, New Managerialism: The Labour Process of State Social Work', *British Journal of Social Work*, 28 (6): 839–862.

—— (2003) *The Social Work Business*, London: Routledge.

Hartshorn, A.E. (1982) *Milestone in Education for Social Work*, London: Carnegie United Kingdom Trust.

Hawkins, P. and Shohet, R. (1989) *Supervision in the Helping Professions: An Individual, Group and Organizational Approach*, Buckingham: Open University Press.

Health Sciences and Practice (2005) *Newsletter*, Summer, retrieved 4 December 2005 at http://www.health.heacademy.ac.uk/publications/newsletter/Newsletter15.pdf.

Henderson, J. and Atkinson, D. (2003) *Managing Care in Context*, London: Taylor & Francis.

Hendrick, H. (1997) *Children, Childhood and English Society*, Cambridge: Cambridge University Press.

Henry, W.P. and Strupp, H.H. (1994) 'The Therapeutic Alliance as Interpersonal Process', in A.O. Horvath and L.S. Greenberg (eds) *The Working Alliance: Theory, Research and Practice*, New York: Wiley and Sons.

Hetherington, R., Cooper, A., Smith, P. and Wiford, G. (1997) *Protecting Children: Messages from Europe*, Lyme Regis: Russell House.

Higham, P. (2005) 'What is Important about Social Work and Social Care', *SSRG [Social Services Research Group] Newsletter*, July.

Hockey, J. and James, A. (2003) *Social Identities across the Life Course*, Basingstoke: Palgrave.

Holland, S. (2000) 'Assessment Relationships: Interactions between Social Workers and Parents in Child Protection Assessments', *British Journal of Social Work*, 30 (2): 149–163.

Holman, B. (2000) *Kids at the Door Revisited*, Lyme Regis: Russell House.

Holt, J. and Rafferty, J. (2005) *Building Skills into the Curriculum: A Guide to Meeting the Requirement for Social Work Degree Students to Achieve Information and Communication Technology Skills*, Social Work and Social Policy Subject Centre, University of Southampton, retrieved 3 March 2006 at http://www.swap.ac.uk/elearning/develop4.asp.

Home Office (2002) *Report of the Independent Committee Chaired by Ted Cantle*, London: Home Office.

—— (2005) *Social Capital: Report on UK Research*, London: Home Office.

Honey, P. and Mumford, A. (1989) *The Manual of Learning Opportunities*, Maidenhead: Peter Honey.

Horvath, A.O. and Greenberg, L.S. (eds) (1994) *The Working Alliance: Theory, Research and Practice*, New York: Wiley and Sons.

Horwath J., and Thurlow C. (2004) 'Preparing Students for Evidence-Based Child and Family Social Work: An Experiential Learning Approach', *Social Work Education*, 23 (1): 7–24.

Howe, D. (1987) *An Introduction to Social Work Theory*, Aldershot: Wildwood House.

—— (1991) 'Knowledge, Power and the Shape of Social Work Practice', in M. Davies (ed.) *The Sociology of Social Work*, London: Routledge.

—— (1998) 'Relationship-Based Thinking and Practice in Social Work', *Journal of Social Work Practice*, 12 (1): 45–56.

Hudson, B. (2002) 'Interprofessionality in Health and Social Care: The Achilles' Heel of Partnership', *Journal of Interprofessional Care*, 16 (1): 7–17.

—— (2005) 'New Labour and the Public Sector: A Tale of Two Green Papers', *Journal of Integrated Care*, 13 (4): 6–11.

Hugman R. (1991) *Power in the Caring Professions*, Basingstoke: Macmillan.

—— (1998) *Social Welfare and Social Value*, Basingstoke: Macmillan.

—— (2005) *New Approaches in Ethics for the Caring Professions*, Basingstoke: Palgrave.

Humphries, B. (2003) 'What Else Counts as Evidence in Evidence-Based Social Work?', *Social Work Education*, 22 (1): 81–91.

—— (2004) 'Taking Sides: Social Work Research as a Moral and Political Activity', in R. Lovelock, K. Lyons and J. Powell (eds) *Reflecting on Social Work: Discipline and Profession*, Aldershot: Ashgate.

Humphries, P. and Camilleri, P. (2002) 'Social Work and Technology: Challenges for Social Workers in Practice: A Case Study', *Australian Social Work*, 55 (4): 251–259.

Hunt, S. (2005) *The Life Course: A Sociological Introduction*, Basingstoke: Palgrave.

Ife, J. (2001) *Human Rights and Social Work*, Cambridge: Cambridge University Press.

International Federation of Social Workers/International Association of Schools of Social Work (IFSW/IASSW) (2000) *The Definition of Social Work*, Berne: IFSW.

—— (2004) *Ethics in Social Work: Statement of Principles*, Berne: IFSW.

Irving, J. (1972) *Victims of Groupthink*, Boston, MA: Houghton Mifflin.

Iversen, T. and Wren, A. (1998) 'Equality, Employment and Budgetary Restraint: The Trilemma of the Service Economy', *World Politics*, 50 (4): 242–256.

Ixer, G. (2003) 'Developing the Relationship between Reflective Practice and Social Work Values', *Journal of Practice Teaching in Health and Social Work*, 5 (1): 7–22.

James, L.R., James, L.A. and Ashe, D.K. (1990) 'The Meaning of Organisations: The Role of Cognition and Values', in B. Schneider (ed.) *Organisational Climate and Culture*, San Francisco, CA: Jossey Bass.

Jessup, G. (1991) *Outcomes: NVQs and the Emerging Model of Education and Training*, London: Falmer.

Johns, R. (2003) 'Application of Web-Based Learning in Teaching Social Work Law', *Social Work Education*, 22 (5): 429–443.

—— (2005) *Using the Law in Social Work* (2nd edn), Exeter: Learning Matters.

Jones, A. (1999) 'Clinical Supervision for Professional Practice', *Nursing Standard*, 17 November, 14 (9): 42–44.

Jones, C. (2001) 'Voices from the Frontline: State Social Workers and New Labour', *British Journal of Social Work*, 31 (4): 547–562.

Jordan, B. (2001) 'Tough Love: Social Work, Social Exclusion and the Third Way', *British Journal of Social Work*, 31 (4): 527–546.

—— (2004) *Sex, Money and Power: The Transformation of Collective Life*, Cambridge: Polity.

—— (2005) 'Social Theory and Social Policy: Choice, Order and Human Well-Being', *European Journal of Social Theory*, 8 (2): 149–170.

Jordan, B. with Jordan C. (2000) *Social Work and the Third Way: Tough Love as Social Policy*, London: Sage.

Josefsson, U. (2003) 'Patients' Online Communities: Experiences of Emergent Swedish Self-Help on the Internet', in M. Huysman, E. Wenger and V. Wulf (eds) *Communities and Technologies*, Dordrecht: Kluwer.

Kadushin, A. (1992) *Supervision in Social Work* (3rd edn), New York: Columbia University Press.

Kadushin, A. and Kadushin, G. (1997) *The Social Work Interview: A Guide for Human Service Professionals* (4th edn), New York: Columbia University Press.

Kahn, A. and Kamerman, S. (1976) *Social Services in an International Perspective*, Washington, DC: US Department of Health, Welfare and Education.

Kahneman, D. (1999) 'Objective Well-Being', in D. Kahneman, E. Diener and N. Schwartz (eds) *Well-Being: The Foundations of Hedonic Psychology*, New York: Russell Square Sage Foundation.

Kahneman, D., Diener, E. and Schwartz, N. (eds) (1999) *Well-Being: The Foundations of Hedonic Psychology*, New York: Russell Sage Foundation.

Kakabadse, A., Bank, J. and Vinnicombe, S. (2004) *Working in Organisations*, Aldershot: Gower Publishing.

Kamerman, S.B. (2002) 'Fields of Practice', in M.A. Mattaini, C.T. Lowery and C.H. Meyer (eds) *Foundations of Social Work Practice: A Graduate Text*, Washington, DC: NASW Press.

Karlsen, S. and Nazroo, J. (2000) *Understanding Health Inequalities*, Milton Keynes: Open University Press.

Kearney, P. (2003) *A Framework for Supporting and Assessing Practice Learning*, Social Care Institute for Excellence position paper no. 2, London: SCIE, retrieved 17 July 2006 at http://www.scie.org.uk/publications/positionpapers/pp02.pdf.

Keene, J. (2001) *Clients with Complex Needs: Interprofessional Practice*, Oxford: Blackwell Science.

Kekes, J. (1993) *The Morality of Pluralism*, Princeton, NJ: Princeton University Press.

Kelly, D. and Harris, J. (1996) *Changing Social Care: A Handbook for Managers*, London: Whiting and Birch.

Kemp, S.P., Whittaker, J.K. and Tracy, E.M. (2000) 'Family Group Conferencing as Person-Environment Practice', in G. Burford and J. Hudson (eds) *Family Group Conferencing: New Directions in Community Centred Child and Family Practice*, New York: Aldine de Gruyter.

Kilcommons, A.M. and Morrison, A.P. (2005) 'Relationships between Trauma and Psychosis: An Exploration of Cognitive and Dissociative Factors', *Acta Psychiatrica Scandinavica*, 112 (5): 351–359.

Kirkpatrick, D.L. (1967) 'Evaluation of Training', in R.L. Craig and L.R. Bittel (eds) *Training and Development Handbook*, New York: McGraw-Hill.

Kirkpatrick, I., Ackroyd, S. and Walker, R. (2005) *The New Managerialism and Public Service Professions: Change in Health, Social Services and Housing*, Basingstoke: Palgrave.

Knowles, M.S (1984) *The Adult Learner: A Neglected Species*, Houston, TX: Gulf.

Koehn, D. (1994) *The Ground of Professional Ethics*, London: Routledge.

Kolb, D.A. (1984) *Experiential Learning: Experience as the Source of Learning and Development*, Englewood Cliffs, NJ: Prentice Hall.

Kolb, D.A. and Fry, R. (1975) 'Towards an Applied Theory of Experiential Learning', in C.L. Cooper (ed.) *Theories of Group Processes*, London: John Wiley.

Koprowska, J. (2003) 'The Right Kind of Telling? Locating the Teaching of Interviewing Skills within a Systems Framework', *British Journal of Social Work*, 33 (3): 291–308.

—— (2005) *Communication and Interpersonal Skills in Social Work*, Exeter: Learning Matters.

Kraut, R., Kiesler, S., Boneva, B., Cummings, J., Helgeson, V. and Crawford, A. (2002) 'Internet Paradox Revisited', *Journal of Social Issues*, 58 (1): 49–74.

Kraut, R., Lundmark, V., Patterson, M., Kiesler, S., Mukopadhyay, T. and Scherlis, W. (1998) 'Internet Paradox: A Social Technology that Reduces Social Involvement and Well-Being?', *American Psychologist*, 53 (9): 1017–1031.

Krieger, N. (2001) 'A Glossary for Social Epidemiology', *Journal of Epidemiology & Community Health*, 55 (10): 693–700.

—— (2005) 'Embodiment: A Conceptual Glossary for Epidemiology', *Journal of Epidemiology & Community Health*, 59 (5): 350–355.

Laming, W.H. (2003) *The Victoria Climbié Inquiry*, Norwich: HMSO.

Lane, R. E. (2000) *The Loss of Happiness in Market Societies*, New Haven, CT: Yale University Press.

Langan, M. (2000) 'Social Services: Managing the Third Way', in J. Clarke, S. Gewirtz and E. McLaughlin (eds) *New Managerialism New Welfare?*, London: Sage.

—— (2003). 'Social Work Inside Out', in V. Cree (ed.) *Becoming a Social Worker*, London: Routledge.

Larson, M.S. (1977) *The Rise of Professionalism: A Sociological Analysis*, Berkeley, CA: University of California Press.

Lawson, H. (ed.) (2001) *Practice Teaching: Changing Social Work*, London: Jessica Kingsley.

Layard, R. (2003) 'Happiness: Has Social Science a Clue?', Lionel Robbins Memorial Lectures, London, School of Economics, 3–5 March.

—— (2005) *Happiness: Lessons from a New Science*, London: Allen Lane.

Leathard, A. (2003) 'Models for Interprofessional Collaboration', in A. Leathard (ed.) *Interprofessional Collaboration: From Policy to Practice in Health and Social Care*, London: Brunner Routledge.

Leicht, K. and Fennell, M. (2001) *Professional Work: A Sociological Approach*, Oxford: Blackwell.

Leonard, M. (2004) 'Social Capital: Evidence from Belfast', *Sociology*, 43 (4): 498–509.

Levin, E. (2004) *Involving Service Users and Carers in Social Work Education*, London: Social Care Institute for Excellence.

Lewis, J. (2001) 'Older People and the Health–Social Care Boundary in the UK: Half a Century of Hidden Policy Conflict', *Social Policy and Administration*, 35 (4): 343–359.

Light, D. (1979) 'Uncertainty and Control in Professional Training', *Journal of Health and Social Behaviour*, 20 (4): 310–322.

Lindsay, J. and Tompsett, H. (1998) *Careers of Practice Teachers in the London & South East Region*, London: Central Council for Education and Training in Social Work.

Lindsay, J. and Walton, A. (2000) *Workforce Planning and the Strategic Deployment of Practice Teachers in Approved Agencies*, retrieved 18 December 2005 at http://www.swap.ac.uk/docs/ac/Practiceteachers.rtf.

Lindsay, T. (2003) 'An Investigation of Group Learning on Practice Placements', Social Policy and Social Work (SWAP), retrieved 28 December 2005 at http://www.swap.ac.uk/docs/swap/GrouplearningTLindsay.rtf.

Lipsky, M. (1980) *Street Level Bureaucracy: Dilemmas of the Individual in Public Service*, New York: Russell Sage Foundation.

Lishman, J. (1994) *Communication in Social Work*, Basingstoke: Macmillan.

Lister, P. (2000) 'Mature Students and Transfer of Learning', in V. Cree and C. McCauley (eds) *Transfer of Learning in Professional and Vocational Education*, London: Routledge.

Lister, R. (2001) 'New Labour: A Study in Ambiguity from a Position of Ambivalence', *Critical Social Policy*, 21 (4): 425–447.

Lloyd, M. (2002) 'Care Management', in R. Adams, L. Dominelli and M. Payne (eds) *Critical Practice in Social Work*, Basingstoke: Palgrave.

London Advisory Services Alliance (LASA) (2000) 'The Samaritans: Saving Lives by Email', *Computanews*, retrieved 11 December 2005 at http://www.lasa.org.uk/cgi-bin/publisher/display.cgi?163-10100-10284+computanews.

London Borough of Greenwich (1987) *A Child in Mind – Report on the Death of Kimberley Carlisle*, London: London Borough of Greenwich.

London Borough of Lambeth (1987) *Whose Child – Report on the Death of Tyra Henry*, London: London Borough of Lambeth.

Lorenz, W. (1994) *Social Work in a Changing Europe*, London: Routledge.

Loxley, A. (1997) *Collaboration in Health and Welfare*, London: Jessica Kingsley.

Luft, J. and Ingham, H. (1955) 'The Johari Window: A Graphic Model of Interpersonal Awareness', *Proceedings of the Western Training Laboratory in Group Development*, Los Angeles, CA: UCLA Extension Office.

Lupton, C. and Nixon, P. (1999) *Empowering Practice? A Critical Appraisal of the Family Group Conference Approach*, Bristol: Policy Press.

Lymbery, M. (1998) 'Care Management and Professional Autonomy: The Impact of Community Care Legislation on Social Work with Older People', *British Journal of Social Work*, 28 (6): 863–878.

—— (2001) 'Social Work at the Crossroads', *British Journal of Social Work*, 31 (3): 369–384.

—— (2004) 'The Changing Nature of Welfare Organisations', in M. Lymbery and S. Butler (eds) *Social Work Ideals and Practice Realities*, Basingstoke: Palgrave.

—— (2005) *Social Work with Older People*, London: Sage.

Lymbery, M. and Butler, S. (eds) (2004) *Social Work Ideals and Practice Realities*, Basingstoke: Macmillan.

Lyons, K. (1999) *International Social Work: Themes and Perspectives*, Aldershot: Ashgate.

Macdonald, G. and Sheldon, B. (1998) 'Changing One's Mind: The Final Frontier?', *Issues in Social Work Education*, 18 (1): 35–55.

Macdonald, K. (1995) *The Sociology of the Professions*, London: Sage.

Marshall, T.H. (1981) *The Right to Welfare and Other Essays*, London: Heinemann.

Maughan, B. and McCarthy, G. (1997) 'Childhood Adversity and Psychosocial Disorders', *British Medical Bulletin*, 53 (1): 156–169.

Mayer, J. (1988) 'Levels of Analysis: The Life Course as a Cultural Construction', in M.W. Riley (ed.) *Social Structure and Human Lives*, London: Sage.

McCluskey, U. (2005) *To Be Met as a Person: The Dynamics of Attachment in Professional Encounters*, London: Karnac.

McDonald, A. (1997) *Challenging Local Authority Decisions*, Birmingham: Venture Press.

McLean, J. (1999) 'Satisfaction, Stress and Control Over Work', in S. Balloch, J. McLean, and M. Fisher (eds) *Social Services: Working under Pressure*, Bristol: Policy Press.

McLeod, E. and Bywaters, P. (2000) *Working for Equality in Health*, London: Routledge.

Meyerson, D.E. (2000) 'If Emotions Were Honoured: A Cultural Analysis', in S. Fineman (ed.) *Emotion in Organizations* (2nd edn), London: Sage.

Mezirow, J. (1994) 'Understanding Transformation Theory', *Adult Education Quarterly*, 44 (4): 222–232.

—— (2000) *Learning as Transformation: Critical Perspectives on a Theory in Progress*, San Francisco, CA: Jossey Bass Wiley.

Midgley, J. (1981) *Professional Imperialism: Social Work in the Third World*, London: Heinemann.

—— (2001) 'Issues in International Social Work', *Journal of Social Work*, 1 (1): 21–35.

Midwinter, E. (1994) *The Development of Social Welfare In Britain*, Buckingham: Open University Press.

Miller, C., Freeman, M. and Ross, N. (2001) *Interprofessional Practice in Health and Social Care: Challenging the Shared Learning Agenda*, London: Arnold.

Mittman, R. and Cain, M. (2001) 'The Future of the Internet in Health Care: A Five-Year Forecast', in R.E. Rice and J.E. Katz (eds) *The Internet and Health Communication: Experiences and Expectation*, Thousand Oaks, CA: Sage.

Morgan, G. (1997) *Images of Organization* (2nd edn), London: Sage.

Morrison, T. (1993) *Staff Supervision in Social Care*, Harlow: Longman.

Muir, H. (2005) 'Learn from Oldham', *Guardian*, 11 May, p. 21.

Mullender A. and Coulshed V. (2001) *Management in Social Work* (2nd edn), Basingstoke: Palgrave.

Munro, E. (1998) *Understanding Social Work: An Empirical Approach*, London: Athlone.

—— (2004) 'The Impact of Audit on Social Work Practice', *British Journal of Social Work*, 34 (8): 1075–1095.

Myers, D.G. (1999) 'Close Relationships and Quality of Life', in D. Kahneman, E. Diener and N. Schwartz (eds) *Well-Being: The Foundations of Hedonic Psychology*, New York: Russell Sage Foundation.

Newman, J. (2001) *Modernising Governance: New Labour, Policy and Society*, London: Sage.

NHS Management Executive (1993) *A Vision for the Future*, London: DH.

Northern Ireland Social Care Council (2003) *Framework Specification for the Degree in Social Work*, Belfast: Department of Health, Social Services and Public Safety.

Nursing and Midwifery Council (NMC) (2004) *The NMC Code of Professional Conduct: Standards for Conduct, Performance and Ethics*, London: NMC, retrieved 20 February 2006 at http://www.nmc-uk.org/(pcft2445mdcgj2uuv2nswd45)/aFramedisplay.aspx?documentID=201.

O'Donoghue, K. (2003) *Restorying Social Work Supervision*, Palmerston North, New Zealand: Dunmore Press.

O'Hagan, K. (ed.) (1996) *Competence in Social Work Practice*, London: Jessica Kingsley.

O'Hara, M. (2006) 'Evidence that the NHS Cuts Deeply', *Guardian Society*, 26 July, p. 3.

Office of National Statistics (ONS) (2005) *Trends in Life Expectancy by Social Class 1972–2001*, retrieved 20 September 2005 at http://www.statistics.gov.uk/statbase/Product.asp?vlnk=8460&Pos=1&ColRank=1&Rank=272.

Oliver, J. and Huxley, P. (1988) 'The Development of Computer Assisted Learning (CAL) Materials for Teaching and Testing Mental Health Social Work in Great Britain: A Review of Four Years Progress', *Journal of Teaching in Social Work*, 2 (2): 21–34.

Onyett, S. (2003) *Teamworking in Mental Health*, Basingstoke: Palgrave.

Opie, A. (2000) *Thinking Teams/Thinking Clients: Knowledge-Based Teamwork*, New York: Columbia University Press.

Organisation for Economic Co-operation and Development (OECD) (2005) *Age of Women and First Childbirth*, retrieved 20 September 2005 at http://www.nationmaster.com/graph-T/hea_age_of_wom_at_fir_chi.

Parker, G. (1990) *Team Players and Teamwork: The New Competitive Business Strategy*, San Francisco, CA: Jossey-Bass.

Parker, J. and Bradley, G. (2003) *Social Work Practice: Assessment, Planning, Intervention and Review*, Exeter: Learning Matters.

Parker, R.A. (1980) *Caring for Separated Children*, London: Macmillan.

—— (1990) *Away from Home: A History of Child Care*, London: Routledge.

Parry, N. and Parry, J. (1979) 'Social Work, Professionalism and the State', in N. Parry, M. Rustin and C. Satyamurti (eds) *Social Work, Welfare and the State*, London: Edward Arnold.

Parton, N. (1985) *The Politics of Child Abuse*, Basingstoke: Macmillan.

—— (2004) 'Post-Theories for Practice: Challenging the Dogmas', in L. Davies and P. Leonard (eds) *Scepticism/Emancipation: Social Work in a Corporate Era*, Aldershot: Ashgate.

Parton, N. and O'Byrne, P. (2000) *Constructive Social Work*, Basingstoke: Macmillan.

Payne, M. (1993) *Linkages: Effective Networking in Social Care*, London: Whiting and Birch.

—— (1995) 'Partnership between Organisations in Social Work Education', *Issues in Social Work Education*, 14 (1): 53–70.

—— (2000a) *Teamwork in Multiprofessional Care*, Basingstoke: Macmillan.

—— (2000b) *Anti–Bureaucratic Social Work*, Birmingham: Venture Press.

—— (2005a) *The Origins of Social Work*, Basingstoke: Palgrave.

—— (2005b) *Modern Social Work Theory* (3rd edn), Basingstoke: Palgrave.

Pellizoni, L. (2003) 'Knowledge, Uncertainty and the Transformation of the Public Sphere', *European Journal of Social Theory*, 6 (3): 227–255.

Peters T. (1988) *Thriving on Chaos*, London: Pan Books.

Phillips, T. (2005) 'After 7/7: Sleepwalking to Segregation', Speech to Manchester Council for Community Relations, 22 September.

Pithouse, A. (1987) *Social Work: The Social Organisation of an Invisible Trade*, Aldershot: Gower.

Plath, D., English, B., Connors, L. and Beveridge, A. (1999) 'Evaluating the Outcomes of Intensive Critical Thinking Instruction for Social Work Students', *Social Work Education*, 18 (2): 207–217.

Pollitt C. (1990) *Managerialism and the Public Services*, Oxford: Basil Blackwell.

—— (2003) *The Essential Public Manager*, Maidenhead: Open University Press.

Popay, J. and Roen, K. (2003) *Types and Quality of Knowledge in Social Care*, SCIE *Knowledge Review 3*, Bristol: Policy Press.

Postle, K. (1999a) '"Things Fall Apart: The Centre Cannot Hold": Deconstructing and Reconstructing Social Work with Older People for the 21st Century', *Issues in Social Work Education*, 19 (2): 23–43.

—— (1999b) 'Care Managers' Responses to Working under Conditions of Postmodernity', unpublished PhD thesis, Department of Social Work Studies. University of Southampton.

—— (2002) 'Working "Between the Idea and the Reality": Ambiguities and Tensions in Care Managers' Work', *British Journal of Social Work*, 32 (3): 335–351.

Postle, K. and Beresford, P. (2005) 'Capacity Building and the Reconception of Political Participation: A Role for Social Care Workers?', *British Journal of Social Work*, published online: doi:10.1093/bjsw/bch330.

Powell, M. (2000) 'New Labour and the Third Way in the British Welfare State: A New and Distinctive Approach', *Critical Social Policy*, 20 (1): 39–60.

Practice Learning Task Force (PLTF) (2004) *First Annual Report*, London: DH.

—— (2005) 'A Model of Group Practice Learning for Use in the BA Social Work Degree', *What Works PLTF*, retrieved 28 December 2005 at http://www.practicelearning.org/index.php?cid=26.

Prasad, R. (2000) 'Poll Reveals Crucial Role of Grandparents in Childcare', *Guardian*, 14 December.

Preston-Shoot, M. (2000) 'Making Connections in the Curriculum: Law and Professional Practice', in R. Pierce and J. Weinstein (eds) *Innovative Education and Training for Care Professionals: A Providers' Guide*, London: Jessica Kingsley.

Preston-Shoot, M., Roberts, G. and Vernon, S. (1997) '"We Work in Isolation Often and in Ignorance Occasionally": On the Experiences of Practice Teachers Teaching and Assessing Social Work Law', *Social Work Education*, (16) 4: 4–34.

—— (1998) 'Developing a Conceptual Framework for Teaching and Assessing Law within Training for Professional Practice: Lessons from Social Work', *Journal of Practice Teaching*, 1 (1): 41–51.

Priestley, M. (2000) 'Adults Only: Disability, Social Policy and the Life Course', *Journal of Social Policy*, 29 (3): 421–439.

—— (2004) *Disability: A Life Course Approach*, Cambridge: Blackwell.

Pritchard J. (1995) 'Supervision or Practice Teaching for Students', in J. Pritchard (ed.) *Good Practice in Supervision*, London: Jessica Kingsley.

Proctor, B. (1987) 'Supervision: A Co-operative Exercise in Accountability', in M. Marken and M. Payne (eds) *Enabling and Ensuring Supervision in Practice*, Leicester: National Youth Bureau.

—— (1991) 'On Being a Trainer and Supervisor for Counselling', in W. Dryden and B. Thorne (eds) *Training and Supervision for Counselling in Action*, London: Sage.

Pusey, M. (2003) *The Experience of Middle Australia: The Dark Side of Economic Reform*, Cambridge: Cambridge University Press.

Putnam, R.D. (2000) *Bowling Alone: The Collapse and Revival of American Community*, New York: Simon & Schuster.

—— (2002) *Democracies in Flux: The Evolution of Social Capital in Contemporary Society*, Oxford: Oxford University Press.

Quality Assurance Agency for Higher Education (QAA) (2000) *Social Policy and Administration and Social Work: Subject Benchmark Statements*, Gloucester: QAA.

—— (2001) *Descriptor for a Qualification at Masters (M) Level*, retrieved 25 July 2005 at http://www.qaa.ac.uk/crntwork/nqf/ewni2001/annex1.htm#4.

Rafferty, J. and Waldman, J. (2006) 'Fit for Social Work Practice', *Journal of Technology for the Human Services*, 24 (2/3): 1–22.

Rampal, R. (2000) 'The HIV/AIDS Epidemic in South Africa: The Current Situation, Future Trends and Intervention', in N.-T. Tan and E. Envall (eds) *Social Work around the World* (Vol. I), Berne: International Federation of Social Workers.

Read, J., van Os, J., Morrison, A.P. and Ross, C.A. (2005) 'Childhood Trauma, Psychosis and Schizophrenia: A Literature Review with Theoretical and Clinical Implications', *Acta Psychiatrica Scandinavica*, 112 (5): 330–351.

Rich, P. (1993) 'The Form, Function, and Content of Clinical Supervision: An Integrated Model', *The Clinical Supervisor*, 11 (1): 137–178.

Richards, S., Ruch, G. and Trevithick, P. (2005) 'Communication Skills Training for Practice: The Ethical Dilemma for Social Work Education', *Social Work Education*, 24 (4): 409–422.

Ritchie, J. (1994) *Report of the Inquiry into the Care and Treatment of Christopher Clunis*, London: HMSO.

Robb, B. (2005) 'Forging Ahead', *Professional Social Work*, March: 12–13.

Roberts, Y. (2006) 'Raped, Beaten and helpless: UK's Sex Slaves', *Observer*, 2 April, pp. 14–15.

Rogers, R. (2004) 'Ethical Technologies of Self and the "Good Jobseeker"', in H. Dean (ed.) *The Ethics of Welfare*, Bristol: Policy Press.

Rose, N. (1996) *Inventing Ourselves: Psychology, Power and Personhood*, Cambridge: Cambridge University Press.

Rowland, D. and Pollock, A. (2004) 'Choice and Responsiveness for Older People in the "Patient Centred" NHS', *British Medical Journal*, 328 (7430): 4–5.

Ruch, G. (2000) 'Self in Social Work: Towards an Integrated Model of Learning', *Journal of Social Work Practice*, 14 (2): 99–112.

—— (2004) '"Self-ish" Spaces: Reflective Practice and Reflexivity in Contemporary Child Care Social Work Practice and Research in the U.K.', in Leopard M. Stoneman (ed.) *Advances in Sociology Research*, Vol. II, Hauppauge, NY: Nova Science.

—— (2005) 'Relationship-Based Practice and Reflective Practice: Holistic Approaches to Contemporary Child Care Social Work', *Child and Family Social Work*, 4 (2): 111–124.

Rutter, M. (1985) 'Resilience in the Face of Adversity: Protective Factors and Resistance to Psychiatric Disorder', *British Journal of Psychiatry*, 147: 598–611.

Rutter, M. and Smith, D. (1995) *Psychosocial Disorders in Young People*, Chichester: Wiley.

Saleebey, D. (2005) *The Strengths Perspective in Social Work Practice* (4th edn), London: Pearson/Allyn & Bacon.

Sapey, B. (1997) 'Social Work Tomorrow: Towards a Critical Understanding of Technology in Social Work', *British Journal of Social Work*, 27 (6): 803–814.

Satyamurti, C. (1981) *Occupational Survival*, Oxford: Blackwell.

Schön, D. (1983) *The Reflective Practitioner*, New York: Basic Books.

—— (1987) *Educating the Reflective Practitioner: Towards a New Design for Teaching and Learning in the Professions*, San Francisco, CA: Jossey-Bass.

—— (1991) *The Reflective Practitioner: How Professionals Think in Action*, Avebury: Ashgate.

Schore, A. (2003a) *Affect Dysregulation and Disorders of the Self*, New York: Norton.

—— (2003b) *Affect Regulation and the Repair of the Self*, New York: Norton.

Scott, R., Ashcroft, J. and Wild, A. (2005) 'Crisis Prevention', in G. Meads and J. Ashcroft with H. Barr, R. Scott and A. Wild, *The Case for Interprofessional Collaboration in Health and Social Care*, Oxford: Blackwell/Centre for Advancement of Inter-Professional Education.

Scottish Executive (2003) *Standards in Social Work Education: Framework for Social Work Education in Scotland*, Edinburgh: Scottish Executive.

—— (2006) *Changing Lives: Report of the 21st Century Social Work Review*, Edinburgh: Scottish Executive.

Seden, J. and Reynolds, J. (2003) *Managing Care in Practice*, London: Taylor & Francis.

Senge, P.M. (1990) *The Fifth Discipline: The Art and Practice of the Learning Organization*, London: Random House.

Senge, P., Jaworski, J., Scharmer, O. and Flowers, B.S. (2005) *Presence: Exploring Profound Change in People, Organizations and Society*, London: Nicholas Brealey.

Shaping Our Lives/Social Care Institute for Excellence (SOL/SCIE) (2005) *A Strategy to Support Service User and Carer Participation in Social Work Education: Proposal to the Department of Health*, London: SOL/SCIE.

Shardlow, S. (2002) 'Values, Ethics and Social Work', in R. Adams, L. Dominelli, and M. Payne (eds) *Social Work: Themes, Issues and Critical Debates*, Basingstoke: Palgrave.

Shardlow, S.M. and Wallis, J. (2003) 'Mapping Comparative Empirical Studies of European Social Work', *British Journal of Social Work*, 33 (7): 921–941.

Sheldon, B. and Macdonald, G. (2000) *Research and Practice in Social Care: Mind the Gap*, Exeter: Centre for Evidence-Based Social Services.

Simon, A. and Agazarian, Y.A. (2003) *SAVI Definitions*, Philadelphia, PA: self-published by Simon.

Sinclair, A. (1995) 'Sex and the MBA', *Organization*, 2 (2): 295–317.

Skills for Care (2005) *Leadership and Management Strategy*, retrieved on 10 November 2005 at http://www.skillsforcare.org.uk/view.asp?id=494.

Smale, G. and Tuson, G. with Biehal, N. and Marsh, P. (1993) *Empowerment, Assessment, Care Management and the Skilled Worker*, London: National Institute of Social Work.

Smale, G., Tuson, G. and Statham, D. (2000) *Social Work and Social Problems: Working Towards Social Inclusion and Social Change*, Basingstoke: Macmillan.

Smith, J. (2002) *Department of Health Press Release*, reference 2002/0241, retrieved 2 June 2005 at http://www.Info.doh.gov.uk/intpress.nsf/page/2002/024111?Open Document.

Social Services Inspectorate (SSI) (1991) *Women in Social Services: A Neglected Resource*, London: DH.

—— (1994) *Inspection of Assessment and Care Management Arrangements in Social Services Departments, October 1993–March 1994*, London: DH.

—— (1997) *Better Management, Better Care: 6th Annual Report of the Chief Inspector of Social Services*, London: DH.

—— (1999) *Meeting the Challenge: Improving Management for the Effective Commissioning of Social Care Services for Older People*, London: DH.

—— (2001) *Modernising Social Services: A Commitment to Deliver: 10th Annual Report of the Chief Inspector of Social Services*, London: DH.

Spitzberg, B.H. (1994) 'The Dark Side of (In)competence', in W.R. Cupach and B.H. Spitzberg (eds) *The Dark Side of Interpersonal Communication*, Hillside: NJ: Lawrence Erlbaum.

Statham, D. (2003) 'Changing Social Work', in V. Cree (ed.) *Becoming a Social Worker*, London: Routledge.

Steyaert, J. (2000) *Digitale vaardigheden, geletterdheid in de informatiesamenleving*, The Hague: Rathenau Institute.

—— (2005) 'Web Based Higher Education, the Inclusion/Exclusion Paradox', *Journal of Technology in Human Services*, 23 (1/2): 67–78.

Sudbery, J. (2002) 'Key Features of Therapeutic Social Work: The Use of Relationship', *Journal of Social Work Practice*, 16 (20): 149–161.

Sullivan, W. (1995) *Work and Integrity: The Crisis and Promise of Professionalism in America*, New York: Harper Business.

Sutton Trust (2005), study reported in the *Guardian*, 10 October.

Tan, N.-T. (ed.) (2004) *Social Work around the World*, Vol. III, Berne: International Federation of Social Workers.

Tan, N.-T. and Dodds, I. (eds) (2002) *Social Work around the World*, Vol. II, Berne: International Federation of Social Workers.

Tan, N.-T. and Envall, E. (eds) (2000) *Social Work around the World*, Vol. I, Berne: International Federation of Social Workers.

Tannen D. (1995) *How Women's and Men's Conversational Styles Affect who Gets Heard, who Gets Credit and what Gets Done at Work*, London: Virago.

Tanner, D. (2001) 'Sustaining the Self in Later Life: Implications for Community-Based Support', *Ageing and Society*, 21 (3): 255–278.

Thomas, K.W. and Kilmann, R.H. (1974) *Conflict Mode Instrument*, Palo Alto, CA: Consulting Psychologists Press (CPP).

Thompson, N. (2002) *People Skills* (2nd edn), Basingstoke: Palgrave.

—— (2003) *Promoting Equality: Challenging Discrimination and Oppression* (2nd edn), Basingstoke: Palgrave.

—— (2005) *Understanding Social Work: Preparing for Practice* (2nd edn), Basingstoke: Palgrave.

Thompson, N., Murphy, M. and Stradling, S. (1994) *Dealing with Stress*, Basingstoke: Macmillan.

Tight, M. (1998) 'Lifelong Learning: Opportunity or Compulsion?', *British Journal of Educational Studies*, 46 (3): 252–263.

Training Organisation for the Personal Social Services (TOPSS) (2002) *National Occupational Standards for Social Work*, Leeds: TOPSS. http://www.skillsforcare. org/files/cd/

Travis, A. (2006) 'There's No Ignoring Probation's Problems', *Guardian*, 29 March, retrieved 7 April 2006 at http://society.guardian.co.uk/comment/column/0,,1741442,00.html.

Trevithick, P. (2003) 'Effective Relationship-Based Practice: A Theoretical Exploration', *Journal of Social Work Practice*, 17 (2): 163–176.

—— (2005) *Social Work Skills: A Practice Handbook* (2nd edn), Buckingham: Open University Press.

Trevithick, P., Richards, S., Ruch, G. and Moss, B. (2004) *Teaching and Learning Communication Skills in Social Work Education, Knowledge Review 6*, London: SCIE/SWAPltsn/The Policy Press.

Tsui, M.S. (2004) *Social Work Supervision: Contexts and Concepts*, Thousand Oaks, CA: Sage.

Turner, B. and Rojek, C. (2001) *Society and Culture: Principles of Scarcity and Solidarity*, London: Sage.

Twining, W. (1967) 'Pericles and the Plumber', *Law Quarterly Review*, 83: 396–426.

United Kingdom Central Council for Nursing, Midwifery and Health Visiting (UKCC) (1995) *Position Statement on Clinical Supervision for Nursing and Health Visiting: Annexe 1 to Registrar's Letter 4/1995*, London: UKCC.

United Nations (1948) *The Universal Declaration of Human Rights*, New York: United Nations.

Valentine, G., Marsh, J. and Pattie, C. (2005) *Children and Young People's Home Use of ICT for Educational Purposes*, London: Department for Education and Skills.

van der Laan, G. (2000) 'Social Work in the Netherlands', in A. Adams, P. Erath and S.M. Shardlow (eds) *Fundamentals of Social Work in Selected European Countries*, Lyme Regis: Russell House.

Waine B. and Henderson J. (2003) 'Managers, Managing and Managerialism', in J. Henderson and D. Atkinson (eds) *Managing Care in Context*, London: Routledge.

Wainwright, D. and Calnan, M. (2002) *Work Stress: The Making of a Modern Epidemic*, Buckingham: Open University Press.

Waldman, J. (2004) *There4me Evaluation Final Report*, University of Southampton, retrieved 12 November 2005 at http://www.sws.soton.ac.uk/t4mstudy/reports.htm.

Waldman. J and Storey, A. (eds) (2004) *Nature of the Medium in a Short Anthology of Perspectives on Practice*, produced as part of the Evaluation Study of There4me, retrieved on 3 March 2006 at http://www.sws.soton.ac.uk/t4mstudy/final/anthology_all.pdf.

Walter, I., Nutley, S., Percy-Smith, J., McNeish, D. and Frost, S. (2004) *Promoting the Use of Research in Social Care Practice*, SCIE Knowledge Review 7, Bristol: Policy Press.

Ward, D. and Hogg, B. (1993) 'An Integrated Approach to the Teaching of Social Work Law', in M. Preston-Shoot (ed.) *Assessment of Competence in Social Work Law*, London: Whiting and Birch.

Webb, S.A. (2001) 'Some Considerations on the Validity of Evidence-Based Practice in Social Work', *British Journal of Social Work*, 31 (1): 57–79.

Weber, M. (1947) *The Theory of Social and Economic Organisation*, translated by A.M. Henderson and T. Parsons, London: William Hodge.

Weinstein, J., Whittington, C. and Leiba, T. (eds) (2003) *Collaboration in Social Work Practice*, London: Jessica Kingsley.

Welsh, L. and Woodward, P. (1989) *Continuing Professional Development: Towards a National Strategy*, London: Further Education Unit.

Wenger, E. (1998) *Communities of Practice: Learning, Meaning and Identity*, Cambridge: Cambridge University Press.

White, V. and Harris, J. (eds) (2001) *Developing Good Practice in Community Care*, London: Jessica Kingsley Publishers.

White, S. and Stancombe, J. (2003) *Clinical Judgement in the Health and Welfare Professions*, Buckingham: Open University Press.

White, V. (2006) *The State of Feminist Social Work*, London: Routledge.

White, V. and Harris, J. (eds) (2004) *Developing Good Practice in Children's Services*, London: Jessica Kingsley Publishers.

Whittington, C. (1983) 'Social Work in the Welfare Network', *British Journal of Social Work*, 13 (1): 265–286.

—— (1999) *Partnership of Social Care and Health*, Supplementary Report on Modernising the Social Care Workforce, TOPSS England, retrieved 12 October 2005 at http://www.topssengland.net/files/PSHIP1(1).pdf.

—— (2003a) *Learning for Collaborative Practice with Other Professions and Agencies: Research Report*, London: DH.

—— (2003b) 'A Model of Collaboration', in J. Weinstein, C. Whittington and T. Leiba (eds) *Collaboration in Social Work Practice*, London: Jessica Kingsley.

—— (2003c) 'Collaboration and Partnership in Context', in J. Weinstein, C. Whittington and T. Leiba (eds) *Collaboration in Social Work Practice*, London: Jessica Kingsley.

—— (2003d) *Learning for Collaborative Practice with Other Professions and Agencies: Summary Report*, London: DH.

Whittington, C. and Bell, L. (2001) 'Learning for Interprofessional and Inter-Agency Practice in the New Social Work Curriculum', *Journal of Interprofessional Care*, 15 (2): 153–169.

Wiggins, R.D., Higgs, P.F.D., Hyde, M. and Blane, D.B. (2004) 'Quality of Life in the Third Age: Key Predictors of the CASP-19 Measure', *Ageing and Society*, 24 (5): 693–708.

Williamson, H. (2000) 'In or Out? How Lesbians Negotiate and Experience Coming Out', in J. Batsleer and B. Humphries (eds) *Welfare, Exclusion and Political Agency*, London: Routledge.

Yelloly, M. and Henkel, M. (1995) *Learning and Teaching in Social Work: Towards Reflective Practice*, London: Jessica Kingsley.

Young, A., Ackerman, J. and Kyle, J. (1998) *Looking On: Deaf People and the Organisation of Services*, Bristol: Policy Press.

Younghusband, E. (1959) *Report of the Working Party on Social Workers in Local Authority Health and Welfare Services*, London: HMSO.

Yuen-Tsang, A.W.K. and Sung, P.P.L. (2002) 'Capacity Building through Networking: Integrating Professional Knowledge with Indigenous Practice', in N.-K. Tan and I. Dodds (eds) *Social Work around the World*, Vol. II, Berne International Federation of Social Workers.

Index